Women as Global Leaders

A Volume in
Women and Leadership: Research, Theory, and Practice

Series Editors
Faith Wambura Ngunjiri, *Concordia College, MN*
Susan R. Madsen, *Utah Valley University*
Karen A. Longman, *Azusa Pacific University*

**Women and Leadership:
Research, Theory, and Practice**

Faith Wambura Ngunjiri,
Susan R. Madsen, and Karen A. Longman, Series Editors

Women and Leadership in Higher Education (2014)
edited by Karen A. Longman and Susan R. Madsen

Women as Global Leaders (2015)
edited by Faith Wambura Ngunjiri and Susan R. Madsen

Women as Global Leaders

edited by

Faith Wambura Ngunjiri
Concordia College, MN

and

Susan R. Madsen
Utah Valley University

INFORMATION AGE PUBLISHING, INC.
Charlotte, NC • www.infoagepub.com

Library of Congress Cataloging-in-Publication Data

CIP record for this book is available from the Library of Congress
http://www.loc.gov

ISBN: 978-1-62396-964-6 (Paperback)
    978-1-62396-965-3 (Hardcover)
    978-1-62396-966-0 (ebook)

Copyright © 2015 Information Age Publishing Inc.

All rights reserved. No part of this publication may be reproduced, stored in a retrieval system, or transmitted, in any form or by any means, electronic, mechanical, photocopying, microfilming, recording or otherwise, without written permission from the publisher.

Printed in the United States of America

CONTENTS

Foreword
    Barbara Kellerman .... *vii*

Introduction
    Faith Wambura Ngunjiri and Susan R. Madsen .... *xi*

PART I: THE STATE OF WOMEN AS GLOBAL LEADERS

1. Introducing Global Leadership: Laying the Groundwork for Women as Global Leaders
   Joyce S. Osland 3

2. Women Leaders: Shaping History in the 21st Century
   Nancy J. Adler 21

PART II: THEORETICAL APPROACHES TO WOMEN'S GLOBAL LEADERSHIP

3. Women and Global Leadership: Three Theoretical Perspectives
   Roya Ayman and Karen Korabik 53

4. Multiple Intelligences of Effective Women Global Leaders: Emotional, Social, and Cultural Competencies
   Julie R. Breithaupt 73

5. Women Leading Through the Lens of Cultural Intelligence
   Joanne Barnes 95

6. Becoming More Themselves: How Can Global Organizations Promote Women's Authentic Leadership?
   Sarah E. Saint-Michel and Valerie Claire Petit 119

7. Global Women Leaders: A Leadership Cartography as a Proposed Approach
   Karin Klenke 141

PART III: DEVELOPING WOMEN AS GLOBAL LEADERS

8. Advancing Women's Executive Development: Effective Practices for the Design and Delivery of Global Women's Leadership Programs
   Mary Ellen Kassotakis and Julnar B. Rizk 163

9. A Master's Degree in Global Leadership: A Story of Development
   Wendy E. Rowe, Cheryl Heykoop, and Catherine Etmanski 187

10. Women's Leadership Learning Through Global Study in Central and South America
    Paige Haber-Curran and Kaitlin Hartley 209

PART IV: STORIES OF WOMEN AS GLOBAL LEADERS

11. What Films Reveal About Women as Global Leaders
    Margie A. Nicholson 233

12. Malala Yousafzai: The Power and Paradox of Global Celebrity
    Carol Burbank 251

13. Beyond the Appendage Syndrome: The Life and Meaning of Golda Meir
    Norman W. Provizer 269

14. What Kind of Leader was Mrs. Thatcher?
    Stephanie Jones 289

About the Authors 305

FOREWORD

Barbara Kellerman

Our interest in, even fixation on leadership is as old as recorded history. Early on there were writings on the subject. And early on there were great minds preoccupied with nothing so much as with how we should be governed—and later with how we should govern ourselves. Names that come to mind extend from Confucius to Plutarch to Locke and beyond—each associated first and foremost with the question of how leaders should lead and, implicitly if not explicitly, how followers should follow—and each similarly concerned with the more general question of what good governance should look like.

By and large, notwithstanding some exceptions to the general rule, this longstanding tradition has been a male enterprise, dominated in every direction by men as opposed to women. Historically, it was mainly men who thought about leadership and left a written record. Historically, men were the subjects of writings about leadership. Though there were always some women leaders—and even a few women global leaders—overwhelmingly leaders historically have been men. And more importantly, historically, leadership overwhelmingly has been conceived of as being appropriate to and suitable for men, not women.

I do not mean to suggest, necessarily, that women and men lead differently. All I am saying here is that historically there has been a presumption that women do or would lead differently if given the chance.

Put slightly differently, the presumptions have been first that leadership work is naturally men's work; and second, that women simply are not suited to the exercise of either power or authority. Arguably, this was for eons so ingrained an understanding that until only recently the very idea of a woman global leader was nearly inconceivable. Plato described a philosopher-king, not a philosopher-queen. Machiavelli's manual was for a prince, not a princess, and Thomas Carlyle's inquiry into historical causation was about the impact of "Great Men" on "the world's history," never "Great Women."

There is, however, an irony here, for such leadership as women were able to exercise was, occasionally, of great consequence. We tend to associate the word *leadership* with formal positions of authority in domains such as politics, business, and the military. But because women have nearly always been denied access to such roles, they sometimes found other ways of creating change, other ways of having an impact. Usually this was in the realm of ideas, the irony to which I refer being that such leadership—intellectual leadership—tends to be of far greater and more enduring import than other, more ordinary kinds of leadership. Consider, for example, the influence of women such as Mary Wollstonecraft, Harriet Beecher Stowe, and Rachel Carson. Although each of these instances took time, the seeds they sowed changed the world.

Still, as the present book attests, it is of the utmost significance that times have changed; that in the second decade of the 21st century there is a book dedicated not simply, not only, to women as leaders, but to women as *global* leaders. Of itself, this is a signifier. Of itself, this book testifies to the idea of a woman as a leader who is no longer so confined or constrained. It testifies to the idea of a woman as a leader who is free to extend her reach as far and as wide as any man. This book should, then, be put in a historical context. It should be understood as a collection of investigations whose time has come, precisely because women now have opportunities to lead that are far more expansive than they were even in the recent past. Though their numbers remain low, they are able in some cases to exercise leadership not only as outsiders, but also as insiders, from the very positions of power and authority to which men forever have had access.

This brings me to the concept of context. In recent years I have become persuaded that the impact of context has been mistakenly marginalized; that those of us who research leadership and followership, teach leadership and followership, and write about leadership and followership pay too little attention, much too little attention, to the environment within which both inevitably are embedded. So now when I discuss leadership in any detail, I invariably discuss what I have come to call the *leadership system*. The leadership system is composed of three equal, independent, and interdependent parts: (a) the leader, (b) the followers or the others, and, (c) the context.

Moreover, I have come to divide context into two conceptually separate and distinct halves: the first is the proximate context, such as the small group or large organization within which we are immediately situated. The second is the distal context, which seems perhaps to be remote, removed, maybe even irrelevant—say, the nation-state—but that turns out to be anything but. Distal context is every bit as relevant to how we lead and follow as is proximate context, and maybe more.

In this sense, the contributors to this book are pioneers; they have placed women leaders specifically in the global context, within which, I might add, every one of us, everywhere, similarly is situated. I wish I could say, if only for the sake of simplicity, that the task that they have set for themselves is easily mastered. But it is not. For those who have edited and authored this volume have taken on—in some cases explicitly, in others implicitly—not only the host of issues that particularly vex women leaders but also the host of issues that vex, even bedevil, the international system.

Let me be clear here. This book is not about the nation-state with which we tend generally to be relatively familiar. Rather it is about the larger world within which the nation-state is itself located—a world with which we tend generally to be relatively less familiar. Many Americans can, for example, tick off at least a few facts and figures pertaining to domestic issues such as government dysfunction, the budget deficit, and our obvious, ubiquitous, decaying infrastructure. But most Americans are much less well informed about Ukraine's continuing conflict with Russia; about Nigeria's problem with homegrown terrorists, specifically Boko Haram; about the return of tensions between China and Japan; or even, notwithstanding America's significant interventions in Iraq and Afghanistan, the bitter struggle between Sunni and Shia Muslims. Anyone who presumes to be a global leader must, moreover, contend with a host of transnational, multinational, international problems—problems that no single nation, no matter how apparently powerful, can possibly address alone. These include, among others, global warming, poverty, and markets that, given their heightened interconnectivity, are inherently less stable or even predictable than they were.

Inevitably this raises questions including what are the skills and capacities required for good leadership at the international level? Do they differ from those required for good leadership at the national level, and if so, how? Is it possible that women might be better suited for global leadership than men? If yes, why would this be, how might this be manifested, and what evidence exists to support any such claim? Some of these questions are, to a degree, addressed in the pages that follow. But obviously the study of women as global leaders is in its infancy. So while the editors of this volume are to be congratulated for taking on so ambitious a task, we should make no mistake—the study of leadership is a challenge that is ongoing.

The study of women and leadership is a challenge that is ongoing. And the study of leadership in the global system is a challenge that also is ongoing. What this means is that when you lash the three together—when the subject at hand is women as global leaders—you are setting the bar extremely high. You are taking a path as yet largely uncharted, which is precisely why this book is as intrepid as it is important.

INTRODUCTION

WOMEN AS GLOBAL LEADERS

Introducing Conceptual, Empirical, and Illustrative Studies

Faith Wambura Ngunjiri and Susan R. Madsen

Whereas the literature on women and leadership has expanded in the last couple of decades, most of the research and studies continue to be about women leading in their own cultural context. Recently, Sheryl Sandberg, the Facebook COO, made headlines as she popularized the topic of women and leadership with her provocative book, *Lean In* (2013), where she argued that there are still challenges to attaining positions of authority, but that women have to play a stronger role in rising up to the challenge. Sandberg recognized that indeed, "men still run the world" (2013, p. 5), and that although "women have the skills to lead in the workplace" (p. 15), challenges continue whether that is because of women limiting their own options, lack of social support, or lack of organizational structures that encourage women to rise to the top.

Long before Sandberg's *Lean In* (2013) became a part of the popular imagination, researchers have extensively argued that there are gender stereotypes and barriers in society that keep women from positions of authority and power (Eagly & Carli, 2003, 2007; Heilman, 2001), because "stereotypes often are a potent barrier to women's advancement to positions of leadership. This assertion is the consensus view" (Koenig, Eagly, Mitchell, & Ristikari, 2011, pp. 616-617). Koenig and colleagues' meta-analysis revealed that there is a reduction in the effect of stereotypes on women's access to leadership positions over the 40 or so years of available research, which is good news indeed. So while gender and culture still matter in leadership (Ayman & Korabik, 2010), the evidence suggests that things are getting better, albeit slowly and in small degrees; there are more women able to attain leadership positions and be effective in playing their roles. There is thus a need for continued studies of women as leaders, more so in this globalizing context, in order to understand what works and then engage in appropriate development activities for emerging women leaders.

Research on a relatively new leadership paradigm, global leadership, has been on the rise in the past two decades, with scholars conceptualizing the various competencies needed to be effective in the global context and arguing for appropriate developmental strategies for enhancing global skills (House, Hanges, Javidan, Dorfman, & Gupta, 2004; Javidan & House, 2001; Jokinen, 2005; Mendenhall, Reiche, Bird, & Osland, 2012; Tubbs & Schulz, 2006). Because this line of research has primarily focused on men, with little looking specifically at women as global leaders, there is a critical need for this volume. Professor Nancy Adler, a pioneer scholar on women as global leaders, eloquently argued that since women are now rising to positions of leadership as heads of countries and corporations, it is no longer a role for men only (Adler, 1996, 1999); in this volume, she updates her earlier seminal research (Adler, 2003) to demonstrate the progress that has been made since she began researching this area in the mid-1990s.

The study of global leadership is a nascent field; there is still no agreement on how to define global leadership, which competencies are needed to be effective in the global context, or how to appropriately develop global leaders (Bird, Mendenhall, Stevens, & Oddou, 2010; Jokinen, 2005; Mendenhall et al., 2012; Osland, 2013; Osland, Bird, & Mendenhall, 2012). In this volume, Professor Joyce Osland, a pioneer in the study of global leadership, adds to the existing literature by providing us with a definition, conceptualization, and recommendations for future research. She recognizes that, with the exception of Adler's pioneering work, not much has been done in the area of women and global leadership, making this volume timely.

Most definitions of global leadership articulate the need for leaders to influence followers' attitudes and behaviors in a global context in order to achieve a common vision and goals and also to incorporate several competencies, including a global perspective or mindset, intercultural competency, and behavioral adaptability (Osland, 2013; Osland, Bird, Mendenhall, & Osland, 2006). Other competencies discussed in the literature include cultural intelligence (Earley, 2002; Hampden-Turner & Trompenaars, 2006), emotional intelligence (Alon & Higgins, 2005), and social intelligence (Crowne, 2007). We continue the conversation in this volume with chapters that utilize qualitative and quantitative measures to explore how women utilize emotional, social, and cultural intelligence in their global leadership roles, a missing element in most previous studies.

OUTLINE OF THE VOLUME

The purpose of this volume then is to explore women's leadership in a global context. Our call for chapters resulted in close to 80 proposals; 14 chapters that cover a wide range of important topics relevant to women and global leadership are included in this volume. Our goal was to provide readers with current conceptualizations and theory related to women as global leaders, recent empirical investigations utilizing qualitative and/or quantitative methods, analyses of global leadership development programs, and case studies or portraits of historical and present-day global women leaders. Built upon the existing literature on global leadership, the various chapters focus specifically on women's experiences crossing borders of language, culture, geography, political, and economic systems in a context of multiplicities, complexities, and flux (Lane, Maznevski, & Mendenhall, 2004; Mendenhall et al., 2012).

A secondary goal of this volume was to respond to the *Asilomar Declaration and Call to Action on Women and Leadership*, written by attendees of the inaugural International Leadership Association's Women and Leadership Conference held at Asilomar Conference Grounds in Pacific Grove, California, in 2013. This seminal document laid out a series of calls to action for scholars, educators, practitioners, policymakers, and others to do more to help girls and women become leaders. Conducting and publishing scholarship that moves this forward provides a critical foundation for increased awareness and understanding toward designing and creating programs and other opportunities for girls and women around the world. This volume helps do just that.

This book is divided into four parts and contains the chapters briefly described below. It presents the state of affairs in terms of women as global leaders, discusses theoretical approaches to women's global leadership, highlights programs and initiatives that focus on developing women to become global leaders, and offers some stories of amazing women who have been or currently are global leaders. This book also presents current demographic realities, sobering struggles and challenges, opportunities that are now before us, and also fresh new thinking about how progress can and must be made.

Part I: The State of Women as Global Leaders

Given the importance of providing foundational information about "The State of Women as Global Leaders," this opening section contains two compelling chapters that establish the current demographics, trends, and areas of concern. Professor Joyce S. Osland from San Jose State University wrote Chapter 1, "Introducing Global Leadership: Laying the Groundwork for Women as Global Leaders." Osland begins by describing the need for global leadership and the scarcity of global leaders. A description of the global context as the crucible that shapes global leaders lays the groundwork for a discussion of the construct definition of global leadership and the distinction between global and domestic leaders. She then provides a brief history of the field's development that includes its multidisciplinary roots. Key research findings are also summarized for the main topics of study—determining what global leadership is and how it is developed. The chapter concludes with a review of the limited research on women global leaders to date and provides directions for future research.

Professor Nancy J. Adler from McGill University wrote the second chapter, titled "Women Leaders: Shaping History in the 21st Century." Whereas most societal commentators continue to review the historical patterns of men's leadership in search of models for 21st century success, Adler argues that few have begun to recognize, let alone appreciate, the equivalent patterns of women's leadership and the potential future contributions that women could make as leaders. She questions, "What could and are women bringing to society as global leaders?" Are we entering an era in which both male and female leaders—rather than primarily men—will literally and symbolically shape history? While rarely recognized or reported in the media, Adler reviews the trend toward women joining men in senior leadership positions that began in the 20th century and is now accelerating in the current century. This chapter was originally published as "Shaping History: Global Leadership in the Twenty-First Century" in Ronald J. Burke and Cary L. Cooper's (Eds.), *Leading in Turbulent Times: Managing in the New World of Work* (2003). It was then subsequently updated and published in Paul R. Sparrow's (Ed.), *Handbook of International Human Resource Management: Integrating People, Process and Context* (2009). And now, Adler has done a thorough update of the global data and literature to offer this insightful chapter on women shaping history as global leaders. The chapter demonstrates that the numbers in both country and corporate leadership, while still miniscule, have steadily increased, offering hope for the future.

Part II: Theoretical Approaches to Women's Global Leadership

The opening chapters that introduce global leadership and provide background on the state of women as global leaders set the stage for a rich discussion on the various approaches that are used as women lead in global settings. Part II of this volume provides descriptions of five chapters that provide insight on this topic and offers creative implications on how progress can be made. Chapter 3, written by Dr. Roya Ayman (Illinois Institute of Technology) and Dr. Karen Korabik (University of Guelph, Canada), is titled "Women and Global Leadership: Three Theoretical Perspectives." This chapter reviews the concepts of gender, culture, and leadership and discusses what is expected of global leaders. They first distinguish between cross-cultural leadership, international or intercultural leadership, and global leadership and discuss the overlap between recognized competencies in mainstream leadership and those required for global leadership. They next define gender and culture and explain why they are essential factors in understanding women's global leadership. Ayman and Korabik provide some examples of women who are global leaders and identify the qualities that make them effective. Finally, they present three theoretical models that delineate the different dynamic processes (i.e., intrapsychic, social interactional, and social structural) that underlie the impact of gender on leadership. In so doing, they provide insights about the key issues that are faced by woman global leaders and how to remedy some of the obstacles they face on their pathway to success. Together, the three models form a theoretical framework about how gender and culture impact on global leadership that facilitates our understanding of global women leaders.

Dr. Julie R. Breithaupt (Global Leadership Development, LLC), moves the conceptual needle forward in Chapter 4, titled "Multiple Intelligences of Effective Women Global Leaders." Her chapter reviews the literature on emotional, social, and cultural intelligences and discusses considerations of these multiple intelligences as competencies for global leadership. These intelligences, acting in concert, provide a strong foundation for effective global leadership. The chapter presents a phenomenological research study that used a framework of emotional, social, and cultural intelligences to understand the experiences of women global leaders. Authentic leadership paired with emotional, social, cultural intelligences, and specialized or technical skills, lead to a powerful combination of capabilities and values that contributed to the women's effectiveness in global leadership roles. The chapter ends with implications for further theory development and practical applications for women's leadership development.

Dr. Joanne Barnes (Indiana Wesleyan University) wrote Chapter 5, titled "Women Leading Through the Lens of Cultural Intelligence." She argues that, whereas there is increasing research on women in leadership, there continues to be a dearth of research on women's leadership in global and culturally diverse settings. Her mixed-method research examined whether women leaders with a high level of cultural intelligence (CQ) had a more positive relationship with their culturally diverse team than women leaders with a low level of CQ. Her research found that experience, language, and training impacted the CQ scores of women leaders, influenced how they interacted with direct reports, and how direct reports perceived the leaders' ability to understand cultural differences. Even though it utilized a small sample, the study illuminates women's experiences in leading culturally diverse teams and recommends training in order to enhance cultural competency for global leadership roles.

Chapter 6 is titled "Becoming More Themselves: How Can Global Organizations Promote Women's Authentic Leadership?" Dr. Sarah E. Saint-Michel (University of Toulouse Capitole, France) and Dr. Valérie Claire Petit (EDHEC Business School, France) focus their chapter on exploring the organizational antecedents for authentic leadership development of women leaders. They cite Eagly's (2005) work that has shown that achieving authentic leadership is more challenging for women who have traditionally been excluded from top leadership roles. They analyze the case of an exemplary global company and suggest that authentic leadership development among female managers may rely on three complementary pillars: a three-dimensional gender-equality corporate policy, a strong commitment to inclusion, and a set of deeply ingrained and humane-oriented corporate values.

Recognizing the complexity of the global context, Dr. Karin Klenke (North Central University and the Leadership Development Institute International) proposes a new approach to interrogating women's experiences as global leaders. In Chapter 7, titled "Global Women Leaders: Leadership Cartography as a Proposed Approach," Klenke introduces leadership cartography (LC) as a paradigm located within the interpretivist tradition and innovative qualitative research method at the confluence of cartography, cognitive mapping, and leadership theories and qualitative methodologies. LC would start with a map of the physical terrain of a country or smaller geographical unit of the female global leader's context and juxtapose it on a mind map that captures her strength, weaknesses, convictions, and values. Klenke posits that LC is potentially positioned to further the study of women as global leaders and address critical issues they face asymmetries of power and power games, patterns of domination, the dysfunctionalities of particular types of leadership, hierarchy, and authority. The chapter concludes with a discussion of Iranian lawyer and human rights activist Shirin Ebadi and Brazilian CEO and business leader Silva Foster to demonstrate what an LC of these two women may look like; it also highlights the importance of the context in which global women leaders enact their leadership. Whereas LC cannot be utilized yet due to a lack of software that can juxtapose cartographic with cognitive maps, Klenke proposes that it offers an alternative approach to explicating the complexity of the global context.

Part III: Developing Women as Global Leaders

The third section of the book focuses leadership development programs aimed at enhancing global leadership knowledge, competencies, and skills, particularly for women. Chapter 8, "Advancing Women's Executive Development: Effective Practices for the Design and Delivery of Global Women's Leadership Programs," focuses on unpacking the value of women's-only programs. The authors, Dr. Mary Ellen Kassotakis (Oracle Corporation) and Julnar B. Rizk (Facebook), argue that the topics of leadership and the development of effective leaders have intrigued researchers for decades, and they state that many renowned universities offer workshops designed to develop leadership skills for female leaders. Similarly, many of today's corporations invest in gender-specific leadership development initiatives. Their chapter explores current research and programs with regard to the development of global women leaders to better understand current goals and practices. They ask and answer the questions: Are there benefits for same-sex learning environments as well as specific design considerations for this target audience? If so, how might women-only development programs be enhanced in order to further the cause of advancing women leaders in the workplace?

Dr. Wendy E. Rowe (Royal Roads University), Dr. Catherine Etmanski (Royal Roads University), and Cheryl Heykoop (International Institute for Child Rights and Development), authored Chapter 9 titled, "A Master's Degree in Global Leadership: A Story of Development." Their chapter describes a master's degree program in global leadership that targets leaders working in the global social purpose public sector—a program that reinforces values of respect, relationship, equity, and compassion. This is a story of program development grounded in existing literature about the complexity of the global context, the application of an intersectional lens, and understanding roles and competencies required of female (and male) global leaders. Additionally, it is based on an underlying assumption that global leadership is a cultural activity that recognizes the broad diversity of people, values, perspectives, beliefs, worldviews, and practices.

Dr. Paige Haber-Curran (Texas State University) and Kaitlin Hartley (University of Alabama) co-authored Chapter 10, "Women's Leadership Learning Through Global Study in Central and South America." These authors examined a 4-week global study program in Central and South America focused on global leadership and social change. The reflections and personal accounts of four college women who participated in the program were examined to identify salient experiences and learning related to self, leadership, and culture/global issues. A discussion of the global study experience through the lens of the women's experiences and learning is presented with implications for developing women as global leaders through leadership education and study abroad.

Part IV: Stories of Women as Global Leaders

The final section of the book includes portraits and analyses of women leaders who serve currently or historically served in global roles. Three chapters provide insights into the lives of Malala Yousafzai, Golda Meir, and Margaret Thatcher, while the fourth, which is the first chapter in this section, offers insights from films about a few other high-profile global leaders.

Margie A. Nicholson (Columbia College, Chicago), wrote Chapter 11 where she shared critical analysis and insights in "What Films Reveal about Women as Global Leaders." She analyzed four films in order to explore theories about women as global leaders: *The Lady*, which profiles Burma's Aung San Suu Kyi; *Bhutto*, a documentary about Pakistan's Benazir Bhutto; *Taking Root: The Vision of Wangari Maathai*, about Kenya's Wangari Maathai; and *Chahinaz: What Rights for Women?* which features Ireland's Mary Robinson and Bahrain's Sheikha Haya Rashed Al Khalifa along with Chahinaz, an emerging young leader from Algeria. The analysis of these women leaders focuses on topics such as their commitment to a vision or mission; their courage and relentless effort; and the roles that popular support, media, the David and Goliath story, multicultural experience, family members, and mentors play in their emergence as global leaders.

In Chapter 12, Dr. Carol Burbank (Storyweaving: Transformational Leadership, Education, and Consulting) wrote "Malala Yousafzai: The Power and Paradox of Global Celebrity." In only five years, Malala has evolved from a vocal advocate for girl's education in Pakistan into a survivor of terrorist violence, global activist, fundraiser, and nearly mythical icon. The key reason for her undeniable success in global spheres, and particularly in developed Western nations, is that she has been adopted as a representative for all Muslim women and girls; a kind of leadership by synecdoche that has more to do with her role as iconic survivor than her activism. This leadership position is both powerful and problematic, offering charismatic visibility and significant resources to her cause, but reinforcing Western propaganda around Muslim conflict. Although she has created a persuasive master frame to challenge the exclusion of girls and women from access to education under Taliban rule, there is little room in her inspiring mytho-political activism to express the complex and culturally specific intersectionality of identities that shape women's cultural roles as leaders in the Islamic world. Burbank argues that leading by synecdoche is a potent form of political and social leadership, but it requires both sacrifice and strategy to maintain without losing the focus of her cause in the complex elaborations of sociopolitical celebrity.

Dr. Norman W. Provizer (Metropolitan State University of Denver) wrote Chapter 13, "Beyond the Appendage Syndrome: The Life and Meaning of Golda Meir." He notes that when Golda Meir emerged as Israel's prime minister in 1969, she became the first woman leader of a significant global actor in the 20th century to reach her position owing nothing to the Appendage Syndrome. Unlike the women prime ministers who preceded her, Meir had no male coattails to help her gain power. In exploring that achievement, Provizer explores the contradictions embodied in Meir that helped her navigate through turbulent seas. Today, we have moved in a number of ways beyond the Appendage Syndrome; and Provizer argues that Meir, driven by a sense of commitment and duty, was a significant pathfinder in that regard.

Chapter 14, "What Kind of Leader Was Mrs. Thatcher?" is the concluding chapter in this section and in this book. Dr. Stephanie Jones (Maastricht School of Management, The Netherlands) questions the role of former British Prime Minister Margaret Thatcher in advancing the cause of women at high levels in global leadership. Considering the context of several frameworks assessing leadership styles, Jones attempts to define her sometimes contradictory approach to leadership. She argues that Thatcher was a truly global leader, but hardly worldly and very British. Though Thatcher had celebrity status, Jones evaluates her leadership as having changed some aspects of British society, but she was authoritarian and directive, intolerant of criticism, and uninterested in alternative viewpoints. Further, Thatcher was charismatic, outspoken, opinionated, and intimidating; she eventually became out of touch with many of her voters. Jones sees Thatcher's legacy both positively and negatively, and argues that as the first and only woman to play that role, she made the concept of women leaders at the highest levels more commonplace.

CONCLUSION

These 14 chapters explored various aspects of women and global leadership, providing readers with conceptualizations, theory developments, relevant approaches, effective leadership development strategies, and case studies of prominent global women leaders. The authors advanced theory by expanding the conceptualizations of leadership, culture, gender, and the globalized context. They help readers see leadership in practice through analyzing the lives of historical figures as well as contemporary leaders. The chapters provide us a way forward by discussing the implications for future research, leadership development, and theory building.

The world is changing faster than ever before, and there are new opportunities for women to emerge as leaders in all types of organizations and efforts that expand beyond the walls of specific countries—but there is still much work to be done. We need more men and women to build, bridge, and blaze pathways for women and leadership around the world. Thus, it is now up to you, the reader, to take the contributions you will read in this book as a foundation for your own leadership theory building, scholarly research, development activities, and/or improved practice.

REFERENCES

Adler, N. J. (1996). Global women political leaders: An invisible history, an increasingly important future. *The Leadership Quarterly, 7*(1), 133–161.

Adler, N. J. (1999). Global women leaders: A dialogue with future history. In D. Cooperrider & J. E. Dutton (Eds.), *Organizational dimensions of global change: No limits to cooperation* (pp. 320–345). Thousand Oaks, CA: Sage.

Adler, N. J. (2003). Shaping history: Global leadership in the twenty-first century. In R. J. Burke & C. L. Cooper (Eds.), *Leading in turbulent times: Managing in the new world of work* (pp. 302–318). Oxford, England: Blackwell.

Alon, I., & Higgins, J. M. (2005). Global leadership success through emotional and cultural intelligences. *Business Horizons, 48*(6), 501–512.

Ayman, R., & Korabik, K. (2010). Leadership: Why gender and culture matter. *American Psychologist, 65*(3), 157.

Bird, A., Mendenhall, M., Stevens, M. J., & Oddou, G. (2010). Defining the content domain of intercultural competence for global leaders. *Journal of Managerial Psychology, 25*(8), 810–828.

Crowne, K. A. (2007). *The relationships among social intelligence, emotional intelligence, cultural intelligence and cultural exposure.* Doctoral dissertation, Temple University, Philadelphia, PA.

Eagly, A. H., & Carli, L. L. (2003). The female leadership advantage: An evaluation of the evidence. *The Leadership Quarterly, 14*(6), 807–834.

Eagly, A. H., & Carli, L. L. (2007). *Through the labyrinth: The truth about how women become leaders.* Boston, MA: Harvard Business School Press.

Earley, P. C. (2002). Redefining interactions across cultures and organizations: Moving forward with cultural intelligence. *Research in Organizational Behavior, 24*, 271–299.

Hampden-Turner, C., & Trompenaars, F. (2006). Cultural intelligence: Is such a capacity credible? *Group Organization Management, 31*(1), 56–63.

Heilman, M. E. (2001). Description and prescription: How gender stereotypes prevent women's ascent up the organizational ladder. *Journal of Social Issues, 57*(4), 657–674.

House, R. J., Hanges, P. J., Javidan, M., Dorfman, P., & Gupta, V. (Eds.). (2004). *Culture, leadership, and organizations: The GLOBE study of 62 societies.* Thousand Oaks, CA: Sage.

Javidan, M., & House, R. J. (2001). Cultural acumen for the global manager: Lessons from project GLOBE. *Organizational Dynamics, 29*(4), 289–305.

Jokinen, T. (2005). Global leadership competencies: A review and discussion. *Journal of European Industrial Training, 29*(3), 199–216.

Koenig, A. M., Eagly, A. H., Mitchell, A. A., & Ristikari, T. (2011). Are leader stereotypes masculine? A meta-analysis of three research paradigms. *Psychological Bulletin, 137*(4), 616.

Lane, H. W., Maznevski, M. L., & Mendenhall, M. E. (2004). Globalization: Hercules meets Buddha. In H. W. Lane, M. Maznevski, M. Mendenhall, & J. Mcnett (Eds.), *The Blackwell handbook of global management: A guide to managing complexity* (pp. 3–25). Malden, MA: Blackwell.

Mendenhall, M. E., Reiche, B. S., Bird, A., & Osland, J. S. (2012). Defining the "global" in global leadership. *Journal of World Business, 47*(4), 493–503.

Osland, J. S. (2013). An overview of the global leadership literature. In M. Mendenhall, J. Osland, A. Bird, G. R. Oddou, M. Maznevski, M. J. Stevens, & G. Stahl (Eds.), *Global leadership: Research, practice and development* (2nd ed., pp. 40–79). London, England: Routledge.

Osland, J. S., Bird, A., & Mendenhall, M. (2012). Developing global mindset and global leadership capabilities. In G. Stahl, I. Bjorkman, & S. Morris (Eds.), *Handbook of research in international human resource management* (2nd ed., pp. 220–252). Cheltenham, England: Elgar.

Osland, J. S., Bird, A., Mendenhall, M., & Osland, A. (2006). Developing global leadership capabilities and global mindset: A review. In G. K. Stahl & I. Bjorkman (Eds.), *Handbook of research in international human resource management* (pp. 197–222). Cheltenham, England: Elgar.

Sandberg, S. (2013). *Lean in: Women, work, and the will to lead.* New York, NY: Alfred A. Knopf.

Tubbs, S. L., & Schulz, E. (2006). Exploring a taxonomy of global leadership competencies and meta-competencies. *Journal of American Academy of Business, Cambridge, 8*(2), 29–34.

PART I

THE STATE OF WOMEN AS GLOBAL LEADERS

CHAPTER 1

INTRODUCING GLOBAL LEADERSHIP

Laying the Groundwork for Women as Global Leaders

Joyce S. Osland

> *We cannot solve our problems by using the same kind of thinking we used when we created them.*
>
> —Albert Einstein (1946)

Einstein is correct that we need a different type of thinking to solve today's problems. For today's global problems and global organizations, we also need a different type of leadership. Global leadership is a growing field of study triggered by globalization and the increased complexity confronting leaders in global organizations. Beginning in the late 1990s, surveys documented the crucial importance of global leadership and the scarcity of global leaders in business (e.g., Black, Morrison, & Gregersen, 1999; Gitsham et al., 2008) as well as government and not-for profit sectors (Bikson, Treverton, Moini, & Lindstrom, 2003). Recent studies continue to confirm this need. Global leadership was identified more than any other

Women as Global Leaders, pp. 3–20
Copyright © 2015 by Information Age Publishing
All rights of reproduction in any form reserved.

option as a key factor for global success in the business sector in a 2012 McKinsey & Company survey. The World Economic Forum's (WEF) 2013 *Global Agenda Outlook* included global leadership in its list of the world's 10 most urgent issues and concluded that the global leadership vacuum "remains the biggest challenge of all for 2013 and beyond" (WEF, 2013, p. 6).

In response to the growing acknowledgement of this need, the number of global leadership training and development programs in both organizations and universities is on the upswing, as is the rate of research production. Nevertheless, from an academic point of view, global leadership is a relatively nascent field of study that, while showing promise and progress, is in an early stage of development. This chapter covers the global context that prompted the need for global leadership in the business sector, provides a construct definition, describes the difference between global and domestic leadership, the multidisciplinary roots of the field, key research findings on global leadership competencies and development, and concludes by reviewing the research on women in global leadership and identifying future research directions.

The Global Context as Crucible

The nature of the global context, with its impact on global organizations and job demands, is the crucible that shapes and challenges global leaders (Osland, Taylor, & Mendenhall, 2009). Scholars have long acknowledged the greater complexity resulting from the pressures and dynamics of global competition (Weber, Festing, Dowling, & Schuler, 1998). For instance, global leaders reported dealing with a range of fluctuating environments that span geographies, cultures, and sociopolitical systems (Rosen, Digh, Singer, & Philips, 2000). According to an IBM study consisting of interviews with 1,500 CEOs in 33 industries across 60 countries, the most challenging aspect of their jobs is complexity (IBM, 2010). With respect to global leadership, Lane, Maznevski, and Mendenhall (2004, p. 197) contend that globalization more accurately connotes "increased complexity," which comprises the following four dimensions:

- *Multiplicity* refers to the increased number and type of issues confronting global leaders. Multiplicity is both "more and different," consisting of more and different competitors, customers, stakeholders, governments, nongovernmental organizations (NGOs), and ways of organizing and conducting business.
- *Interdependence* among a host of stakeholders, sociocultural, political, economic, and environmental systems implies that global

leaders have to attend to and manage more complex systems of human and technological interaction than domestic leaders.
- *Ambiguity* derives from the lack of information clarity, equivocality or multiple interpretations of information, and confusion about cause-effect relationships. Cross-cultural differences add even more ambiguity with respect to interpreting cues and signals, identifying appropriate actions, and pursuing plausible goals in the global context.
- *Flux* refers to the rapid rate of change in the global context, involving quickly transitioning systems, shifting values, and emergent patterns of organizational structure and behavior.

Therefore, global leadership is leadership under conditions of extreme complexity, which, at a minimum, requires human adaptations in cognition and behavior. For this reason, Osland and her colleagues (Osland, Bird, & Oddou, 2012) coined the term "extreme leadership" as a metaphor for global leadership that describes the difference between global and domestic leadership. People engaged in extreme sports typically began by learning domestic sports; while seeking greater challenge and adventure, they learned to adapt to the demands of more grueling and difficult forms of sport, often traveling to other countries in the process. Likewise, global leaders typically mastered domestic leadership and eventually adapted and learned how to deal with the greater complexity and challenges inherent in global work. This begs the questions "Who are global leaders?" and "How is this phenomenon defined?"

Global Leadership Defined

Well-known political, diplomatic, military, and spiritual leaders, such as Mahatma Ghandi, Martin Luther King Jr., Mother Theresa, Nelson Mandela, and Alexander the Great, are among the first names that come to mind when most people hear the term "global leader." Carlos Ghosn—Chairman, President, and CEO of Nissan and Renault—is one of the most famous global leaders in the business field (Stahl & Brannen, 2013). In today's globalized world, more and more people who are not household names and who work farther down the hierarchical pyramid in global organizations are engaged in global leadership. Employees who work on multicultural teams, have subordinates from different cultural backgrounds, work virtually around the globe, have jobs with a global scope, work across organizational boundaries in other countries, and/or merge together global organizations can all be categorized as a type of global leader. Scholars have recently begun work on a global leader taxonomy and a construct definition to aid sample selection (Mendenhall, Reiche, Bird, & Osland, 2012; Reiche, Mendenhall, Bird, & Osland, 2014).

One of the largest obstacles in advancing the field is the lack of a construct definition and the resulting indiscriminate mixing of samples and research evidence (Mendenhall et al., 2012, 2014; Reiche et al., 2014). Confusion concerns the distinction between domestic/global leaders, between global leaders/global managers, and among expatriate/comparative/global leadership. Therefore, vetting and understanding global leadership findings should always begin with a careful look at the researchers' selection criteria and definition of global leadership. After reviewing the definitions employed in the field, Mendenhall and his colleagues (Mendenhall et al., 2012; Reiche et al., 2014) proposed a definition to advance the ongoing construct definition debate:

> The process of influencing others to adopt a shared vision through structures and methods that facilitate positive change while fostering individual and collective growth in a context characterized by significant levels of complexity, flow and presence. (Mendenhall et al., 2012, p. 500)

This definition includes parameters that specify what is *not* global leadership. For instance, it is not simply domestic leadership plus intercultural competence. Neither is it simply expatriate leadership, comparative leadership, nor global management. These fields, however, have been identified as the multidisciplinary roots of global leadership, based on a review of the literature (Osland, 2013a). The literature on domestic leadership appears to have had the least impact on the global leadership field to date.

Osland and colleagues have delineated distinctions between domestic and global leadership (Osland & Bird, 2006; Osland et al., 2012; Osland et al., 2009). The greater complexity in the global context has resulted in qualitative differences between domestic and global work (Dalton, Ernst, Deal, & Leslie, 2002; Shin, Morgeson, & Campion, 2007). Traditional leadership does not mention or emphasize some key global leadership skills, such as extensive boundary spanning (Osland et al., 2009). The developmental path is not exactly the same—key global leadership lessons come from cultural experiences (McCall & Hollenbeck, 2002). As noted above, global leadership has additional multidisciplinary intellectual roots (Osland, 2013a). There are, however, both shared similarities *and* differences of degree and kind between domestic and global leadership (Osland, Bird, Mendenhall, & Osland, 2006).

GLOBAL LEADERSHIP RESEARCH

Although global leaders exist in all fields, international management scholars have produced the most research with their studies on business people.

The early publications in the 1990s were based on extrapolations from the domestic leadership literature, interviews, focus groups, or observations from the authors' consulting or training experiences. The publication rate for empirical studies has doubled recently, but it is a relatively small literature base of fewer than 40 empirical articles (for reviews, see Osland, 2013b and Osland, Li, & Wang, 2014a; for a compendium of research in the field, see Mendenhall et al., 2013). The identification of competencies and to a lesser degree, global leadership development, are the primary topics studied. Table 1.1 summarizes the foundational studies in the field. The following sections describe three different approaches to understanding global leadership—competency studies, job analysis, and expert cognition—and a summary of global leadership development.

Table 1.1. Examples of Global Leadership Foundational Research

Construct Definition	Jokinen (2005); Mendenhall et al. (2012); Osland et al. (2012)
Scope of GL Tasks	Caligiuri (2006); Osland et al. (2013)
Competencies	Bird (2013); Black et al. (1999); Bird et al. (2010); Caligiuri & Tarique (2009); Gitsham et al. (2008); Wills & Barham (1994)
Assessment Instruments	Bird et al. (2010); Bird & Stevens (2013); Kets de Vries, Vrignaud, & Florent-Treacy (2004)
Training & Development	Caligiuri & Tarique (2012); Li et al. (2013); McCall & Hollenbeck (2002); Miska, Stahl & Mendenhall (2013); Oddou & Mendenhall (2013); Pless et al. (2011, 2012); Terrell & Rosenbusch (2012); Tompson & Tompson (2013)

Source: Osland and Wang (2014a).

The Content Approach—Global Leadership Competencies

Scholars have identified numerous competencies, well over 50 in number, related to global leadership effectiveness (cf. Adler, 1997b; Black et al., 1999; Brake, 1997; Gitsham et al., 2008; Goldsmith, Greenberg, Robertson, & Hu-Chan, 2003; Gundling, Hogan, & Cvitkovich, 2011; Holt & Seki, 2012; Jokinen, 2005; Lobel, 1990; McCall & Hollenbeck, 2002; Rosen et al., 2000; Wills & Barham, 1994; Yeung & Ready, 1995). Mendenhall and Osland (2002) categorized them into six dimensions, as shown in Figure 1.1. The first overarching competency, called *Intercultural Competencies*, consists of relationship skills, traits, and cognitive orientation. These competencies concern interactions and relationships at the interpersonal and small-group level. The second overarching competency, *Global Business Competencies*, comprises global business expertise, global organizing expertise, and visioning. Its macrofocus relates to global business knowledge and skills. Bird (2013) recently categorized the content domain of global leadership as *Business and Organizational Acumen, Managing People and Relationships*, and *Managing Self*. Gitsham and his colleagues (2008) identified three clusters of competencies: context, complexity, and connectedness.

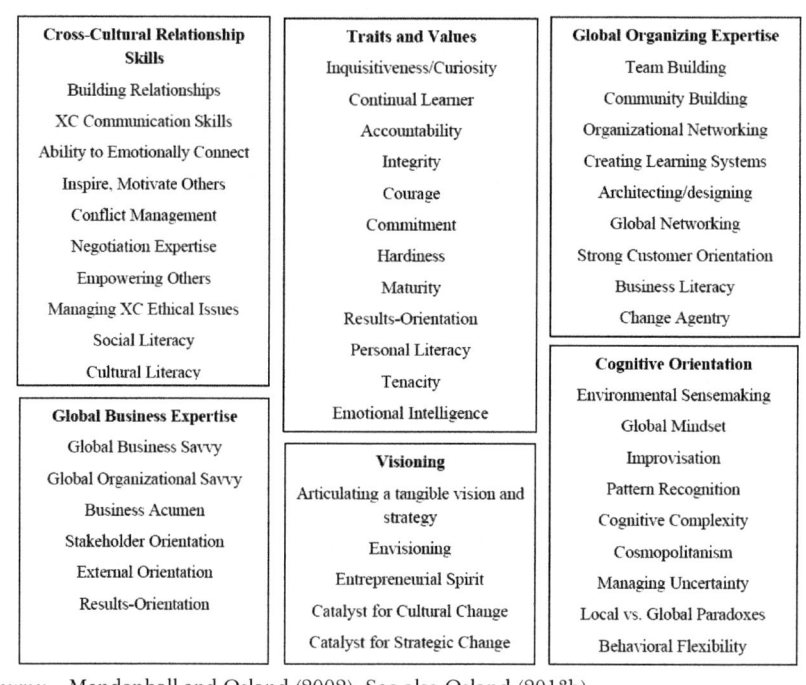

Source: Mendenhall and Osland (2002). See also Osland (2013b).

Figure 1.1. Dimensions of global leadership.

The Pyramid Model, yet another way to order the competencies, includes scaffolded levels: global knowledge, threshold characteristics (integrity, humility, inquisitiveness, and resilience), attitudes and orientations (cognitive complexity and cosmopolitanism), interpersonal skills (mindful communication, creating and building trust, and multicultural teaming), and system skills (spanning boundaries, building community and social capital, architecting, leading change, influencing stakeholders, and making ethical decisions). The system skills are metaskills that incorporate competencies at lower levels. The Pyramid Model, shown in Figure 1.2, was originally developed by a team of international management scholars in a modified Delphi technique (Bird & Osland, 2004) and later adapted and expanded to incorporate global leadership findings (Osland, 2013b).

Source: Bird & Osland, 2004; Osland, 2013.

Figure 1.2. Pyramid model of global competencies.

The various frameworks for organizing global leadership competencies (Bird, 2013; Gitsham et al., 2008; Jokinen, 2005; Mendenhall & Osland, 2002; Osland, 2013b) have overlapping and nonexclusive categories (Jokinen, 2005). Certain competencies surface repeatedly, such as cognitive complexity, behavioral flexibility, intercultural competence, learning ability, and integrity. The content domain for the intercultural competence dimension consists of perception management, relationship management, and self-management factors (Bird, Mendenhall, Stevens, & Oddou, 2010). In sum, global leadership is a multidimensional construct with both micro- and macroelements.

The content approach to identify *what global leadership is* has yielded important findings, but it is not sufficient. Such research does not tell us which competencies are most important in which situations or what types of global leaders or global jobs require which subset of competencies. We have yet to identify the boundary conditions for global leadership competencies, although we know that leadership requirements are contingent on level, culture, situation, functions, and operating units (Conger & Ready, 2004). Furthermore, the competency approach does not explain why exemplary global leaders succeed despite glaring weaknesses. In a study of the top 25 business leaders of our time (Pandaya & Shell, 2005), no one possessed all the attributes that were identified. McCall and Hollenbeck (2002) discovered that effective global leaders performed their jobs in different ways with different talents. Thus, the global leadership field would benefit from acknowledging the reality of the imperfect "incomplete leader" (Ancona, Malone, Orlikowski, & Senge, 2007) and devoting more attention to varied global leader profiles and the interactive processes they employ.

The Job Analysis Approach

Caliguiri (2006), trained as an industrial and organizational psychologist, carried out a job analysis based on surveys and focus groups that identified 10 global leader tasks:

- works with colleagues from other countries,
- interacts with external clients from other countries,
- interacts with internal clients from other countries,
- often speaks another language at work,
- supervises employees who are of different nationalities,
- develops a strategic business plan on a worldwide basis,
- manages a worldwide budget,
- negotiates in other countries or with people from other countries,
- manages foreign suppliers or vendors, and
- manages risk on a worldwide basis for their unit.

This list was then used to measure global leader effectiveness in a large multinational sample identified by HR personnel as global leaders engaged in global work (Caligiuri & Tarique, 2012). Personality characteristics (extraversion, openness to experience, and conscientiousness) and cultural experiences (both within and outside the organization) predicted dynamic cross-cultural competencies: tolerance of ambiguity, cultural flexibility, and reduced ethnocentrism. In turn, these competencies predicted higher effectiveness ratings by the global leaders' superiors, indicating that they serve as mediators between developmental cultural experiences and the Big 5 personality characteristics that were measured. Caligiuri and Tarique's findings are very helpful, but they do not provide much insight into how global leaders approach their work or how they behave as they carry out these tasks.

Expert Cognition

Osland and her colleagues (Osland, Bird, Oddou, & Osland, 2013) took a step closer to determining the process of global leadership in their study of expertise. They carried out a qualitative study using cognitive task analysis on global change initiatives led by nominated effective global leaders. These expert global leaders described their work context as precarious, ambiguous, and involving huge challenges and numerous multiplicities (more and different entities and organizations) (Osland et al., 2012). All of their critical incidents involved teamwork and consisted mainly of problem solving, strategic thinking, boundary spanning, and stakeholder management. Their key global skills comprised dealing with ambiguity, reading people very closely to gauge their reactions and bridge intercultural communication gaps, engaging in conscious managerial "code-switching" to be effective in different situations, using stakeholder dialogue and boundary-spanning expertise, and interacting with the environment via different types of sense-making (Osland, 2010). In many cases, their missions were challenges in uncharted waters that no one had ever attempted. They dealt with the ambiguity and uncertainty this caused by relying on an acquired problem-solving process, choosing the right team members, building trust among the team, and trusting the team and their own capacity to figure things out as they went along (Osland et al., 2013).

Global Leadership Development

The term "both born and made" (Black & Morrison, 2014) is frequently used with respect to global leadership development (Black et al., 1999). People have to be ready, willing, and able to work hard at personal development (Björkman & Mäkelä, 2013; Oddou & Mendenhall, 2013); some are better equipped to become global leaders or to take advantage of development methods than others due to personal characteristics (Caligiuri & Tarique, 2014).

The process models of global leadership development (Black et al., 1999; McCall & Hollenbeck, 2002; Osland & Bird, 2013) involve personal transformation, growing out of crucible experiences that occured over time, in an unpredictable nonlinear fashion (Osland, Bird, & Mendenhall, 2012). Expatriation has long been viewed as the most effective way to develop global leaders (Black et al., 1999; McCall & Hollenbeck, 2002), but less expensive and time-consuming methods also develop global leadership competencies. Nonwork-related intercultural experiences, international service learning, short-term global business travel, multicultural team experience, action learning projects, reflection, global leadership assessment centers, assessment instruments and 360-degree feedback, personal development plans, executive coaching, cross-cultural mentoring, outdoor learning experiences, and traditional training are other paths to global leadership development (Oddou & Mendenhall, 2013). Research has not yet compared the efficacy of these different methods. Caligiuri and Tarique's (2012) research documented that cross-cultural experiences should be both high-contact and highly challenging. They also found that extraversion, openness, emotional stability, motivation, language skills, and prior experience accelerated intercultural competence gains from cross-cultural experiences. Cognitive ability, prior knowledge, and personality traits also accelerated the knowledge gain in cross-cultural training. Thus, both personal characteristics and the "treatment" (i.e., the specific training methodology) must be considered. Fitzsimmons, Lee, and Brannen (2013) suggested another relevant personal characteristic after summarizing new research on *marginals*, defined as bicultural (or multicultural) individuals who have internalized more than one culture. Because marginals do not identify strongly with any culture, they are simultaneously cultural insiders and outsiders who have already mastered some challenges that are similar to those faced by global leaders. Therefore, marginals may have the potential to be good candidates for global leadership roles and training programs (Fitzsimmons et al., 2013). Research is also emerging on methods to develop culture-related aspects of global leadership, such as cultural intelligence (Li, Mobley, & Kelly, 2013), cultural self-awareness (Wernsing & Clapp-Smith, 2013) and global mindset (Clapp-Smith & Hughes, 2007).

International service learning programs (ISLPs), whose purpose is to develop socially responsible global leaders who contribute to society and the triple bottom line (economic, social, and environmental value), are receiving growing attention by companies and scholars (c.f. Voegtlin, Patzer & Scherer, 2012). These programs, sometimes called the corporate version of Peace Corps (O'Neill, 2011), reflect the expanded stakeholder expectations and ethical challenges confronting global leaders. High potential trainees are selected, given predeparture training, work in a developing country with local people on service projects or small businesses, and then undergo a debriefing. In a model ISLP, PricewaterhouseCooper's Ulysses program (Pless, Maak, & Stahl, 2011, 2012), the following competencies—cultural empathy awareness, ethical literacy, interpersonal skills, and relationship management—were developed simultaneously at the cognitive, affective, and behavioral levels. This development was triggered by the ensuing demands or learning mechanisms: (a) resolving cultural and ethical paradoxes, (b) constructing a new "life-world"—a new perspective of self and the world to survive and make sense of their daily experiences in the challenging cross-cultural contexts they were in, and (c) coping with the adversity and strong emotions that were kindled as they confronted realities they had never experienced (Pless et al., 2011). In a similar program, IBM's Corporate Service Corps (CSC) has sent 2,400 global leadership trainees in 200 teams to 30 countries to work on local projects. The results are a significant increase in cultural adaptability, teaming skills, and employee satisfaction;

furthermore, 100% reported that they were more likely to complete their careers at IBM after their CSC experience (Marquis & Kanter, 2010).

Assessment measures typically serve three nonexclusive functions in global leadership development: (a) selection of high-potential employees for development programs or global leadership positions; (b) self-awareness and personal growth within training and development programs; and (c) pre- and postmeasures for program evaluation and assessment purposes. The most commonly used instruments (in alphabetical order) in business and educational institutions include the following: Cross-Cultural Adaptability Inventory (CCAI), Cultural Intelligence (CQ), Global Competencies Aptitude Assessment (GCAA), Global Competencies Inventory (GCI), Global Executive Leadership Inventory (GELI), Global Mindset Inventory (GMI), Intercultural Effectiveness Scale (IES), Intercultural Readiness Check (IRC), and the Multicultural Personality Questionnaire (MPQ). For a review of these assessment instruments, see Bird and Stevens (2013). Using cognitive behavior therapy, Mendenhall and his colleagues (Mendenhall, Arnardottir, Oddou, & Burke, 2013; Mendenhall, Burke, Arnardottir, Oddou, & Osland, in press) described the successful use of personal development plans in MBA courses based on assessment results.

Women in Global Leadership

One of the first descriptions of a corporate global leadership development program was one targeted at women (Adler, Brody, & Osland, 2000, 2001a, 2001b). The company was Bestfoods, a global food company subsequently bought by Unilever. The consultants (co-authors) partnered with Laura Brody, Director of Diversity and Development, to design the week-long Women's Global Leadership Forum attended by 55 women and many of the senior male executives. Its purpose was to (a) increase the global competitiveness of Bestfoods; (b) develop the global leadership skills of Bestfoods' most highly talented and senior women; (c) create an internal network among them to facilitate their global effectiveness; and (d) develop both global and local recommendations via action learning projects for enhancing Bestfoods' ability to support the career advancement and success of an increasing number of such women. In addition to personal growth, the Forum produced practical recommendations adopted by the company, an effective women's network, and an increased Balanced Scorecard goal for women global leaders, set by senior managers.

In addition to carrying out global leadership development efforts, Nancy Adler (1996, 1997a, 1997b) was the first to study women global leaders (see also Calas & Smircich, 1993). Early global leadership research had a predominance of males in the samples, so Adler's research counterbalanced this tendency. She employed archival data and interviews with a sample of senior women global leaders in business and politics from 60 countries. The women in her sample held positional power. She identified a rapid increase in women presidents and prime ministers, from zero in the 1950s to 21 in the 1990s. More than 60% of the total women in the world who ever served as prime ministers or presidents ($n = 47$) came into office during this decade (Adler, 2001). As of April 2014, there are 19 women prime ministers or presidents (CFWD, 2014).

The number of female CEOs in the United States is increasing, if slowly. In 1996, Catalyst (1996) reported that 2.6% of Fortune 500 chairpersons and CEOs were women; in 2014, this percentage is 4.6% (Catalyst, 2014). According to Catalyst (2014), 46 women are currently CEOs of Fortune 1000 companies, which represent 4.6% of companies. Globally, 14% of companies have women CEOs, women hold 19% of board seats and 24% of senior management roles (IBR, 2013). Higher percentages of women CEOs are found in Asia, specifically South Korea, China, and the Philippines.

Adler's (1996) principle findings were that women global leaders came from diverse backgrounds with no predictable path to leadership. Surprisingly, they were not selected or elected only in women-friendly companies or countries. Their selection represented hope, change, and unity to others. They were driven by vision rather than hierarchical status. They used broad-based popular support instead of traditional, hierarchical party or structural support. Their path to power was through lateral transfers, not a traditional trajectory up the hierarchy. Finally, they leveraged the increased visibility they received as women or "the first woman."

Directions for Future Research

Several scholars have recently identified the gaps in global leadership research (Khilji, Davis, & Cseh, 2010; Maznevski, Stahl, & Mendenhall, 2013; Osland, 2013b; Osland, Li, & Wang, 2014a, 2014b; Reiche & Mendenhall, 2013; Steers, Sanchez-Runde, & Nardon, 2012). To date, there are no global leadership theories, just models and frameworks.

Another important weakness is *construct definition*. The field would benefit from a generally accepted unifying construct definition. It would be helpful if scholars could specify how global leaders differ from global managers and domestic leaders in terms of roles, behavior, and cognitive processes.

Competency identification is the most advanced area in the field, but further research is needed to bridge the *micro-macro divide* (Maznevski et al., 2013). For example, are there capabilities with respect to teams and organizations or particular types of global strategy that have yet to be identified?

There are no observational studies of actual *global leader behavior* nor a comparison of male and female behavior. Similarly, we do not know how global leaders adapt their behavior when performing different tasks in different types of global leader jobs in different contexts. In general, we need more process models to help us understand how global leaders interact with their environment and how it affects them.

While we have process models of *global leadership development* that are supported by research (McCall & Hollenbeck, 2002; Mendenhall et al., in press; Osland & Bird, 2013), they have yet to be empirically tested. Research is starting to appear on specific development methods; however, there is a dearth of longitudinal or comparative studies of methodologies that measure cost-benefits and training transfer.

The research on *assessment instruments* is growing, particularly in the intercultural competence domain of global leadership and global leadership behaviors. However, more numerous and more rigorous assessments are needed in certain areas, such as other domains of competencies, the degree of complexity in the global context so this can be controlled in studies, dynamic processes, and contingencies that impact global leadership.

Very little research exists on *global leadership effectiveness*. Scholars could develop performance measures and identify antecedents as well as contingencies that impact effectiveness and styles (Osland et al., 2014a, 2014b).

Finally, there have been no subsequent studies only focusing on women global leaders until this volume. The number of males and females in today's research samples are less imbalanced, but some of them still reflect the lower number of women at high levels or in certain industries, such as high tech. One possible area for future research would be to determine whether the findings Adler (1996, 1997a, 1997b) identified have changed in the past two decades.

My hope is that this volume will broaden our understanding of women global leaders and contribute to an increase in their numbers. To return to Einstein's quotation at the beginning of the chapter, the seriousness of today's global problems is such that we need not only different thinking and leadership, but widespread diversity and a strong representation of women among those taking an active role to find solutions.

REFERENCES

Adler, N. J. (1996). Global women political leaders: An invisible history, an increasingly important future. *Leadership Quarterly*, 7(1), 133–161.

Adler, N. J. (1997a). Global leaders: A dialogue with future history. *International Management*, 1(2), 21–33.

Adler, N. J. (1997b). Global leadership: Women leaders. *Management International Review*, 37(1), 171–196.

Adler, N. J. (2001). Global leadership: Women leaders. In M. Mendenhall, T. M. Kühlmann, & G. K. Stahl (Eds.) *Developing global business leaders: Policies, processes and innovations* (pp. 72–98). Westport, CT: Quorum.

Adler, N. J., Brody, L., & Osland, J. S. (2000). The Women's Global Leadership Forum: Enhancing one company's global leadership capability. *Human Resource Management, 39*(2/3), 209–225.

Adler, N. J., Brody, L. & Osland, J. S. (2001a). Advances in global leadership: The Women's Global Leadership Forum. *Advances in global leadership* (Vol. 2, pp. 351–383). Greenwich, CT: JAI.

Adler, N. J., Brody, L. & Osland, J. S. (2001b). Going beyond twentieth century leadership: A CEO develops his company's global competitiveness. *Cross-Cultural Management: An International Journal, 8*(3/4), 11–32.

Ancona, D., Malone, T. W., Orlikowski, W. J., & Senge, P. M. (2007). In praise of the incomplete leader. *Harvard Business Review, 85*(2), 92–100, 156.

Bikson, T. K., Treverton, G. F., Moini, J., & Lindstrom, G. (2003). *New challenges for international leadership: Lessons from organizations with global missions.* Santa Monica, CA: RAND.

Bird, A. (2013). Mapping the content domain of global leadership competencies. In M. E. Mendenhall, J. S. Osland, A. Bird, G. Oddou, M. Maznevski, G. Stahl, & M. Stevens (Eds.), *Global leadership: Research, practice and development* (2nd ed., pp. 80–96). London, England: Routledge.

Bird, A., Mendenhall, M., Stevens, M., & Oddou, G. (2010). Defining the content domain of intercultural competence for global leaders. *Journal of Managerial Psychology, 25*(8), 810–828.

Bird, A., & Osland, J. S. (2004). Global competencies: An introduction. In H. W. Lane, M. L. Maznevski, M. E. Mendenhall, & J. McNett (Eds.), *The Blackwell handbook of global management: A guide to managing complexity* (pp. 57–80). Malden, MA: Blackwell.

Bird, A., & Stevens, M. (2013). Assessing global leadership competencies. In M. E. Mendenhall, J. S. Osland, A. Bird, G. Oddou, M. Maznevski, G. Stahl, & M. Stevens (Eds.), *Global leadership: Research, practice and development* (2nd ed., pp. 113–140). London, England: Routledge.

Björkman, I., & Mäkelä, K. (2013). Are you willing to do what it takes to become a senior global leader? Explaining the willingness to undertake challenging leadership development activities. *European Journal of International Management, 7*(5), 570–586.

Black, J. S., & Morrison, A. J. (2014). *The global leadership challenge.* London, England: Routledge.

Black, J. S., Morrison, A. J., & Gregersen, H.B. (1999). *Global explorers: The next generations of leaders.* New York, NY: Routledge.

Brake, T. (1997). *The global leader: Critical factors for creating the world class organization.* Chicago, IL: Irwin.

Calas, M. B., & Smircich, L. (1993). Dangerous liaisons: The "feminine-in-management" meets "globalization." *Business Horizons, 36*(2), 71–81.

Caliguiri, P. (2006) Developing global leaders. *Human Resource Management Review, 16*(2), 219–228.

Caligiuri, P., & Tarique, I. (2009). Predicting effectiveness in global leadership activities. *Journal of World Business, 44*(3), 336–346.

Caligiuri, P., & Tarique, I. (2012). Dynamic cross-cultural competencies and global leadership effectiveness. *Journal of World Business, 47*(4), 612–622.

Caligiuri, P., & Tarique, I. (2014). *Individual-level accelerators of global leadership development.* In J. S. Osland, M. Li, & Y. Wang (Eds.), Advances in global leadership (Vol. 8, pp. 251–268). Bingley, England: Emerald.

Catalyst. (1996, February 28). *1996 Catalyst census of women corporate officers and top earners of the Fortune 500.* Retrieved from http://www.catalyst.org/knowledge/1996-catalyst-census-women-corporate-officers-and-top-earners-fortune-500

Catalyst. (2014, September 19). *Women CEOs of the Fortune 1000.* Retrieved from http://www.catalyst.org/knowledge/women-ceos-fortune-1000

CFWD. (2014). *Women presidents and prime ministers July 2014.* Retrieved from http://www.cfwd.org.uk/uploads/PresidentsandPrimeMinistersJuly2014.pdf

Clapp-Smith, R., & Hughes, L. (2007). Unearthing a global mindset: The process of international adjustment. *Journal of Business and Leadership: Research, Practice and Teaching, 3*(1), 99–107.

Conger, J., & Ready, D. (2004). Rethinking leadership competencies. *Leader to Leader, 32*, 41–48.

Dalton, M., Ernst, C., Deal, J., & Leslie, J. (2002). *Success for the new global manager: What you need to know to work across distances, countries and cultures.* San Francisco, CA: Jossey-Bass/Center for Creative Leadership.

Einstein, A. (1946, June 23). Only then shall we find courage. *New York Times Magazine.*

Fitzsimmons, S. R., Lee, Y., & Brannen, M. Y. (2013). Demystifying the myth about marginals: Implications for global leadership. *European Journal of International Management, 7*(5), 587–603.

Gitsham, M. et al. (2008, December). *Developing the global leader of tomorrow.* Conference presentation at the 1st Global Forum for Responsible Management Education, United Nations, New York.

Goldsmith, M., Greenberg, C., Robertson, A., & Hu-Chan, M. (2003). *Global Leadership: The next generation.* Upper Saddle River, NJ: Prentice Hall.

Gundling, E., Hogan, T., & Cvitkovich, K. (2011). *What is global leadership? 10 key behaviors that define great global leaders.* Boston, MA: Intercultural.

Holt, K., & Seki, K. (2012). Global leadership: A developmental shift for everyone. *Industrial and Organizational Psychology, 5*(2), 196–215.

IBM. (2010). *Capitalizing on complexity: Insights from the 2010 Global CEO Study.* Fishkill, NY: IBM.

IBR. (2013). *Women in senior management: Setting the stage for growth.* Grant Thornton International Business Report 2013. Retrieved from http://www.grantthornton.ie/db/Attachments/IBR2013_WiB_report_final.pdf

Kets de Vries, M. F. R., Vrignaud, P., & Florent-Treacy, E. (2004). The global leadership life inventory: Development and psychometric properties of a 360-degree feedback instrument. *International Journal of Human Resource Management, 15*(3), 475–492.

Jokinen, T. (2005). Global leadership competencies: A review and discussion. *Journal of European Industrial Training, 29*(2/3), 199–216.

Khilji, S., Davis, E. G., & Cseh, M. (2010). Building competitive advantage in a global environment: Leadership and the mindset. In T. Devinney, T. Pedersen, & T. Tihanyi (Eds.), *The past, present and future of international business and management (Advances in international management)* (Vol. 23, pp. 353–373). Bingley, England: Emerald.

Lane, H. W., Maznevski, M. L., & Mendenhall, M. E. (2004). Hercules meets Buddha. In H. W. Lane, M. Maznevski, M. E. Mendenhall, & J. McNett (Eds.), *The handbook of global management: A guide to managing complexity* (pp. 3–25). Malden, MA: Blackwell.

Li, M., Mobley, W., & Kelly, A. (2013). When do global leaders learn best to develop cultural intelligence? An investigation of the moderating role of experiential learning style. *Academy of Management Learning & Education, 12*(1), 32-50.

Lobel, S. A. (1990). Global leadership competencies: Managing to a different drumbeat. *Human Resource Management, 29*(1), 39–47.

Marquis, C., & Kanter, R. M. (2010). *IBM: The corporate service corps.* Harvard Business School Case 9-409-106. Boston, MA: Harvard Business School Press.

Maznevski, M., Stahl, G., & Mendenhall, M. (2013). Towards an integration of global leadership practice and scholarship: Repairing disconnects and heightening mutual understanding. *European Journal of International Management, 7*(5), 493–500.

McCall, M., & Hollenbeck, G. P. (2002). *Developing global executives: The lessons of international experience.* Boston, MA: Harvard Business School Press.

McKinsey. (2012). *McKinsey global survey results: Managing at global scale.* London, England: McKinsey.

Mendenhall, M., Arnardottir, A., Oddou, G., & Burke, L. (2013). Developing cross cultural competencies in management education via cognitive behavior therapy. *Academy of Management Education & Learning, 12*(3), 436–451.

Mendenhall, M., Burke, L., Arnardottir, A., Oddou, G., & Osland, J. (in press). Making a difference in the classroom: Developing global leadership competencies in business school students. In L. Zander (Ed.), *Handbook of global leadership research: Making a difference.* Cheltenham, England: Elgar.

Mendenhall, M. & Osland, J. S. (2002). *An overview of the extant global leadership research.* Symposium presentation, Academy of International Business, San Juan, Puerto Rico.

Mendenhall, M., Osland, J. S., Bird, A., Oddou, G., Maznevski, M., Stevens, M., & Stahl, G. (Eds.). (2013). *Global leadership: Research, practice, and development.* London, England: Routledge.

Mendenhall, M., Reiche, B. S., Bird, A., & Osland, J. S. (2012). Defining the "global" in global leadership. *Journal of World Business, 47*(4), 493–503.

Miska, C., Stahl, G., & Mendenhall, M. (2013). Intercultural competencies as antecedents of responsible global leadership. *European Journal of International Management, 7*(5), 550–569.

Oddou, G. R., & Mendenhall, M. E. (2013). Global leadership development. In M. E. Mendenhall, J. S. Osland, A. Bird, G. R. Oddou, M. L. Maznevski, M. J.

Stevens, & G. K. Stahl (Eds.), *Global leadership: Research, practice, and development* (2nd ed., pp. 215–239). London, England: Routledge.

O'Neill, H. (2011, May 24). Corporate America embracing their version of the Peace Corps. *Workforce*. Retrieved from http://www.workforce.com/articles/corporate-america-embracing-their-version-of-the-peace-corps

Osland, J. S. (2010). Expert cognition and sense-making in the global organization leadership context: A case study. In U. Fisher & K. Moser (Eds.), *Informed by knowledge: Expert performance in complex situations* (pp. 23–40). New York, NY: Taylor & Francis.

Osland, J. S. (2013a). The multidisciplinary roots of global leadership. In M. E. Mendenhall, J. S. Osland, A. Bird, G. R. Oddou, M. L. Maznevski, M. J. Stevens, & G. K. Stahl (Eds.), *Global leadership: Research, practice, and development* (2nd ed., pp. 21–39). New York, NY: Routledge.

Osland, J. S. (2013b). An overview of the global leadership literature. In M. E. Mendenhall, J. S. Osland, A. Bird, G. R. Oddou, & M. L. Maznevski, M. J. Stevens, & G. K. Stahl (Eds.), *Global leadership: Research, practice, and development* (2nd ed., pp. 40–79). New York, NY: Routledge.

Osland, J., & Bird, A. (2006) Global leaders as experts. In W. H. Mobley & E. Weldon (Eds.), *Advances in global leadership* (Vol. 4., pp. 123–142). Oxford, England: Elsevier.

Osland, J., & Bird, A. (2013). Process models of global leadership development. In M. E. Mendenhall, J. S. Osland, A. Bird, G. R. Oddou, & M. L. Maznevski, M. J. Stevens, & G. K. Stahl (Eds.), *Global leadership: Research, practice, and development* (2nd ed., pp. 97–112). New York, NY: Routledge.

Osland, J. S., Bird, A., & Mendenhall, M. (2012). Developing global mindset and global leadership capabilities. In G. Stahl, I. Björkman, & S. Morris (Eds.), *Handbook of research in international human resource management* (2nd ed., pp. 220-252). Cheltenham, England: Elgar.

Osland, J., Bird, A., Osland, Mendenhall, M., & Osland, A. (2006). Developing global leadership capabilities and global mindset: A review. In G. Stahl & I. Bjorkman (Eds.), *Handbook of research in international human resource management* (pp. 197–222). Cheltenham, England: Elgar.

Osland, J. S., Bird, A., & Oddou, G. (2012). The context of expert global leadership. In W. H. Mobley, Y. Wang, & M. Li (Eds.), *Advances in global leadership* (Vol. 7, pp. 107–124). Bingley, England: Emerald.

Osland, J. S., Bird, A., Oddou, G., & Osland, A. (2013). Exceptional global leadership as cognitive expertise: In the domain of global change. *European Journal of International Management*, 7(5), 517–534.

Osland, J., Li, M., & Wang, Y. (2014a). Introduction: The state of global leadership research. In J. Osland, M. Li, & Y. Wang (Eds.), *Advances in global leadership* (Vol. 8, pp. 17–34). Bingley, England: Emerald.

Osland, J., Li, M., & Wang, Y. (2014b). Conclusion: Future directions for advancing global leadership research. In J. Osland, M. Li, & Y. Wang (Eds.), *Advances in global leadership* (Vol. 8, pp. 351–364). Bingley, England: Emerald.

Osland, J., Taylor, S., & Mendenhall, M. (2009). Global leadership: Challenges and lessons. In R. Steers & R. Bhagat (Eds.), *Handbook of cultural variations in work* (pp. 245–271). Oxford, England: Blackwell.

Pandaya, M., & Shell, R. (2005). *Lasting leadership*. Upper Saddle River, NJ: Pearson Education/Wharton.

Pless, N. M., Maak, T., & Stahl, G. (2011). Developing responsible global leaders through international service learning programs: The Ulysses experience. *Academy of Management Learning and Education, 10*(2), 237–260.

Pless, N. M., Maak, T., & Stahl, G. K. (2012). Promoting corporate social responsibility and sustainable development through management development: What can be learned from international service learning programs? *Human Resource Management, 51*(6), 873–903.

Reiche, B. S., & Mendenhall, M. (2013). Looking to the future. In M. E. Mendenhall, J. S. Osland, A. Bird, G. R. Oddou, M. L. Maznevski, M. J. Stevens, & G. K. Stahl, (Eds.), *Global leadership: Research, practice and development* (2nd ed., pp. 260–268). New York, NY: Routledge.

Reiche, B. S., Mendenhall, M., Bird, A., & Osland, J. S. (2014). *A taxonomy of global leadership*. Presented at the Academy of International Business, Vancouver, Canada.

Rosen, R., Digh, P., Singer, M., & Philips, C. (2000). *Global literacies: Lessons on business leadership and national cultures*. New York, NY: Simon & Schuster.

Shin, S. J., Morgeson, F. P., & Campion, M. A. (2007). What you do depends on where you are: Understanding how domestic and expatriate work requirements depend upon the cultural context. *Journal of International Business Studies, 38*(1), 64–83.

Stahl, G. K., & Brannen, M. Y. (2013). Building cross-cultural leadership competence: An interview with Carlos Ghosn. *Academy of Management Learning & Education, 12*(3), 494–502.

Steers, R. M., Sanchez-Runde, C., & Nardon, L. (2012). Special issue: Leadership in a global context. *Journal of World Business, 47*(4), 479–483.

Terrell, R. S., & Rosenbusch, K. (2012). How global leaders develop. *Journal of Management Development, 32*(10), 1056–1079.

Tompson, H. B., & Tompson, G. H. (2013). The focus of leadership development in MNCs. *International Journal of Leadership Studies, 8*(1), 6–14.

Voegtlin, C., Patzer, M., & Scherer, A. (2012). Responsible leadership in global business: A new approach to leadership and its multi-level outcomes. *Journal of Business Ethics, 105*(1), 1–16.

Weber, W., Festing, M. Dowling, P. J., & Schuler, R. S. (1998). *Internationales personalmanagement*. Weisbaden, Germany: Gabler Verlag.

Wernsing, T., & Clapp-Smith, R. (2013). Developing global leaders through building cultural self-awareness. *European Journal of International Management, 7*(5), 535–549.

Wills, S., & Barham, K. (1994). Being an international manager. *European Management Journal, 12*(1), 49–58.

World Economic Forum (WEF). (2013). *Global agenda outlook 2013*. Retrieved from http://www.weforum.org/reports/global-agenda-outlook-2013

Yeung, A. K., & Ready, D. A. (1995). Developing leadership capabilities of global corporations: A comparative study of eight nations. *Human Resource Management, 34*(4), 529–547.

CHAPTER 2

WOMEN LEADERS

Shaping History in the 21st Century

Nancy J. Adler

> *We have a responsibility in our time, as others have had in theirs, not to be prisoners of history, but to shape history.*
>
> —Former U.S. Secretary of State Madeleine K. Albright (1997)

Shaping history; that is the challenge of global leadership—creating a 21st century in which organizations enhance, rather than diminish, civilization. For global leaders, economic viability is necessary, but no longer sufficient for organizational, let alone societal, success.

None of us can claim that the 20th century left a legacy of worldwide success, a success defined by peace, prosperity, compassion, and sustainability. In reflecting on the inheritance left to our children from the 20th century, many people feel ashamed. Yes, we have advanced science and technology, but at the price of a world torn asunder by a polluted environment, cities infested with social chaos and physical decay, an increasingly skewed income distribution that condemns large portions of the population to poverty (including people living in the world's most affluent societies),

---

The current chapter has been updated, revised, and is published with the permission of Wiley. Original copyright details at the end of the chapter.

Women as Global Leaders, pp. 21–50
Copyright © 2015 by Information Age Publishing
All rights of reproduction in any form reserved.

and rampant physical violence that continues to kill people in ostensibly limited wars and seemingly random acts of aggression. No, society did not exit the 20th century with pride. Unless we collectively learn to treat each other and our planet in a more civilized way, it may soon become blasphemy to even consider ourselves a civilization (Rechtschaffen, 1996).

BEGINNING THE 21st CENTURY

With the 20th century now history, have the opening years of the current century given us hope? Unfortunately, no. If anything, many economic and societal trends appear to be heading in the wrong direction. We need look no further than at the number of children who live in abject poverty to be humbled into silence, if not despair. Review just a few of the facts from the first year of this century.

September 2001 opened with the U.N.-sponsored World Conference Against Racism in Durban, South Africa.[1] As the world watched with high expectations, the conference drowned in a cacophony of intolerance, expressed by official delegates from more than 160 countries as well as by thousands of representatives of nongovernmental organizations. "The meeting, which was intended to celebrate tolerance and diversity, became an international symbol of divisiveness" (Swarms, 2001, p. A1). According to the world press, the results reflected "less a new international unity than a collective exhaustion" (Slackman, 2001, p. A1).

One week later, on September 11th, terrorists destroyed New York's World Trade Center, killing more than 3,000 people. In the immediate aftermath, while stock markets plummeted, public rhetoric and behavior became increasingly susceptible to simplistic definitions of good and evil and calls for large-scale military retaliation. The escalation of ignorance-based hatred attempting to pit the Western world against Islamic communities and nations became palpable. Perhaps the danger, absurdity, and pain can be best symbolized by the fate of a woman living far from both Durban and the World Trade Center. As the woman, a Montreal physician, made her usual hospital rounds the week after the terrorist attacks, she was strangled. Why? Strictly because she was Muslim. Her status as a medical doctor and good citizen, working daily to save the lives of her fellow human beings, was obliterated in the eyes of her attacker solely because she wore a headscarf that symbolizes a religion he failed to understand.

Hate and intolerance, optimism reduced to hopelessness, compassion eclipsed by anger, and ignorance motivating senseless action—is this the scenario that will define the rest of the century, that will define our children's and our children's children's future? Possibly, but not necessarily. Hope for a better future rests largely with the quality of business, political, and societal leadership offered by women and men worldwide.

Although from the perspective of the first year of this century it would seem otherwise, the 21st century need not become a time of terrorism, intolerance, fear, and deteriorating economic equality. It also could herald an era of unprecedented worldwide prosperity, communication, and innovation, led in large part by global organizations and companies (Adler, 2006, 2008, 2010; Friedman, 2006). The ability of global companies to work successfully across cultures, however, while better than the track record of participants attending U.N.-sponsored racism conferences, remains problematic. Historically, three quarters of all international joint ventures fail.[2] One wonders, at times, why societies choose to continue to become more globally interconnected and companies choose to continue to expand beyond their borders, when the track record of global cross-cultural relations remains so dismal.[3] Weaving the people of the world together, whether in companies or in society at-large, is clearly not easy. Our current approaches beg for new—or perhaps ancient-but-forgotten—perspectives. Is it not possible to imagine a world defined by peace and prosperity in the 21st century (see Fort & Schipani, 2004)? Would not our wisest global leaders know how to guide us in creating such a world? Is this only a naïvely idealistic assumption? Perhaps, but not historically. Such visionary leadership only appears naïve from the parochial perspective of the last 9,000 years.

As archaeologists and other scholars have observed, there have always been legends and writings about an earlier, more harmonious and peaceful age (Eisler, 1987).[4] *The Bible*, for example, tells us of the Garden of Eden. But many people assume that these are only idyllic fantasies, expressing universal yearnings and seemingly exaggerated aspirations. Only now, thanks to new findings and scientific dating methods, are archaeologists exposing facts that support the supposed myths and fantasies of our distant past (Gimbutas, 1991).

New excavations reveal that these alleged legends derive not from idealistic fantasies but from folk memories about real flesh and blood people who organized their societies along very different lines from our own. At Chatal Huyuk and Hajilar, for example, both located in modern-day Turkey, archaeologists date communities to 7000 B.C.E., 90 centuries ago. These peaceful communities were located in the middle of fertile plains, not in defensible positions against stone cliffs or atop mountains nor surrounded by moats, walls, or other defense systems. Their art, moreover, shows no sign of either individual-or community-level violence. Excavations reveal only minimal indications of hierarchy.

Just as Columbus' discovery that the world was not flat made it possible for our ancestors to "find" a world that, in fact, had been here all along, the archaeologists' findings are allowing us to rediscover prosperous communities that interacted peacefully and cooperatively with their neighbors (Eisler, 1987). Their findings allow us to ground supposedly naïve, unattainable idealism in the reality of history. Perhaps not coincidentally, women led most of these ancient communities.

ARE IDYLLIC SOCIETIES POSSIBLE AGAIN?

What would it take to remarry such idealism with contemporary global realities? First, we would need to again believe that prosperity and a civilized way of living together on this planet are possible; that 21st-century humanity is capable of success, broadly defined.[5] To that end, the archaeologists' findings are crucial. We know that we achieved such success at one time; the only question is whether we can achieve it again.[6] Second, we would need to believe that change is possible; that society is capable of moving from a world organized around war and violence, the extremes of poverty and wealth, and an overall mentality of scarcity, to one organized around peace, prosperity, compassion, and abundance.[7] And third, we would need to move from discrete local perspectives to broadly encompassing global perspectives. We would need to move away from divisiveness and return to more unifying images and strategies. For humanity to embrace each of the beliefs needed to create a healthy, economically vibrant, sustainable global society, we would need approaches to leadership that differ quite markedly from those offered by most leaders in recent history.

Where is society to find leaders to guide it toward beliefs that differ so markedly from those of the recent past? Whereas most societal commentators continue to review the historical patterns of men's leadership in search of models for 21st century success, few have begun to recognize, let alone appreciate, the equivalent patterns of women's leadership and the potential future contributions that women could make as leaders. What are women bringing to society as global leaders? Are we entering an era in which both male and female leaders, rather than primarily men, will literally and symbolically shape history?

WOMEN LEADING COUNTRIES AND COMPANIES: NO LONGER MEN ALONE

While rarely recognized or reported in the media, the trend toward women joining men in senior leadership positions began in the 20th century and is accelerating in the current century. The pattern is easiest to see when observing leaders of countries. Whereas in the past almost all political leaders were men, the number of women selected to serve as president or prime minister of their country since the mid-20th century has increased markedly, albeit from a negligible starting point. As highlighted in Table 2.1 and Figure 2.1, of the 126 women who have served as president or prime minister of her country, none came into office in the 1950s (or the 1940s), just 3 came into office in the 1960s, 6 in the 1970s, 11 in the 1980s, 37[8] in the 1990s, 39 in the 2000s, and already 30 in the first 3 years of the current decade. If the early years of this decade are indicative of the trend, 92 women will come into office in the 2010s, more than the combined total of women (57) serving as president or prime minister in the entire 20th century. Countries as dissimilar as France, India, Rwanda, South Korea, and Sri Lanka have all selected women to lead them. Whereas the increase is impressive, the total is not. Given that there are more than 195[9] countries in the world, many with both a president and a prime minister, and each with multiple leaders since the mid-20th century, a total of 126 women in more than a half century is neither a large nor an impressive number.

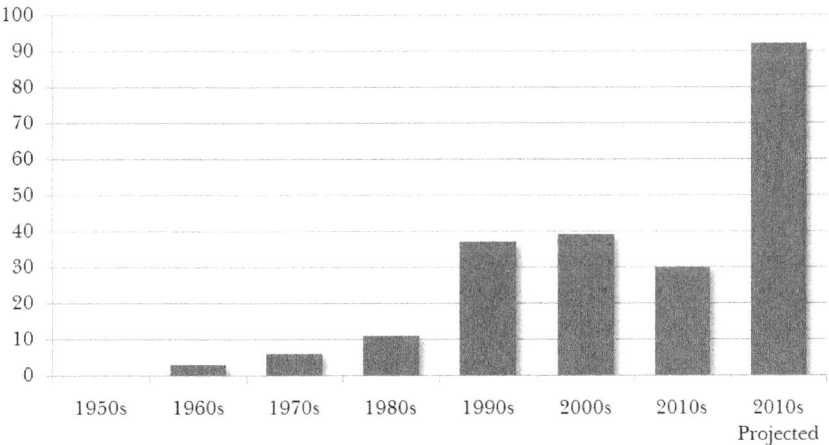

Figure 2.1. Women political leaders: Numbers increasing (data as of April 2014).

Table 2.1. Women Political Leaders: A Chronology

Country	Name	Office	Date
Sri Lanka	Sirimavo Bandaranaike	Prime Minister	1960–1965; 1970–1977; 1994–2000
India	Indira Gandhi	Prime Minister	1966–1977; 1980–1984
Israel	Golda Meir	Prime Minister	1969–1974
Argentina	Isabel Perón	President	1974–1976
Central African Rep.	Elizabeth Domitien	Prime Minister	1975–1976
Netherlands Antilles	Lucinda da Costa Gomez–Matheeuws	Prime Minister	1977
Portugal	Maria de Lourdes Ruivo da Silva Pintasilgo	Prime Minister	1979 (5 mo.)
Bolivia	Lidia Gueiler Tejada	Interim President, Prime Minister	1979–1980 (8 mo.)
Great Britain	Margaret Thatche	Prime Minister	1979–1990
Dominica	Mary Eugenia Charles	Prime Minister	1980–1995
Iceland	Vigdís Finnbógadottir	President	1980–1996
San Marino	Maria Lea Pedini Angelini	Captain Regent	1981 (6 mo.)
Norway	Gro Harlem Brundtland	Prime Minister	1981; 1986–1989; 1990–1996
Yugoslavia	Milka Planinc	Prime Minister	1982–1986
Malta	Agatha Barbara	President	1982–1987
Guinea Bissau	Carmen Pereira	Acting President (Head of State)	1984 (3 days)
San Marino	Maria Lea Pedini Angelini	Captain Regent	1984 & 1989/90 (each 6 mo.)
Norway	Gro Harlem Brundtland	Prime Minister	1981; 1986–1989; 1990–1996
Yugoslavia	Milka Planinc	Prime Minister	1982–1986
Malta	Agatha Barbara	President	1982–1987
Guinea Bissau	Carmen Pereira	Acting President (Head of State)	1984 (3 days)
San Marino	Gloriana Ranocchini	Captain Regent	1984 & 1989/90 (each 6 mo.)

(Table continues of next page)

Table 2.1. (Continued)

Country	Name	Office	Date
Netherlands Antilles	Maria Liberia–Peters	Prime Minister	1984–1986; 1989–1994
The Philippines	Corazon Aquino	Executive President	1986–1992
Pakistan	Benazir Bhutto	Prime Minister	1988–1990; 1993–1996
Lithuania	Kazimiera–Danute Prunskiene	Prime Minister	1990–1991
Haiti	Ertha Pascal–Trouillot	Acting President	1990–1991
Burma (Myanmar)	Aung San Suu Kyi	Elected President**	1990–**
German Democratic Republic	Sabine Bergmann–Pohl	Chairman of the Volksammer (Staatspräsident)/ Acting Head of State	1990 (6 mo.)
Ireland	Mary Robinson	President	1990–1997
Nicaragua	Violeta Chamorro	Executive President	1990–1997
Bangladesh	Khaleda Zia	Prime Minister	1991–1996; 2001–2006
San Marino	Edda Ceccoli	Captain Regent	1991–1992 (6 mo.)
France	Edith Cresson	Prime Minister	1991–1992
Poland	Hanna Suchocka	Prime Minister	1992–1993
San Marino	Patrizia Busignani	Captain Regent	1993 (6 mo.)
Canada	Kim Campbell	Prime Minister	1993 (5 mo.)
Burundi	Sylvia Kinigi	Acting Head of State/President	1993–1994 (4 mo.)
Faroe Islands	Marita Petersen	Prime Minister	1993–1994
Rwanda	Agatha Uwilingiyimana	Prime Minister	1993–1994
Turkey	Tansu Çiller	Prime Minister	1993–1996
Netherlands Antilles	Susanne Camelia–Romer	Prime Minister	1993; 1998–1999
Bulgaria	Reneta Indzhova	Interim Prime Minister	1994–1995 (3 mo.)
Sri Lanka	Chandrika Kumaratunga	Exec. President & Prime Minister	1994–2005
Haiti	Claudette Werleigh	Prime Minister	1995–1996
Bangladesh	Hasina Wajed	Prime Minister	1996–2001

(Table continues of next page)

Table 2.1. (Continued)

Country	Name	Office	Date
Liberia	Ruth Perry	Chair, Council of State	1996–1997
Ecuador	Rosalia Arteaga	Acting Executive President	1997 (3 days)
Bermuda	Pamela Gordon	Premier	1997–1998
Bosnian Serb Republic	Biliana Plavsic	President	1997–1998
Ireland	Mary McAleese	President	1997–2011
New Zealand	Jenny Shipley	Prime Minister	1997–1999
Guyana	Janet Jagan	Prime Minister, President	1997–1999
Norway	Anne Enger Lahnstein	Acting Prime Minister	1998 (24 days)
Bermuda	Jennifer Smith	Premier	1998–2003
Lithuania	Irena Degutienë	Acting Prime Minister	1999 (22 days)
Mongolia	Nyam–Osoryn Tuyaa	Acting Prime Minister	1999 (9 days)
Switzerland	Ruth Dreifuss	President	1999 (1 yr.)
San Marino	Rosa Zafferani	Captain Regent	1999 (6 mo.); 2008–2009 (6 mo.)
Latvia	Vaira Vike-Freiberga	President	1999–2007
Panama	Mireya Moscoso	Executive President	1999–2004
New Zealand	Helen Clark	Prime Minister	1999–2008
San Marino	Maria Domenica Michelotti	Maria Domenica Michelotti	2000 (6 mo.)
Finland	Tarja Halonen	President	2000–2012
Philippines	Gloria Macapagal–Arroyo	Executive President	2001–2010
Sénégal	Madior Boye	Prime Minister	2001–2002
Indonesia	Megawati Sukarnoputri	Executive President	2001–2004
South Korea	Chang Sang	Acting Prime Minister	2002 (20 days)
Serbia	Natasa Micic	Acting President	2002–2004
São Tomé & Principe	Maria das Neves de Souse	Prime Minister	2002–2003; 2003–2004

(Table continues of next page)

Table 2.1. (Continued)

Country	Name	Office	Date
Finland	Anneli Jäätteenmäki	Prime Minister	2003 (2 mo.)
Peru	Beatriz Merino	Prime Minister	2003 (6 mo.)
Netherlands Antilles	Mirna Louisa–Godett	Prime Minister	2003–2004
Georgia	Nino Burdzhanadze	Acting Executive President	2003–2004; 2007–2008 (2 mo.)
San Marino	Valeria Ciavatta	Captain Regent	2003–2004 (6 mo.);
Macedonia	Radmila Sekerinska	Acting Prime Minister	2004 (2 x 1 mo.)
Austria	Barbara Prammer	Acting Joint Head of State	2004 (3 days)
New Caledonia	*Maria–Noëlle Thérmereau	President	2004–*
Mozambique	Luisa Días Diogo	Prime Minister	2004–2010
The Bahamas	Cynthia A Pratt	Acting Prime Minister	2005 (1½ mo.)
São Tomé & Principe	Maria do Carmo Silveira	Prime Minister	2005–2006
Ukraine	Yuliya Tymoshenko	Prime Minister	2005; 2007–2010
San Marino	Fausta Morganti	Captain Regent	2004–2005 (6 mo,)
Germany	*Angela Merkel	Chancellor	2005–*
South Africa	*Ivy Matsepe–Casaburri	Acting President	2005 (4 dys); 2008
Liberia	*Ellen Johnson–Sirleaf	President	2006–*
Chile	*Michelle Bachelet	President	2006–2010; 2014–*
Jamaica	*Portia Simpson–Miller	Prime Minister	2006–2007; 2012–*
South Korea	Han Myung–sook	Prime Minister	2006–2007
Switzerland	Micheline Calmy–Rey	President of the Confederation	2007 2011
Israel	Dalia Itzik	Acting President Interim President	2007
India	Pratibha Patil	President	2007–2012
Argentina	*Cristina Fernández de Kirchner	Executive President	2007–*

(Table continues of next page)

Table 2.1. (Continued)

Country	Name	Office	Date
San Marino	Assunta Meloni	Captain Regent	2008–2009 (6 mo.)
Moldova	Zinaida Grecianîi	Prime Minister	2008–2009
Haiti	Michèle Pierre-Louis	Interim President	2009 (4 mo.)
Gabon	Rose Francine Rogombé	Acting Prime Minister	2009 (2 mo.)
Madagascar	Cécile Manorohanta	Acting Prime Minister	2009 (2 mo.)
Iceland	Jóhanna Sigurðardóttir	Prime Minister	2009–2013
Croatia	Jadranka Kosor	Prime Minister	2009–2011
Lithuania	*Dalia Grybauskaité	President	2009–*
Switzerland	Doris Leuthard	President	2010 (1 yr.)
Kyrgyzstan	Roza Otunbayeva	President	2010–2011
Bermuda	Paula Cox	Premier	2010–2012
Costa Rica	*Laura Chinchilla Miranda	President	2010–*
Brazil	*Dilma Vana Linhares Rousseff	President	2011–*
Trinidad and Tobago	*Kamla Persad-Bissessar	Prime Minister	2010–*
Finland	Mari Kiviniemi	Prime Minister	2010–2011
Australia	Julia Gillard	Prime Minister	2010–2013
Slovakia	Iveta Radičová	Prime Minister	2010–2012
San Marino	Maria Luisa Berti	Captain Regent	2011 (6 mo.)
Peru	Rosario Fernández	Prime Minister	2011 (4 mo.)
Kosovo	Atifete Jahjaga	President	2011–*
Mali	Mariam Kaïdama Sidibé	Prime Minister	2011–2012
Thailand	*Yingluck Shinawatra	Prime Minister	2011–*
Guinea Bissau	Adiatu Djalo	Prime Minister	2012 (2 mo.)
Switzerland	Eveline Widmer-Sclumpf	President of the Confederation	2012 (1 yr.)
Mauritius	Monique Agnès Ohsan-Bellepeau	Acting President	2012 (7 mo.)

(Table continues of next page)

Table 2.1. (Continued)

Country	Name	Office	Date
Serbia	Slavica Dukić–Dejanović	Acting President	2012 (2 mo.)
Malawi	*Joyce Banda	President	2012–*
San Marino	Denise Bronzetti	Captain Regent	2012 (6 mo.)
South Korea	*Park Geun–hye	President	2013–*
Slovenia	*Alenka Bratušek	Prime Minister	2013–*
Turkish Republic of Northern Cyprus	Sibel Siber	Prime Minister	2013 (3 mo.)
Transnistria	*Tatyana Turanskaya	Prime Minister	2013–*
San Marino	Antonella Mularoni	Captain Regent	2013 (6 mo.)
Sénégal	*Aminata Touré	Prime Minister	2013–*
Norway	*Erna Solberg	Prime Minister	2013–*
Latvia	*Laimdota Straujuma	Prime Minister	2014–*
Central African Republic	*Catherine Samba–Panza	Acting Head of State	2014–*
Malta	*Marie–Louise Coleiro Preca	President	2014–*

Notes: * = Currently in office as of April 2014; ** = Party won 1990 election but prevented by military from taking office, Nobel Prize laureate. List includes a total of 126 women political leaders and 79 countries/political jurisdictions; includes all jurisdictions, including those such as San Marino, that are extremely small, as well as those that lack universal recognition, such as the Turkish Republic of Northern Cyprus and Transnistria, and those whose women leaders were in office for a very short time. Sources: Individual country histories and aggregate summaries, including Guide to Women Leaders at www.guide2womenleaders.com. © Nancy J. Adler, April 2014

Are the increasing numbers a new trend? Yes. As highlighted in Table 2.2, of the 126 women leaders, almost two-thirds (79) were the first women that their respective countries had ever selected to lead them. Ruth Dreifuss, for example, became President of Switzerland in 1999 after a 700-year history of male-led democracy. A total of 27 of the 79 countries that have had a woman leader have already selected more than one woman to lead them. Two countries, Switzerland and the Netherlands Antilles, have already elected four women leaders. Six countries have already elected three women leaders to serve them (Bermuda, Finland, Haiti, Lithuania, Norway, and South Korea), and 18 countries have already selected two

Table 2.2. Countries Having Selected One or More Women Political Leaders Between 1950–2014*

Twelve Women Leaders (1)	Costa Rica
San Marino	Croatia
Four Women Leaders (2)	Dominica
Switzerland	Ecuador
Netherlands Antilles	Faroe Islands
Three Women Leaders (6)	France
Bermuda	Gabon
Finland	Georgia
Haiti	German Democratic Republic
Lithuania	Germany
Norway	Great Britain
South Korea	Guyana
Two Women Leaders (18)	Indonesia
Argentina	Jamaica
Bangladesh	Kosovo
Central African Republic	Kyrgyzstan
Guinea Bissau	Malawi
Iceland	Mali
India	Myanmar (Burma)
Ireland	Macedonia
Israel	Madagascar
Latvia	Mauritius
Liberia	Moldova
Malta	Mongolia
New Zealand	Mozambique
Two Women Leaders (18)	New Caledonia
Peru	Nicaragua
The Philippines	Pakistan
São Tomé & Principe	Panama
Sénégal	Poland
Serbia	Portugal
Sri Lank	Rwanda
One Woman Leader (52)	Slovakia
Austria	Slovenia
Australia	South Africa
The Bahamas	Thailand
Bolivia	Transnistria
Bosnian Serb Republic	Trinidad and Tobago
Brazil	Turkey
Bulgaria	Turkish Rep. of Northern Cyprus
Burundi	Ukraine
Canada	Yugoslavia
Chile	

Notes: * = as of April 2014; Total countries between 1950–2014 having selectedat least one woman leader ($n = 79$), more than one woman leader ($n = 27$), just one woman leader ($n = 52$), and total women political leaders ($n = 126$). List includes all jurisdictions, including those such as San Marino, that are extremely small, as well as those that lack universal recognition, such as the Turkish Republic of Northern Cyprus and Transnistria. List includes Burma/Myanmar, even though the elected leader was not seated.

women leaders. One country is an outlier: the Republic of San Marino, a micro-state surrounded by Italy which claims to be the oldest surviving sovereign state and constitutional republic in the world. It has had 12 women hold their most senior leadership position, that of captain regent. The countries that have selected multiple women to lead them are highly diverse—culturally, geographically, politically, and economically.

Given these trends, there is no question that more women will be leading countries in the 21st century than have ever done so before. Already in the opening years of this century, 69 additional women have been selected to lead their countries.

Women Leading Companies

Are there similar increases in the number of women leading major corporations (e.g., Adler, 1997a, 1997b, 1999b, 2002b, 2002c, 2005, 2007, 2011; Adler & Izraeli, 1994)? Whereas the patterns among business leaders are not as clear as those among political leaders, surveys suggest that an increasing number of women are leading global companies. The initial numbers, however, are very small; even smaller, proportionally, than those of women leading countries. Even including executives who have held positions below the number one position in their companies, women still held less than 5% of the most senior management positions in the United States and less than 2% of all senior management positions in Europe at the end of the last century.[10] Moreover, not until the late 1990s did either the *Fortune* top 30 or the *FTSE (Financial Times Stock Exchange)* 100 include a woman among their lists of leading CEOs.[11] As shown in Tables 2.3 and 2.4, by the beginning of 2014, the *Fortune 500* still included only 23 women CEOs, and the *Fortune* 1000 similarly included only an additional 23 women CEOs, a mere 4.6% of both lists.[12] As shown in Table 2.5, at the close of 2013, the UK's *FTSE 100* similarly included only four women CEOs (4%).[13] Not dissimilarly, as highlighted in Table 2.6, only 5% (25) of the CEOs listed on Canada's *Financial Post 500* in 2013 were women. Contrary to popular belief, however, women's scarcity in leading major corporations does not reflect their absence as leaders of global companies. Unlike their male counterparts, most women chief executives either create their own entrepreneurial enterprises or assume the leadership of a family business.[14]

Women Leading: A Worldwide Trend, Not a Local Peculiarity

Similar to women-led countries, women-led businesses exist almost everywhere in the world. They are not clustered in just the few countries

Table 2.3. Global Women Business Leaders: Women CEOs of Fortune 500 Companies

	2013 Fortune 500	Companies Ranked 1–500	23 Women CEOs (4.6%)
1.	Mary Barra	General Motors	#7
2.	Meg Whitman	Hewlett Packard	#15
3.	Virginia Rometty	IBM	#20
4.	Patricia A. Woertz	Archer Daniels Midland Company	#27
5.	Indra K. Nooyi	PepsiCo, Inc.	#43
6.	Marillyn Hewson	Lockheed Martin	#59
7.	Ellen J. Kullman	DuPont	#72
8.	Irene B. Rosenfeld	Mondelez International	#88
9.	Phebe Novakovic	General Dynamics	#98
10.	Carol M. Meyrowitz	The TJX Companies, Inc.	#115
11.	Ursula M. Burns	Xerox Corporation	#131
12.	Lynn J. Good	Duke Energy	#145
13.	Deanna M. Mulligan	Guardian	#238
14.	Sheri S. McCoy	Avon Products Inc.	#252
15.	Debra L. Reed	Sempra Energy	#281
16.	Denise M. Morrison	Campbell Soup	#338
17.	Heather Bresch	Mylan	#374
18.	Ilene Gordon	Ingredion Incorporated	#386
19.	Jacqueline Hinman	CH2M Hill	#415
20.	Kathleen M. Mazzarella	Graybar Electric	#465
21.	Gracia C. Martore	Gannett	#467
22.	Mary Agnes (Maggie)	Wilderotter- Frontier Communications	#492
23.	Marissa Mayer	Yahoo	#494

Table 2.4. Global Women Business Leaders: Women CEOs of Fortune 1000 Companies

	2013 Fortune 1000	Companies Ranked 501–1000	23 Women CEOs (4.6%)
1.	Beth E. Mooney	KeyCorp	#510
2.	Cindy B. Taylor	Oil States International Inc.	#537
3.	Karen W. Katz	The Neiman Marcus Group Inc.	#547
4.	Laura J. Alber	Williams-Sonoma	#582
5.	Elizabeth Smith	Bloomin' Brands	#590
6.	Patricia Kampling	Alliant Energy	#655
7.	Constance H. Lau	Hawaiian Electric Industries Inc.	#656
8.	Tamara L. Lundgren	Schnitzer Steel Industries	#661
9.	Mindy F. Grossman	HSN	#666
10.	Kimberly Harris	Puget Sound Energy	#673
11.	Amy Miles	Regal Entertainment	#742
12.	Diane M. Sullivan	Brown Shoe Company	#788
13.	Sandra Cochran	Cracker Barrel	#793
14.	Debra Cafaro	Ventas	#807
15.	Gayla Delly	Benchmark Electronics	#821
16.	Kay Krill	ANN Inc.	#842
17.	Denise Ramos	ITT	#861
18.	Patti S. Hart	International Game Technology	#899
19.	Andrea Ayers	Convergys	#906
20.	Judy McReynolds	Arkansas Best Corp.	#927
21.	Linda Massman	Clearwater Paper	#981
22.	Eileen McDonnell	Penn Mutual Life Insurance	#990
23.	Jane Elfers	Children's Place Retail Stores	#999

Source: Catalyst*—http://www.catalyst.org/knowledge/women-ceos-fortune-1000
– Data as of January 15, 2014.

Note: * List as of April 2014. List prepared by Catalyst and based on the Fortune 1000 list of companies published by Fortune magazine in May or June of each year. The number and rank of companies remains unchanged throughout the year until a new list is published. Catalyst updates their list throughout the year whenever a woman becomes CEO or departs a CEO position at any listed company. Catalyst lists women CEOs on the date they officially take over their positions. Note that Susan N. Story is scheduled to become CEO of American Water Works Company, Inc. (#731) on May 9, 2014.

Table 2.5. Global Women Business Leaders: Women CEOs of FTSE 100 Companies (UK)

Women Leading 2013 FTSE 100 Companies:* 4 Women CEOs (4%)

Liv Garfield	Severn Trent
Alison Cooper	Imperial Tobacco
Carolyn McCall	easyJet
Angela Ahrendts	Burberry

Source: https://uk.finance.yahoo.com/news/severn-trent-ceo-lifts-women-100841091.html – Data as of November 18, 2013.

Note: * As reported by Yahoo! UK and Ireland/Reuters in "New Severn Trent CEO lifts women FTSE 100 bosses to four" November 18, 2013, at: https://uk.finance.yahoo.com/news/severn-trent-ceo-lifts-women-100841091.html (Note that the FTSE is the London, England based Financial Times Stock Exchange.)

Table 2.6. Global Women Business Leaders: Women CEOs/Heads of Financial Post 500 Companies (Canada)

Women Leading Canada's 2013 *Financial Post 500* Companies: 25 Women (5%)

1.	Shelley Broader	Wal-Mart Canada Corp.	#12
2.	Louise Wendling	Costco Wholesale Canada Ltd. (SVP)	#24
3.	Jacynthe Côté	Rio Tinto Alcan Inc.	#43
4.	Monique F. Leroux	Mouvement des caisses Desjardins	#47
5.	Dianne Craig	Ford Motor Co. of Canada Ltd.	#49
6.	Nancy C. Southern	ATCO Ltd.	#97
7.	Kathy Bardswick	Co-operators Financial Services Ltd.	#125
8.	Linda S. Hasenfratz	Linamar Corporation	#126
9.	Gianna Manes	ENMAX Corp.	#127
10.	Karen H. Sheriff	Bell Aliant Regional Communications Inc.	#148
11.	Shelley Martin	Nestlé Canada Inc.	#168
12.	Dawn Farrell	TransAlta	#170
13.	Zoë Yujnovich	Iron Ore Co. of Canada	#190
14.	Sophie Brochu	Gaz Métro, Inc.	#193
15.	Karen Gavan	The Economical Mutual Insurance Group	#205
16.	Mandy Shapansky	Xerox Canada, Inc.	#267
17.	Elaine Campbell	AstraZeneca Canada Inc.	#286

(Table continues on next page)

Table 2.6. (Continued)

Women Leading Canada's 2013 *Financial Post 500* Companies: 25 Women (5%)

18.	Marilyn McLaren	The Manitoba Public Insurance Corp.	#305
19.	Heather M. Reisman	Indigo Books & Music Inc.	#322
20.	Marie-Claude Houle	EBC Inc.	#368
21.	Tamara Vrooman	Vancouver City Savings Credit Union	#383
22.	Ellen J. Moore	Chubb Insurance Company of Canada	#391
23.	Gabrielle Chevalier	Solutions 2 Go Inc.	#405
24.	Eva Carissimi	Noranda Income Fund.	#414
25.	Tracy Redies	Coast Capital Savings Credit Union	#447

Source: Catalyst*—http://www.catalyst.org/knowledge/women-ceos-and-heads-financial-post-500 – Data as of January 22, 2014.

Note: * List of companies published by the Financial Post in June of each year. Whereas the Financial Posts leaves the number and rank of companies unchanged throughout the year, Catalyst updates the list whenever a woman becomes CEO/Head or departs from a CEO/Head position at any of the listed companies. Catalyst includes women starting on the date they officially assume their position. Current calculations are based on the 491 companies which have CEOs/Heads or for which the CEO or Head could be determined by the Catalyst Information Center.

Table 2.7. Global Women Business Leaders: Global Diversity—20th-Century Leaders (Worldwide)

Examples of women led-companies with revenues over U.S. $1 billion, or for banks with assets over U.S. $1 billion, already in the 20th century:

Ernestina Herrera de Noble, Argentina, $1.2 billion: President and editorial director of Grupo Clarin, the largest-circulation Spanish newspaper in the world.

Francine Wachsstock, Belgium, $2.25 billion: President of the board of administrators, La Poste, Belgium's state-owned post office and largest employer.

Beatriz Larragoiti, Brazil, $2.9 billion: Vice president (and owner) of Brazil's largest insurance company, Sul America S.A.

Maureen Kempston Darkes, Canada, $18.3 billion: President and General Manager of General Motors of Canada.

Ellen R. Schneider-Lenne, Germany, $458 billion in assets: Member of the Board of Managing Directors, Deutsch Bank AG, responsible for operations in the U.K. (deceased).

Nina Wang, Hong Kong, $1-2 billion in assets: Chairlady of Chinachem Group, property development.

(Table continues on next page)

Table 2.7. (Continued)

Tarjani Vakil, India, $1.1 billion in assets: Chairperson and managing director, Export-Import Bank of India, highest ranking female banking official in Asia.

Margaret Heffernan, Ireland, $1.6 billion: Chairman, Dunnes Stores Holding Company, largest retailing company in Ireland.

Galia Maor, Israel, $35.6 billion in assets: CEO of Bank Leumi le-Israel.

Gloria Delores Knight, Jamaica, $1.86 billion in assets: President and managing director, The Jamaica Mutual Life Assurance Society, largest financial conglomerate in English-speaking Caribbean (deceased).

Sawako Noma, Japan, $2 billion: President of Kodansha Ltd., largest publishing house in Japan.

Harumi Sakamoto, Japan, $13 billion: Senior managing director, the Seiyu, Ltd., a supermarket and shopping centre operator expanding throughout Asia.

Khatijah Ahmad, Malaysia, $5 billion: Chairman and managing director, KAF Group of Companies, financial services group.

Merce Sala i Schnorkowski, Spain, $1.1 billion: CEO of Renfe, Spain's national railway system, currently helping to privatize Colombian and Bolivian rail and selling trains to Germany.

Antonia Ax:son Johnson, Sweden, $6 billion: Chair, The Axel Johnson Group, retailing and distribution, more than 200 companies.

Elisabeth Salina Amorini, Switzerland, $2.8 billion: Chairman of the board, managing director, and chairman of the group executive board, Societe Generale de Surveillance Holding S.A., the world's largest inspection and quality control organization, testing imports and exports in more than 140 countries.

Emilia Roxas, Taiwan, $5 billion: CEO, Asiaworld Internationale Groupe, multinational conglomerate.

Additional examples of countries with women leading companies with revenues over $250 million:

Donatella Zingone Dini, Costa Rica, $300 million: Zeta Group, fifth largest business in Central America, conglomerate.

Nawal Abdel Moneim El Tatawy, Egypt, $357 million in assets: Chairman, Arab Investment Bank.

Colette Lewiner, France, $800 million: Chairman and CEO, SGN-Eurisys Group, world's largest nuclear fuels reprocessing company.

Jannie Tay, Singapore, $289 million: Managing director, The Hour Glass Limited, high end retailer of watches.

Aida Geffen, South Africa, $355 million: Chairman and managing director, Aida Holdings Ltd., residential commercial real estate firm.

Ann Gloag, United Kingdom, $520 million: Stagecoach Holdings Plc; Europe's largest bus company.

Liz Chitiga, Zimbabwe, $400 million: General manager and CEO, Minerals Marketing Corporation of Zimbabwe; in foreign-currency terms, the biggest business in Zimbabwe.

Note: * Based on Kelly (1996); CEOs of *Fortune 500* firms based on *Fortune 500* list as reported at http://money.cnn.com/magazines/fortune/fortune500/womenceos/

considered to be female friendly—those countries providing women with equal property rights; equal access to education, health care, and employment; and equal protection under law. The women leaders come from the world's largest and smallest countries, the world's richest and poorest countries, and the world's most socially and economically advantaged and disadvantaged countries. They come, moreover, from every geographical region, represent all six of the world's major religions, and lead companies in a wide range of industries. The changing trend toward women's leadership is a broad-based, worldwide phenomenon, not a trend limited to a few particularly pro-women countries, industries, or regions. Moreover, most major corporations that select women as senior business leaders are not those that have implemented the most advanced female–friendly policies, such as daycare centers, flextime, and other equal employment opportunities. Among the 61 American *Fortune 500* companies employing women as chairmen, CEOs, board members, or one of the top five earners, for example, only three are companies that *Working Woman* identified as the most favorable for women employees.

As can be seen, the trends among political and business leaders appear similar. More women are leading global firms than ever before, with the vast majority being the first woman whom their particular firm has ever selected to hold such a senior position. Based on these trends, we can easily predict that women's voices will become a more common and therefore more important addition to the world's global leadership dialogue during the 21st century. Change is not only possible, it has already begun to happen.

GLOBAL LEADERSHIP: NUMBERS ARE NOT ENOUGH

Increasing the number of women in senior leadership positions is certainly a necessary condition for equity, but it is not a sufficient condition for shaping history. The fundamental challenge is not simply to select more women as senior leaders. Rather, it is to provide a form of leadership in the world that will foster global society's survival and prosperity.

Based on research observing women managers, many people have predicted that women leaders would exhibit a new sought after 21st century leadership style, incorporating new, more inclusive, trustworthy, and humanistic approaches. They base their predictions on research studies that have concluded that a disproportionate number of women exhibit many, if not all of the following qualities:

> empathy, helpfulness, caring, and nurturance; interpersonal sensitivity, attentiveness to and acceptance of others, responsiveness to their needs and motivations; an orientation toward the collective interest and toward integrative goals such as group cohesiveness and stability; a preference for

open, egalitarian, and cooperative relationships, rather than hierarchical ones; and an interest in actualizing values and relationships of great importance to community. (Fondas, 1997, p. 260)

By contrast, the traits that have been culturally ascribed to men include

an ability to be impersonal, self–interested, efficient, hierarchical, tough minded, and assertive; an interest in taking charge, control, and domination; a capacity to ignore personal, emotional considerations in order to succeed; a proclivity to rely on standardized or "objective" codes for judgment and evaluation of others; and a heroic orientation toward task accomplishment and a continual effort to act on the world and become something new or [different]. (Fondas, 1997, p. 260)

To date, however, no research that has focused on senior leaders (rather than employees or managers) exists to support or refute claims that women would make more effective 21st century leaders than would men. Not surprisingly, similar to men, women exhibit a wide range of leadership visions, approaches, and levels of effectiveness (Adler, 2002b, 2002c). One need look no further than the ouster on corruption charges of Turkey's former prime minister Tansu Çiller or the demise of Sotheby's former CEO Diana Brooks (indicted, along with Sotheby's former chairman Alfred Taubman on criminal conspiracy and price-fixing charges) to know that women leaders, like their male counterparts, are neither perfect nor a universal solution to the world's or any particular company's problems.[15]

Do some women exhibit exemplary styles of leadership? Yes; not all women, but certainly many give us reason for hope, especially those not mimicking the style of leadership of most 20th century male leaders. Ireland's first woman president, Mary Robinson, for example, brilliantly took her commitment to human rights into the presidency of Ireland, transforming the position from one of ceremony to one of substance. She then let go of the presidency (a typically feminine use of power, "letting go") in order to continue her human rights agenda on a broader, worldwide scale at the United Nations. Aung San Suu Kyi, the legally elected leader of Burma (Myanmar) was incarcerated in her own home by the military for more than a decade. While under house arrest, the military dictatorship even denied her the right to see her husband one last time before he died of cancer. Given her situation, does Suu Kyi advocate annihilating the military dictatorship that imprisoned her and her people for so long? No, to this day, she fearlessly advocates dialogue—words, not guns—a unity strategy typically attributed to what many consider to be a more feminine approach to leadership.

Agatha Uwilingiyimana, the former prime minister of Rwanda, similarly exemplifies the courage it takes to break with traditional leadership approaches and to use unifying strategies—strategies many attribute to a more feminine approach. By 1993, the level of violence in Rwanda had forced the Hutus and Tutsis to seriously consider signing a peace agreement. But who would have the courage to publicly sign such a paper with a sworn enemy? No one relished the risk, as extremists on both sides condemned those who would consider signing as traitors. At that crucial moment in Rwanda's history, no man would accept the risk of becoming a peacemaking prime minister. In July 1993, shortly before the genocide, it was Uwilingiyimana, in the name of peace and unity, who agreed to serve her country as prime minister. Less than a month later, the peace agreement was signed. Less than a year later, extremist Hutus began hunting down and killing Tutsis and moderate members of the Hutu government. Agatha Uwilingiyimana, a moderate Hutu, was one of the first to be murdered. Although reported as a Tutsi murder in the Western press, Uwilingiyimana was killed by her own people, extremist Hutus who rejected her attempts at unity and peace.

Is the situation in Rwanda so extreme that it would be inappropriate for the rest of the world to attempt to learn anything from Uwilingiyimana's story? The answer is a resounding no. Think for a moment of some of the other women leaders with whom we are perhaps more familiar. Former President of the Philippines, Corazon Aquino, like Uwilingiyimana, also believed in building coalitions with the opposition. She invited members of both her own and the opposition party to join her presidential cabinet. The world press, viewing her leadership through the obsolete lens of divisive 20th century perspectives, labeled her invitation to the opposition as the naïve act of a housewife who does not know what it means to be president. In response, Aquino explained that she never again wanted political differences to be resolved by murder. She wanted to preclude the possibility that any person would have to watch the political assassination of his or her spouse as she had been obliged to when her husband, Benigno Aquino, opposition leader at the time, was murdered on the tarmac upon his return to the Philippines. In her cabinet, animated discussion replaced murder as the accepted form of political discourse.

Aquino, similar to Mary Robinson in Ireland, refused to run for a second term because she believed that democracy, not her longevity as president, was more important. Having lived through years of Marcos' dictatorship, she believed that Filipinos deserved to choose a new president after she had served her initial 6-year term. Each of these leaders went outside of the patterns of history and said, "Enough! There has to be a better way."

Are the stories of more inclusive leadership all stories of political leaders? Of course not. Rebecca Mark, for example, as CEO of Enron Development Corporation, negotiated the first major commercial agreement among Arabs and Israelis following the Oslo Peace Accords.[16] Rebecca Mark saw coalition building, including links across groups that the world had always viewed as enemies, as smart business. Did people question her judgment? Of course they did. Did she do what had not been done before? Yes. As Rebecca Mark's decisions show, true leadership, by definition, is not the act of the usual.[17]

As both business and political leaders, women regularly challenge conventional wisdom in their approach to leadership. Britain's Anita Roddick, founder and former CEO of the Body Shop, for example, regularly challenged conventional practice in the beauty and healthcare industry. She challenged conventional product design, for example, by not allowing animal testing. The Body Shop challenged the conventional marketing strategies of its competitors by not promising women unattainable beauty. The company challenged convention in its organization design and strategic intent by tying societal commitments to product strategies long before corporate social responsibility came into vogue. Sweden's Antonia Ax:son Johnson, CEO of a fourth-generation, 200-year-old family business, the Ax:son Johnson Group, eliminated all war- and violence-related toys from her company's department stores. Although such toys would have increased revenues, they were not consistent with Ax:son Johnson's concept of "the good company."

PEOPLE'S ASPIRATIONS: HOPE, CHANGE, AND UNITY

To understand the dynamics of the 21st century, we must go beyond strictly attempting to assess if, or how, women's approaches to leadership differ from those of their male counterparts. We know that they differ in some cases, but certainly not in all, or perhaps even most. Given the absence of consistently substantiated differences and, at the same time, the rapid increase in the number of women leaders (especially in the last decades), we must ask why countries and companies worldwide—for the first time in modern history and after so many years of male-dominated leadership—are choosing women to lead them, often for the first time. It appears that people worldwide may want what all women symbolize, but what only some women leaders in fact exhibit.

Leadership Symbolism: The Possibility of Change

Perhaps the most powerful and attractive symbolism of women leaders is the possibility of significant change. When a woman is chosen as the first woman to become president, prime minister, or CEO—when no other woman has ever held such an office in the particular country or company, and when few people thought that she could be selected—people begin to believe that other, more substantive and less symbolic changes are also possible. The combination of a woman being an outsider at senior leadership levels previously controlled by men and of her beating the odds in attaining a top position provides powerful public imagery supporting the possibility of broad-based societal and organizational change. The fact that most women in senior leadership positions, to date, are the first women to assume those positions, underscores the beginning not just of symbolic change, but of real change. Mary Robinson's presidential acceptance speech captures the unique event of Ireland electing its first woman president coupled with the possibility of national change:

> I was elected by men and women of all parties and none, by many with great moral courage who stepped out from the faded flags of Civil War and voted for a new Ireland. And above all by the women of Ireland ... who instead of rocking the cradle rocked the system, and who came out massively to make their mark on the ballot paper, and on a new Ireland.[18]

The fact that women who become leaders are perceived to differ from their male counterparts (whether or not they actually do) fosters the sense that change is possible. In Kenya, for example, when Charity Ngilu became the first woman to run for president, many Kenyans saw her as representing "a complete break with [the] divisive tribal politics of the past" (McKinley, 1997, section 1, p. 3). As one Kenyan observed, "Charity is talking about unity, and this unity will unite both men and women.... If we vote for a man, there will be no change. With a woman, there will have to be a big change" (McKinley, 1997, section 1, p. 3).

The symbolism supporting the possibility of change is almost identical in the business world, where most women CEOs are "firsts"; not only the first woman, but also often the first outsider that the company has selected to lead them.[19] Notable examples include Marjorie Scardino, the first woman, first outsider, and first American to become CEO of Britain's Pearson Plc, as well as the first woman to lead a *FTSE* (*Financial Times Stock Exchange*) *100* firm; Carly Fiorina, the first woman and first outsider to lead Hewlett Packard, a *Fortune 500* top-30 firm; and Charlotte Beers, the first woman and the first outsider whom Ogilvy & Mather Worldwide had ever brought in to lead their worldwide advertising business.

Leadership Symbolism: The Possibility of Unity

In addition to the possibility of change, women also symbolize unity— and women leaders are no exception. Nicaragua's former president Violetta Chamorro, for example, became a symbol of national unity following her husband's assassination. Emphasizing her commitment to unity, Chamorro even claimed that, beyond reconciliation, she had no ideology (Benn, 1995). Chamorro's ability to bring her four adult children—two of whom were prominent Sandinistas, while the other two equally prominently opposed the Sandinistas—together every week for Sunday dinner achieved near legendary status in war-torn Nicaragua (Saint-Germain, 1993). Chamorro gave symbolic hope to her nation that it too could find peace based on a unity that would bring all Nicaraguans together. The fact that the behavior of a woman leader who created family unity became a symbol for national unity is neither surprising nor coincidental.

On the basis of similar dynamics, Pakistan's former Prime Minister Benazir Bhutto and the Philippines' former President Corazon Aquino each came to symbolize unity for their strife-torn countries. As the scope of governments' influence and companies' operations expand to encompass the world, the desire and need for unifying strategies increase. Currently, women symbolize the hope for unity within multinational constituencies and multicultural contexts.

The hope that women leaders will foster unity and inclusiveness is heightened by the ways in which many women gain access to power. In contrast to many of their male counterparts, many women leaders have developed and used broad-based popular support rather than relying primarily on traditional, hierarchical political-party or corporate-structural support. This broad-based inclusiveness, often seen as a precursor of other hoped for unifying strategies, has been particularly apparent among the aspiring women political leaders who often are not seriously considered as potential candidates by their country's main political parties. They are consequently forced to gain support directly from the people (which, of course, is a profoundly democratic process).

Mary Robinson, for example, campaigned in more small communities in Ireland than any previous presidential candidate before either her party or the opposition took her seriously. The opposition later admitted that they did not seriously consider Robinson's candidacy until it was too late to stop her (Finlay, 1990). Similarly, Corazon Aquino, whose campaign and victory were labelled the People's Revolution, held more than 1,000 rallies during her campaign, while Ferdinand Marcos, the incumbent, held only 34 (Col, 1993). Likewise, Benazir Bhutto, who succeeded in becoming Pakistan's first woman and youngest prime minister, campaigned in more communities than any politician before her. Only later did her own party take her seriously (Anderson, 1993; Weisman, 1986).

In business, the disproportionate number of women who choose to start their own companies echoes the same pattern of broad-based support. Rather than attempting to climb the corporate ladder and to break through the glass ceiling into senior leadership positions in established corporations, these entrepreneurial women build their success directly in the marketplace. The types of broad-based support developed by women political leaders and entrepreneurs differ only in their source, with the former enjoying support directly from the electorate and the latter gaining support from the marketplace. In both cases, the base of support is outside of the traditional power structure and hierarchy, and therefore more representative of new and more diverse opinions and ideas. Women leaders' sources of support, and therefore of power, more closely reflect the flattened network of emerging 21st century organizations and society than they do the more centralized and limited power hierarchies defining most 20th century organizations.

SHAPING HISTORY

Former Czech Republic President Vaclav Havel (1994) described the world as "going through a transitional period, when something is on the way out and something else is painfully being born" (p. A27). During such a transition, it is not surprising that people worldwide are attracted to women leaders' symbolic message of bringing positive change, hope, and the possibility of unity. The interplay of women's and men's styles of leadership will define the contours and potential success of 21st century society. The risk is in encapsulating leaders—both women and men—in approaches that worked well in the 20th century but foretell disaster for the 21st century. The challenge is in the urgency and complexity. However, as poet David Whyte (1994) enjoins us, "The journey begins right here, in the middle of the road, right beneath your feet. This is the place. There is no other place, there is no other time" (p. 27).

ACKNOWLEDGMENTS

This chapter was originally published as Adler, Nancy J. (2003) "Shaping History: Global Leadership in the Twenty-First Century" in Ronald J. Burke and Cary L. Cooper (eds.), *Leading in Turbulent Times: Managing in the New World of Work*. Oxford: Blackwell: pp. 302–318. The chapter was subsequently updated and published in Paul R. Sparrow (ed.) (2009) *Handbook of International Human Resource Management: Integrating People, Process and Context*. West Sussex, United Kingdom: Wiley: 461–482.

NOTES

1. The official title of the U.N. Conference was the United Nations' World Conference Against Racism, Racial Discrimination, Xenophobia and Related Intolerance.
2. A. T. Kearney study reported in Haebeck, Kroger, & Trum (2000) and in Schuler and Jackson (2001). The same study, as cited by Schuler and Jackson,

concludes that "only 15 percent of mergers and acquisitions in the U.S. achieve their objectives, as measured by share value, return on investment and post-combination profitability." For research on the instability of international joint ventures, see summary by Yan and Zeng (1999). Although the definitions (complete termination versus significant change of ownership) and overall results vary, numerous studies have reported substantial international joint venture instability, including 55% termination reported by Harrigan (1988), 49% termination reported by Barkema and Vermeulen (1997); and 68% instability through termination or acquisition reported by Park and Russo (1996). Also see Gary Hammel's classic 1991 article.
3. For a notable exception, see the description of the Norway-based global company, Norske Skog, in Adler (2002a).
4. Section excerpted and adapted from Eisler's insightful 1987 book (see book jacket).
5. The contemporary discussion on global corporate citizenship addresses the possibility, and the necessity for companies to simultaneously do good and do well (see, among others, Cooperrider & Adler, 2006; Adler 2002a, 2010, 2008; Hart, 2005; Hawken, Lovins, & Lovins, 1999; Laszlo, 2003; Lovins, Lovins, & Hawken, 2000; McDonough & Brangart, 2002; Prahalad, 2005; Prahalad & Hammond, 2002; and Prahalad & Hart, 2002).
6. The logic of building future success based on past success in inherent the appreciative inquiry strategies (see Cooperrider, Whitney, & Stavros, 2003) and other strength-based approaches (see Cameron, Dutton, & Quinn, 2003, among others).
7. See the initial work on positive psychology (Seligman, 1998, 2003; Seligman and Csikszentmihalyi, 2000; Synder & Lopez, 2002), which was then led to positive organizational scholarship (Cameron, Dutton & Quinn, 2003).
8. Burma (renamed Myanmar by the military junta) selected Aung San Suu Kyi, but the military imprisoned her, rather than allowing her to be seated and to serve the country as president.
9. The calculation of the number of countries in the world depends on the definition of a country. There are currently (2014) 195 widely recognized sovereign states (193 U.N. members plus two U.N. observer states). However, there are 201 countries if partially recognized states (such as Taiwan, Kosovo, and Northern Cyprus) are included, some of which have had women leaders. The number rises to 204 if both partially recognized and de facto states (such as Nagorno-Karabakh, Transnistria, and Somaliland) are included, at least one of which has had a woman leader. For purposes of this paper, the most conservative, 195, number has been used, based on 2014 data. Source: http://www.polgeonow.com/2011/04/how-many-countries-are-there-in-world.html
10. United States statistics based of the research of Catalyst as originally published by Wellington (1996). European statistics reported in Dwyer et al. (1996).
11. Carly Fiorina, former CEO of Hewlett–Packard and Marjorie Scardino, CEO of Pearson Plc.
12. As reported by Catalyst at: http://www.catalyst.org/knowledge/women-ceos-fortune-1000

13. As reported by *Yahoo! UK and Ireland/Reuters* in "New Severn Trent CEO lifts women FTSE 100 bosses to four" November 18, 2013, from https://uk.finance.yahoo.com/news/severn-trent-ceo-lifts-women-100841091.html
14. For a discussion of women who are global entrepreneurs, see Adler (1999a, 1999c).
15. For a description of the case against Sotheby's former chairman, A. Alfred Taubman, on criminal conspiracy charges for a price-fixing scheme with archrival auction house, Christie's, see the business press in November-December 2001, including the *New York Times* reporting (see, for example, Blumenthal & Vogel (2001).
16. Note that this was long before the demise in 2001 of Enron, under the leadership chairman Kenneth L. Lay. Among many other business articles covering Enron's downfall, see Oppel and Atlas (2001).
17. When Enron collapsed, Rebecca Mark was one of the few executives who was not indicted.
18. Speech in the RDS, Dublin, 9 November 1990 as reported in Finlay (1990, p. 1).
19. See the discussion of women who are firsts often being "double strangers" and acting as the "thin edge of the wedge" (Czarniawska & Sevon, 2005).

REFERENCES

Adler, N. J. (1997a). Global leaders: A dialogue with future history. *International Management, 1*(2), 21–33.

Adler, N. J. (1997b). Global leadership, women leaders. *Management International Review, 37*(1), 171–196.

Adler, N. J. (1999a). Global entrepreneurs: Women, myths, and history. *Global Focus, 11*(4), 125–134.

Adler, N. J. (1999b). Global leaders: Women of influence. In G. Powell (Ed.), *Handbook of gender and work* (pp. 239–261). Thousand Oaks, CA: Sage.

Adler, N. J. (1999c). Twenty-first-century leadership: Reality beyond the myths. In A. M. Rugman (Series Ed.) & R. Wright (Ed.), *International entrepreneurship: Globalization of emerging business, Vol 7. Research in global strategic management* (pp. 239–261). Greenwich, CT: JAI.

Adler, N. J. (2002a). Global companies, global society: There is a better way. *Journal of Management Inquiry, 11*(3), 255–260.

Adler, N. J. (2002b). Global managers: No longer men alone. *International Journal of Human Resource Management, 13*(5), 743–760.

Adler, N. J. (2002c). Women joining men as global leaders in the new economy. In M. Gannon & K. Newman (Eds.), *Handbook of cross-cultural management* (pp. 236–249). Oxford, England: Blackwell.

Adler, N. J. (2005). Leading beyond boundaries: The courage to enrich the world. In L. Coughlin, E. Wingard, & K. Hollihan (Eds.), *Enlightened power: How women are transforming the practice of leadership* (pp. 350–366, 505–507). San Francisco, CA: Jossey–Bass.

Adler, N. J. (2006). Corporate global citizenship: Successfully partnering with the world. In G. Suder (Ed.), *Corporate strategies under international terrorism and adversity* (pp. 177–195). Cheltenham, England: Elgar.

Adler, N. J. (2007). One world: Women leading and managing worldwide. In D. Bilimoria & S. K. Piderit (Eds.), *Handbook on women in business and management* (pp. 330–355). Cheltenham, England: Elgar.

Adler, N. J. (2008). Global business as an agent of world benefit: New international business perspectives leading positive change. In A. Scherer & G. Palazzo (Eds.), *Handbook of research on global corporate citizenship* (pp. 374–401). Cheltenham, England/Northampton, MA: Elgar.

Adler, N. J. (2010). Corporate citizenship. In C. Laszlo, K. Christensen, D. Fogel, G. Wagner, & P. Whitehouse (Eds.), *The encyclopedia of sustainability, Vol. 2. The business of sustainability* (pp. 79–82). Great Barrington, MA: Berkshire.

Adler, N. J. (2011). Women leading and managing worldwide. In A. Pinnington & A. Harzing (Eds.), *International human resource management* (3rd ed., pp. 507–537). London, England: Sage.

Adler, N. J., & Izraeli, D. (Eds.). (1994). *Competitive frontiers: Women managers in a global economy.* Cambridge, MA: Blackwell.

Albright, M. K. (1997, June 6). Harvard commencement address. *The New York Times*, p. A8.

Anderson, N. F. (1993). Benazir Bhutto and dynastic politics: Her father's daughter, her people's sister. In M. A. Genovese (Ed.), *Women as national leaders* (pp. 41–69). Newbury Park, CA: Sage.

Barkema, H., & Vermeulen, F. (1997). What differences in the cultural backgrounds of partners are detrimental for international joint ventures? *Journal of International Business Studies, 28*(4), 845–864.

Benn, M. (1995, February). Women who rule the world. *Cosmopolitan*.

Blumenthal, R., & Vogel, C. (2001, December 4). Trial prosecutor depicts ex–chief of Sotheby's as price fixer. *The New York Times*, p. A20.

Cameron, K. S., Dutton, J. E., & Quinn, R. E. (Eds.). (2003). *Positive organizational scholarship.* San Francisco, CA: Berrett–Kohler.

Col, J. (1993). Managing softly in turbulent times: Corazon C. Aquino, president of the Philippines. In M. A. Genovese (Ed.), *Women as national leaders* (pp. 13–40). Newbury Park, CA: Sage.

Cooperrider, D., & Adler, N. J. (2006). *The global forum on business as an agent of world benefit: Management knowledge leading positive change.* Concept paper, Weatherhead School of Business, Case Western Reserve University, Cleveland, OH.

Cooperrider, D. L., Whitney, D., & Stavros, J. M. (2003). *Appreciative inquiry handbook.* Bedford Heights, OH: Lakeshore.

Czarniawska, B., & Sevon, G. (2005). *The thin end of the wedge: Foreign women professors as double strangers in academia.* Gothenburg, Sweden: Gothenburg Research Institute.

Dwyer, P., Johnston, M., & Lowry, L. (1996, April 15). Europe's corporate women. *Business Week*, pp. 40–42.

Eisler, R. (1987). *The chalice and the blade: Our history, our future.* San Francisco, CA: Harper & Row.

Finlay, F. (1990). *Mary Robinson: A president with a purpose.* Dublin, Ireland: O'Brien.

Fondas, N. (1997). The origins of feminization. *Academy of Management Review, 22*(1), 257–282.
Fort, T. L., & Schipani, C. A. (2004). *The role of business in fostering peaceful societies.* Cambridge, England: Cambridge University Press.
Friedman, T. L. (2006). *The world is flat: A brief history of the twenty-first century.* New York, NY: Farrar, Straus and Giroux.
Gimbutas, M. (1991). *The civilization of the goddess: The world of old Europe.* San Francisco, CA: Harper.
Haebeck, M. H., Kroger, F., & Trum, M. R. (2000). *After the mergers: Seven rules for successful post-merger integration.* New York, NY: Prentice Hall/FT.
Hammel, G. (1991). Competition for competence and inter-partner learning within international strategic alliances. *Strategic Management Journal, 12*(1), 83–103.
Harrigan, K. R. (1988). Strategic alliances and partner asymmetries. In F. Contractor & P. Lorange (Eds.), *Cooperative strategies in international business* (pp. 205–226). Lexington, MA: Lexington.
Hart, S. L. (2005). *Capitalism at the crossroads.* Upper Saddle River, NJ: Wharton School Publishing (Pearson Education).
Havel, V. (1994, July 8). The new measure of man. *The New York Times*, p. A27.
Hawken, P., Lovins, A., & Lovins, L. H. (1999). *Natural capitalism: Creating the next industrial revolution.* Boston, MA: Little Brown.
Kelly, C. (1996). 50 world-class executives. *Worldbusiness, 2*(2), 20–31.
Laszlo, C. (2003). *The sustainable company: How to create lasting value through social and environmental performance.* Washington, DC: Island.
Lovins, A. B., Lovins, H., Hawken, P., Reinhardt, F., Shapiro, R., & Magretta, J. (2000). *Harvard Business Review on business and the environment.* Boston, MA: Harvard Business School.
McDonough, W., & Braungart, M. (2002). *Cradle to cradle.* New York, NY: North Point.
McKinley, J. C., Jr. (1997, August 3). A woman to run Kenya? One says, "why not?" *The New York Times* (world late edition), Section 1, p. 3.
Oppel, R. A., Jr., & Atlas, R. D. (2001, December 4). Hobbled Enron tries to stay on its feet. *The New York Times*, pp. C1, C8.
Park, S. H., & Russo, M. V. (1996). When competition eclipses cooperation: An event history analysis of joint venture failure. *Management Science, 42*(6), 875–890.
Prahalad, C. K. (2005). *The fortune at the bottom of the pyramid: Eradicating poverty through profits.* Upper Saddle River, NJ: Wharton School Publishing (Pearson Education).
Prahalad, C. K., & Hammond, A. (2002). Serving the world's poor, profitably. *Harvard Business Review, 80*(9), 48–57.
Prahalad, C. K., & Hart, S. L. (2002). The fortune at the bottom of the pyramid. *Strategy + Business, 26*(1), 2–14.
Rechtschaffen, S. (1996). *Timeshifting.* New York, NY: Bantam Doubleday/Dell Audio.
Saint-Germain, M. A. (1993). Women in power in Nicaragua: Myth and reality. In M. A. Genovese (Ed.), *Women as national leaders* (pp. 70–102). Newbury Park, CA: Sage.

Schuler, R. S., & Jackson, S. E. (2001, October 22). Seeking an edge in mergers and acquisitions. *The Financial Times*, Special Section, Part Two: People Management.

Seligman, M. P. (1998). *Learned optimism: How to change your mind and your life* (2nd ed.). New York, NY: Free Press.

Seligman, M. E. P. (2003). Positive psychology: Fundamental assumptions. *Psychologist*, 126–127.

Seligman, M. E. P., & Csikszentmihalyi, M. (2000).Positive psychology: An introduction. *American Psychologist, 55*(1), 5–14.

Slackman, M. (2001, September 9). Divisive U.N. race talks end in accord. *The Los Angeles Times*, p. A1.

Snyder, C. R., & Lopez, S. J. (Eds.). (2002). *Handbook of positive psychology*. New York, NY: Oxford University Press.

Swarns, R. L. (2001, September 9). Race talks finally reach accord on slavery and Palestinian plight. *The New York Times*, p. A1.

Weisman, S. R. (1986, April 11). A daughter returns to Pakistan to cry for victory. *The New York Times*, p. 12.

Wellington, S. W. (1996). *Women in corporate leadership: Progress and prospects.* New York, NY: Catalyst.

Whyte, D. (1994). *The heart aroused.* New York, NY: Currency Doubleday.

Yan, A., & Zeng, M. (1999). International joint venture instability: A critique of previous research, a reconceptualization, and directions for future research. *Journal of International Business Studies, 30*(2), 397–414.

PART II

THEORETICAL APPROACHES TO WOMEN'S GLOBAL LEADERSHIP

CHAPTER 3

WOMEN AND GLOBAL LEADERSHIP

Three Theoretical Perspectives

Roya Ayman and Karen Korabik[1]

The 21st century has witnessed technological advances that have allowed us to overcome vast distances, bringing the world of work closer to the analogy of a global village. Events occurring in one part of the world no longer remain merely international news; instead, such news can have a direct impact on individuals, businesses, and governments around the world. In this environment, the need for effective global leaders is accentuated. It is now more important than ever before for those in leadership positions to adopt a global mindset and consider the global consequences of their decisions.

Many examples exist of women around the world who have taken the helm and demonstrated global leadership. As Adler (2002) stated, global leadership is no longer only for men. Among existing global women leaders are Indira Nooyi, the CEO of Pepsi; Kristin Lagarde, head of International Monitory Fund; and Angela Merkel, Germany's chancellor. They not only are competent leaders, but they also possess a vision beyond their company or country. After examining these global women leaders' leadership style through what they have said and done, it is evident that they are aware of the worldwide impact of their decisions. For this reason, they have more diverse perspectives and use more inclusive processes when forming decisions.

In an interview with Nooyi, Cramer (2012) quoted her saying,

> So across the world we have unleashed the power of our people to come up with ideas to reduce, recycle, replenish the environment and we are making great progress by reducing how much water we use in our manufacture and the carbon footprint that we put on the environment.

Lagarde has a very strong financial background and is using her position at the international bank to establish policies that help bring about fairness in the distribution of wealth (James, 2014). Merkel has gained the attention of many around the globe due to her strength of character, her fortitude on principle, and her ability to manage uncertainty and diversity. Friend and foe alike are in admiration of her competency in handling the economy and politics of a complex European Union world. These women serve as role models for successful global leaders.

Even though there is increasing literature on global leadership and its effectiveness (e.g., Mendenhall et al., 2013), there is still debate about exactly what global leadership is and how it should be defined. For example, scholars often have used the terms global leadership and international leadership synonymously (Ayman, 2004; Osland, 2013). Additionally, most research regarding the development and assessment of global leaders has relied on samples of existing leaders who are primarily men.

In this chapter, we first distinguish between the concepts of cross-cultural leadership, international leadership, and global leadership. We discuss the narrowing of the gap between recognized competencies in mainstream leadership and global leadership. We argue that global leadership must embrace diversity and explain the role that culture and gender play in developing global leaders. Finally, we present three theoretical models to illustrate the different dynamics that underlie the extent to which women global leaders are able to be successful.

LEADERSHIP IN A GLOBAL CONTEXT

In this section, we begin by distinguishing between the concepts of cross-cultural leadership, international leadership, and global leadership in recognition of the need for conceptual clarity. We start with explaining cross-cultural leadership.

Cross-Cultural Leadership

The Global Leadership and Organizational Behavior (GLOBE) project is an example of large-scale cross-cultural leadership research (House, Hanges, Javidan, Dorfman, & Gupta, 2004). As part of GLOBE, data were collected from leaders and their subordinates in over 62 countries around the world. The aim of the project was to examine the extent to which leadership behavior is culturally universal and to compare leadership ideals in various regions and countries across the world to one another. While a very important contribution, the GLOBE project looked only at leaders operating within their own culture. Therefore, it did not really address matters pertaining to leaders who engage across cultures. Specifically, knowing how leaders in a given culture are perceived by their followers in that same culture is of value, but it does not tell us about how these leaders would relate to followers from another country or culture. This is because there is an added complexity when leaders cross country boundaries, something Lewis (1999) referred to as "when cultures collide."

International Leadership

International or intercultural leadership deals with the issue of how the behavior displayed by a manager from one culture is received by people in another culture. International leaders come from one culture to be sojourners or expatriates in another culture. When they move to another country, they bring with them their own particular set of values and they remain protectors of the interests of their home country. International leaders must deal with processes of acculturation and cultural adjustment (Mendenhall & Oddou, 1985).

Specific cultural competencies, which have been called cultural intelligence, have been identified as contributing to the success of international leaders. These competencies have been conceptualized as consisting of four components: the metacognitive, cognitive, motivational, and behavioral (Early & Ang, 2003). The metacognitive competency component entails having awareness about a cross-cultural situation and being able to develop a strategy to deal effectively with it. This includes being sensitive to the situation, planning with foresight for what may occur in the interaction, and checking or examining the degree of alignment. The cognitive component involves having knowledge or information about various cultural groups and how they differ from one's own. The motivational component deals with having the drive or motivation to adjust to cultural differences. Finally, the behavioral component entails having a behavioral repertoire extensive enough to engage in the needed normative behavior (verbal or nonverbal) in different social settings. Several studies have established the reliability and validity of these competencies in fostering the success of international leaders (see Bird & Stevens, 2013 for a review).

In practice, however, most of those in charge of the training and development of international leaders invariably use an approach that involves teaching leaders only about how people in different countries work and interact (Lewis, 1999). Unfortunately, this enhances only one of the necessary cultural competencies, that of having knowledge about how others differ from oneself.

Hampden-Turner and Trompenaars (2000) contended that, when working in cross-cultural contexts, the capacity to reconcile value differences serves to foster business success. They have identified six dimensions of cultural diversity and argue that both poles of each dimension need to be reconciled. The dimensions are (a) universalism-particularism, (b) individualism-communitarianism, (c) specificity-diffusion, (d) achieved status-ascribed status, (e) inner-direction or outer-direction, and (f) sequential-synchronous time. Through many examples, the authors have demonstrated how the two sides of each dimension need to coexist and that having the ability to see the situation from more than one perspective allows a leader to have a broader perspective and be more inclusive. In this way, instead of dictating their position with the power of status or wealth, leaders have the ability to negotiate the similarity and differences of perspectives more effectively.

Most research on culture and leadership has adopted an *etic* approach and focused on validating leadership models developed in North America across cultures. From this we can infer whether a particular behavior or process is acceptable to be used by managers in other cultures (Ayman & Korabik, 2010). In this sense, the emphasis has been on comparative leadership, and the approach is not cross-cultural (Osland, 2013) or even international. A few studies (e.g., GLOBE) have also employed an *emic* approach and have been aimed at understanding the expectations or normative behaviors of leadership within various cultures. Concepts like benevolent paternalism (Ayman & Chemers 1983), paternalism (Aycan, 2006) or *guanxi* (Wong, Tinsley, Law, & Mobley, 2003) have been recently developed to represent leadership processes occurring within particular cultures as scholars around the world explore factors that affect leadership and leadership effectiveness in different cultural contexts.

Only a small number of studies have examined intercultural or international leadership. Thomas and Ravlin (1995) showed that by training foreign managers in the ways of managers in the United States, American employees had a more favorable reaction to them. In another study, Chen and Tjosvold (2007) examined dyads of American managers with Chinese subordinates. Their results demonstrated that when the Chinese concept of *guanxi* (personal relationship) was included, it had a major impact on the openness of the interaction between the subordinate and the manager. As Ayman and Korabik (2010) pointed out, there are very few studies of this type and more are warranted.

Global Leadership

Most trainers and authors use the terms international leadership, intercultural leadership, and global leadership interchangeably (Osland, 2013). However, in essence, global leadership and international leadership are potentially intertwined, yet distinct phenomena (Ayman, 2004). Some scholars claim that just because someone is the leader of a company in the global economy, it makes them a global leader, but this is not necessarily so. There are specific characteristics that differentiate global leaders from international leaders.

One agreed-upon distinguishing factor is that a global leader needs to have a special mindset. Although many models of what this means exist, we extrapolate on the concept here by referring to two. Osland (2013) adapted Bird and Osland's (2004) global competencies and put forth a pyramid model where the foundation layer consists of global knowledge. The next layer consists of particular traits (e.g., integrity, humility, inquisitiveness, and resilience), and the one above that includes attitudes and orientations, such as having cognitive complexity and a cosmopolitan attitude. For example, being cosmopolitan, as opposed to parochial, includes being open to new ideas, able to deal with uncertainty in an immediate situation, and able to explore a variety of alternatives. These traits and attitudes can then manifest themselves in interpersonal skills like mindful communication and building trusting multicultural teams. The top layer of their model is labeled "system skills" and includes things like ethical decision making, leading change, and architecting and building community.

A second model is that of Javidan and his colleagues (Javidan, Teagarden, & Bowen, 2010). They have identified three major competency categories. The first is having intellectual capital, which is global business savvy, cognitive complexity, and cosmopolitan outlook. The second is psychological capital or having passion for diversity, thirst for adventure, and self-assurance. The third is social capital or the ability to connect with people across cultures and social groups and treat them with empathy and respect. This can be demonstrated by having intercultural empathy, the ability to build credibility and maintain a diverse social network of people from divergent cultures and experiences, and the ability to inquire about and listen to those who are different from oneself.

In essence, global leaders think about the consequences of their actions, not only as they relate to their firm or their country, but also as they relate to humanity and the globe. They consider multiple perspectives and scenarios at the same time. For instance, Andrew Liveris, the CEO of Dow Chemical (2012), voiced concern not only about Dow's situation or about benefits to the United States, but also about providing solutions to humanity's challenges by being attentive to a three-prong approach to sustainability: environmental, economic, and social responsibility. He is an example of a global leader, not only because he travels, not only because he leads a workforce that is international, not even because he is a Greek-Australian-American. It is because, in addition to all of that, he has a sense of responsibility to the world now and for the future.

Some scholars view international leadership as a precursor to developing global leadership (McCall & Hollenbeck, 2002). This is because some of the competencies associated with international leadership are needed for international leaders to develop into global leaders. However, not all international leaders are or become global leaders. Many international leaders are merely expatriates and sojourners who enjoy traveling and being a foreigner in other lands. A global leader has empathy and appreciation for diverse viewpoints and life experiences, enjoys learning about them, and considers them in future plans.

GLOBAL LEADERSHIP AND MAINSTREAM LEADERSHIP THEORIES

The field of leadership has evolved as new leadership styles are being recognized from transformational (Bass, 1985; Judge & Piccolo, 2004) and charismatic leadership (DeGroot, Kiker, & Cross, 2000; House, 1977) to servant leadership (Liden, Wayne, Zhou, & Henderson, 2008). No matter what the style, there has been an ever-stronger emphasis on authenticity in leadership. Authentic leadership is not a distinct style but rather a form of principle-based leadership which seems to have close association with global leadership. Avolio and his colleagues (Walumbwa, Avolio, Gardner, Wensing, & Peterson, 2008) have articulated authentic leadership as incorporating four major dimensions: self-awareness, relational transparency, internalized moral perspective, and balanced processing. We review these and compare them with the global leadership dimensions we presented earlier.

Self-awareness is the capacity to see one's self as others do. This ability to check oneself in the mirror requires a certain level of humility and integrity, and it is a necessary precursor to developing empathy toward the others with whom one is collaborating. Relational transparency requires leaders to be open and honest in their relationships with others. This quality includes being able to accept one's own limitations while praising others for their strengths (Walumbwa et al., 2008).

Fairness and moral values are critical in an authentic leader as they are for global leaders. However, for global leaders, the definition of ethics and moral values goes beyond the issue of fair and equitable treatment of minority and majority group members alike. It also entails having the moral courage to act based on principles, being aware of the necessity to reconcile opposing values, and being mindful of how every decision one makes impacts everyone else (Walumbwa et al., 2008).

Balanced processing refers to the process by which a leader makes decisions (Walumbwa et al., 2008). This dimension focuses on insuring that the leader not only is surrounded with similarly minded people but also engages those who see the situation very differently. Thus, it is incumbent upon the leader to include diverse and even conflicting viewpoints and through an exchange of ideas to integrate these to arrive at a more inclusive perspective. All of the qualities necessary for authentic leadership are also very relevant to global leadership. It appears, therefore, that contemporary leadership models have become more sensitive to the need to develop leaders who have the capacity to be global leaders. The merging of the two lines of work is encouraging and promising.

With regard to women global leaders, several questions arise: Are the same requisite qualities needed for men and women alike? Do men and women both have the capacity to have these qualities? If women show the same qualities as men, will they garner the same support and positive evaluations from others? Are there factors particular to women that give them a potential advantage as global leaders?

DEFINITIONS OF GENDER AND CULTURE

Gender

Before discussing the impact of gender on leadership, it is first necessary to distinguish between sex, which is a biological process, and gender, which is a psychosocial process. Sex refers to whether someone is biologically a male or a female, whereas gender refers to whether someone is, or considers themselves, a man or a woman. In other words, gender encompasses all of the psychosocial ramifications of biological sex. These are extremely wide-ranging and affect all aspects of our daily lives (Korabik, 1997).

The distinction between sex and gender is important because not all people who are biologically male consider themselves to be men nor do all biological females consider themselves to be women. More importantly, however, it is essential to distinguish sex from gender to keep from making two unwarranted assumptions. The first is that of biopsychological equivalence (or equating sex and gender with one another) and the second is biological essentialism (or the belief that behavior is solely attributable to biological causes) (Bem, 1993; Shields, 2013). When these assumptions are made, gender is not viewed as an aspect of social identity, but instead as a biologically based difference that is innate, natural, inevitable, and attributable to nonchangeable causes (Shields, 2013). Moreover, based on these supposed differences, individuals are assigned to distinct, nonintersecting categories, which form the basis for stereotypes.

Gender-related stereotypes affect perceptions and attributions and can result in prejudice and discrimination (Korabik, 1999; Shields, 2013). The implications of conflating sex and gender are profound. For example, it results in the tendencies to (a) accept stereotypes as facts, (b) see the categories of male/man and female/woman in and of themselves as being the explanation for why behavior occurs, (c) overestimate between group differences and underestimate within group differences, and (d) ignore the impact of any differences that are due to context, power, and status (Shields, 2013). Because of this, researchers who fail to clearly distinguish sex from gender risk leaving their findings open to misinterpretation about what is causing their effects (Korabik, 1999). In this chapter, we focus on psychosocial causes and confine ourselves to discussing issues related to gender.

Gender is a multidimensional construct. As such, it includes both external and internal aspects. The external or observable aspect is one's appearance as a man or a woman, which we refer to here as physical gender. This self-presentation is affected by one's self-identity and in turn influences the perceptions, attributions, and evaluations of others. The internal aspect of gender encompasses a variety of intrapsychic gender-related traits and attitudes (Korabik, 1999).

Culture

Culture is the psychosocial impact of membership in a social group with similar history, experiences, values, and normative behaviors. In research, it has either been defined as observable or unobservable (Ayman, 2004). In studies of the more observable aspect of culture, people are usually grouped by country of origin or ethnic origin based on the color of their skin, the shape of their eyes, the texture of their hair, or their accent in language. This is done based on observers' perceptions. However, sometimes these characteristics also impact the social identity of individuals and their adherence to membership in one cultural group or another.

The intrapsychic aspects of culture refer to cultural values such as individualism/collectivism, power distance, uncertainty avoidance, focus on quality or quantity in life (Hofstede, 1984), orientation toward time (polychronicity), and gender equality (traditional versus egalitarian). These are values that individuals hold; and while there may be similarity between those who live in proximity to one another and who have similar historical experience, referred to as national culture (Hofstede, 1984; House, Hanges, & Ruiz-Quitanilla, 1997), they also may vary within a country or ethnic group. In most investigations, cultural differences are studied by looking at either visible or invisible cultural markers (Ayman & Korabik, 2010). There are advantages and limitations when researchers focus on only one or the other of these types of markers, and the use of both can strengthen the interpretation of their results.

THREE MODELS OF GENDER, CULTURE, AND GLOBAL LEADERSHIP

Gender and societal culture are important to both global and international leaders. In studying how leadership is related to gender or culture, it is necessary to understand that leadership is not only a manifestation of one's own values, motives, and aspirations. It also is a process involving social interactions with others whose values and cultural assumptions may be different from ones own (Ayman & Korabik, 2010; Bass, 1991). For this reason, it is important to consider both the characteristics of women global leaders and how others perceive a woman global leader. To explore these dynamics, we offer three models (see also Ayman & Korabik, 2010; Korabik & Ayman, 2007) that focus on how different gender-related processes impact leadership: the intrapsychic model, the social interaction model, and the social structural model.

Gender as an Intrapsychic Process

The first model delineates the impact of internal processes or the importance of the intrapsychic characteristics of leaders. One aspect of these is gender-role orientation, which refers to gender-related personality traits that are acquired through gender-role socialization (Cook, 1985). These internal personality characteristics are theorized as falling in two separate bipolar dimensions, which are independent of both biological sex and physical gender. Thus, both men and women have both masculine (argentic/instrumental) and feminine (communal/ expressive) characteristics in their personalities (Bem, 1974; Spence, Helmreich, & Stapp, 1975). This means that not all men are masculine nor are all women feminine. Moreover, being high on masculinity or agency does not mean that a person is low on femininity or communion; and being high on femininity does not mean that a person is low on masculinity or agency. Individuals who have high amounts of both agentic and communal traits are considered to be androgynous (Cook, 1985).

In terms of leadership, support for the intrapsychic perspective comes from research showing that gender-role orientation is a better predictor of leadership behavior than is either biological sex or physical gender. For example, Eagly and Johnson's (1990) meta-analysis showed that men and women in actual positions of leadership did not differ in their considerate or structuring leadership behavior. Moreover, studies have demonstrated that instrumental traits are associated with task-oriented or initiating structure leadership behaviors and competencies; expressive traits are associated with person-oriented or consideration leadership behaviors and competencies; and androgyny is associated with both structure and consideration (Korabik, 1996; Korabik & Ayman, 1987, 1989a, 1994; Stephens, 2004). Furthermore, not only do androgynous leaders perceive themselves to be significantly more effective than either masculine or feminine leaders, but their supervisors also rate androgynous managers as being the most effective (Korabik & Ayman, 1989b).

Androgyny also has been linked to a transformational leadership style, and the more leaders report being androgynous and transformational, the more both they themselves and their subordinates report lower job stress and higher job satisfaction (Korabik, Ayman, & Purc-Stephenson, 2001). Other research has demonstrated that androgynous individuals have greater behavioral flexibility and a wider behavioral repertoire, which helps them adapt to a greater range of situational demands (Cook, 1985). As it pertains specifically to leadership, research has shown that androgynous individuals are more likely to be able to switch roles in a flexible, adaptive manner to take on whatever leadership function is lacking in a group and that they are higher in social intelligence (Korabik, 1981, 1982, 1990; Zugec & Korabik, 2003).

Although some characteristics and competencies of effective global leaders are gender-neutral in nature (e.g., motivation, integrity, moral values), many others are associated with androgyny. Among these are planning and decision making; empathy, tolerance, concern for others, and sensitivity to their feelings; flexibility and an extensive behavioral repertoire; and openness, cognitive complexity, and tolerance for ambiguity (Cook, 1985; Korabik & Ayman, 1989a). Theoretically, men and women should be equally likely to posses the qualities that make them androgynous leaders. However, androgyny may be more advantageous for women leaders than it is for men (Kark, Waismel-Manor, & Boas, 2012; Korabik &

Ayman, 1989a). Women leaders are often involved in a delicate balancing act. They must conform to a narrow band of acceptable behavior. They cannot act too masculine or they risk violating the norm of acceptable behavior for women. Likewise, they cannot act too feminine or they risk being seen as poor managers. Androgyny offers women a way out of this dilemma. It allows them to have characteristics that correspond to the ideal of the masculine leader while retaining the feminine qualities that society expects of them (Korabik & Ayman, 1989a).

Androgynous women leaders, therefore, seem to have many of the characteristics that are necessary to be effective global leaders, such as the abilities to fit into different cultural contexts, relate to people with different cultural values, and see the implications of their decisions for a wide variety of people in a wide range of circumstances. Based on anecdotal observation, women like Indra Nooyi and Christine LeGarde, who appear to be androgynous, fare well as global leaders. For example, in a recent interview, Indra Nooyi (Serwer, 2014) came across both as a strong traditional CEO and one with nurturing values. That is, it was apparent that she was able to connect with her employees on a personal level and use individualized consideration toward them in her leadership. She also displayed an awareness of the complexity of her situation and the diversity of what she refers to as the social ecosystem, and she was focused on bringing about the betterment of society at-large.

A second intrapsychic gender-related characteristic that might affect the performance of women global leaders is gender-role ideology, which refers to gender-related beliefs, values, and attitudes. This construct is conceptualized as falling on a continuum ranging from traditional to egalitarian values and attitudes about the roles of men and women in society. In leadership situations, the leaders and followers may hold contradictory or varying beliefs about appropriate gender roles, which may result in problems.

Gender as a Social Interaction Process

In contrast to our first model, which is based on intrapsychic gender-related characteristics, in our next two models we examine processes related to gender as an external characteristic. Here we explore the dynamics arising from perceptions and judgments of women leaders based on the fact that they are women rather than men.

The first of these models is founded on the notion that the social interactions that take place between a leader and others are gendered in nature. As Ayman (1993) has noted, men and women leaders will have different types of social interactions with their men and women supervisors and subordinates, and these will influence the outcomes experienced by each party. This is because social interactions are a function of gender-related beliefs and expectations both about the self (schemas) and about others (stereotypes). In addition, these processes are influenced by situational cues (e.g., the gender-typed nature of tasks, skewed gender ratios in groups) that make gender more or less salient and induce priming.

In social interactions, the external or physical aspect of gender (whether someone appears to be a man or a woman) is far more salient to others than the intrapsychic aspects of gender. Here a person's physical gender acts as a cue for the formation of stereotypes. There is abundant evidence that stereotypes can develop based solely on the differential distribution of individuals to social roles without any basis in fact. Gender-role stereotypes are ubiquitous and play a major role in affecting perceptions, judgments, and evaluations of men and women (Korabik, 1997). For example, stereotypes about women result in the attributions that they lack ability and that their effective performance is due solely to luck. This leads to judgments that women are less competent leaders than men and has the effect of making it harder for them to legitimize their authority (Korabik, 1997). Another consequence is that women are subjected to double standards of evaluation so that they must do more and work harder to get ahead (Korabik, 1997). Gender-based stereotypes result in gender-biased decision making that affects personnel selection, compensation, and promotion and produces a system of systemic discrimination against women (Korabik, 1997).

There are some circumstances under which negative evaluations of women leaders are even more likely to occur. One is when role incongruence is perceived to exist. In leadership situations, it is much easier for men leaders to be in a role-congruent position than it is for women leaders (Eagly & Carli, 2007). This is because research in many countries around the world has established that incongruence exists between the stereotype of a prototypical woman (feminine) and that of a prototypical leader (masculine) (Schein, 2001; Schein, Mueller, Lituchy, & Liu, 1996). Women leaders are also more likely to be devalued in situational contexts where gender is primed (Korabik, 1997). Thus, women leaders are often at a disadvantage when they (a) are being evaluated on masculine-stereotyped behaviors and competencies, (b) rely on a leadership style that is overly masculine, (c) are operating in settings with a preponderance of men, or (d) are being evaluated by their male subordinates (Eagly, Karau, & Makhijani 1995; Eagly, Makhijani, & Klonsky, 1992).

These dynamics can act as obstacles to the success of women leaders, making it more difficult for them to attain and keep positions of global leadership. In their seminal work, Eagly and Carli (2007) have argued that, instead of these barriers forming a glass ceiling, they function more like a labyrinth or maze that women must negotiate on their path to leadership.

While women aspiring to global leadership, similar to men, need to build their competencies such as their technical skills, cultural intelligence, and global mindedness, these are not sufficient for them to be successful. They also must be cognizant of the additional impediments that they face due to the gender dynamics described above, have an understanding of how to overcome them, and be able to position themselves to manage the expectations of those with whom they interact. In this respect, culture may play a role. For example, Asian management styles have been noted to be more relationship-focused (Triandis, 1993). Because this is more consistent with the stereotype of women, it may be easier for women global leaders to be accepted in Asian cultures.

Gender as a Social Structural Process

Our third model examines processes related to gender as an ascribed status characteristic that influences access to power and resources. A number of theories (e.g., expectation states theory and status characteristics theory) are particularly useful in explicating the dynamics that result from the structural inequality in societies (Ridgeway, 1992). Due to the prevalence of patriarchies in most societies around the world, men are generally granted greater power of legitimacy and privilege than are women. Because of this, different outcomes often will be attained by men leaders and women leaders due to perceived status differentials. Because women are seen as having lower social standing than men, they do not get as much time when speaking in groups, and when they do express their opinions they are often ignored by others. In addition, their perceived lower status may make it more difficult for women leaders to gain access to power and resources compared to men leaders. This may undercut the extent to which they can achieve goals and bring about change. Moreover, the lower social status that is attributed to leaders who are women and people of color can result in ingroup/outgroup dynamics that favor the ingroup (Korabik, 1997). Some of the consequences of this for lower status individuals include having their failures accentuated, the devaluation of their accomplishments by others, being subjected to unwelcoming environments, and exclusion from majority networks (e.g., old boys' networks) (Ibarra, Carter, & Silva, 2010; Korabik, 1997).

Research has shown that issues of status and power may be particularly salient when women leaders are interacting with men subordinates. For example, women managers with men subordinates experience lower LMX than when they have women subordinates (Green, Anderson, & Shiver, 1996). In addition, a transformational leadership style appears to be less effective for women leaders with men subordinates than for men leaders with women subordinates (Ayman, Korabik, & Morris, 2009). These results may arise because men, who are used to being in a privileged position and as having higher status than women, experience identity threat, which leads them to derogate woman leaders.

Sometimes, however, factors other than gender play a role in determining status and the access to power. One example is in societies with strict caste or class divisions where a woman who comes from the upper class or an elite family may be accorded privileges that her counterpart in a less hierarchical culture may not experience. While among her equals she still may not have the same status as a man in her society, her legitimate power is well situated over men of lower social class than her own. For example, historically, we can see in Iran during the Quajar period (19th century) that the mother of the king was more powerful than the minsters and other government officials. A similar situation is the proverbial "power behind the throne" phenomenon, which is when women gain indirect power and influence through the control they have over a powerful man.

Even in societies like India and Pakistan, which have very traditional views about women's roles, we've seen women such as Benazir Bhutto and Indira Gandhi emerge as leaders partially due to their family connections. Social connections can also be related to status. Thus, in China, women with connections to the Communist Party or those with greater *guanxi* have more access to leadership positions and social influence. Limited educated manpower and a high need for knowledge also can be another factor with which, in more traditional societies, women who are highly educated can get the respect they deserve.

These additional forms of status can act to override the lower status that women have as a function of their gender and provide them with power and resources that they might not otherwise have had available to them. However, this does nothing to change the *status quo* or to equalize access to power and privilege for the less fortunate. Thus, there may be many women with the potential to be global leaders who will not be able to attain such positions due to their lack of access to the necessary power and resources.

SUMMARY AND CONCLUSION

As globalization has become more widespread, the need for global leaders has become more imperative. In this chapter, we have distinguished global leadership from cross-cultural and international leadership. We have discussed the competencies that are necessary for the success of global leaders and compared these to those of authentic leaders. We also have provided some examples of women who are global leaders and identified the qualities that make them effective. In addition, we have defined gender and culture and have tried to explain why they are key factors in global leadership. We have presented three theoretical models delineating the different dynamic processes that underlie the impact of gender on leadership.

In doing so, we have demonstrated the necessity of differentiating between the effects that are due to the internal characteristics of leaders themselves and those that are due to others' perceptions and observations of them. Thus, a global woman leader's own intrinsic characteristics and values will be what primarily guide her decisions and actions. By contrast, society and her employees' judgments about her will be based on stereotypes, perceived role incongruence, and perceptions about her status and privilege. When doing research on women global leaders, therefore, it is critical to be attentive to the source of information. In other words, information obtained from women leaders themselves via self-reports about their own characteristics may not coincide with reports and evaluations obtained from their superiors and subordinates. Researchers should be careful to articulate their theory about what is driving their effects (i.e., intrapsychic, social interactional, or social structural processes) and formulate their research designs accordingly.

As our discussion of these dynamics illustrates, we would expect few differences between men and women global leaders in the qualities they have or in their potential for global leadership. However, due to the additional impediments faced by women global leaders, they might not be able to garner the same support and positive evaluations from others, even when they show the same competencies as men. In addition, it should be noted that the three processes that we have discussed do not operate in isolation from one another. Rather, there are complex interactions among them, which it is beyond the scope of this chapter to discuss. Taken together, these provide a theoretical framework for understanding the multiple factors that impact upon women in leadership positions (Korabik & Ayman, 2007.

Moreover, culture also plays an important role. It would not be surprising, therefore, if women in some modern societies with more aptitude than men experience more hindrances than do women in traditional societies. What becomes important is that women in traditional societies still need to have the requisite mindset and competencies for global leadership and that women in modern societies, who many may have the needed competencies, are respectful of the needed connections and social bonds.

It is incumbent upon women aspiring to positions of global leadership, not only to understand the requisite characteristics and competencies that they need to have, but also to understand the wide variety of gender dynamics that they will encounter. Therefore, global women leaders need to become conversant in how to handle them. Organizations should help to clear the pathway for women to attain positions of global leadership by identifying promising women and providing them with development and training opportunities and mentorship experiences. Moreover, they need to instruct all employees on how gender dynamics operate in the workplace, be alert for situations where gender-related barriers to women's performance might arise, and act to remove these.

There has been very little research on women global leaders. Most studies thus far have been biographical or autobiographical and thus have limitations with regard to who is providing the information and who is interpreting it. At this time, due to the limited number of women in the global arena, this may be our only source on which to base the initial development of programs and training aimed at them. Clearly, much more research is needed before we have a comprehensive understanding about who women global leaders are, how they attain their positions, what obstacles they encounter, and what makes them successful. In this chapter, we have discussed three types of processes that form the basis for a theoretical framework. This framework should be useful in guiding future research efforts on this important topic.

NOTE

1. The order of authorship is alphabetical and both authors contributed equally to this chapter.

REFERENCES

Adler, N. J. (2002). Global managers: No longer men alone. *International Journal of Human Resource Management, 3*(5), 743–760.

Aycan, Z. (2006). Paternalism: Towards a conceptual refinement and operationalization. In U. Kim, K. S. Yang, & K. K. Hwang (Eds.), *Indigenous and cultural psychology: Understanding people in context* (pp. 445–466). New York, NY: Springer.

Ayman, R. (1993). Leadership perception: The role of gender and culture. In M. M. Chemers & R. Ayman (Eds.), *Leadership theory and research: Perspectives and directions* (pp. 137–166). New York, NY: Academic.

Ayman, R. (2004). Culture and leadership. In C. Spielberger (Editor in Chief), *Encyclopedia of applied psychology* (Vol. 2., pp. 507–519). San Diego, CA: Elsevier.

Ayman, R., & Chemers, M. M. (1983). The relationship of supervisory behavior ratings to work group effectiveness and subordinate satisfaction among Iranian managers. *Journal of Applied Psychology, 68*(2), 338–341.

Ayman, R., & Korabik, K. (2010). Leadership: Why gender and culture matter. *American Psychologist, 65*(3), 157–170. doi:10.1037/a0018806

Ayman, R., Korabik, K., & Morris, S. (2009). Is transformational leadership always perceived as effective? Men subordinates' devaluation of women transformational leaders. *Journal of Applied Social Psychology, 39*(4), 852–879.

Bass, B. M. (1985). *Leadership performance beyond expectations.* New York, NY: Academic.

Bass, B. M. (1991). *Bass & Stogdill's handbook of leadership* (3rd ed.). New York, NY: Free Press.

Bem, S. L. (1974). The measurement of psychological androgyny. *Journal of Consulting and Clinical Psychology, 42*(2), 155–162.

Bem, S. L. (1993). *The lenses of gender.* New Haven, CT: Yale University Press.

Bird, A., & Osland, J. (2004). Global competencies: An introduction. In H. Lane, M. Maznevski, M. Mendenhall, & J. Mc Nett (Eds.), *Handbook of global management* (pp. 57-80). Oxford, England: Wiley-Blackwell.

Bird, A., & Stevens, M. J. (2013). Assessing global leadership competencies. In M. E. Mendenhall, J. S. Osland, A. Bird, G. Oddou, M. L. Maznevski, M. J. Stevens, & G. K. Stahl (Eds.), *Global leadership: Research, practice, development* (2nd ed., pp. 113-140). New York, NY: Routledge/Taylor & Francis.

Chen, N. Y., & Tjosvold, D. (2007). Guanxi and leader member relationships between American managers and Chinese employees: Open minded dialogue as mediator. *Asia Pacific Journal of Management, 24*(2), 171–189. doi:10.1007/s10490-006-9029-9

Cook, E. P. (1985). *Psychological androgyny.* New York, NY: Pergamon.

Cramer, J. (2012). A quote by Indra Nooyi on environment, sustainability, and corporate social responsibility. *GAIAM life.* Retrieved from http://blog.gaiam.com/quotes/authors/indra-nooyi/61012

DeGroot, T., Kiker, D. S., & Cross, T. C. (2000). A meta-analysis to review organizational outcomes related to charismatic leadership. *Canadian Journal of Administrative Sciences, 17*(4), 356–371.

Eagly, A. H., & Carli, L. (2007). *Through the labyrinth.* Boston, MA: Harvard Business School Press.

Eagly, A. H., & Johnson, B. T. (1990). Gender and leadership style: A meta-analysis. *Psychological Bulletin, 108*(2), 233–256.

Eagly, A. H., Karau, S. J., & Makhijani, M. G. (1995). Gender and the effectiveness of leaders: A meta-analysis. *Psychological Bulletin, 117*(1), 125–145.

Eagly, A. H., Makhijani, M. G., & Klonsky, B. G. (1992). Gender and the evaluation of leaders: A meta-analysis. *Psychological Bulletin, 111*(1), 3–22.

Early, C., & Ang, S. (2003). *Cultural intelligence: Individual interactions across cultures.* Stanford, CA: Stanford University Press.

Green, S. G., Anderson, S. E., & Shiver, S. L. (1996). Demographic and organizational influence on leader-member exchange and related work attitude. *Organizational Behavior and Human Decision Processes, 66*(2), 203–214.

Hampden-Turner, C., & Trompenaars, F. (2000). *Building cross-cultural competence: How to create wealth from conflicting values.* New Haven, CT: Yale University Press.

Hofstede, G. (1984). *Culture's consequences: International differences in work related values.* Beverly Hills, CA: Sage.

House, R. J. (1977). A 1976 theory of charismatic leadership. In J. G. Hunt,, & L. L. Larson (Eds.), *Leadership: The cutting edge* (pp. 189–207). Carbondale: Southern Illinois University Press.

House, R. J., Hanges, P. J., Javidan, M., Dorfman, P. W., & Gupta, V. (Eds.). (2004). *Culture, leadership, and organizations: The GLOBE study of 62 societies*. Thousand Oaks, CA: Sage.

House, R. J., Hanges, P. J., & Ruiz-Quitanilla, A. (1997). GLOBE: The global leadership and organizational behavior effectiveness research program. *Polish Psychological Bulletin, 28*(3), 215–254.

Ibarra, H., Carter, M. N., & Silva, C. (2010, September). Why men still get more promotions than women? Your high-potential females need more than just well-meaning mentors. *Harvard Business Review*, 80–86.

James, D. (2014, April 4). *IMF will address global inequality, says Managing director Christine Lagarde*. Retrieved from http://therealnews.com/t2/index.php?option=com_content&task=view&id=31&Itemid=4&jumival=11725

Javidan, M., Teagarden, M., & Bowen, D. (2010). Making it overseas. *Harvard Business Review, 88*(4), 109–113.

Judge, T. A., & Piccolo, R. F. (2004). Transformational and transactional leadership: A meta-analytic test of their relative validity. *Journal of Applied Psychology, 89*(5), 755–768.

Kark, R., Waismel-Manor, R., & Boas, S. (2012). Does valuing androgyny and femininity lead to a female advantage? The relationship between gender-role, transformational leadership and identification. *The Leadership Quarterly, 23*(3), 620–640

Korabik, K. (1981, March). *Androgyny and leadership: An integration*. Paper presented at the meeting of the Association for Women and Psychology, Boston, MA. (ERIC Document Reproduction Service No. ED208-274)

Korabik, K. (1982, August). *Sex-role orientation and leadership: Further explorations*. Paper presented at the annual meeting of the American Psychological Association, Washington, DC. (ERIC Document Reproduction Service No. ED223-963)

Korabik, K. (1990). Androgyny and leadership style. *Journal of Business Ethics, 9*(4/5), 9–18.

Korabik, K. (1996). Gender, leadership style, and managerial effectiveness. *Proceedings of the meeting of the International Association of Management*. Toronto, ON, Canada.

Korabik, K. (1997). Applied gender issues. In S. W. Sadava & D. R. McCreary (Eds.), *Applied social psychology* (pp. 292–302). Upper Saddle River, NJ: Prentice Hall.

Korabik, K. (1999). Sex and gender in the new millennium. In G. N. Powell (Ed.), *Handbook of gender in organizations* (pp. 3–16). Thousand Oaks, CA: Sage.

Korabik, K., & Ayman, R. (1987, August). *Androgyny and leadership style: A conceptual synthesis*. Paper presented at the annual meeting of the American Psychological Association, New York, NY. (ERIC Document Reproduction Service ED291-032)

Korabik, K., & Ayman, R. (1989a). Should women managers have to act like men? *Journal of Management Development, 8*(6), 23–32.

Korabik, K., & Ayman, R. (1989b). Androgyny and managerial effectiveness. In J. McGuire (Ed.), *Proceedings of the Administrative Sciences Association of Canada annual conference: Women in management* (pp. 1–9). Montreal, Quebec.

Korabik, K., & Ayman, R. (1994, July). *Sex-role orientation and self-perception of managerial ability*. Paper presented at the meeting of the International Congress of Applied Psychology, Madrid, Spain.

Korabik, K., & Ayman, R. (2007). Gender and leadership in the corporate world: A multiperspective model. In Chin, J. L., Lott, B., Rice, J. K., & Sanchez-Hucles, J. (Eds.), *Women and leadership* (pp. 106-124). Malden, MA: Blackwell.

Korabik, K., Ayman, R., & Purc-Stephenson, R. (2001, June). *Gender-role orientation and transformational leadership*. Paper presented at the conference on Gender, Work, and Organizations, Keele University, Staffordshire, England.

Lewis, R. D. (2000). *When cultures collide: Managing across cultures*. Naperville IL: Brealey.

Liden, R. C., Wayne, S. J., Zhou, H., & Henderson, D. (2008). Servant leadership: Development of a multidimensional measure and multi-level assessment. *The Leadership Quarterly, 19*(2), 161–177.

Liveris, A. (2012). *Andrew N. Liveris speech at AHC awards gala 2012* [Video]. Retrieved from https://www.youtube.com/watch?v=G0kcDOpuEP0

McCall, M. W., Jr., & Hollenbeck, G. P. (2002). *The lessons of international experience: Developing global executives*. Boston, MA: Harvard Business School Press.

Mendenhall, M., & Oddou, G. (1985). Dimensions of expatriate acculturation: A review. *Academy of Management Review, 10*(2), 39–47.

Mendenhall, M. E., Osland, J. S., Bird, A., Oddou, G., Maznevski, M. L., Stevens, M. J., & Stahl, G. K. (2013). *Global leadership: Research, practice, development* (2nd ed). New York, NY: Routledge/Taylor & Francis.

Osland, J. S. (2013). An overview of the global leadership literature. In M. E. Mendenhall, J. S. Osland, A. Bird, G. Oddou, M. L. Maznevski, M. J. Stevens, & G. K. Stahl (Eds.), *Global leadership: Research, practice, development* (2nd ed., pp. 40-79). New York, NY: Routledge/Taylor & Francis.

Ridgeway, C. L. (Ed.). (1992). *Gender, interaction, and inequality*. New York, NY: Springer-Verlag.

Schein, V. E. (2001). A global look at psychological barriers to women's progress in management. *Journal of Social Issues, 57*(4), 675–688.

Schein, V. E., Mueller, R., Lituchy, T., & Liu, J. (1996). Think manager-think male: A global phenomenon? *Journal of Organizational Behavior, 17*(1), 33–41.

Serwer, A. (2014, January 28). (Say wha???) The CEO who writes her employees' parents. *Fortune Magazine*. Retrieved from http://management.fortune.cnn.com/2014/01/28/say-wha-the-ceo-who-writes-her-employees-parents/

Shields, S. A. (2013). Gender and emotions: What we think we know, what we need to know, and why it matters. *Psychology of Women Quarterly, 37*(4), 423–435.

Spence, J. T., Helmreich, R., & Stapp, J. (1975). Ratings of self and peers on sex-role attributes and their relation to self-esteem and the conception of masculinity and femininity. *Journal of Personality and Social Psychology, 32*(1), 29–39.

Stephens, H. E. (2004). *Gender-role orientation and leadership effectiveness*. Unpublished master's thesis, Guelph, ON, Canada: University of Guelph.

Thomas, D. C., & Ravlin, E. C. (1995). Reponses of employees to cultural adaptation by foreign manager. *Journal of Applied Psychology, 80*(1), 133–146.

Triandis, H. C. (1993). The contingency model in cross-cultural perspectives. In M. M. Chemers, & R. Ayman (Eds.), *Leadership theory and research: Perspectives and directions* (pp. 167–188). New York, NY: Academic.

Walumbwa, F. O., Avolio B. J., Gardner, W. L. Wernsing, T. S., & Peterson, S. J. (2008). Authentic leadership: Development and validation of a theory-based measure. *Journal of Management, 34*(1), 89–126.

Wong, C. S., Tinsley, C., Law, K. S., & Mobley, W. H. (2003). Development and validation of a multidimensional measure of guanxi. *Journal of Psychology in Chinese Societies, 4*(1), 43–69.

Zugec, L., & Korabik, K. (2003, June). *Multiple intelligences, leadership, and androgyny.* Paper presented at the annual meeting of the Canadian Psychological Association, Hamilton, ON.

CHAPTER 4

MULTIPLE INTELLIGENCES OF EFFECTIVE WOMEN GLOBAL LEADERS

Emotional, Social, and Cultural Competencies

Julie R. Breithaupt

Global leaders face greater complexity than domestic leaders. Global leaders must be culturally sensitive, knowledgeable of other nations, and understand boundaries that span organizations (Beechler & Baltzley, 2008). Increased globalization and a rise in multinational organizations have led to a need for global leaders who are effective (Cohen, 2010). Global leadership researchers have sought to identify personality characteristics and competencies essential for effective global leadership and how these capabilities could be developed (Jokinen, 2005). A plethora of competencies and traits attributed to effective global leadership has been identified (Osland, 2008). However, research has not empirically determined if any are universal or how gender and individual characteristics contribute to effective global leadership. The purpose of this chapter is to explicate how emotional, social, and cultural intelligences together contribute to the effectiveness of women as global leaders. It is based on a qualitative study of 14 women serving in global leadership roles in different industries. The chapter begins with a discussion of the concept of multiple intelligences and three competencies important for global leadership.

Believing that the intelligence quotient (IQ) as a single measure of competence does not capture all aspects of human intelligence, Gardner (1983) introduced a theory of multiple intelligences. He posited that intelligences are competences derived from various combinations of abilities, talents, and mental skills. Gardner initially proposed that there are seven independent intelligences. This theory has advanced over time; however there is no consensus on how many types of intelligence exist (Gardner, 2006). More recently, the impact of multiple intelligences on leadership effectiveness has gained the interest of researchers, scholars, and practitioners.

Scholars suggest that emotional, social, and cultural intelligences are important competencies for global leaders (Alon & Higgins, 2005; Boyatzis, 2008). While intellectual intelligence is an important leadership trait, a meta-analysis of 151 studies examining intelligence and leadership found that this relationship is not as important as previously believed (Judge, Colbert, & Ilies, 2004). Judge and colleagues pose that high levels of intelligence only lead to effective leadership if a leader possesses other leadership competencies.

Emotional and social intelligences have been shown to be important for leadership effectiveness (Kerr, Garvin, Heaton & Boyle, 2006; Rockstuhl, Seiler, Ang, Van Dyne & Annen, 2011; Rosete & Ciarrochi, 2005; Zaccaro, 2002). Cultural intelligence increases the likelihood that global leaders will be effective in cross-cultural interactions (Earley & Mosakowski, 2004; Ng, Van Dyne, & Ang, 2009) and may further enact other global leadership competencies (Mendenhall, 2011). The combination of these intelligences may provide a strong foundation for effective global leaders.

EMOTIONAL INTELLIGENCE

The concept of emotional intelligence (EQ) was introduced over two decades ago (Salovey & Mayer, 1990) and is distinct from intellectual intelligence (Riggio & Reichard, 2008). EQ was originally described as a subset of social intelligence that involved the ability to monitor one's own and others' emotions to guide thoughts and actions. An ability model of EQ includes four constructs of perceiving emotions, using emotions, understanding emotions, and managing emotions (Salovey & Mayer, 1997). Perception of emotions involves the ability to convey and read one's own and others' emotions to manage relationships. Individuals can use emotions to stimulate creativity and make better decisions. Understanding emotions involves recognizing emotions and understanding how they are related. Managing emotions requires self-awareness and having the ability to be engaged or dissonant from emotions.

Daniel Goleman is credited with popularizing EQ. Goleman (1998) defined EQ as "the capacity for recognizing our own feelings and those of others, for motivating ourselves and for managing emotions well in ourselves and in our relationships" (p. 317). Building upon Salovey and Mayer's (1997) ability model of EQ, Goleman (1998) proposed a mixed model of EQ by further adding personality traits. This model included five constructs: knowing one's emotions, managing emotions, self-motivation, recognizing others' emotions, and handling relationships. This EQ model has undergone revisions and presently consists of four domains, including self-awareness, self-management, social awareness, and relationship management (Goleman, Boyatzis, & McKee, 2013). In this model, self-awareness encompasses self-confidence and awareness of personal strengths and weaknesses, in addition to recognizing one's emotions and how they affect others (Goleman, 2000). Self-awareness is critical to EQ because it is linked to emotional control and empathy, which are important for management of relationships (Goleman et al., 2013).

As a global leadership competency, EQ increases the likelihood that a leader will be effective in complex situations when conditions are uncertain (Emmerling & Boyatzis, 2012). A leader with EQ is better equipped to understand their own and others' emotions and use this information to achieve successful leadership (Boyatzis, 2009). A study of 27 international sales managers from four different cultural clusters reported that EQ was critical for effective leadership (Reilly & Karounos, 2009). An empirical study of more than 358 managers in 37 countries in a global pharmaceutical company observed a strong relationship between EQ and its high performing leaders, particularly on competencies of self-awareness and self-management (Cavallo & Brienza, 2006).

EQ may pose a female advantage to global leaders (Chugh & Sahgal, 2007). Some studies show that women score higher on measures of EQ than men (Mandell & Pherwani, 2003; Rivers, Brackett, Salovey, & Mayer, 2007). Other studies demonstrate that EQ is associated with transformational leadership (Lam & Higgins, 2012; Mandell & Pherwani, 2003), a leadership style frequently embraced by women leaders (Bass & Riggio, 2006). A study of 176 Australian female managers across multiple industries indicated that women leaders who adopted a transformational leadership style exhibited high levels of EQ (Downey, Papageorgiou, & Stough, 2006). Moreover, in a study of 2,816 male and female executives in 149 countries, women executives (20% of the population studied) rated themselves higher in EQ as did their male and female colleagues (Ibarra & Obodaru, 2009). Researchers have only begun to explore these relationships.

SOCIAL INTELLIGENCE

The concept of social intelligence (SQ) is not new. It was first introduced by Thorndike (1920) as a purely cognitive construct. However, researchers lost interest in it because it was too broad (Salovey & Mayer, 1990) and closely related to IQ (Goleman, 2006). Recently, neuroscientists have shown that neural circuits are actively involved in the conscious and unconscious detection of others' emotions, finding that SQ is underpinned biologically (Goleman & Boyatzis, 2008). A more recent concept of SQ includes important elements related to human aptitudes for relationships and nonverbal communication that ensue when people interact (Goleman, 2006). As such, SQ involves social awareness or what one senses about others and social facility or how this information is used in relationship management (Goleman, 2006).

Leadership manifests itself in a relational or social context, thus effective leaders build relationships and social networks within and outside of their organizations. As a competency, Boyatzis (2008) defined SQ as "the ability to recognize, understand, and use emotional information about others that leads to or causes effective or superior performance" (Boyatzis, 2008, p. 8). SQ is important to help leaders interpret social situations and influence followers toward goals (Zacccaro, 2002). As social complexity rises with positional authority, SQ becomes of greater importance to achieve effective organizational leadership (Riggio, 2002).

Competencies of SQ and EQ overlap in their emphasis on social awareness and relationship management (Boyatzis, 2008) but are distinct from cognitive skills that underlie intellectual intelligence (Earley, 2002). EQ and SQ are deemed to be culturally bound and lack direct application to cross-cultural contexts (Earley & Peterson, 2004). However, empirical evidence suggests that the social competences associated with social awareness and relationship management are predictive of cultural intelligence (Moon, 2010).

CULTURAL INTELLIGENCE

Achieving effective cross-cultural leadership is one of the most critical challenges for global leaders (Beechler & Javidan, 2007). Cultural intelligence (CQ) is a relatively new construct defined as "an individual's capability to function and manage effectively in a culturally diverse setting" (Ang et al.,

2007, p. 337). CQ is critical for global leaders because the influence of native cultural values and norms can hinder cultural adjustment (Earley, 2002). What is understood about an international culture, its traits, norms, social cues, and behaviors is one part of CQ. Another part involves awareness of behavioral and cultural preferences and being able to interpret and respond appropriately to different social cues in cross-cultural interactions. CQ increases the likelihood that global leaders will be open-minded, nonjudgmental, and display cultural sensitivity (Ng et al., 2009).

CQ has advantages over other proposed intercultural competencies like global mindset. CQ is grounded in cognitive psychology and contemporary theories of intelligence (Earley & Ang, 2003; Sternberg, 1986). While global mindset is popular, there is no clear definition or agreement on what competencies constitute this construct (Beechler & Javidan, 2007). Unlike global mindset, CQ focuses solely on an individual's capability to effectively interact in culturally diverse contexts (Ang et al., 2007).

CQ is a multidimensional construct composed of four components: cognitive, metacognitive, motivational, and behavioral (Earley, 2002). The cognitive component pertains to acquired knowledge of other cultures that enables strategies to process new and unfamiliar information (Earley, 2002). Metacognition links knowledge and skills with culturally intelligent behavior by eliciting self-regulation (Thomas et al., 2008). CQ's emphasis on metacognition differentiates it from SQ and EQ (Earley & Peterson, 2004) because self-awareness and social awareness do not guarantee behavioral flexibility in unfamiliar cultural situations (Earley, 2002). An assessment of CQ in 140 participants reported that individuals who visited foreign countries for purposes of education and work had significantly higher CQ scores for metacognition than other participants (Crowne, 2008).

The motivational component of CQ involves being open-minded, persistent, and confident to act in culturally appropriate ways (Earley, Ang, & Tan, 2006). Effective cross-cultural interactions stem from having a strong motivation to develop interpersonal relationships with those who are culturally different (Thomas et al., 2008). Furthermore, the motivational component of CQ has been shown to predict adjustment of individuals working globally (Templer, Tay, & Chandrasekar, 2006).

The behavioral component of CQ goes beyond knowledge of how one should act and reflects how one does act in social situations, despite acquired cognition (Ang et al., 2007). It involves adapting to cross-cultural situations and developing a behavioral repertoire of culturally learned behaviors as well as flexibility of one's verbal and nonverbal responses (Earley & Peterson, 2004). The ability to withhold judgment and actions in order to select an appropriate behavioral response is critical for global leaders in cross-cultural interactions (Triandis, 2006).

Compared to other types of intelligence, CQ is unique in its focus on intercultural settings. CQ is predictive of task performance, cultural adaptation, cultural judgment, and decision-making (Ang et al., 2007). EQ and SQ assume a cultural familiarity that may not extend across borders, as social norms and behaviors are not universal (Earley & Peterson, 2004). A recent study of multiple intelligences in 126 Swiss military leaders showed that CQ significantly predicted cross-border effectiveness, whereas EQ was only predictive of domestic leadership effectiveness (Rockstuhl et al., 2011). Global leaders with high EQ or SQ are better equipped to empathize and interact with others; however, CQ is needed because these intelligences lack cultural context.

RESEARCH METHODS

Over the past two decades, a number of studies have been conducted to begin to understand global leadership (Osland, 2008). Researchers studying leadership and global leadership have largely focused on males, and as a result, the perspective of gender has not been addressed in the development of leadership theories (Eagly & Chin, 2010). There is much theory on how leaders develop, yet there is little empirical evidence to understand how these processes might be different for women (Ely & Rhode, 2010). This study provides an opportunity to gain new perspectives on women's global leadership. Qualitative research was conducted to explore what it means to be a woman who is an effective leader in a global context (Rood-Breithaupt, 2013). Using hermeneutic phenomenological methods and a conceptual framework of multiple intelligences as a guide, this study focused on the lived experiences of 14 women global leaders.

Phenomenology seeks to identify the essences or meanings of experiences about a particular phenomenon as individuals describe their lived experiences (Moustakas, 1994). Therefore, a purposive criterion-based sampling strategy was used to select 14 women with appropriate global leadership experience for participation. The availability of women global leaders is limited and their cultural contexts vary. To avoid potential confounding factors stemming from national differences, all of the participants were U.S. citizens. Given that few women have achieved a senior managerial or a top management role and their geographic dispersion, informal social networks and a snowball approach were utilized to identify global women leaders who were qualified for the study.

After ethics approval and signed informed consent were obtained, informal interviews were utilized to collect autobiographical data, typical of phenomenological studies. The interviews provided the means to explore and gather stories of the women's lived experiences as global leaders. To maintain anonymity and confidentiality, the women's names, any names of other people, and names of organizations were de-identified and assigned pseudonyms. The interview transcripts were sent to participants to solicit their feedback and ensure the accuracy of their described experiences. Transcriptions were analyzed and coded following the modified Van Kaam method and steps for analysis of phenomenological data described by Moustakas (1994).

The participants were drawn from seven different business sectors including global business consulting, health care, hospitality, marketing, telecommunications, transportation, and the U.S. State Department. Of the women studied, 12 were Caucasian and two were African American. The age range of participants varied, with the majority of participants in the 40–49 year and 50–59 year age categories. One younger woman was in the 30–39 year age category and three older women in the 60–69 year age category. Four participants were fluent in at least one other language in addition to English, and 10 of the 14 women had at least one child.

All women had 4-year college degrees. Nine women had advanced degrees with either a master's degree or an MBA. The highest organizational levels achieved by the participants included two chief executive officers, one president, four vice presidents, one diplomat, one co-pilot, three directors, and two senior managers. Years of international experience ranged from more than 5 years to over 25 years, with most participants having at least 15 years of experience in a global leadership role. All organizations except for one were privately held. Headquarters for nine organizations were in the United States, four had headquarters located in Europe, and one was headquartered in the Middle East.

FINDINGS AND DISCUSSION

As the women shared their experiences in global leadership roles, common themes of self-awareness, self-confidence, building relationships, authenticity, and cultural acumen emerged. These themes begin to form the essence of what it means to be a woman who effectively leads in a global context. The themes are presented in the context of current literature with supportive descriptions from the women's interview transcripts.

Self-Awareness

The majority of women described experiences where they had to overcome gender stereotyping. Through self-awareness of a need to be more or less assertive, early in their careers these women recognized the need to adjust their leadership style in order to interact effectively with male bosses and subordinates. Referring to a male boss, one woman said,

> I definitely found that showing that level of initiative and let's say aggressiveness was not treated the same way as if a male would have done it. So I changed my behavior in order to be more acceptable to him and apparently less threatening.

A woman with responsibility for managing foreign physicians from cultures where women are not typically in leadership roles, had difficulty gaining their respect despite having positional authority. To gain their respect, she said, "I had to be more direct and firm, [adopting] more of a male style of interaction." A number of women credited coaches and mentors for opening their eyes to the effects of assertiveness. One woman said, "I've very early on in my career had that input that allowed me to kind of manage my style so that I could be palatably direct, if there's such a way of phrasing that." Self-awareness, a key component of EQ, was important in enabling the women to recognize the effects of assertiveness and adjust their leadership style.

Assertiveness is a masculine trait commonly associated with male leadership (Schein, 2007). Globally, assertive qualities are recognized as male traits, and communal qualities are recognized as female traits (Eagly & Carli, 2007). Women in leadership roles often find themselves in a double bind where being assertive is incongruent with societal prescriptions for females (Eagly & Carli, 2007). To overcome the double bind resulting from gender stereotyping, these women, using their EQ, changed their behavior to be more acceptable to others. Affirmed by two women,

> You have to work harder and you have to speak softer and prepare more, even as a boss. And sometimes, it's just exhausting, but you know, I have no other recourse.

> Stereotypes exist and sometime creep up in the back of your head and makes you feel like well, maybe I should just keep my voice silent ... as opposed to just being a leader and saying what I need to say anyway, despite the discomfort.

Self-Confidence

Self-confidence is an important part of an individual's EQ (Goleman, 2000). Men typically exhibit more self-confidence than women (Goleman & Boyatzis, 2008), and male confidence is suggested to perpetuate male dominance in leadership (Reuben, Rey-Biel, Sapienza & Zingales, 2012). Many women battled their own self-doubt and found that being well prepared and understanding their strengths and weaknesses raised their self-confidence. Statements by four women reflect their experiences:

> I overprepare and I go in knowing that I know what I am talking about.

> I had to let go of fear. That's the first thing ... you have to start to say to yourself, look, you've done the homework. Your work is fine. Just deliver it!

> You need to know yourself and you need to know what you are good at and what you are not good at and you need to be okay with it.

> There is a tendency of women to view themselves and maybe to think about the things that they don't have, more than the things that they do have. Believing that you have what you need to do the job is really important and projecting that.

Being well prepared and recognizing personal strengths and weaknesses was an important strategy to raise the women's level of self-confidence and belief in their success.

In male-dominated fields, all of the women said that their knowledge and expertise in their fields of specialty was essential. Many women further said that they had to prove their competence. Women typically face higher standards for leadership competence than men (Eagly & Carli, 2007). These quotes reflect the women's experiences:

> I think if you know anybody who works in the male-dominated field as a woman, you always feel like you have to have all of your stuff.

> Being well prepared and confident in your knowledge base helps people to recognize and respect your competence. Once competence is firmly established, it is much easier to establish trust and build relationships.

> Being able to sell your capabilities comes secondary, because if you have technical knowledge, people know that you're competent and then you don't need to work really hard to get them to understand or agree on how to approach things.

Sharing knowledge with people who are culturally different and having the confidence to act in culturally appropriate ways is an important part of SQ and CQ.

Building Relationships

As cross-cultural work has grown in response to globalization and the rapid changes ensuing from technology and competition, researchers pose that relational skills have increased in importance (Gentry, Harris, Baker, & Leslie, 2008). Women leaders are more apt to use relational skills and give more attention to development of interpersonal relationships than men (Eagly & Johnson, 1990). This was echoed by the women in this study. Most women expressed that relationships are critical to being successful as a global leader. As one woman put it, "That's how things get done because you're building your sphere of influence through relationship building." Women typically score higher on measures of SQ than men, particularly on sensing nonverbal emotions of others (Goleman, 2006). Another woman concurred: "The female part of it is the relationship building skills that I could use." Relational qualities are beginning to become recognized as important for effective leadership in addition to male leadership traits (Koenig, Mitchell, Eagly, & Ristikari, 2011).

Developing and managing relationships requires skills involving both EQ and SQ. Building relationships with people who come from different cultural backgrounds further requires CQ. Many women developed strong relationships with their direct reports, teams, peers, and colleagues in different countries that led to trust and mutual respect. One woman said, "The only way you can understand other cultures is by establishing relationships." She fully immersed herself in new cultures by establishing relationships with employees at every level. She put herself in their shoes, went to their homes for dinner, and met the family members. This helped her begin to understand what is important to people in other cultures. Building relationships over a meal or cup of coffee proved to be useful to the women's exercise of global leadership.

Using social facility to influence and shape the outcome of conversations is an important component of SQ (Goleman, 2006). As global leaders, being able to persuade and influence others is important to achieving organizational goals. One woman had a boss who was prescient in his views. She understood what he was saying and possessed better communication skills than he did. She became his voice and eventually earned the respect of her male colleagues. She said, "I did a huge amount of persuasion and that was my main job, to persuade people … I didn't initially have a lot of resources, and gradually I ended up building a team, but it was constantly me having to persuade others." Knowing how to say something was as important as what is said in a conversation. As posed by one woman, to say, "I have experienced that before, and this is the way it is going to work if we do that," is a way to express one's experience that is not easily questioned.

Understanding how an audience will perceive what is said and having the ability to choose how and what to say involves social facility (Riggio, 2002).

Women are less likely to receive formal leadership training and development opportunities than men (Hoyt, 2013). Receiving little organizational assistance for professional development, the majority of women used their ability to build and establish informal mentoring relationships. When the women started a job in a new organization or a new country, they built a new informal network. From their networks, some colleagues grew into mentors or sponsors and became their advocates. These relationships were vital for career development and obtaining important feedback. Mentors and sponsors helped them obtain visible assignments as well as increase their specialized knowledge and potential for advancement. Mentoring was important at all stages of the women's careers. The importance of networks in career advancement is beginning to be recognized (O'Neil, Hopkins, & Sullivan, 2011).

Most women viewed networks as key facilitators of their effectiveness as global leaders. They relied on the relationships established in their networks for support. They could count on individuals in their network to back them up and support them in key meetings. One woman said that she is often asked to get things done in a time frame that requires bypassing normal procedures. Using her internal networks, she knows who to approach to cut through the bureaucracy and accomplish the task. Leveraging networks requires relationship management skills involving both EQ and SQ. Networks are instrumental in developing relationships, building partnerships, and linking one's capabilities with global connections (Jokinen, 2005).

Recognizing the power base in existence requires social awareness and knowing how the social world works (Goleman, 2006). The women in the study at the vice president level or higher were more intentional in the relationships they formed and the networks they built. They possessed a higher level of SQ. They developed relationships with people that were in the power base of their organization. One woman said,

> Stepping out perhaps sometimes of a comfort zone beyond the people that you really connect with and feel comfortable, to reaching out to some of those who aren't as natural colleagues or natural business associates and building relationships there ... a concerted effort on that is quite important.

She further added, "Men have that natural sense for who are the power players. Women have to think about it a little bit harder." Women typically lack influential individuals in their networks (Ibarra, Carter, & Silva, 2010; O'Neil et al., 2011).

The women in this study described themselves as being empathetic. Empathy is a key component of EQ, important for establishing and managing relationships. Empathy is further universal in not being culturally bound (Jokinen, 2005). Having moved up through the ranks to their leadership roles, empathy enabled them to understand others. One woman said, "To be a good leader you have to be a follower. You have to be able to take orders before you can really give them." Another woman reflected, "In managing people under me, I've always tried to understand where they are coming from, understand their job, and empathize with them."

Authenticity

Global work involves being able to communicate with people from many cultures. The majority of the women described encountering language barriers in global work. While most people who work for multinational companies are fluent in English, it is a first language for approximately 5% of the world's population (Livermore, 2010). Little research has been done to understand the impact of language on diversity management (Harzing & Feely, 2008). In response to communication challenges, many women described becoming active listeners and adjusting their behavioral interactions by speaking slowly and using body language to convey attention. They provided honest feedback and consciously avoided the use of phrases or slang that would not be understood in non-American cultures. They were empathetic toward others who struggled to find the right words in English. One woman told a Korean physician who kept apologizing for his poor English, "Look, you're doing much better in English than I would do in Korean." Another woman said, "It is just a question of reading your audience so that you can be more effective with them." Enacting behaviors which show cultural consciousness in cross-cultural interactions reflect use of the metacognitive component of CQ. Moreover, displays of empathy and listening with receptivity show use of EQ and SQ.

The majority of women said that effective communication was critical to their success. One woman said, "Being able to communicate with conviction, yet warmth and passion is important … communication comes in a variety of ways, it can't be one of condescension or I had to be nice to you. It has to come from the heart!" Many women described communication as being effective when it was authentic so that it would serve as a foundation to establish their integrity, build trust and relationships. One woman said, "I'm honest and fair, and I think that approach works better with subordinates who may be hesitant that they will not be treated well or will be given a fair shake." Authentic conversations can renew commitment and improve collaboration (Showkeir & Showkeir, 2008).

Honesty was valued highly by these women. The following quotes reflect the women leaders' perception of honesty in cross-cultural interactions:

> It was really about being honest and acknowledging our uniqueness.

> I have to trust in humanity and believe that most people want to do the right thing.

> You just need to be honest. People know when you are not telling the truth.

The women earned trust from their teams, colleagues, and subordinates by being honest. Honesty and integrity are well-respected universal values (House, Hanges, Javidan, Dorfman, & Gupta, 2004). One woman, speaking about her direct reports. added, "I was always honest with them and I always told them what I expected from them.... They told me they appreciate that honesty, even when we have to go over bad things."

Social facility involves engaging in behaviors that are perceived by others as authentic (Goleman, 2006). Building relationships and establishing connections through the use of authentic conversation shows the women's use of SQ. Overall, the women's style of leadership was one that was positive, transparent, and grounded in personal integrity, and honesty. One woman reflected,

> My leadership style is one that is based upon honesty, one that is based upon fairness, one that is based upon accountability, and one that's based upon the discipline of listening, learning, and then responding. It took me awhile to get here.

The women built trust by sharing their vision with their teams and direct reports. One woman leader summed it up thusly:

> So you need to have very clear power so everybody understands that vision or North Star against which you're operating. I think the second thing is you need to have very authentic communication because that builds trust, and then I think that the relationship building in its sense of support is also really critical.

Another woman echoed, "The team needs to have shared vision and then the relationships amongst the team members are important so that everyone has respect and trust for each other."

Authentic communication and having a positive leadership style that is based on values of honesty, integrity, and transparency lend themselves to authentic leadership. When probed about their leadership style, most women described themselves using terms related to authenticity and acting in accordance with their true self:

> I lead by example.

> I can't run somebody else's race. I want to run my own race.

> What I've learned is that I just want to be me now.

Consistent with these descriptions, Luthans, Norman, and Hughes (2006) found that authentic leadership, unlike other forms of leadership, is not a particular style of leadership. If an individual is true to oneself, then the individual will be true to their core values, providing a normative guide to one's actions (George, 2003).

The core values of these women are consistent with some of the universal attributes of effective leadership identified in Project GLOBE (House et al., 2004). Ethical attributes of effective leaders identified in the GLOBE study included character and integrity, altruism, collective motivation, encouraging, and empowering others (Johnson, 2009). These attributes suggest that global leaders who are effective show respect and dignity for humankind. Universal leadership attributes are also important for global leaders, as these facilitators of effective leadership transcend cultural boundaries (Jokinen, 2005). Moreover, Eagly (2005) suggested that authenticity is relational in that a leader embraces values that are readily identified and accepted by followers.

Cultural Acumen

Cultural differences can pose a significant barrier in conducting business. Several women experienced cultural prejudice and had to dispel the notion that Americans want to tell everyone else what to do. One woman overcame this barrier by living overseas for 2 months and getting to know her team on a personal level, establishing respect and trust.

> They thought I was going to come in and tell them what to do. They have a little bit more respect for me because they understood where I came from a bit more, not just being on the phone trying to control and direct things.

Another woman was able to connect with her German colleagues on a social level, and through this connection she was able to establish relationships. Enacting the motivational component of CQ, these women found ways to be accepted at an individual level.

As the women became more experienced in cross-cultural situations, they learned to adapt and expand their behavioral repertoires. One woman found that humor was useful to break the ice with her foreign team. Caution is appropriate here: humor is difficult to gauge in multicultural interactions and involves skillful awareness of one's audience and involves not only self-awareness but social awareness. In the absence of face-to-face interactions in Web-based meetings, many women described being very aware of the tone of the communication and making sure their voices were friendly. Communication is not only verbal but physical. The women adopted ways to control showing their emotions through body language. In face-to-face meetings and on video teleconferences, one woman found it best to sit erect with both hands clasped together on the table to show others that she was giving her undivided attention to the conversation. With the help of an executive coach, one woman learned not to display facial expressions that showed disagreement or annoyance. Managing emotions requires self-awareness and control of emotional responses (Goleman et al., 2013).

All of the women had a very positive cosmopolitan outlook and fully embraced the challenge of working across cultures. The following quotes from three of the participants demonstrate their cosmopolitan outlook:

> When you are working in an international setting, you have to understand the customs. You have to understand where those customs and those cultural traits are coming from ... I had to understand them and then lead from that standpoint.

> When I would go to a new place or meet new people, I would be much more circumspect in initial comments that I would make because I realized how making a mistake is part of the first impression that you are establishing.

> I've always been very interested in different cultures and the way that they work and pretty accepting of the fact that there's a whole lot of ways to get the same things done and not one of them is more right or wrong than the other. They're just different, and so I often seek first to understand and I think that helps enormously.

As these women were immersed in cross-cultural work, they made mistakes and learned from their experiences to adjust their leadership styles. In response to the urgency of a particular situation in Central America, one woman raised her voice in giving direction. Later she learned that the local people perceived that she had been yelling at them. Confrontation is not the norm in this culture, so she learned to moderate her voice. Two women, expatriates in Asia-Pacific, gathered input from their teams, but found it was less collaborative than it would have been in the United States because in those cultures, the preference was for the leader to just make the decision. The more experiences they gained across cultures, the more effective they became in applying CQ in their work.

Learning from cultural experiences is an important cognitive component of CQ (Ang et al., 2007). Many women acknowledged adjusting their leadership style depending on the country in which they were interacting. One woman said she would be more direct and outspoken in Austria, whereas in Japan she would ask more questions to gain her team's input as opposed to telling them what she thought they should do, because they might appear to agree just out of being respectful. Other women had similar experiences in needing to ask more questions when working with teams in Hong Kong and Taiwan. Working with Arab men, one woman learned that she should never come out and say "No." She had to find creative ways to show respect by asking questions and then proposing an action. The women frequently described refraining from providing immediate responses in conversations until they could speak diplomatically to the situation. Such behaviors are consistent with self-management in EQ and the behavioral component of CQ.

CONCLUSIONS AND IMPLICATIONS

Multiple intelligences provided a solid foundation for effective global leadership of the women studied. As the women described their experiences, it became evident that EQ, SQ, and CQ were important to their global leadership effectiveness. Some women leaders were stronger on some components of these intelligences than others. Overall, high levels of EQ and SQ were observed. As these women increased their cognitive knowledge and interactions with other cultures, their CQ increased. As a relational process, leadership is molded by context (McCallum & O'Connell, 2009), and for this reason, CQ, in addition to EQ and SQ, was important in helping these women communicate and build relationships across borders.

While the cross-cultural relevance of EQ and SQ is widely debated, these intelligences were just as important as CQ to the effectiveness of these women global leaders. Adhering to positive attitudes and values of honesty, transparency, empathy, and integrity led them to embrace an authentic style of leadership. Authentic leadership speaks to the true power of an individual's character. The authentic leadership of these women paired with EQ, SQ, CQ, and their technical competencies provided a powerful combination of leadership skills and values that contributed to their effectiveness in global leadership roles.

The results of this study expand our knowledge of global leadership from the experiences of women leaders. Due to the qualitative design of this study and inclusion of 14 participants, these results cannot be generalized to the larger population of women global leaders. In spite of the small sample size and the fact that all the participants were U.S. women working globally, the study provides a useful starting point for understanding women as global leaders. Future studies should explore the importance of EQ, SQ, and CQ in women global leaders in different countries, including comparative studies across different contexts and utilizing quantitative measures of the three intelligences.

Lack of consensus on competencies needed for global leadership leaves a gap in the understanding of what is needed to be an effective leader in a global context. This study suggests that EQ, SQ, and CQ are important for women in global leadership roles. Organizations and individuals should learn about these intelligences and take initiatives to develop these competencies. Personality traits in the mixed model of EQ would be difficult to change and would require long-term intervention. However, other aspects of these intelligences such as self-awareness, social awareness, and cultural awareness could be developed by executive coaching or training and development using available tools for assessment. Organizational opportunities for expatriate or extended work assignments in other countries can further help develop CQ.

Informal mentors and sponsors were instrumental in contributing to the development and effectiveness of these women global leaders. Mentoring is well recognized as an important tool for receiving advice and feedback as well as for career development of women (Ehrich, 2008). If informal mentoring provides the best chance for the career development and advancement of women, then women must be intentional and strategic in the informal mentoring relationships they seek and build. Overall, this study shines a light on what enables these 14 global women leaders to be successful and suggests personal and organizational strategies to develop women as global leaders.

REFERENCES

Alon, I., & Higgins, J. M. (2005). Global leadership success through emotional and cultural intelligences. *Business Horizons, 48*(6), 501–512.

Ang, S., Van Dyne, L., Koh, C., Ng, K. Y., Templer, K. J., Tay, C., & Chandrasekar, M. A. (2007). Cultural intelligence: Its measurement and effects on cultural judgment and decision making, cultural adaptation and task performance. *Management and Organization Review, 3*(3), 335–371.

Bass, B. M., & Riggio, R. E. (2006). *Transformational leadership*. Mahwah, NJ: Erlbaum.

Beechler, S., & Baltzley, D. (2008). Creating a global mindset. *Chief Learning Officer, 7*(6), 40–45.

Beechler, S., & Javidan, M. (2007). Leading with a global mindset. In M. Javidan, R. M. Steers, & M. A. Hitt (Eds.), *Advances in international management: Vol. 19. The global mindset* (pp. 131–170). Oxford, England: JAI.

Boyatzis, R. E. (2008). Competencies in the 21st century [Editorial]. *Journal of Management Development, 27*(1), 5–12.

Boyatzis, R. E. (2009). Competencies as a behavioral approach to emotional intelligence. *Journal of Management Development, 28*(9), 749–770.

Cavallo, K., & Brienza, D. (2006). Emotional competence and leadership excellence at Johnson & Johnson. *Europe's Journal of Psychology, 2*(1). doi:10.5964/ejop.v2i1.313

Chugh, S., & Sahgal, P. (2007). Why do few women advance to leadership positions? *Global Business Review, 8*(2), 351–361.

Cohen, S. L. (2010). Effective global leadership requires a global mindset. *Industrial and Commercial Training, 42*(1), 3–10.

Crowne, K. A. (2008). What leads to cultural intelligence? *Business Horizons, 51*(5), 391–399.

Downey, L. A., Papageorgiou, V., & Stough, C. (2006). Examining the relationship between leadership, emotional intelligence and intuition in senior female managers. *Leadership & Organization Development Journal, 27*(4), 250–264.

Eagly, A. (2005). Achieving relational authenticity in leadership: Does gender matter? *Leadership Quarterly, 16*(3), 459–474.

Eagly, A. H., & Carli, L. L. (2007). *Through the labyrinth: The truth about how women become leaders.* Cambridge, MA: Harvard Business School Press.

Eagly, A. H., & Chin, J. L. (2010). Diversity and leadership in a changing world. *American Psychology, 65*(3), 216–224.

Eagly, A. H., & Johnson, B. T. (1990). Gender and leadership style: A meta-analysis. *Psychological Bulletin, 108*(2), 223–256.

Earley, P. C. (2002). Redefining interactions across cultures and organizations: Moving forward with cultural intelligence. *Research in Organizational Behavior, 24*, 271–299.

Earley, P. C., & Ang, S. (2003). *Cultural intelligence: An analysis of individual interactions across cultures.* Stanford, CA: Stanford University Press.

Earley, P. C., Ang, S., & Tan, J. S. (2006). *CQ: Developing cultural intelligence at work.* Stanford, CA: Stanford University Press.

Earley, P. C., & Mosakowski, E. (2004). Cultural intelligence. *Harvard Business Review, 82*(10), 139–146.

Earley, P. C., & Peterson, R. S. (2004). The elusive cultural chameleon: Cultural intelligence as a new approach to intercultural training for the global manager. *Academy of Management Learning and Education, 3*(1), 100–115.

Ehrich, L. C. (2008). Mentoring and women managers: Another look at the field. *Gender in Management: An International Journal, 23*(7), 469–483.

Ely, R. J., & Rhode, D. L. (2010). Women and leadership: Defining the challenges. In N. Nohria & R. Khurana (Eds.), *Handbook of leadership theory and practice* (pp. 377–410). Cambridge, MA: Harvard Business Press.

Emmerling, R. J., & Boyatzis, R. E. (2012). Emotional and social intelligence competencies: Cross-cultural implications. *Cross Cultural Management, 29*(1), 4–18.

Gardner, H. (1983). *Frames of mind.* New York, NY: Basic.

Gardner, H. (2006). *Multiple intelligences: New horizons in theory and practice.* New York, NY: Basic.

Gentry, W. A., Harris, L. S., Baker, B. A., & Leslie, J. B. (2008). Managerial skills: What has changed since the late 1980s. *Leadership & Organization Development Journal, 29*(2), 167–181.

George, B. (2003). What is authentic leadership? *Harvard Management Update, 8*(10), 3.

Goleman, D. (1998). *Working with emotional intelligence.* New York, NY: Bantam.

Goleman, D. (2000). Leadership that gets results. *Harvard Business Review, 78*(2), 78–93.

Goleman, D. (2006). *Social Intelligence.* New York, NY: Bantam Dell.

Goleman, D., & Boyatzis, R. (2008, September). Social intelligence and the biology of leadership. *Harvard Business Review, 8*(9), 74–81.

Goleman, D., Boyatzis, R., & McKee, A. (2013). *Primal leadership: Unleashing the power of emotional intelligence.* Cambridge, MA: Harvard Business Press.

Harzing, A. W., & Feely, A. J. (2008). The language barrier and its implications for HQ-subsidiary relationships. *Cross-cultural Management: An International Journal, 15*(1), 49–61.

House, R. J., Hanges, P. J., Javidan, M., Dorfman, P. W., & Gupta, V. (2004). *Culture, leadership and organizations: The GLOBE study of 62 societies.* Thousand Oaks, CA: Sage.

Hoyt, C. L. (2013). Women and leadership. In P. G. Northouse (Ed.), *Leadership theory and practice* (pp. 349–382). Thousand Oaks, CA: Sage.

Ibarra, H., Carter, N. M., & Silva, C. (2010). Why men still get more promotions than women. *Harvard Business Review, 88*(9), 80–126.

Ibarra, H., & Obadaru, O. (2009, January). Women and the vision thing. *Harvard Business Review, 87*(1), 62–70.

Johnson, C. E. (2009). *Meeting the ethical challenges of leadership.* Thousand Oaks, CA: Sage.

Jokinen, T. (2005). Global leadership competencies: A review and discussion. *Journal of European Industrial Training, 29*(3), 199–216.

Judge, T. A., Colbert, A. E., & Ilies, R. (2004). Intelligence and leadership: A quantitative review and test of theoretical propositions. *Journal of Applied Psychology, 89*(3), 542–552.

Kerr, R., Garvin, J., Heaton, N., & Boyle, E. (2006). Emotional intelligence and leadership effectiveness. *Leadership & Organizational Development, 27*(4), 265–279.

Koenig, A. M., Mitchell, A. A., Eagly, A. H., & Ristikari, T. (2011). Are leader stereotypes masculine? A meta-analysis of three research paradigms. *Psychological Bulletin, 137*(4), 616–642.

Lam, C. S., & Higgins, E. R. (2012). Enhancing employee outcomes: The interrelated influences of managers' emotional intelligence and leadership style. *Leadership & Organizational Development Journal, 33*(2), 149–174.

Livermore, D. (2010). *Leading with cultural intelligence.* New York, NY: AMACOM.

Luthans, F., Norman, S., & Hughes, L. (2006). Authentic leadership. In R. J. Burke & C. L. Cooper (Eds.), *Inspiring leaders* (pp. 84–104). New York, NY: Routledge.

Mandell, B., & Pherwani, S. (2003). Relationship between emotional intelligence and transformational leadership style: A gender comparison. *Journal of Business and Psychology, 17*(3), 387–404.

McCallum, S., & O'Connell, D. (2009). Social capital and leadership development. *Leadership & Organizational Development Journal, 30*(2), 152–166.

Mendenhall, M. E. (2011, December). Three necessary questions for global leadership development in India. *Vikalpa, 36*(4), 17–23.

Moon, T. (2010). Emotional intelligence correlates of the four-factor model of cultural intelligence. *Journal of Managerial Psychology, 25*(8), 876–898.

Moustakas, C. (1994). *Phenomenological research methods.* Thousand Oaks, CA: Sage.

Ng, K., Van Dyne, L., & Ang, S. (2009). From experiential learning: Cultural intelligence as a learning capability for global leader development. *Academy of Management Learning & Education, 8*(4), 511–526.

O'Neil, D. A., Hopkins, M. M., & Sullivan, S. E. (2011). Do women's networks help advance women's careers? *Career Development International, 16*(7), 733–743.

Osland, J. S. (2008). An overview of the global leadership literature. In M. E. Mendenhall, J. S. Osland, A. Bird, G. R. Oddou, & M. L. Maznevski (Eds.), *Global leadership* (pp. 34–63). New York, NY: Routledge.

Reilly, A. H., & Karounos, T. J. (2009, February). Exploring the link between emotional intelligence and cross-cultural leadership effectiveness. *Journal of International Business and Cultural Studies, 1*, 1–13.

Reuben, E., Rey-Biel, P., Sapienza, P., & Zingales, L. (2012). The emergence of male leadership in competitive environments. *Journal of Economic Behavior & Organization, 83*(1), 111–117.

Riggio, R. E. (2002). Multiple intelligences and leadership: An overview. In R. E. Riggio, S. E. Murphy, & F. J. Pirozzolo (Eds.), *Multiple intelligences and leadership* (pp. 1–6). Mahwah, NJ: Erlbaum.

Riggio, R. E., & Reichard, R. J. (2008). The emotional and social intelligences of effective leadership: An emotional and social skill approach. *Journal of Managerial Psychology, 23*(2), 169–185.

Rivers, S. E., Brackett, M. A., Salovey, P., & Mayer, J. D. (2007). Measuring emotional intelligence as a set of mental abilities. In G. Matthews, M. Zeidner, & R. D. Roberts (Eds.), *The science of emotional intelligence: Knowns and unknowns* (pp. 230–257). New York, NY: Oxford University Press.

Rockstuhl, T., Seiler, S., Ang, S., Van Dyne, L., & Annen, H. (2011). Beyond general intelligence (IQ) and emotional intelligence (EQ): The role of cultural intelligence (CQ) on cross-border leadership effectiveness in a globalized world. *Journal of Social Issues, 67*(4), 825–840.

Rood-Breithaupt, J. (2013). *Multiple intelligences for effective global leadership: Women as authentic leaders* (Unpublished doctoral dissertation). Eastern University, St. Davids, PA.

Rosete, D., & Ciarrochi, J. (2005). Emotional intelligence and its relationship to workplace performance of effective leadership. *Leadership & Organization Development Journal, 26*(5), 388–399.

Salovey, P., & Mayer, J. D. (1990). Emotional intelligence. *Imagination, Cognition, and Personality, 9*(4), 45–56.

Salovey, P., & Mayer, J. D. (1997). What is emotional intelligence? In P. Salovey & D. Sluyter (Eds.), *Emotional development and emotional intelligence: Implications for educators* (pp. 3–13). New York, NY: Basic.

Schein, V. E. (2007). Women in management: Reflections and projections. *Women in Management Review, 22*(1), 6–18.

Showkeir, J., & Showkeir, M. (2008). *Authentic conversations.* San Francisco, CA: Berret-Koehler.

Sternberg, R. J. (1996). *Successful intelligence.* New York, NY: Simon & Schuster.

Templer, K. J., Tay, C., & Chandrasekar, N. (2006). Motivational cultural intelligence, realistic job previews, and realistic living conditions, and cross-cultural adjustment. *Group and Organization Management, 31*(1), 154–173.

Thorndike, E. L. (1920). Intelligence and its uses. *Harper's Magazine, 140,* 227–235.

Thomas, D. C., Elron, E., Stahl, G., Ekelund, B. Z., Ravlin, E. C., Cerdin, J. L., ... Lazarova, M. B. (2008). Cultural intelligence: Domain and assessment. *International Journal of Cross Cultural Management, 8*(2), 123–143.

Triandis, H. C. (2006). Cultural intelligence in organizations. *Group & Organization Management, 31*(1), 20–26.

Zaccaro, S. J. (2002). Organizational leadership and social intelligence. In R. E. Riggio, S. E. Murphy, & F. J. Pirozzolo (Eds.), *Multiple intelligences and leadership* (pp. 29–54). Mahwah, NJ: Erlbaum.

CHAPTER 5

WOMEN LEADING THROUGH THE LENS OF CULTURAL INTELLIGENCE

Joanne Barnes

The 21st century welcomed many changes and challenges in the workplace and within the field of leadership. Women working in for-profit and not for profit organizations are now being promoted to top leadership positions. The U.S. Bureau of Labor Statistics (2013a) reported that over 51% of women now make up management and professional positions within organizations. Furthermore, women are now being considered for expatriate positions more than in the past 20 years. Yet with this increase, there is still not enough understanding of how women expatriates demonstrate and lead with cultural intelligence.

This research builds on the existing empirical studies that have focused primarily on leadership skills and styles of women and how these relate to a woman's ability to be successful in a global environment. The purpose of this study goes beyond the examination of leadership styles by focusing on how cultural intelligence catalyzes women to be successful in an ever-changing, diverse landscape.

Even though women have continually moved through the ranks of the organization and taken on more leadership roles, challenges continue to exist. Organizations are more diverse and the leaders are interacting with many cultures. The ability to lead across diverse cultures will not only require appropriate leadership styles, cultural knowledge, and cultural savvy, but also cultural intelligence (CQ).

Global leadership no longer refers only to leadership across borders; it includes leadership in a multicultural environment. Adler (2002) opined that organizations no longer examine global leadership from a male-only context, and current global leaders must recognize the existing talent within their organization regardless of gender. Organizations doing business in a global context with a multiculturally diverse workforce, supplier base, and customer base more often select their leaders (both men and women) based on their qualifications, not their gender (Adler, 2002; Cole & McNulty, 2011).

More importantly, organizations must recognize there is a difference between global and domestic leadership. Both men and women will require different skills to be effective in a global/multicultural environment than those used in a domestic, homogeneous environment. To date, the majority of research on women working in global leadership has been comparative in nature and examines leadership differences and styles between men and women (Eagly, Johannesen-Schmidt, & van Engen, 2003; Eagly & Chin, 2010; Eagly & Johnson, 1990). Eagly and Chin (2010) suggested that women leaders "are expected to take charge and approach leadership in the same ways as their male colleagues" (p. 218). Yet these same women leaders are also expected to display characteristics and traits normally associated with women, such as empathetic, warm, and friendly (Eagly & Chin, 2010). The question remains: Are these gendered characteristics effective across cultures? Are global leadership competencies nongendered, and what are the cultural competencies needed for women to be successful in a multicultural world?

GLOBAL LEADERSHIP

There are multiple definitions of culture; for the purpose of this research, the definition developed by Kroeber and Kluckhohn (1952), stating that culture is the collective beliefs, values, behaviors, customs, and attitudes that uniquely identify members of one society from another will be used. To be effective working across cultures, women in global and multicultural leadership roles must be able to define culture in order to understand its importance as a foundational competency.

Cultural competencies are the skills needed to be successful when working with an ethnic and diverse workforce. Researchers throughout the years have focused on cultural dimensions. Kluckhohn and Strodtbeck (1961) developed a model of cultural dimensions which included (a) relationship with nature, (b) relationship with people, (c) human activities, (d) relationship with time, and (e) human nature. Other researchers (Hall & Hall, 1990; Hofstede, 1980; Trompenaars, 1993) used the Kluckhohn and Strodtbeck model and further defined cultural dimensions to include items such as power distance, masculinity-femininity, time, space, individualism-collectivism, and universalism-particularism (Nardon & Steers, 2011). These dimensions focused on specific behaviors that were generalized across different cultures; however, they did not provide global competencies for the leader. Most cultural dimensions can be referred to as tenents of cultural knowledge, necessary for the global leader but not a part of their development.

Global Leadership and Cultural Competencies

Jokinen (2005) conducted a literature review of several global leadership competencies that did not include gender-specific competencies, but resulted in a categorization of desired skills. These fundamentals are self-awareness, engagement in personal transformation, and inquisitiveness. Self-awareness can be defined as having an understanding of one's own assumptions and values. Engagement in personal transformation can be related to having an entrepreneurial attitude connected to self-development and growth, and finally, inquisitiveness can be referred to as the willingness to step out of one's comfort zone and learn about things that are unfamiliar to them. Jokinen (2005) categorized the global leadership skills into three broad categories: (a) behavioral, (b) mental, and (c) fundamental core. Behavioral skills are social, network management, and knowledge; mental skills include optimism, self-regulation, social judgment, and acceptance of complexity and its contradictions; while the fundamental core includes "self-awareness, engagement in personal transformation, and inquisitiveness" (Jokinen, 2005, p. 204).

Mendenhall and Osland (2002) and Osland (2013) inferred that global leadership competencies can be categorized into "core characteristics, context-specific abilities, and universal leadership skills" (Osland, 2013, p. 65). To further examine these competencies, Mendenhall and Osland (2002) suggested there are six dimensions of global leadership with related attendant competencies (see Figure 5.1). Bird (2013) further narrowed these competencies to include (a) business and organizational acumen, (b) managing people and relationships, and (c) managing self.

Global Leadership Dimensions

with attendant competencies

Relationship Skills
Close Personal Relationships
CC Communication Skills
"Emotionally Connect" Ability
Inspire, Motivate Others
Conflict Management
Negotiation Expertise
Empowering Others
Managing CC Ethical Issues

Organizing Expertise
Team Building
Community Building
Organizational Networking
Creating Learning Systems
Strong Operational Codes
Global Networking
Strong Customer Orientation

Traits
Curiosity/Inquisitiveness
Continual Learner
Learning Orientation
Accountability
Integrity/Courage
Commitment
Hardiness
Maturity
Results/Orientation

Cognitive
Environmental Sensemaking
Global Mindset
Thinking Agility
Improvisation
Pattern Recognition
Cognitive Complexity
Cosmopolitanism
Managing Uncertainty
Local vs. Global Paradoxes

Business Expertise
Global Business Savvy
Global Organizational Savvy
Business Acumen
Total Organizational Astuteness
Stakeholder Orientation
Results-Orientation

Vision
Articulating a tangible vision and strategy
Envisioning
Entrepreneurial Spirit
Catalyst for Cultural Change
Change Agentry
Catalyst for Strategic Change
Empowering, Inspiring

Source: Osland, J. (2013). Used with permission.

Figure 5.1. Mendenhall and Osland's literature review results: The six dimensions of global leadership and their competencies.

With the overwhelming amount of literature related to global leadership competencies and skills, the degree that intelligence, specifically cultural intelligence, influences one's success in cross-cultural, global, intercultural, and multicultural environments is an important element. To date, there have been few studies that have examined global/multicultural leadership competencies and the relationship to cultural intelligence; there are even fewer studies that have examined this phenomenon as it relates to women leaders in global/multicultural context. In order to comprehend the importance of cultural intelligence for women in leadership, it is imperative that a definition that fits the context of CQ be examined: "Cultural intelligence refers to a person's capability to adapt effectively to new cultural contexts" (Earley & Ang, 2003, p. 59).

CULTURAL INTELLIGENCE

The various types of intelligences provide an individual with a coping mechanism to try and adapt to continuous changing circumstances. Earley and Ang (2003) suggested that the most common view of intelligence examines attributes at the biological, mental, motivational, or behavioral level. Ng and Earley (2006) included cultural and contextual factors as influencers of intelligence within distinct environments. Building on the research of Earley and Ang, Ang and Van Dyne (2008) stated that CQ was built on Sternberg's framework of intelligence, therefore resulting in four factors of cultural intelligence: (a) cognitive reflects general knowledge and knowledge structures about cultural difference, (b) metacognitive reflects the mental capability to acquire and evaluate cultural knowledge, (c) motivational reflects the mental capacity to direct and sustain energy toward function and performing in intercultural situations, and (d) behavioral reflects the capability to flex behaviors to fit different cultural contexts (Ang & Van Dyne, 2008). According to Van Dyne, Ang, and Nielsen (2007), CQ is essential to an individual's "personal, interpersonal, and work-related implications given the wide-ranging effects of globalization and diversity throughout most of the world" (p. 345). The nomological network of CQ proposed by Ang and Van Dyne (2008) further supports the importance of CQ and its relationship to individual effectiveness. Ang and Van Dyne described the nomological network as consisting of four major relationships: distal factors, intermediate/intervening constructs, other correlates, and individual and interpersonal outcomes. These constructs are foundational in cultural intelligence. The four factors of cultural intelligence are discussed in some detail in the following sections.

Cognitive CQ

Cognitive CQ assists an individual in understanding the values, norms, and behaviors that are carried out in different cultural environments. Cognitive CQ is an important component for "decision-making in culturally-diverse settings" (Van Dyne et al., 2012, p. 300). The cognitive dimensions of CQ are the subdimensions of cultural-general knowledge and context-specific knowledge. Cultural-general knowledge is defined as "the universal elements that constitute a cultural environment" (Van Dyne et al., 2012, p. 301) and reflects how an individual understands the differences and similarities of various cultures. Context-specific knowledge is defined as "declarative knowledge about manifestations of cultural universals in a specific domain and procedural knowledge of how to be effective in that domain" (Van Dyne et al., 2012, p. 302). This type of knowledge is also referred to as an insider's understanding of a specific culture, and the individual often gains this knowledge through experiences with other cultures.

Metacognitive CQ

As discussed earlier, cognitive CQ deals with one's understanding of cultural differences: metacognitive CQ is our conscious cultural awareness and executive processing during cross-cultural interactions (Ang & Van

Dyne, 2008). The three subdimensions of metacognitive CQ are planning, awareness, and checking. Planning is an individual's ability to determine strategies prior to entering a culturally diverse situation. It requires having a descriptive plan prior to the engagement and considering the unexpected and how to react to it. Awareness is defined "as knowing about cultural thinking and knowledge of self and others in real time" (Van Dyne et al., 2012, p. 299). The subdimension of awareness is the ability to understand our own cultural beliefs, behaviors, norms, and values (self) and those of others in a specific cultural context. The final subdimension of metacognitive CQ is checking. Checking is the process in which an individual examines their own assumptions and beliefs of other cultures and how they differ from one's actual experiences within the culture.

Motivational CQ

Motivational CQ, also referred to as CQ Drive, is our ability to confidently adapt to and show interest in multicultural environments. Motivational CQ is composed of the subdimensions of intrinsic and extrinsic motivation and self-efficacy. In a cross-cultural or multicultural context, intrinsic motivation is our ability to find value in the experience; whereas, extrinsic motivation comes from our ability to find value from "tangible, personal benefits" (Van Dyne et al., 2012, p. 304), such as expatriate assignments, leading multicultural teams, incentives, and rewards. One's self-efficacy is the ability to have self-confidence during collaborations with multicultural groups and in culturally diverse settings.

Behavioral CQ

The final dimension is behavioral CQ. This dimension is our ability to act appropriately in multicultural settings. It defines our ability to change or moderate our behavior to lessen the misunderstandings that may occur when interacting with different cultures. The subdimensions include verbal and nonverbal behaviors and speech acts. Verbal behaviors are our ability to use accent and tone during our communication with other cultures. Nonverbal behaviors include our facial expressions, body gestures, and paralinguistic. Finally, speech acts is defined "as flexibility in manner of communicating specific types of messages such that requests, invitations, apologies, gratitude, disagreement, and saying 'no' are expressed appropriately" (Van Dyne et al., 2012, p. 305).

These competencies and their subdimensions are essential for women leading in a multicultural environment as their span of control continues to grow to include a more diverse workforce and expatriate assignments. This means that women leaders who have the skills not only understand cross-cultural and intercultural differences, but interact successfully in diverse cultural settings.

THE IMPORTANCE OF CULTURAL INTELLIGENCE FOR WOMEN LEADERS

The landscape of organizations is continually changing. Totally domestic-focused businesses have gone by the wayside as competition has demanded organizations to become more global. Even without the competition, the changing demographics of the workforce are requiring leaders to understand the complexities and nuances of various cultures. The Bureau of Labor Statistics (BLS) October 2013 report stated,

> In 2012, employed Asian and White women were more likely than other women to work in management, professional, and related occupations—47 percent of Asian women and 43 percent of White women. By contrast, 34 percent of employed Black women and 26 percent of employed Hispanic women worked in this occupational group. (BLS, 2013b, pp. 3–4)

These figures represent just a sample of the changes of the face of the domestic workforce as it relates to women in leadership and management positions. However, the composition of the overall workforce is also changing. The Bureau of Labor Statistics (2013a) projected that by the year 2020, the workforce will continue to become more diversified. Adler (2002) proffered that as organizations no longer impose boundaries for women as global leaders, they are also recognizing the importance of selecting individuals who possess the necessary skills to be effective and successful. Even though men and women may be perceived to lead differently, a high level of cultural intelligence can give the leader the additional tools to be successful. Adler further suggested this success is based on the leader's ability to "adopt the thinking and behavioral patterns of the dominant culture" (p. 753).

RESEARCH METHODS

The intent of this research was to address whether women who had a high level of cultural intelligence were perceived to be more successful in global and multicultural contexts than those who had a low level of cultural competence. The researcher hypothesized that "$H1_A$: Women leaders who possess a high level of cultural intelligence (CQ), as measured by the

E-CQS, will be perceived to be more successful than women who possess a low level of CQ in a global or multicultural context."

To test the hypothesis, a mixed method study was employed. The Enhanced Cultural Intelligence Scale (E-CQS) was used for quantitative data collection (see Table 5.1) and two questionnaires were utilized for the qualitative interviews; one for the leaders and one for the followers. Women leaders who were either in a global leadership position or led a multicultural team were asked to complete the E-CQS; based on their results, four women who completed the E-CQS and scored moderate to high in all domains of CQ with an aggregate score of moderate to high in overall CQ, and two leaders who had scored low in all domains of CQ were randomly selected for interviews using the leadership questionnaire. To ensure another perspective was included, each leader was asked to provide the email addresses for six of their direct reports. The leaders had to have a minimum of 10 direct reports to participate in the study. Three direct reports were contacted to complete the questionnaire on their leader.

Table 5.1. Sample Item Questions of the Expanded Cultural Intelligence Scale (the E-CQS)

Subdimension	Example Item
Metacognitive CQ	
Planning	I develop action plans before interacting with people from a different culture.
Awareness	I am aware of how my culture influences my interactions with people from different cultures.
Checking	I adjust my understanding of a culture while I interact with people from that culture.
Cognitive CQ	
Culture-General Knowledge	I can describe the different cultural value frameworks that explain behaviors around the world.
Culture-Specific Knowledge	I can describe the ways that leadership style differ across cultural settings.
Motivational CQ	
Intrinsic interest	I truly enjoy interacting with people from different cultures.

(Table continues on next page)

Table 5.1. (Continued)

Subdimension	Example Item
Extrinsic interest	I value the status I would gain from living or working in a different culture.
Self-efficacy to adjust	I am confident that I can persist in coping with living conditions in different cultures.
Behavioral CQ	
Verbal behavior	I change my use of pause and silence to suit different cultural situations.
Nonverbal behavior	I modify how close or far apart I stand when interacting with people from different cultures.
Speech acts	I modify the way I disagree with others to fit the culture setting.

© Cultural Intelligence Center, 2011. Adapted and used by permission of the Cultural Intelligence Center.
Note: Use of these items is granted to academic researchers for research purposes only.[1]

There were 15 women who completed the E-CQS, and of those that were completed, 11 were usable. All six of the leaders selected for the qualitative questionnaires returned completed questionnaires (four leaders with moderate to high CQ and two leaders with low CQ). Examples of the leader questions were

1. Please explain your most challenging aspect of leading a global and/or multicultural team.
2. What is your least challenging aspect of leading a global and/or multicultural team?
3. What is your understanding of being a culturally or globally competent leader?
4. List any training programs you have been involved in which have had the focus of developing cultural or global competency and/or skills.
5. Of the programs listed, which one was the most and least beneficial?
6. How do you believe your direct reports see you as a leader? Select one response and explain your selection:

    a. Possesses intercultural competence
    b. Possesses cultural intelligence
    c. Accepts cultural differences

d. Embraces cultural differences
   e. Treats everyone the same

Of the 12 questionnaires sent to the direct reports of leaders with high CQ, 10 were complete and usable; six direct reports of leaders (three for each leader) with low CQ were complete and usable. Examples of the direct report questions were

1. How does your leader show inclusiveness in an ethnically diverse group?
2. In what ways, if any, does your leader show an interest and understanding of other cultures?
3. Based on your interaction with your leader, to what degree do you feel she is culturally competent?
4. How has your leader demonstrated adaptability to proactively plan and guide multicultural team meetings? Explain.
5. List your leader's strongest skills that you have observed demonstrated in a multicultural situation.
6. Explain any weaknesses, if any, that your leader has displayed in a multicultural situation

Basic demographic information was collected for each participant in the study (leader and direct report). Most leader respondents were between the age of 35 and 44, had been in a leadership position for at least 5 years, lived in at least three countries (this was determined as a long-term stay of one year or more), visited one to three countries, and spoke at least two languages (including their native language). The majority of direct reports who participated in the study were between the ages of 35 and 44, had been employed with their current organization for at least 5 years, and had been with their current leader for at least 5 years. The majority were bilingual.

RESULTS AND DISCUSSION

To best determine how cultural intelligence assisted in the development of four women leaders, a qualitative questionnaire was used to gauge what influences in their career were different from the two women leaders who scored low in CQ. The themes discussed below demonstrate the differences in the two groups of women, as well as the areas of convergence.

Women Leaders Self-Perceptions

The discussion of themes includes all six leaders who completed the quantitative and qualitative portion of the study. Leaders with moderate to high cultural intelligence are identified as Leader A, B, C, or D. Leaders with low cultural intelligence are identified as Leader E or F.

Interestingly, the primary theme that emerged for all women irrespective of their CQ score in response to the first question (please explain your most challenging aspect of leading a global and/or multicultural team?) was the lack of support within their current organization to provide solutions related to gender leadership stereotype. Leader A, with high cultural intelligence stated,

> My team is made up of men and women from a total of three different countries. Unfortunately, two of the men are from a country and culture that does not view women as leaders. At first I tried to ignore the comments and sometimes insubordination, but I found that the overall morale of the team went down. Then I stood up to them, and that was not successfully. Finally, I went to my leadership and asked for advice ... the response was comical, I was told to toughen up and make the men follow instructions. One of my leaders said, "Man up and just handle it." I often wonder why our employees are not trained on cultural understanding and respect for the existing hierarchy, be it male or female.

Leader F, who had low CQ, stated,

> My challenge is leading in a male-dominated organization where no one respects my decisions or authority. I was promoted to this position because of my experience in the organization and working successfully in global sales. Now I struggle to understand my value to the organization because of the lack of respect and support I get. I have one employee from Eastern Europe who will continually ask my supervisor what he should do after I have given him an assignment. Disturbingly, my supervisor will change my assignment to keep the employee happy.

Other themes that emerged in order of occurrence were (a) lack of recognition of their skills and knowledge, (b) viewed as too empathetic, and (c) no confidant available to discuss concerns with. Although these challenges existed for women with both high and low cultural intelligence, women with high cultural intelligence were more likely to overcome the obstacle. For example, Leader A further stated that even though she will often face opposition, she uses her knowledge of the organization and the job to give assignments. Men who do not believe she should be in a leadership position will complete tasks because they are assigned and supported with information.

Challenging Aspects of Leading Across Cultures

The next question revealed some significance in responses: What is your least challenging aspect of leading a global and/or multicultural team? Leaders A through D felt that their experience in or with cultures was helpful. Leader C suggested she was good at building relationships and because of this, the team, regardless of cultural make-up, worked well under her leadership. Leader C has lived in three different countries as an expatriate and now leads a virtual global team where members live in South America, while she is based in the United States. A common theme from Leaders E and F was that, the majority of the time, the team was cohesive and problems were resolved internally.

The responses from those with moderate to high CQ aligns with earlier studies. Amiri, Moghimi, and Kazemi (2010) found that metacognitive CQ did have an effect on employees' performance and behavior. Individuals with high metacognitive CQ are more apt to determine how to interact with other cultures based on their knowledge and understanding of the culture. Furthermore, Amiri et al. opined individuals with high cognitive CQ are more apt to clearly communicate job requirements and expectations.

Leaders who have a cohesive team environment are often strong in relational skills and conflict management. Engle, Elahee, and Tatoglu (2013) hypothesized that individuals with higher metacognitive CQ are more effective at problem solving in cross-cultural or multicultural environments. The direct reports of leaders with high CQ (moderate to high metacognitive CQ) indicated that their leaders were effective at conflict management and problem resolution. This aligns with the earlier studies conducted by Huang (2010) and Van Dyne, Ang, and Koh (2008). Van Dyne et al. further viewed metacognition as being critical to cultural intelligence as it focuses on one's consciousness of other cultures and how to interact with those cultures.

Literature has suggested that women in leadership face many challenges, and women who are leading in a global environment face even more challenges. Caligiuri and Lazarova (2002) argued that challenges faced by women as global leaders are different than those faced by men in the same capacity. They suggested that women have both work and nonwork challenges. However, the greatest challenge is the ability to adapt to the "cultural norms towards working women" (p. 762) from the host country. Eagly and Chin (2010) agreed, positing that women face the challenge where many cultures view leadership as a masculine trait. As a result of the challenges, cross-cultural adaptation and leadership in a multicultural environment may be more difficult if the women leader does not have a moderate to high level of cultural intelligence.

Understanding Cultural and Global Competence

The next question was critical in determining how these women (moderate to high CQ and low CQ) understood what it meant to be a culturally or globally competent leader. Table 5.2 provides a list of the most frequent responses for both groups of leaders. There were two common responses, communication and training. However, training was not ranked as high for Leaders A through D as it was for Leaders E and F (see Table 5.2).

Table 5.2. Global and Culturally Competent Leadership Traits Based on Level of Cultural Intelligence (CQ)

Leaders With Moderate to High CQ	*Leaders With Low CQ*
Being flexible during intercultural interactions	Behaving the same during intercultural interactions
Having appropriate communication styles	Communicating with all individuals the same regardless of culture
Seeking to actively learn about cultures they are working with	Displaying no interest in learning about other cultures
Accepting expatriate assignments to develop as a global leader	Lacking in expatriate assignments and experience
Visiting other countries for at least 3 months	Limiting visits or the time spent living outside of their native country for less than 3 months.
Learning at least one other language other than their native language	Failing to learn an additional language or languages. Only spoke their native language
Receiving mentor(s) from another country	Mentoring from individuals from other countries was not available
Completing global and/or intercultural training	Training for global and intercultural competence not part of their leadership development plan

As for the question related to training programs, the responses may account for the differences in rating the importance of training for those with moderate to high CQ and those with low CQ. Leader B discussed that her organization conducts mandatory training for each leader who has global responsibilities. There are four trainings they must attend, one per quarter; however, the information does not seem to change. Leaders B stated, "If the training was geared more to developing a global mindset, then it could be beneficial. Right now, we just attend and walk away with little to no new knowledge." Leader E stated,

> My organization does not have a formal training program for global leaders. When I was promoted to my current position, I went to a two-week course on leadership and company policies and goals. It did not prepare me to lead my current workgroup. My group sits in the same area, but we are so diverse. Since our group is made up of members who come from Europe, Asia and the US, we often find we can't communicate with one another. Don't get me

wrong, it's not the language, it's the way we communicate direct, indirect, and the hidden messages in our conversations. I wish I had some training on what it is like to work with other cultures and how to communicate effectively between cultures. This may not mean a lot to some, but I think it would really help me and my team.

Whereas Leader B's organization offered training that did not help with the global context, Leader E did not get any training at all. Both recognize the need for global leadership/cultural competence relevant training.

Rehg, Gundlach, and Grigorian (2012) posited, "Training in CQ becomes a strategic human resource management function leading to successful cross-cultural business interactions" (p. 217). They further hypothesized that individuals who have received cultural intelligence training will have a higher level of cognitive CQ than they did prior to the training. In this research, the participants who had training had a higher level of cognitive CQ than those who did not. These participant's scores in the subdimension of cultural-general knowledge could be attributed to the training they received.

Communication was important to both groups. Those with moderate to high CQ were confident in the way they related to their direct reports with verbal and nonverbal communication. Both Leaders A and B stated they had learned how to pay attention to the nonverbal cues with working in other cultures. By picking up on what was not being said, they have been able to change the way they communicate to fit the individual and the context. Leaders E and F rated communication skill as number one on the list of global or cultural competencies. Leader E stated, "If you can't talk with your employees, you might as well work alone." Additionally, those leaders with moderate to high cultural intelligence inferred they had little to no difficulty communicating with cultures different from their own. These results are supported by an earlier study in which Brislin, Worthley, and Macnab (2006) found that individuals who are culturally intelligent would be more selective in the communication to others. Because of the selectivity, often negative, implicit messages are not sent during the communication process.

Leaders Views of Followers' Evaluation of Their Cultural Competency

The leaders were asked what they believed their followers thought about their leadership in a multicultural context. None of the leaders believed their direct reports thought they were interculturally competent or had cultural intelligence. Leader B and D selected "accepts cultural differences." Leader B explained that it was a conscious choice to work on not being judgmental. "I know people are different, even if we are all from Michigan, so accepting the differences of people from other cultures is just something I do." Leader D explained her acceptance of cultures as something she grew up doing. She described her situation as follows:

> My family lived in Germany when I was in my teens; many of my friends were German, and as a teenager I did not focus on the differences. Now as an adult, I look at people for who they are and not how different they are from me.

Leader A selected "embraces cultural differences," and provided insight to a celebration she initiated in her group during her first 6 months as the leader.

> When I first moved to my new area, no one seemed to talk to each other outside of the normal day-to-day meetings or explanations of work. At lunch everyone went their own way; there were a few groups of people, but for the most part, it was every man for himself. At one of my monthly meetings I told the group that effective immediately we would be hosting a group lunch twice a month. After the moans, I explained we were going to celebrate our different cultures with food and music and one person from our team would be given a budget to host the lunch. This was met with caution and some support. The first lunch celebrated France … we learned a few French words, had some amazing food and good conversation. This continued until every culture was represented. Now we celebrate a lunch every other month, but I hope my employees know I appreciate what they bring to our group besides their knowledge of our business processes.

Leader C chose "treats everyone the same." She further explained,

> I believe my employees recognize that I am here to get a job done. It doesn't matter where they come from, I am here to lead us to success, I don't have time to look past their work and examine where they are from.

Even though the leaders with moderate to high CQ selected various responses, their replies align with individuals who are culturally intelligent. Each respondent demonstrated behaviors and characteristics of high CQ. Ang, Van Dyne, and Tan (2011) found that individuals with high metacognitive CQ are aware of how they interact with other cultures and what communication methods they use. The leaders in this research demonstrated mindfulness, which is a characteristic of individuals with high metacognitive CQ. The participants in this research who scored moderate to high in cognitive CQ demonstrated characteristics such as being able to understand the differences and similarities of those who work for them or interact with. Ang et al. opined that high cognitive CQ can assist individuals in understanding "the systems that shape and cause patterns of social interaction within a culture" (p. 590). In the area of motivational CQ, Leader A was successful in demonstrating attributes of an individual who was high in motivational CQ. Ang et al. defined motivational CQ as "the capability to direct attention and energy toward learning about and functioning in culturally diverse situations" (p. 590). They further discussed the criticality of this dimension to cultural intelligence and suggested an individual with high motivational CQ will be moved to determine how to best function in different cultural settings.

The final dimension of cultural intelligence is behavioral CQ. Behavioral CQ examines one's ability to be flexible in her verbal, nonverbal, and speech acts (Ang et al., 2011). Themes that emerged from the qualitative interviews included changing or choosing words to be more appropriate for the cultural situation, changing the inflection and tone of voice, and checking nonverbal behaviors for accuracy within the cultural context. Van Dyne et al. (2012) discussed the importance of one having a high behavioral CQ, as demonstrated by the participants in this research. A high behavioral CQ is expressed when individuals can "overcome the natural human tendency to rely on habits … they show their behavioral flexibility in intercultural settings" (p. 306).

The two leaders with low CQ also responded to the same questions. Both leaders believe their direct reports would view them as leaders who treat everyone the same. Leader E simply declared, "I work towards being fair and just. I have not had a complaint from anyone that works for me about unfair treatment. I just follow HR [human resource] guidelines." Leader F did not elaborate on her response. She only added, "It's a struggle to treat everyone the same when I do not always understand why they do or say certain things." Unlike the leaders with moderate to high CQ, Leaders E and F did not recognize the importance of changing their behaviors when interacting with individuals who were culturally different. Typically, individuals with low CQ have a tendency to accept stereotypes of other cultures. When treating everyone the same, leaders with low CQ did not adapt to the different cultures and were not flexible.

Direct Reports Perceptions of Leaders Cultural Competency

Direct reports of leaders with moderate to high CQ found their leaders to be inclusive in various parts of the decision-making process and to recognize each member of the team for their unique contributions. The direct reports further categorized their leaders as inquisitive and interested in cultures beyond their own. This type of behavior not only demonstrates high CQ, but also shows the leader to be more ethnorelative than ethnocentric (Hammer, Bennett, & Wiseman, 2003).

In the area of cultural competence and cultural intelligence, direct reports found their leaders with high CQ to be accepting of differences and related that acceptance to cultural competence. They further implied the leaders had a degree of culture-general knowledge, but could improve their context-specific knowledge. These areas of knowledge are related to cognitive CQ. Even though the leaders scored moderate to high in metacognitive CQ, direct reports did not view the leaders as being good at planning, a subdimension of metacognitive CQ. However, direct reports for each leader did acknowledge their ability for awareness and checking when dealing with other cultures.

Leaders Strengths and Weaknesses

Direct reports were asked to identify strengths and weaknesses of their leaders. Leaders with moderate to high CQ were found to have strengths in the areas of (a) listening, (b) relationships, (c) communication and consultation, and (d) understanding. Their weaknesses were (a) lack of ability to fully understand the team's point of view, and (b) generalizing across cultures. The responses regarding weaknesses were interesting as they did not align with the general strengths of the leaders. Because leaders in the group could have been toward the low end of moderate, this would account for the responses of some direct reports.

Direct reports for the leaders with low CQ found their leaders to have little to no interest in the group or what they could offer to the team. Many believed they were not part of a team and worked in silos more than as a group. This was attributed to the leader's lack of bringing the group together and being inclusive. Motivational CQ includes the subdimensions of intrinsic motivation, extrinsic motivation, and self-efficacy to adjust (Van Dyne et al., 2012). Leaders who scored low in CQ were viewed by their direct reports has having little to no interest in what their countries were like and a lack of sensitivity as it relates to norms and behaviors of other cultures, to the extent that accents were often mocked. Individuals with low motivational CQ may often not be interested or driven to either learn about other cultures or are less likely to interact with other cultures, which can result in ethnocentric attitudes and behaviors (Hammer et al., 2003; Van Dyne et al., 2012). These leaders were also viewed as having no or little empathy toward different cultures and lacked listening skills.

Direct reports were asked to identify the strengths and weaknesses of their leaders with low CQ, and no strengths came forth. Direct reports viewed these leaders as ethnocentric and having only one worldview without recognizing there are other worldviews and cultures. The weaknesses mentioned included that the leaders did not appreciate the diversity of the group and the diverse view each member brought to the team. Further, the leaders did not display listening skills, which affected the direct reports ability to function effectively in teams and within the organization. Cseh (2003) argued that listening is one of many skills needed by leaders to assist in developing team cohesiveness in a multicultural environment.

Leaders CQ Levels and Perceptions

There is a distinct difference in how direct reports of leaders with moderate to high CQ and low CQ perceive the cultural competence and intelligence of their leaders. Leaders who scored moderate to high in cultural intelligence were more engaged with their direct reports and recognized the cultural differences each member brought to the team. The direct reports of leaders with moderate to high cultural intelligence had a strong relationship with their leaders and felt communication impacted the success of the team. Janssens and Cappellen (2008) found global managers with a high degree of CQ were more flexible, used a variety of communication tools, and were able to use their nonverbal behavior to support their verbal behavior when communicating with different cultures. The high level of engagement of leaders with high CQ in this study was supported by the views of their direct report. The leaders also used a variety of verbal and nonverbal behaviors to ensure messages where understood in the appropriate cultural context. The assumption could be made that the leaders who had a high level of CQ in this study developed their cultural intelligence through experiences with other cultures, as well as having received cultural awareness and language training. Janssens and Cappellen (2008) reported that "cross-cultural interactions—interacting simultaneously with foreign colleagues across multiple cultures on an equal basis—extends the behavioral, motivational, and metacognitive dimensions of CQ" (p. 368). The four leaders who participated in the qualitative portion of the study scored high in motivational CQ and the subdimensions of extrinsic and intrinsic motivation. They were also high in metacognitive CQ. In the subdimensions of planning and awareness, they scored high, and in the subdimension of checking, they scored moderate. All four scored high in behavioral CQ, and three scored high and one scored moderate in cognitive CQ. In comparison, the two leaders who scored low in overall CQ also scored low in all four domains and low or moderate in the subdimensions.

The relationship between leaders with low CQ and their direct reports was less favorable than that of their counterparts with high CQ. Ng, Van Dyne, and Ang (2009) noted, "Leaders who are low in specific CQ capabilities will have the tendency to short-circuit the experiential learning cycle" (p. 239), thus not being able to draw and learn from the interactions they have with other cultures. As noted by the direct reports of leaders with low cultural intelligence, they perceived their leaders had little to no regard for cultural differences and demonstrated little empathy toward the diverse workforce.

CONCLUSION AND IMPLICATIONS

The sample for the study was small but provided insights on the importance of cultural intelligence in women leaders. Whether women have a different leadership style from their men counterparts or not, cultural intelligence is gender neutral. Eagly and Johannesen-Schmidt (2001) argued gender roles and understanding the way one leads are connected. They described attributes associated to gender roles as agentic or communal. "Agentic characteristics, which are ascribed more strongly to men than women" (p. 783) can be viewed as assertiveness, aggressiveness, and forceful behaviors. Women, on the other hand, are thought to have communal characteristics. These characteristics can be described as showing concern for others, being sympathetic and nurturing, and having the ability to interpersonally sensitive. Templer, Tay, and Chandrasekar (2006) examined all dimensions of cultural intelligence. The results of their study indicated global leaders who have high CQ, regardless of their gender, will be more successful in a global environment.

The women in this study who scored moderate to high in cultural intelligence had lived and/or worked in another country and spoke a second language. They recognized the benefits of ethnic cultural diversity in a multicultural and/or global environment and how the differences enhanced the performance of the team. A common theme that emerged from the qualitative questionnaire was that, with all the other leadership skills and training, the leaders needed to be engaged with other cultures and accept cultural behaviors and norms. Ng and Earley (2006) posited the success of leaders working in a global environment requires cultural intelligence. They further opined, "CQ is a capability that is posited to predict, but is distinct from, the actual outcome" (p. 8). Amiria et al. (2010) wrote that the more diverse the culture makeup is within organizations, the greater the need for leaders to have an intercultural skillset. They further posited, "Cultural intelligence has emerged as an important factor in effective performance and interactions inside and among various cultural environments" (p. 418). Leaders in this research who had high CQ understood other cultures and were able to successfully interact with ethnically diverse individuals, whereas those with low CQ were not as successful.

The leaders also stated that they must be inclusive to effectively learn about other cultures and increase cultural intelligence. By pointing out the similarities between cultures rather than focusing on the differences, these women were able to gain the trust of their direct reports and have them share about their cultures openly without feeling there were other motives. The common themes related to skills that the four women leaders attributed to their cultural intelligence and success within the multicultural environment included (a) having empathy for others, (b) seeking and accepting multiple viewpoints, (c) listening, (d) being open and trusting, and (e) creating an environment that supports inclusiveness through behavior and modeling.

The women who scored low in cultural intelligence discussed the need for more development and training. This group of women did not have support from their leadership. Their leaders wanted them to be goal-oriented and task-focused. This resulted in the women with low CQ focusing little to no energy in developing team cohesiveness with their members. They also believed it will be important to their future success to build stronger relationships with their teams.

The study of cultural intelligence is relatively new. As an emerging field of study in leadership, cultural and cross-cultural competencies, global leadership, and intercultural effectiveness, there are many opportunities to study this concept. The current literature on CQ has covered many phenomenon; however, few if any studies have examined CQ in the context of women in global or multicultural leadership positions. This study has shown women can be effective in a global or multicultural environment and that cultural intelligence is an important skillset for their success.

Organizations should not be hesitant to promote or hire women into positions that require cultural interactions. Cultural intelligence can be a predictor to the success of women leading in an intercultural context. Providing intercultural experiences and cultural training can improve a leader's CQ and improve the working relationship they have with direct reports. Leaders with high CQ have a greater potential for working with a team that has strong morale, and positive morale leads to goal attainment and job satisfaction. Because cultural intelligence can be learned, organizations can develop women to be successful leaders and contributors to the organization regardless of the ethnic and culture diversity that may exist.

NOTE

1. For information on using the items or scale for purposes other than academic research (e.g., consultants and nonacademic organizations), send an e-mail to cquery@culturalq.com

REFERENCES

Adler, N. J. (2002). Global managers: No longer men alone. *International Journal of Human Resource Management, 13*(5), 743–760. doi:10.1080/09585190210125895

Amiria, A. N., Moghimi, S. M., & Kazemi, M. (2010). Studying the relationship between cultural intelligence and employees' performance. *European Journal of Scientific Research, 42*(3), 418–427.

Ang, S., & Van Dyne, L. (2008). Conceptualization of cultural intelligence: Definition, distinctiveness, and nomological network. In S. Ang & L. Van Dyne (Eds.), *Handbook of cultural intelligence: Theory, measurement, and applications* (pp. 177–191). Armonk, NY: Sharpe.

Ang, S., Van Dyne, L., & Tan, M. L. (2011). Cultural intelligence. In R. J. Sternberg & S. B. Kaufman (Eds.), *Cambridge handbook on intelligence* (pp. 582–602). New York, NY: Cambridge University Press.

Bird, A. (2013). Mapping the content domain of global leadership competencies. In M. E. Mendenhall, J. S. Osland, A. Bird, G. R. Oddou, M. L. Maznevski, M. J. Stevens, & G. K. Stahl (Eds.), *Global leadership: Research, practice & development* (pp. 80–96). New York, NY: Routledge.

Brislin, R., Worthley, R., & Macnab, B. (2006). Cultural intelligence: Understanding behaviors that serve people's goals. *Group & Organization Management, 31*(1), 40–55. doi:10.1177/1059601105275262

Bureau of Labor Statistics (BLS). (2013a). Current Population Survey. Table 11: Employed persons by detailed occupation, sex, race, and Hispanic or Latino ethnicity. *Annual Averages 2012*. Retrieved from http://www.bls.gov/cps/cpsaat11.htm

Bureau of Labor Statistics (BLS). (2013b, October). *Labor force characteristics by race and ethnicity, 2013*. Report 1044. Labor Force Characteristics by Race and Ethnicity. Retrieved from http://www.bls.gov/cps/cpsrace2013.pdf

Caligiuri, P., & Lazarova, M. (2002). A model for the influence of social interaction and social support on female expatriates' cross-cultural adjustment. *International Journal of Human Resource Management, 13*(5), 761–772. doi:10.1080/09585190210125903

Cole, N., & McNulty, Y. (2011). Why do female expatriates "fit-in" better than males? *Cross Cultural Management, 18*(2), 144–164. doi:http://dx.doi.org/10.1108/13527601111125996

Cseh, M. (2003). Facilitating learning in multicultural teams. *Advances in Developing Human Resources, 5*(1), 26–40. doi:10.1177/1523422302239181

Eagly, A. H., & Chin, J. (2010). Diversity and leadership in a changing world. *American Psychologist, 65*(3), 216–224. doi:10.1037/a0018957

Eagly, A. H., & Johannesen-Schmidt, M. C. (2001). The leadership styles of women and men. *Journal of Social Issues, 57*(4), 781–797.

Eagly, A. H., Johannesen-Schmidt, M. C., & van Engen, M. L. (2003). Transformational, transactional, and laissez-faire leadership styles: A meta-analysis comparing women and men. *Psychological Bulletin, 129*(4), 569–591. doi:10.1037/0033-2909.129.4.569

Eagly, A. H., & Johnson, B. T. (1990). Gender and leadership style: A meta-analysis. *Psychological Bulletin, 108*(2), 233–256. doi:10.1037/ 0033-2909.108.233

Early, C. P., & Ang, S. (2003). *Cultural intelligence: Individual interactions across cultures.* Stanford, CA: Stanford Business Books.

Engle, R. L., Elahee, M. N., & Tatoglu, E. (2013). Antecedents of problem-solving cross-cultural negotiation style: Some preliminary evidence. *Journal of Applied Management and Entrepreneurship, 18*(2), 83–102.

Hall, E. T., & Hall, M. R. (1990). *Understanding cultural differences.* Yarmouth, MA: Intercultural Press.

Hammer, M. R., Bennett, M. J., & Wiseman, R. (2003). Measuring intercultural sensitivity: The Intercultural Development Inventory. *International Journal of Intercultural Relations, 27*(4), 421–443.

Hofstede, G. (1980). *Culture's consequences: International differences in work-related values.* Beverly Hills, CA: Sage.

Huang, L. (2010). Cross-cultural communication in business negotiations. *International Journal of Economics and Finance, 2*(2), 196–199.

Janssens, M., & Cappellen, T. (2008). Contextualizing cultural intelligence: The case of global managers. In S. Ang & L. Van Dyne (Eds.), *Handbook on cultural intelligence: Theory, measurement and applications* (pp. 356–371). Armonk, NY: Sharpe.

Jokinen, T. (2005). Global leadership competencies: A review and discussion. *Journal of European Industrial Training, 29*(2/3), 199–216. doi:10.1108/03090590510591085

Kluckhohn, F. R., & Strodtbeck, F. L. (1961). *Variations in value orientations.* Evanston, IL: Row, Peterson.

Kroeber, A. L., & Kluckhohn, C. K. (1952). *Culture: A critical review of concepts and definitions.* Cambridge, MA: Peabody Museum.

Mendenhall, M. E., & Osland, J. S., (2002, June). *Mapping the terrain of the global leadership construct.* Paper presented at the Academy of International Business, Puerto Rico.

Nardon, L., & Steers, R. M. (2011). The culture theory jungle: Divergence and convergence in models of national culture. In R. S. Bhagat & R. M. Steers (Eds.), *Cambridge handbook of culture, organizations, and work* (pp. 3–22). New York, NY: Cambridge University Press.

Ng, K. Y., & Earley, P. C. (2006). Culture and intelligence: Old constructs, new frontiers. *Group and Organization Management, 31(1),* 4–19. doi:10.1177/1059601105275251

Ng, K. Y., Van Dyne, L., & Ang, S. (2009). Developing global leaders: The role of international experience and cultural intelligence. In W. H. Mobley, Y. Wang, & M. Li (Eds.), *Advances in global leadership* (Vol. 5, pp. 225–250). Bingley, England: Emerald.

Osland, J. (2013). An overview of the global leadership literature. In M. E. Mendenhall, J. S. Osland, A. Bird, G. R. Oddou, M. L. Maznevski, M. J. Stevens, & G. K. Stahl (Eds.), *Global leadership: Research, practice & development* (pp. 40–79). New York, NY: Routledge.

Rehg, M. T., Gundlach, M. J., & Grigorian, R. A. (2012). Examining the influence of cross-cultural training on cultural intelligence and specific self-efficacy. *Cross Cultural Management: An International Journal, 19*(2), 215–232. Retrieved from http://dx.doi.org/10.1108/13527601211219892

Templer, K. J., Tay, C., & Chandrasekar, N. A. (2006). Motivational cultural intelligence: Realistic job preview, realistic living conditions preview, and cross-cultural adjustment. *Group and Organization Management, 31(1)*, 154–173. doi:10.1177/1059601105275293

Trompenaars, F. (1993). *Riding the waves of culture.* London, England: Brealey.

Van Dyne, L., Ang, S., & Koh, C. (2008). Development and validation of the CQS: The cultural intelligence scale. In S. Ang, & L. Van Dyne (Eds.), *Handbook on cultural intelligence: Theory, measurement and applications* (pp. 16–38). Armonk, NY: Sharpe.

Van Dyne, L., Ang, S., Ng, K. Y., Rockstuhl, T., Tan, M. L., & Koh, C. (2012). Subdimensions of the four factor model of cultural intelligence: Expanding the conceptualization and measurement of cultural intelligence. *Social and Personality Psychology Compass, 6(4)*, 295–313.

Van Dyne, L., Ang, S., & Nielsen, T. M. (2007). Cultural intelligence. In S. Clegg & J. Bailey (Eds.), *International encyclopedia of organization studies, Volume 1* (pp. 345–350). Thousand Oaks, CA: Sage.

CHAPTER 6

BECOMING MORE THEMSELVES

How Can Global Organizations Promote Women's Authentic Leadership?

Sarah E. Saint-Michel and Valérie Claire Petit

> The best compliment I have ever received in my career: "You really haven't changed, you've just become more of yourself."
>
> —Oprah Winfrey, Stanford Commencement Address (2008)

> Demand respect. Accept your success. Be lenient with others and yourself. Affirm your convictions. Learn from others. Enjoy your loved ones. Have fun at work. Exist by and for yourselves. Never give in. Do it for you. Do it for your business.
>
> —Sophie Bellon, Vice-President of the Sodexo Group (2013, para. 16)

Most large companies, at least in appearance, wish to see women succeed and recognize their leadership. According to Kalev, Kelly, and Dobbin (2006), to do this they implement policies that are based more or less on three pillars. The organizational pillar sets up structures of responsibility whose mission is to set formal goals and to define action plans, while the behavioral pillar aims to educate employees by making them aware of discriminatory practices and gender stereotypes that underlie them. The last pillar—the network pillar—supports the inclusion of women through mentoring and networking. If these policies can more or less significantly increase the proportion of women in management positions, reduce gender stereotypes, or provide women with familiar, professional role models, we may still ask ourselves if they are offering real conditions for women to express their genuine leadership.

Different cultures, just like organizations, are quick to develop gendered leadership stereotypes and expectations that exclude women from the leader's category and therefore from leadership positions. It is in this context that female managers receive a new injunction that invites them to cultivate authenticity, which is now described as the basis of positive leadership forms. But how can one be oneself—a woman—when this in itself appears to be incongruous for a leader (Eagly, 2005; Eagly & Chin, 2010)? What can be done in organizations to enable women to be both themselves and leaders?

What can a global company do to enable women managers to be both themselves and recognized as legitimate leaders? In this chapter, we narrate the case of the Sodexo Group, which provides an example of what can be done, not only to promote women in leadership positions (which most companies are trying to achieve) but also to enable them to genuinely assert their personal leadership in an authentic way. The first section will introduce the case of the Sodexo Group, describe its policies and initiatives, and also highlight the original culture and the values that bind the employees of the company. In the second section, we discuss the difficulty for women to develop authentic leadership because of the particular conflict between the gender role and that of a leader, and we discuss what companies can do to enable women to become authentic leaders. The third section builds on the case of Sodexo, which puts forward positive propositions and invites academics as professionals to further explore this issue, which seems essential for women's leadership, especially in global enterprises or cultural variations in role expectations that complicate the task for future leaders.

INTRODUCING SODEXO

At Sodexo, promoting women is a strategic issue supported by the whole top management team. According to Sophie Bellon (2013), board member and daughter of the founder, "Ten years ago, when Michel Landel organized the first meeting on this theme with the leaders of the group, it was revolutionary. Perhaps even more so for us, the French and Europeans, who were used to assuming our double life in silence" (para. 1). According to Fortune Magazine's 2013 corporate reputation survey, Sodexo was ranked as the most admired company among leading global companies in the Diversified Outsourcing Services sector ("Sodexo named," 2013). As a French private employer with 428,000 employees worldwide, it is also the 18th largest employer in the world (Sodexo, 2014). The group is present in 80 countries and generates a turnover of €18 billion. Sodexo is a French company with a global presence, and serves as a good example in female leaders' promotion.

Case Methodology

The case of Sodexo is one of the three exploratory cases that are part of a large research project conducted in France, the United Kingdom, and the United States. The purpose of this project was to ask whether companies promoting gender equality, diversity, and inclusion demonstrated a more efficient and authentic leadership, especially among women. We used a mix-method approach, including a qualitative exploratory study, as well as a quantitative study made up of the results of a questionnaire survey conducted among hundreds of respondents. The Sodexo case was the first company studied in our sample and helped us to put forward research propositions and hypothesis about the organizational conditions of women's leadership and authenticity.

The case is built from an impressive number of documents produced by the company on diversity management, inclusion, and gender equality, as well as on a series of semistructured interviews. We were able to interview some of the key players in the company, including the future chairman of the board of directors of the Sodexo Group, the European director of diversity, and the manager for diversity within the human resources department of France. We then interviewed 15 managers, men and women, from different group entities. With each one, we conducted hour-long semistructured interviews on the themes of diversity and leadership. Finally, over a period of 3 years, we met with the group managers on the topic of leadership and gender. These participant observations allowed us to understand the corporate culture and values as well as the managerial perceptions and practices of leadership.

The Three Dimensions of Sodexo's Gender Equality Policy

If the Sodexo case is exemplary in terms of diversity management, particularly in the promotion of gender equality, this is because the company policy in this area combined the three classic pillars of an effective diversity policy (Kalev et al., 2006). Firstly, the establishment of structures of responsibility that supports organizational change, then the education and training of employees that supports behavioral change, and finally the development of networking and the mentoring that fight against social isolation of women. Below we describe how, since 2011, the Sodexo Group has developed each of its pillars in a systematic way, which allowed them, in just 3 years, to get the first significant results in terms of women's leadership.

Effective Structures of Responsibility

In the Sodexo case, the effective structure of responsibility is impressive; in 2007, the new CEO, Michel Landel, decided to create the diversity department, which reports directly to the Global Executive Committee. This affiliation has done a lot for the legitimacy of the structure and the team set-up. Seven years later, by 2014, the department consisted of a full team, including a group director based in the United States and her team, a European director based in Europe and his team, and several country diversity officers. According to comments made by the Director of the Diversity Department during an interview, "Our role is to accompany each country in developing its own strategy and the deployment of its plan of action." He further explained, "Diversity policy is diverse! Each country can launch initiatives provided they are faithful to the values of the companies." Sodexo is guided by four values, and three have been a part of the company since Pierre Bellon started the company in 1966: spirit of service, team spirit, and spirit of progress. Recently, a fourth value, the spirit of inclusion, has been added. For the managers we interviewed, this is not an artificial addition. The company has always been diverse and inclusive, but the diversity policy was made official to increase employees' awareness and understanding.

Gender equality is part of the five dimensions of the diversity policy (with disability, cultural diversity, sexual orientation, and generations); it is also the oldest and the one most heavily invested in and structured. In 2009, Sodexo Women's International Forum for Talent (SWIFT) was created and became the main structure of responsibility for gender equality and women talent recognition. SWIFT is a committee made up of 34 senior managers, men and women from 15 countries, whose mission is to reflect on ways to make progress in gender equality and women's inclusion within Sodexo.

Solidly attached to the group's general management and the company's values, the diversity department and SWIFT are very influential. This is Sodexo's first strong point. However, as Kalev et al. (2006) pointed out, structure in itself is not enough; it must be provided with enforcement power and, in particular, by setting targets for managers. This is precisely the case at Sodexo. Within the company, women represent 54% of the staff, but the percentage drops when management and director positions are considered. In 2009, CEO Michel Landel made a commitment to increase the number of women managers from 19% to 25% by 2015. The managers in charge of recruitment are constantly reminded of this objective, and top management teams are asked to be exemplary. In 2012, 43% of the group executive committee and 38% of the board of directors were made up of women, and in 2016 the group will be chaired by a woman, Sophie Bellon, who is very committed to gender equality. Sophie Bellon and Michel Landel regularly take a stance, inside and outside the company, on the importance of the fight against gender inequality and the positive benefits of diversity in a company. According to the CEO, "Diversity is an ongoing battle that must continue unabated and with unwavering convictions" (Landel, 2010, p. 7). This unanimity and fundamental standpoint within the top management reinforce and legitimize the goals set for managers. Finally, it must be added that Sodexo has signed numerous commitments and agreements with public authorities, trade unions or their partners, and customers or contractors. The company is also regularly assessed and rated by organizations such as Catalyst and DiversityInc. For example, in 2012, Sodexo received prestigious awards in North America for diversity and inclusion policies, making it an excellent example of a company that invests in gender parity goals.

Education and Training Programs

The second pillar of the diversity policy is awareness and training. According to Landel, "For my part, I am convinced that diversity and inclusion is a business case for the company ... we must give it the means to achieve its ambitions and invest in training. Educate, train, is the basis of everything" (2010, p. 8).

Most companies engaged in gender equality offer their managers and employees programs to help raise their awareness of sexual discrimination at work and the gender stereotypes that sustain them. Sodexo became involved in this aspect at an early stage. The company set up communication tools on stereotypes and gender equality. These include video clips, conferences, and a recently introduced newsletter titled *Gender Balance*, which focuses on the objectives and actions conducted at Sodexo. In terms of training, a seminar was offered to 30,000 managers to increase awareness of the stereotypes and also learn to work together on these issues. Called the *Spirit of Inclusion*, the seminar reveals the philosophy of the Sodexo Group policy of gender equality that focuses on including everyone. Beyond this training, numerous initiatives have been launched and experimented with in various countries. For example, in France, where "gender" itself is a word with negative connotation, the diversity officer used humor when inviting managers to a one-woman show. Performed by a French actress, it narrates the ups and downs of a female manager who had just joined the board of directors.

Networking and Mentoring Programs

The third pillar of the diversity policy is the fight against women's isolation, which, according to the Sodexo approach, becomes a positive support for the inclusion of women. The company encouraged networking at an early stage and counted 13 Sodexo women's networks in the world, including unis-Vers in France, Go-Gender in Australia, Network in Chile, winG in the United States, and Women Work in the UK and Ireland. The mentoring programs are also implemented under the instigation of SWIFT; in 2009, 260 women participated in a sponsorship in order to develop their leadership, and in 2013 there were more than 1,000 participants.

Why is Sodexo Succeeding?

The commitment and the results of Sodexo in terms of gender equality is a unique case in France and worldwide. Pierre Bellon, who still chairs the group, founded the company in the south of France in 1966. In 2013, the first 40 listed companies in France were all run by men, with more than 90% of seats in the executive committees and 76% on the board of directors seats held by men. The latter figure recently increased following the 2011 state law on gender equality that established a balanced representation of both genders on the board of directors of listed companies. Sodexo is one particular case in its country and culture (Mediterranean), but also its original business (restaurants) has been traditionally dominated by men (Hofstede, 1993). The company's success is a result of three factors: conjunction, the role played by executive directors, and female leadership development.

The first factor is that of the conjunction. The works of Kalev et al. (2006) on the efficiency of diversity policies, particularly on the promotion of women, leads to two conclusions: first, the most effective way of promoting gender equality is the implementation of an accountability structure. Second, other types of interventions are only effective provided it is combined with this structure. This is precisely the strategy that Sodexo has chosen by implementing both a diversity policy with an accountability structure and effective interventions.

The second factor is the role played by executive directors. If diversity management was not directly linked to the group's general management, and if the directors were not actively involved in the various committees such as SWIFT or the diversity council in France and did not constantly communicate with such conviction about the importance of diversity and the value of women in the company, it is certain that the progress of gender equality would be much slower. The testimony of one manager highlights how the speeches of the directors are integrated in practice even beyond legal obligation: "We do not engage in positive discrimination and in any case this is prohibited; but on the other hand we take part in the positive action." Sophie Bellon (2013) once said, "I always want to have two final CV's, one for a man and one for a woman, and I will choose the most competent" (para. 6). As vice-president of the group, Bellon plays a more determining role in terms of the promotion of women. Her proactive speeches on the promotion of women by the company, exhortations to self-confidence, accountability toward women, and of course her personal success story, make her an effective role model for women managers in the company. One of them told us, "The very fact that she exists, that we are led by a woman changes everything. We can actually say that this is possible!"

These first two factors explain why the Sodexo group does better than the average global enterprise in promoting women leaders. However, by both studying the case and working with the managers of the company, another factor emerged that has not been explored in the scientific and practitioner literature. There is something else at Sodexo that, beyond the formal goals and numbers, supports female leadership development. This helps women to consider themselves as leaders and to be considered by others as genuine leaders. This third factor will be discussed in more depth in the following section.

WOMEN AND AUTHENTIC LEADERSHIP

Authentic leadership theory highlights the virtue of authenticity and the lessons from the ancient philosophers who emphasized this fundamental truth—that self-knowledge prevents leaders from hubris and destructive behaviors. This current leadership paradigm, therefore, assumes that to be effective and positive leaders, we have to be authentic—to know ourselves and to act in a way that is true to ourselves (Avolio & Gardner, 2005; Gardner, Cogliser, Davis, & Dickens, 2011). But what happens when being ourselves also means differing from the leadership expectations and stereotypes? This is the paradoxical injunction that female managers often have to deal with and the challenge that organizations must face if they want to develop female leaders.

Authentic Leadership

Based on the concept of authenticity, the authentic leadership theory (see Gardner et al., 2011 for a review) has emerged in leadership literature from the intersection of leadership, ethics, and positive organizational behavior (Cameron, Dutton, Quinn, & Wrzensniewski, 2003; Luthans, 2002). Walumbwa, Avolio, Gardner, Wernsing, and Peterson (2008) defined authentic leadership along four dimensions as a

> pattern of leader behavior that draws upon and promotes positive psychological capacities and a positive ethical climate, to foster greater self-awareness, and internalized moral perspective, balanced processing information, and relational transparency on the part of leaders working with followers, fostering positive self-development. (p. 94)

The first dimension, *self-awareness*, refers to a deep understanding of one's "true-self," of one's strengths and weaknesses and the multifaceted nature of self. The second dimension, *relational transparency*, reflects on how leaders promote trust through disclosure and a transparent manner, including sharing information and expressions of one's true thoughts and feelings while attempting to minimize displays of inappropriate behavior (Kernis, 2003). The third dimension, *balanced processing*, highlights how leaders show that they objectively analyze all relevant information before making a decision (Gardner, Avolio, Luthans, May, & Walumbwa, 2005). And the fourth dimension, *internalized moral perspective*, refers to an internalized and integrated form of self-regulation (Ryan & Deci, 2003). This process of self-regulation is conducted by internal higher moral standards and values, and it results in expressed decision making and behavior that are consistent with their own values (Avolio & Gardner, 2005).

What happens to managers who would like to develop authentic leadership? According to Avolio and Luthans (2006), authentic leadership development is "the process that draws upon a leader's life course, psychological capital, moral perspective, and a highly developed supporting organizational climate to produce self-awareness and self-regulatory behavior, which in turn fosters continuous, positive self-development resulting in veritable, sustained performance" (p. 2). Authentic leadership development is a complex process that is difficult to reach (Cooper, Scandura, & Schriesheim, 2005). From an individual and relational perspective, achieving authentic leadership development becomes possible when followers believe that their leader acts in an authentic manner and decides to trust in their leader. Therefore, an authentic followership appears, whereby a developmental process emerges that is characterized by "heightened levels of followers' self-awareness and self-regulation, leading to a positive follower development and outcome" (Avolio & Gardner, 2005, p. 322). However, reaching such a relationship with followers implies that the leader-follower relationship is free from bias and stereotypes, and this is especially difficult for women leaders (Eagly, 2005). From an organizational perspective, authentic leadership development requires a highly supportive context and developed culture. Not all the organizations are able to provide their managers such a positive climate and a secure environment for authenticity.

Women and Authentic Leadership Development

Developing authentic leadership remains a difficult challenge for female managers and at the same time a neglected issue in the literature. As far as we know, the only exception to this assumption is the work done by Eagly (2005) who discussed it from a relational perspective. She explained that authentic leadership is based on relational processes between leader and followers built on two components: the leader endorses values that promote interest of the larger community and conveys these values to followers; and the followers identify with these values and accept them as valuable for the group. Therefore, relational authenticity draws upon two sides: first, a process of persuasion and negotiation between leader and team members, where the leader communicates on his/her personal values and convictions, which in turn leads to followers' identification with their leader; and second, a process of mutual exchange between leader and follower appears where the trust between two parts is fundamental. Followers also play a central role in this process by bestowing upon the leader legitimacy and trust. Without these two elements, an unauthenticated relational process could appear and lead to detrimental work outcomes such as work withdrawal (Avolio, Gardner, Walumbwa, & May, 2004).

Achieving relational authenticity with followers is particularly challenging for women because of gender stereotypes, which shape followers expectations and can bias the leader-follower relationships. Stereotypes have been defined as "cognitive structures that contain the perceiver's knowledge, beliefs, and expectancies about some human group" (Hamilton & Trolier, 1986, p. 133). Stereotypes could bias social interactions through perceptual and behavioral confirmation processes (Merton, 1948). Gender stereotypes suggest that women are perceived as communal (e.g., caring and nurture), whereas men are perceived as agentic (e.g., independent and powerful). These expectations are thought to stem from traditional gender roles, such as women taking charge of domestic tasks and men devoted to the role of breadwinner (Eagly, 1987). Gender stereotypes have been found to influence people's perception of women and men's leadership styles (Eagly, Makhijani, & Klonsky, 1992; Lyness & Heilman, 2006), which in turn could create gendered workplace discrimination (Heilman & Eagly, 2008).

To explain this phenomenon of prejudice toward women leaders, two main theories offer a theoretical framework. Heilman (2001) articulated the lack-of-fit model between women's attributes (e.g., communal characteristics) and the attributes required to succeed in a leadership role. Eagly and Karau (2002) also promoted this idea in their incongruity role theory; the mismatch between women stereotyped gender role (e.g., communal characteristics) and stereotype of leader role (e.g., agentic characteristics) produces biased evaluations. Therefore, in both the lack-of-fit model (Heilman, 2001) and the role congruity theory (Eagly & Karau, 2002), these expectations about female attributes induce two kinds of norms: *descriptive beliefs* "designate what women and men *are* like" (Heilman, 2012, p. 114, emphasis in original), which are consensual expectations about what member groups do, and *prescriptive beliefs* designate injunctive norms about "what women and men *should be* like" (p. 114, emphasis in original), which are consensual expectations about what group members ideally would do (Cialdini & Trost, 1998). Therefore, women in leadership positions are the targets of two forms of prejudice: less favorable evaluation of potential to leadership functions compared to their male counterparts; and less favorable evaluation of actual leadership behavior because agentic behavior is perceived as less desirable in women than men (Eagly, Johannesen-Schmidt, & van Engen, 2003).

Although some recent research indicates that women seem more natural in leadership roles, indicating a less masculine leadership stereotype and better effectiveness of leadership displayed by women (Koenig, Eagly, Mitchell, & Ristikari, 2011; Zenger & Folkman, 2012), we suggest that achieving relational authenticity with followers must be particularly challenging for women in leadership positions (Eagly, 2005; Wang, Chiang, Tsai, Lin, & Cheng, 2013). For example, when women *authentically* display agentic behaviors in leadership roles, followers tend to devaluate leadership style compared to men because agentic traits displayed by women are viewed as violating the prescriptive stereotype (Rudman & Glick, 1999). This phenomenon is called the backlash effect, defined as social and economic repercussions for disconfirming a prescriptive stereotype (Rudman, 1998; Rudman & Glick, 1999). Thus, women who violate injunctive norms about femininity in the broadest sense face social penalties that likely carry over to the evaluation of leadership style (Heilman & Parks-Stamm, 2007). Conversely, women leaders acting *authentically* with communal attributes, such as kindness and generosity, are associated with incompetence and suffer from prejudice because they are viewed as not well equipped to succeed in a leadership position (Jamieson, 1995). In both cases, reaching authentic leadership and achieving a relational process with followers free from bias seems particularly difficult for women in leadership positions.

Research conducted by Eagly (2005) offers us a critical approach to the current paradigm in leadership theory; it raises the awareness about the practical implications for managers, especially those who are from the minority groups. It also invites us to think about the necessary conditions for authentic leadership development, especially for women. In line with Eagly's work, we will discuss the practical implications of authentic leadership for women with a complementary approach that focuses on the role played by the organizational context rather than the leader-follower relationships.

HOW TO PROMOTE AUTHENTIC FEMALE LEADERS

As previously shown, Sodexo did very well in terms of diversity policies, but policy excellence is only a prerequisite for organizations to promote female leaders and authentic leadership among women. We suggest that building a climate of inclusion and cultivating strong and positive corporate values are at the core of providing a conductive context for female authentic leaders.

Cultivating an Inclusion Climate

Our first proposition is that organizations that actively promote inclusion are more likely to enable women to be themselves and to display authentic leadership. There are two different but related approaches to managing diversity: diversity management and inclusion management (Roberson, 2006). Diversity management focuses on reducing the bias in key personnel decision-making and organizational demography (Ely & Thomas, 2001), whereas inclusion management focuses on "removal of obstacles to the full participation and contribution of employees in organization" (Roberson, 2006, p. 217). Diversity climate is defined as the "employees' shared perceptions of the degree to which a firm is thought to utilize fair employee policies and socially integrate underrepresented employees into the work setting" (McKay, Avery, & Morris, 2009, p. 768). In contrast, inclusive climate designates the "degree to which an employee is accepted and treated as an insider by others in work system" (Shore et al., 2011, p. 1266). According to Nishii (2012), the climate for inclusion includes three dimensions: (a) fair employment practices, (b) the integration of differences and "the openness in which employees can act and engage in core aspects of their self-concept and/or multiples identities without suffering unwanted consequences" (p. 1756), and (c) the integration of diverse perspectives from employees through the process of decision making.

In the case of Sodexo, the company has not only developed effective practices in diversity management but also built a climate of inclusion along these three dimensions. First, they implemented fair employment practices as described by one Sodexo manager: "Diversity in Sodexo implies to promote women in different managerial positions. I have seen many actions on operational jobs such as cooking jobs and waiters." This is also reflected in recruitment decisions, access to training, and promotion decisions. Second, Sodexo engages in the integration of differences, whereby employees regularly highlight the integration of difference at work. The following employee quote captures that idea well: "Diversity means including diverse people, namely, various cultures, various social background, and various genders. There is a real willingness here to promote diversity at all hierarchical levels." Third, the integration of diverse perspectives at Sodexo through the decision-making processes is also promoted, illustrated below in one manager's perspective:

> Gender equality and diversity at work involves more people in the decision, and having a variety of different viewpoints makes things all the more complicated in terms of leadership. I have to explain, and must be clear about our decision-making, but I think that we have to be more efficient on the way we lead.

In diverse contexts, leaders are expected to create a common sense in order to integrate all employees with different ideas or viewpoints. These inclusive leadership practices, such as information access, participation in the decision-making process, and freedom from stereotypes, contribute to the establishment of a climate that favors the expression of "true-self" without fear of judgment (Ely & Thomas, 2001; Shore et al., 2011).

One of the lessons we learned from the Sodexo case is that an inclusive climate may have a significant impact on the leadership culture and therefore on leadership stereotypes. At Sodexo, diversity practices and an inclusive climate shape the leadership role. One interviewee stated,

> When I integrate disabled people in my team, I need to take time to explain the new challenge, to take time to gather all the fears and motives of my team. But today, this experience is a real success, and I can share this success because the challenge has been a success, a real solidarity between group members has emerged.

It seems that they also shape a leadership culture that builds on individualized consideration, participation, and communication. Beyond the inclusion climate, there is an inclusive leadership culture at Sodexo (Shore et al., 2011).

As far as we know, there is no research exploring the relationship between diverse and inclusive organizations and the leadership displayed by managers, especially women and minority leaders. Based on the Sodexo case, we make two propositions: First, we believe that this kind of inclusion climate makes it easier for individuals to be themselves, including when individuals do not quite correspond to the universally recognized stereotype of a manager or leader. As a result, women working for inclusive organizations should encounter fewer difficulties in recognizing and securing recognition of their personality and leadership. Second, we suggest that such an inclusion climate encourages development in a managerial role. Part of the mission of managers at Sodexo is to positively recognize differences and above all to integrate these differences so that everyone can work together and feel like full-fledged members of the company community. We believe that companies with a strong climate of inclusion also display a more inclusive leadership culture and model. Such inclusive behavior on the part of leaders could also favor the emergence of more diverse—and therefore more female—leaders in the future.

Building on Positive Corporate Values

Beyond the inclusion climate, the company's values also play a central role in the culture. For several months we talked to company managers not only about their representations and practices of leadership but also about their perceptions and experience of diversity and coeducation. It quickly became apparent that diversity in leadership was systematically reported and evaluated for congruence with the company's values: service spirit, team spirit, and spirit of progress. Moreover, the notions of respect for others and openness to others were constantly discussed. This was illustrated by experiences and cited as distinctive characteristics of the company, as one cook's manager indicated:

> Respect for people is very important ... the person is really at the center of everything. This is not the case in all companies. I think it's very special to Sodexo. Sodexo is a global company, and we have an obligation to be open-minded on a par with all culture, in all countries, so that there is cultural wealth in Sodexo.

According to this employee's perspective, Sodexo's strategic position through its established presence worldwide creates a feeling of belonging to a large community with shared values and standards, which in turn reinforces the feeling of belonging (Shore et al., 2011). One manager stated, "As I have frequently affirmed, Sodexo's values are instilled in us, and when you are placed in a leadership position you must incorporate Sodexo's values." These quotes highlight the importance of corporate values in building the common purpose of Sodexo community members.

When addressing the issue of diversity, managers refer to the positive impact it has on company performance, as do the company's directors. But what convinces them more than anything is the compatibility between this policy and the values of Sodexo, such as the emphasis on service quality. One employee stated, "Because Sodexo is a services company, we have to be attentive to the specific needs of customers and to have diversity and gender equality to represent the customers' needs." Values come up again and again in the comments made by the managers, especially when we asked them to speak about their management and leadership styles. When it comes to management practices, we discovered that there are not, strictly speaking, any models or standards in terms of leadership. In fact, for the managers of Sodexo, that which links the managerial community and that which makes a leader is the ability to share and support the three core values of the company. The rest, including leadership style, belongs to each manager. As one manager explained, "At Sodexo there is a culture that everyone respects; but then in management or leadership, everyone uses their own style."

The role played by values and company culture in the development of authentic leadership has yet to be the subject of specific research. Based on the Sodexo case, we have two propositions to make on this point. First, we suggest that positive values that are shared collectively support a strong climate of inclusion. This is clear from the Sodexo case, where the company's inclusion climate and values are inextricably linked and reinforce one another. Through its corporate values, Sodexo affirms a specific organizational climate that nurtures a sense of belonging to a specific large community. Corporate values serve to assimilate all of the differences that threaten employees as insiders when they conform to the dominant norms of the culture (Shore et al., 2011). At the same time, Sodexo values the uniqueness of employees through the promotion of differences. A video available on the company website shows one employee commenting, "At Sodexo, diversity is a wide range of multiple identities, characters, individuals, personalities, color, and sex; in fact everyone is different and unique," explains a manager (Sodexo Group, 2012). According to the "integration-and-learning" practices perspective on diversity (Ely & Thomas, 2001, p. 240), to manage the uniqueness of the employees and the HRM practices, leaders have to manage the differences, and research on stereotypes shows that giving information about out-group members and about stereotyping may reduce bias (Fiske, 1998). Second, we posit that strong values can partly erode and transcend stereotypes, in particular those relating to gender and leadership. This suggests that the expectations placed on leaders are less influenced by gender stereotypes and more sensitive to individual differences, and that they ultimately give each person the opportunity to be unique and use this uniqueness as a solid basis for his or her leadership. This has important consequences for women. Their recognition as leaders depends less on their *fit* with the stereotypical leader than on company values.

IMPLICATIONS FOR THEORY AND PRACTICE

The aim of this chapter was to offer a case study for professionals and researchers working on female leadership and also to suggest theoretical and managerial implications. The Sodexo case helps us better understand what companies can do if they wish to promote women to senior positions and allow each individual to recognize themselves and to be recognized by others as a leader without having to disguise their own personality.

Implications for Theory and Future Research

In theoretical terms, this exploratory research makes four contributions. First, it provides an example of policies to ensure equality between men and women and the promotion of female employees to formal leadership positions. This case study offers a qualitative illustration of what Kalev and his colleagues (2006) had already demonstrated quantitatively; the importance of creating structures that establish responsibility combined with policies designed to educate and combat isolation. The Sodexo case illustrates that companies must act to address all pillars if they wish to advance the cause of women.

Second, while some studies have been conducted on authentic leadership and its impact on followers (Gardner et al., 2011), this research focuses on the antecedents of authentic leadership and explores the supportive organizational conditions that foster authentic leaders. While previous research on the antecedents of authentic leadership centers on the role of intra-individual personality (Jensen & Luthans, 2006), our case study builds on the seminal research by highlighting the role of organizational climate. By cultivating an inclusive climate that fosters respect for individual differences, Sodexo has created favorable conditions in which leaders can act authentically. Future research may wish to probe how diversity and inclusion policies across organizations may support authentic leadership development within those organizations.

Third, drawing on the seminal work of Eagly (2005), our findings enrich previous research on women and authentic leadership (Eagly, 2005; Eagly & Chin, 2010) by examining a particular context in which organizational conditions encourage women to display authentic leadership. While authentic leadership theorists seem to underestimate the role played by organizational context, as well as the differences between leaders from majority and minority groups (Eagly, 2005), our findings highlight the role played by organizational policies. As suggested by Shore et al. (2011), "very little research has investigated the internal organizational processes that create inclusion" (p. 1277). Our findings stress the role played by top management philosophy and the importance of corporate values in creating an inclusive climate that encourages women to act in an authentic way and in favoring women's access to leadership positions. Our study offers insights into the promotion of authentic female leadership by examining how Sodexo uses genuine diversity and inclusion policies to encourage women to act with authenticity. Thus, fostering authentic leadership involves creating the organizational conditions needed to support such leadership.

Finally, this study may offer some interesting new avenues for future research. By paving the way for exploratory research that links the notion of an inclusive climate with authentic leadership, our results highlight the role of an inclusive and diverse climate in fostering favorable conditions for authentic female leadership. While we are now seeing demands for authentic leadership, a source of organizational effectiveness (Gardner et al., 2011), it appears that organizations play a central role in fostering equal access to authentic female leadership. Moreover, the idea of inclusive leadership has emerged to describe a set of behaviors that builds on positive humane values (e.g., respect, consideration, and solidarity) and the integration of differences as a motivational process for the whole community of followers (Shore et al., 2011). Future research could extend previous results from other organizational settings using alternative research methods such as quantitative data.

Implications for Practice

To highlight the practical implications of this research, we will use an anecdote. While this manuscript was being written, one of the authors, Valérie Petit, interviewed the future chairman of the company who expressed dismay at the departure of a woman with considerable potential and one of the managers interviewed as part of this research. The author was initially surprised to see so much emotion and attention paid to a manager so far removed from the company's Executive Committee. The CEO felt that her departure represented a failure: the company's efforts to build a climate of inclusion were not yet sufficient to counterbalance the influence of a manager on a woman's career. She explained that "all it takes is for a managerial relationship to turn sour, and those with potential become discouraged and feel that the company does not recognize their talent." When asked what she intended to do, she said she would do two things: wait one year (the manager had decided to pursue an MBA) and then convince the woman to return; and above all, pursue her efforts to increase the level of inclusion in the company. This anecdote reveals that even in a company like Sodexo, where every effort is made to promote women at all levels of the organization, the careers of women remain fragile.

In practical terms, the Sodexo case suggests three possible courses of action. First, in spite of the failure described above, Sodexo acts as a source of inspiration for any company that truly wishes to advance the cause of women and allow them to develop their leadership skills. Its success is mainly due to the combination of three dimensions of its equality and diversity policies: (a) the creation of dedicated structures establishing responsibility and high levels of sincere commitment on the part of senior management, (b) an intensive and large-scale training and development program targeting stereotypes in particular, and (c) the development of networking and mentoring program initiatives.

Second, this case study should encourage company leaders to evaluate their climate of inclusion and reflect on the impact it has on the recognition of female leadership. This is what the CEO of Sodexo highlights in the previous anecdote: she feels that inclusion is the key to enabling women to express their leadership with authenticity. But this is not just a key that can open doors for women; it will do so for anyone struggling with a poor fit attributed to leadership stereotyping. Sodexo believes that promoting women is just one among many positive outcomes of the mindset of inclusion that is shared by the majority of employees. The company's strategy is to approach female leadership in a way that is positive and cohesive through the notion of inclusion. It is a strategy that could inspire other companies aspiring to create more inclusive environments as well.

Finally, the Sodexo case should encourage professionals to consider two key factors of success. The first is the nature and strength of company values. The second is the role played by intermediary managers who sometimes destroy leadership talents. This is what one female manager who left the group explained during her interview:

> I really wanted the position, but as usual, I thought that I did not have all the skills to take on this job. But I said to myself, "Well, if they trust me...." " In addition, I had mentoring, so it put me in a dynamic, telling myself, "Sodexo is pushing me and trusts me," but if I had not had all that, maybe I would have refused, saying, "They are crazy, I'm going to fail."

This extract shows the extent to which one's belief in one's capacity for leadership is a fragile sentiment that is highly dependent on the manager's perspective. This is definitely an issue that HR professionals and top managers must bear in mind: how to ensure a balance in the role played by managers when it comes to encouraging leadership talents.

CONCLUSION

Through the Sodexo case study, we stress the importance of effective organizational conditions in promoting gender equality and diversity equality. Therefore, our research highlights the role played by three combined factors: an effective structure of responsibility that supports diversity policies, education and training programs on diversity practices for Sodexo employees, and networking and training programs to fight against the isolation of women. These three dimensions of Sodexo's approach to gender equality are indicative of the success of its diversity and gender equality policies, expressed by the increasing numbers of women in various leadership roles, as well as the rewards provided by external metrics such as Catalysts, Time's Top 50 employers for women in 2014, and DiversityInc Top 50.

The Sodexo case offers practitioners an example of a successful diversity and inclusion strategy for advancing women in leadership. We hope that we have provided sufficient inspiration for future researchers to further explore the relationship between diversity and inclusion policies, authentic leadership, and female leadership development.

REFERENCES

Avolio, B. J., & Gardner, W. L. (2005). Authentic leadership development: Getting to the root of positive forms of leadership. *The Leadership Quarterly, 16*(3), 315–338. doi:10.1016/j.leaqua.2005.03.001

Avolio, B. J., Gardner, W. L., Walumbwa, F. O., & May, D. R. (2004). Unlocking the mask: A look at the process by which authentic leaders impact follower attitudes and behaviors. *The Leadership Quarterly, 15*(6), 801–823.

Avolio, B. J., & Luthans, F. (2006). *The high impact leader: Moments matter accelerating genuine leadership development.* New York, NY: McGraw-Hill.

Bellon, S. (2013, October 30). Les femmes: nouveaux modèles de réussite. *Huffpost.* Retrieved from http://www.huffingtonpost.fr/sophie-bellon/les-femmes-nouveaux-modeles_b_4174539.html

Cameron, K. S., Dutton, J. E., Quinn, R. E., & Wrzensniewski, A. (2003). Developing a discipline of positive organizational scholarship. In K. S. Cameron, J. E. Dutton, & R. E. Quinn (Eds.), *Positive organizational scholarship* (pp. 361–370). San Francisco, CA: Berrett-Koehler.

Cialdini, R. B., & Trost, M. R. (1998). Social influence: Social norms, conformity and compliance. In D. Gilbert, S. Fiske & G. Lindzey (Eds.), *The handbook of social psychology* (Vol. 2, pp. 151–192). New York, NY: McGraw-Hill.

Cooper, C. D., Scandura, T. A., & Schriesheim, C. A. (2005). Looking forward but learning from our past: Potential challenges to developing genuine leadership theory and genuine leaders. *The Leadership Quarterly, 16*(3), 475–493. doi:10.1016/j.leaqua.2005.03.008

Eagly, A. H. (1987). *Sex differences in social behavior: A social-role interpretation*. Hillsdale, NJ: Erlbaum.

Eagly, A. H. (2005). Achieving relational authenticity in leadership: Does gender matter? *The Leadership Quarterly, 16*(3), 459–474. doi:10.1016/j.leaqua.2005.03.007

Eagly, A. H., & Chin, J. L. (2010). Diversity and leadership in a changing world. *American Psychologist, 65*(3), 216–224. doi:10.1037/a0018957

Eagly, A. H., Johannesen-Schmidt, M. C., & van Engen, M. L. (2003). Transformational, transactional, and laissez-faire leadership styles: A meta-analysis comparing women and men. *Psychological Bulletin, 129*(4), 569–591. doi:10.1037/0033-2909.129.4.569

Eagly, A. H., & Karau, S. J. (2002). Role congruity theory of prejudice toward female leaders. *Psychological Review, 109*(3), 573–598. doi:10.1037//0033-295x.109.3.573

Eagly, A. H., Makhijani, M. G., & Klonsky, B. G. (1992). Gender and the evaluation of leaders A meta-analysis. *Psychological Bulletin, 111*(1), 3–22.

Ely, R. J., & Thomas, D. A. (2001). Cultural diversity at work: The effects of diversity perspectives on work group processes and outcomes. *Administrative Science Quarterly, 46*(2), 229. doi:10.2307/2667087

Fiske, S. (1998). Stereotyping, prejudice, and discrimination. In D. T. Gilbert, S. Fiske, & G. Lindzey (Eds.), *Stereotyping, prejudice and discrimination* (4th ed., Vol. 2, pp. 357–411). New York, NY: McGraw-Hill.

Gardner, W. L., Avolio, B. J., Luthans, F., May, D. R., & Walumbwa, F. (2005). "Can you see the real me?" A self-based model of genuine leader and follower development. *The Leadership Quarterly, 16*(3), 343–372. doi:10.1016/j.leaqua.2005.03.003

Gardner, W. L., Cogliser, C. C., Davis, K. M., & Dickens, M. P. (2011). Authentic leadership: A review of the literature and research agenda. *The Leadership Quarterly, 22*(6), 1120–1145. doi:10.1016/j.leaqua.2011.09.007

Hamilton, D. L., & Trolier, T. K. (1986). Stereotypes and stereotyping: An overview of the cognitive approach. In J. Dovidio & S. L. Gaertner (Eds.), *Prejudice, discrimination and racism* (pp. 127–163). New York, NY: Academic.

Heilman, M. E. (2001). Description and prescription: How gender stereotypes prevent women's ascent up the organizational ladder. *Journal of Social Issue, 57*(4), 657–674.

Heilman, M. E. (2012). Gender stereotypes and workplace bias. *Research in Organizational Behavior, 32*(1), 113-135. doi:10.1016/j.riob.2012.11.003

Heilman, M. E., & Eagly, A. H. (2008). Gender stereotypes are alive, well and busy producing workplace discrimination. *Industrial and Organizational Psychology, 1*(4), 393–398.

Heilman, M. E., & Parks-Stamm, E. J. (2007). Gender stereotypes in the workplace: Obstacles to women's career progress. In S. J. Correll (Ed.), *Social psychology of gender: Advances in group processes* (Vol. 24, pp. 47–77). Greenwich, CT: JAI/Elsevier.

Hofstede, G. (1993). Cultural constraints in management theories. *Academy of Management Executive, 7*(1), 81–94.

Jamieson, K. H. (1995). *Beyond the double bind: Women and leadership*. New York, NY: Oxford University Press.

Jensen, S. M., & Luthans, F. (2006). Relationship between entrepreneurs' psychological capital and their authentic leadership. *Journal of Managerial Issues, 2*(18), 254–273.

Kalev, A., Kelley, E., & Dobbin, F. (2006). Best practices or best guesses? Assessing the efficacy of corporate affirmative action and diversity policies. *American Sociological Review, 71*(4), 589–617.

Kernis, M. H. (2003). Toward a conceptualization of optimal self-esteem. *Psychological Inquiry, 14*(1), 1–26.

Koenig, A. M., Eagly, A. H., Mitchell, A. A., & Ristikari, T. (2011). Are leader stereotypes masculine? A meta-analysis of three research paradigms. *Psychological Bulletin, 137*(4), 616–642. doi:10.1037/a0023557

Landel, M. (2010). Carrières au feminin: marathon ou course d'obstacles? *Les cahiers de Centrale Marseille, 9*, 7–9. Retrieved from http://carrieres-au-feminin.blogs.centraliens-marseille.fr/list/la-revue-est-telechargeable-ici/431019509.pdf

Luthans, F. (2002). The need for and meaning of positive organizational behavior. *Journal of Organizational Behavior, 23*(6), 695–706.

Lyness, K. S., & Heilman, M. E. (2006). When fit is fundamental: Performance evaluations and promotions of upper-level female and male managers. *Journal of Applied Psychology, 91*(4), 777–785. doi:10.1037/0021-9010.91.4.777

McKay, P. F., Avery, D. R., & Morris, M. A. (2009). A tale of two climates: Diversity climate from subordinates' and managers' perspectives and their role in store unit sales performance. *Personnel Psychology, 62*(4), 767–791.

Merton, R. K. (1948). The self-fulfilling prophecy. *Antioch Review, 8*(3), 193-210.

Nishii, L. H. (2012). The benefits of climate for inclusion for gender-diverse groups. *Academy of Management Journal, 56*(6), 1754-1774. doi:10.5465/amj.2009.0823

Roberson, Q. (2006). Disentangling the meanings of diversity and inclusion in organizations. *Group and Organization Management, 31*(2), 212–236. doi:10.1177/1059601104273064

Rudman, L. A. (1998). Self-promotion as a risk factor for women: The costs and benefits of counter stereotypical impression management. *Journal of Personality and Social Psychology, 74*(3), 629–645.

Rudman, L. A., & Glick, P. (1999). Feminized management and backlash toward agentic women: The hidden costs to women of a kinder, gentle image of middle managers. *Journal of Personality and Social Psychology, 77*(5), 1004–1010.

Ryan, R. M., & Deci, E. L. (2003). On assimilating identities to the self: A self-determination theory perspective on internalization and integrity within cultures. In M. R. Leary & J. P. Tangney (Eds.), *Handbook of self and identity* (pp. 253–272). New York, NY: Guilford.

Sodexo. (2014). Career springboard [website]. Retrieved from http://sodexousa.com/usen/media/press-releases/2013/Sodexo-Fortune-Most-Admired-2013.aspx

Sodexo Group. (Producer). (2012). I'm Sodexo [Video file]. Retrieved from https://www.youtube.com/watch?v=kytGDih1LlE

Sodexo Named one of the "World's Most Admired Companies" by Fortune Magazine. (2013, March 4). Retrieved from http://sodexousa.com/usen/media/press-releases/2013/Sodexo-Fortune-Most-Admired-2013.aspx

Shore, L. M., Randel, A. E., Chung, B. G., Dean, M. A., Ehrhart, K. H., & Singh, G. (2011). Inclusion and diversity in work groups: A review and model for future research. *Journal of Management, 2011*(37), 1262–1289. doi:10.1177/0149206310385943

Walumbwa, F. O., Avolio, B. J., Gardner, W. L., Wernsing, T. S., & Peterson, S. J. (2008). Authentic leadership: Development and validation of a theory-based measure. *Journal of Management, 34*(1), 89–126. doi:10.1177/0149206307308913

Wang, A.-C., Chiang, J. T.-J., Tsai, C.-Y., Lin, T.-T., & Cheng, B.-S. (2013). Gender makes the difference: The moderating role of leader gender on the relationship between leadership styles and subordinate performance. *Organizational Behavior and Human Decision Processes, 122*(2), 101–113. doi:10.1016/j.obhdp.2013.06.001

Winfrey, O. (2008) Stanford commencement address [Video file]. Retrieved from https://www.youtube.com/watch?v=Bpd3raj8xww

Zenger, J. H., & Folkman, J. R. (2012, April 4). Gender shouldn't matter, but apparently it still does. *Harvard Business Review*. Retrieved from http://blogs.hbr.org/2012/04/gender-shouldnt-matter-but-app/

CHAPTER 7

GLOBAL WOMEN LEADERS

Leadership Cartography as a Proposed Approach

Karin Klenke

Over the past 25 years, multinational companies (MNCs) have proliferated and globalization has moved from periphery to center stage. Although globalization is not a new phenomenon, global leadership is a nascent field of inquiry that has received much less attention than traditional leadership. According to Mobley and Dorfman (2003), the culprits are the relative dearth of leadership talent, the inadequacy of global leadership development processes, and the continued derailment of international executives. As a result, global leadership qualifies as an adolescent theory (Sonpar & Golden-Biddle, 2008), mainly because it has yet to reach paradigmatic consensus (Glynn & Raffaelli, 2010). Brodbeck and Eisenbeiss (2014) concluded that "as organizations increasingly face global markets and operate across national borders, career paths become more and more international, and management assignments are most likely to involve multicultural contexts" (p. 672).

Within the field of global leadership is an even smaller but growing body of research that specifically addresses global women leaders (e.g., Adler,

1996; Klenke, 2011; Suutari, 2002). Many forces that were drivers of globalization, such as rapidly changing technologies, changing demographics, flattened horizontal networks as preferred organizational structures, market and cost competitiveness, and the emergence of a global supraculture that permits common visions and understandings above and beyond the clashes of customs, myths, and civilizations (O'Hara-Devereaux & Johansen, 1994), are also instrumental in propelling women's ascent to global leadership in a variety of contexts ranging from politics and business to arts and sciences. Globalization has become a force that transforms time and place, impacting cultural groups in a temporally and spatially differentiated manner, empowering some while impoverishing others.

In her groundbreaking article, Adler (1996) identified 25 global women leaders who have led countries and governments in diverse political and socioeconomic contexts around the world. In 2012, a total of 20 women leaders were elected, appointed, or succeeded their predecessors. As of July 14, 2013, the number of women in power worldwide had dropped to 19. Globally, women have achieved the highest levels of leadership as political leaders such as presidents, prime ministers, or chancellors of countries, for example, Angela Merkel of Germany, Cristina Fernandez de Kirchner of Argentina, Yingluck Shinawatra of Thailand, Ellen Johnson Sirleaf of Liberia, Tarja Halonen of Finland, Dallia Grysbauskaite of Lithuania, to name a few. In business, Indra Nooyi leads PepsiCo as CEO and chairperson of the second largest food and beverage business in China, India, and Russia. Anne Lauvergeon, CEO of Areta, heads a nuclear company in France that sells uranium, reactors, and waste storage equipment. Reports of global women business leaders in Asian countries include India, China, and Japan. Iranian lawyer and human rights and democracy activist Shirin Ebadi and Kenyan environmental and political activist Wangari Maatai received the Nobel Prize for their work as global peace leaders.

Leadership is a powerful discourse characterized by dichotomies such as the leader-follower bifurcation and dilemmas based on opposing paradigms. Leadership Cartography (LC) is positioned to enter this discourse by expanding critical leadership theory and research. The purpose of this chapter is to introduce LC as a proposed qualitative research method, arguing that this methodology is particularly relevant to the study of women as global leaders (Klenke, 2004a, 2005a). I define LC as the confluence of research methods used in leadership and feminist studies, geography, archaeology, cartography, and cognitive mapping. More specifically, LC is a comprehensive methodology, combining paradigm and method by employing comprehensive maps based on geography, critical cartography (Crampton & Krygier, 2006) as a derivative of critical theory (e.g., Delgado & Stefancic, 2012; Sim & Van Loon, 2001) and cognitive mapping, a qualitative technique that can be used to produce causal mind maps (Stoddart,

Leach, & Dawson, 2000; Wood, 1992). Whereas I cannot provide an actual LC in this chapter due to the lack of availability of the technology to construct a map that includes both cartographic and cognitive components, I offer this approach as a potential future method for studying the complexity of women as global leaders.

LEADERSHIP CARTOGRAPHY DEFINED

Like leadership studies, cartography is multidisciplinary, housed in the physical and social sciences as well as the humanities. Cartography was usually defined as "the art and science of representing the earth's physical features geographically" (Crone, 1978, p. xi), but in recent years a broader outlook has emerged. In 1964, for instance, the British Cartographic Society (n.d.) defined cartography as "the science, and technology of making maps, together with their study as scientific documents and works of art" (para.1). When defined this way, cartography covers all types of maps representing the Earth (terrestrial), including religious maps, any heavenly body (celestial), and astrological diagrams (Harley & Woodward, 1987; Wallis & Robinson, 1987).

The focus of this chapter is on a specific type of map, which I labeled leadership cartography. Using the metaphor of a three-legged stool, LC rests on three major disciplinary contributors: cartography, critical cartography, and cognitive mapping; and it is embedded in leadership theories and qualitative research methods. Furthermore, there are other secondary disciplines that contribute to LC, including archaeology, religion, history, management, and information science, to name a few. Finally, I treat LC as both a paradigm and a research method in the qualitative tradition as discussed below. LC is particularly relevant to the study of women as global leaders because it facilitates the analysis of visual (maps) and textual data, which allows for comparative research of leaders in different countries. In other disciplines, such as anthropology, visual methodologies such as the use of photographs are widely used. Yet there is not a single study on women as global leaders that has utilized visual data, even though the technologies are available due to advances in photography as well as the availability of videos, works of art, or websites for visual analyses.

Foundational Discipline: Cartography

One of the foundational disciplines undergirding cartography is geography. As Curry (2002) noted, the geographer's method of inquiry concentrates on asking two essential questions: Where are things located? And why are they located there? Thus, the discipline of geography is concerned primarily with interpreting and explaining the occurrence, distribution, and interrelationships of the physical and cultural elements that can be discerned in the landscape. But a cartographer's understanding of globalization does not stop here. Harley (1990) called our attention to the importance of ethics and social theory in cartography. The author argued that the absence of a social dimension in cartography theory has led to a lack of representation that is related to cartography's theoretical isolation behind disciplinary barriers and to its lack of social relevance in a practical sense. Harley makes a case for the retention of topographical maps on the grounds that they can offer a democratic and humanistic form of geographical knowledge. Hartley's work on maps as representations and sites of power knowledge has been particularly instrumental and reflects the influence of poststructuralists such as Foucault and Derrida (Crampton, 2001).

Leadership cartography, like the geography of the sea and land, takes place in a turbulent, ever-changing environment. Currents and wind patterns shift, storms alter the contours of sandbars and shoals. Organization are characterized by complexity and uncertainty, many are teetering on the edge of chaos (Marion & Uhl Bien, 2000; Regine & Lewin, 2000; Schneider & Somers, 2006; Uhl-Bien, Marion, & McKelvey, 2007). These types of organizations require a new breed of leaders with different competencies, which I have described elsewhere, including the ability to manage paradox (Klenke, 2014), and emotional, cultural, and spiritual intelligence (Klenke, 2004b). In short, contemporary global organizations call for a new leadership and a new paradigm. LC is intended as one approach to fill this gap.

Foundational Theory: Critical Cartography

According to Crampton and Krygier (2006), critical cartography is a new set of mapping practices and theoretical critique grounded in critical theory (e.g., Sim & Van Loon, 2001). Sim and Van Loom (2001) argued that the last few decades have seen an explosion in the production of critical theories, with deconstructionists, poststructuralists, postmodernists, second-wave feminists, new historicists, cultural materialists, postcolonialists, Black critics, and queer theorists, among a host of others, all vying for our attention. The world around us can look very different depending on the critical theory that serves as a lens through which we filter organizational and environmental information. As a result, this significant range of possible interpretations can leave many leadership scholars feeling confused and frustrated.

The relationship between cartography and critical cartography is analogous to the relationship between critical management studies (CMS) and critical leadership studies (CLS), a growing area of interest particularly in European leadership research, which views power as central to leadership dynamics (Alvesson & Spicer, 2012; Collinson, 2011). These authors pointed out that CSL builds on CMS to highlight the numerous interrelated ways in which power, identity, and context are embedded in leadership dynamics. Although heterogeneous and diverse, critical perspectives share a focus on the situated power relations and leader identity through which leadership discursive practices are socially constructed (Ford, 2006; Tourish, 2014). Here again, LC can be extremely powerful as researchers explore themes of influence and the leader identity of global women leaders.

Crampton and Krygier (2006) emphasized that because critical cartography is grounded in critical theory, it differs from academic cartography in that it links geographical knowledge with power and thus is political. According to this view, critical cartography situates maps within specific relations of power and does not treat them as neutral scientific documents. Pickles (2004) agreed when he pointed out that maps are active; they actively construct knowledge, exercise power, and can be powerful means of promoting social change. Crampton and Krygier (2006) concluded that in critical cartography theoretical, inquiry seeks to determine the social relevance of mapping and its ethics and power relations.

Foundational Discipline: Cognitive Mapping

Tolman (1948) was credited with the development of the *cognitive map* construct. He defined a cognitive map as a type of mental representation that allows an individual to acquire, code, store, and decode information about the relative locations and attributes of phenomena in their everyday or metaphorical spatial environment. A cognitive map approach to organizations begins with the recognition that organizational members edit their own institutional experiences into patterns of personal knowledge. A representation of that knowledge is called a cognitive map; it consists of the concepts and relationships an individual uses to understand organizational situations. If we consider all possible types of relations among concepts, we have a cognitive map. If we limit ourselves to mapping only causal relations, then we talk about a more specific form of cognitive map called a *cause map* (Weick & Bougon, 1986). According to Weick and Bougon, "organizations exist largely in the mind" (1986, p. 102). Weick (1979) asked, "What do managers do?" (p. 42) He argued that managerial work can be viewed as managing myths, images, symbols, and labels. Furthermore, Weick proposed that "managers traffic in images, and as such, the appropriate role of the manager may be evangelist rather than accountant" (p. 42). Cognitive maps have been studied in various fields such as psychology, education, cartography, management, urban planning, and history (Knight, 2002). However, they have been rarely utilized in leadership research.

Huff (1990) asserted that managers must know two things about cognitive maps. First, they must be aware of the functions of such maps. However, Huff is quick to point out that knowledge about map functions, by itself, offer little concrete guidance for managers in attempting to utilize these tools. As is the case with physical maps, the helpfulness of cognitive maps depends on one's ability to choose the right map or right set of maps. The utility of cognitive maps also depends on the user's ability to locate current position, desired new positions, and routes between them. The second thing managers need to know, then, is how to identify appropriate maps and then how to draw on the information they convey (Fiol & Huff, 1992).

Furthermore, Fiol and Huff (1992) contended that a particular difficulty of complex organizations is that the maps that are available, or can be made available through research, convey only parts of the relevant terrain. Moreover, they often conflict and are in a state of flux. To benefit from the expanding technology of cognitive mapping, managers must be able to compare alternative options concerning current locations, improved positions, and the routes between them. These interrelated activities draw on different types or aspects of cognitive maps. Beyond knowing the general functions of cognitive maps, then, managers must learn to recognize and balance the interdependent aspects of multiple maps.

Niccolini (1999) described the Self-Q-Test, a precursor of cognitive maps, as a sophisticated step-by-step technique developed by Bougon (1992) to plot individual and organizational causal maps. According to Bougon, the Self-Q-Test is based on the combination of self-interviews with a number of structured activities to identify networks of concepts connected by causal relations (causal map) without requiring the interviewee to generate complex abstract representation. The Self-Q-Test, according to its inventor, "is non-directive and nonreactive, because it transfers much of the responsibility for the organization, execution and validation of data gathering and map construction from the interviewer to the interviewee" (Bougon, 1992, p. 843). Interviewees are asked to formulate their own questions on the topic of interest, and the researcher then transforms the questions into concepts and constructs. Bougon (1992) proposed that causal maps tell us a story of relationships from which conflict and politics are completely absent.

A variety of cognitive/causal mapping software programs are on the market. In this research, I have used Cognizer (Clarkson & Hodgkinson, 2005) and Decision Explorer to construct cognitive maps for global women leaders. Huff (1990) pointed out that most cognitive/causal mapping programs fall within a general class of procedures that he categorized as methods for revealing understanding of "influence causality and systems dynamics" (p 16.). Both Cognizer and Decision Explorer were specifically developed for use in the context of ideographic research. Within the

Cognizer system, the term *construct* is used to define nodes incorporated within maps. Decision Explorer is an ideas mapping tool that has been described as a data management and analysis tool (Ackerman, Eden, & Cropper, 1992), albeit not in the code and retrieve mode, but it deals solely with qualitative data (ideas). It is also a visual thinking tool. This program helps researchers to develop visual representations of people's thoughts and the relationships between them, encouraging reflection and making ideas explicit and shareable.

Foundational Discipline: Leadership Theory and Associated Qualitative Methods

Leadership theories, from their humble beginnings known as trait theory, which focused on individual characteristics of the leader, have broadened significantly over the past two decades and produced a range of new theories that embrace followers, context, culture, and technology. We now evidence a wide array of alternative models characterized by a focus on core concepts such as spirituality (e.g., Fry, 2003, 2005), authenticity (e.g., Avolio & Gardner, 2005; Avolio, Gardner, Walumbwa, Luthans, & May, 2004; Harter, 2001: Klenke, 2005b), chaos and complexity (e.g., Marion & Uhl-Bien, 2001; Schneider & Somers, 2006, Uhl-Bien et al., 2007), relationality (Uhl-Bien, 2006), invisible leadership (Hickman & Sorensen, 2014), ethics (Brown & Treviño, 2006; Ciulla, 2004), technology (e.g., Avolio, Kahai, & Dodge, 2001), as well as bringing followership into leadership dynamics (e.g., Chaleff; 2009; Tourish, 2014).

Leadership Cartography as Paradigm

Because a paradigm is a worldview, spanning ontology, epistemology, and methodology, the quality of scientific research conducted within a paradigm has to be judged on its own paradigmatic terms (Klenke, 2004a, 2008). I argued elsewhere (Klenke, 2005a) that both leadership studies and cartography are positioned between a positivistic worldview, grounded in the search for universal truth, a worldview increasingly dominated by postmodern thought and the emphasis on context (Klenke, 1996; Osborn, Hunt, & Jauch, 2000). Since I am treating leadership cartography as a paradigm, our worldview or belief system as researchers has to be recognized as an important influence upon our research, intrinsically linked to ontological, epistemological, and methodological assumptions. As Krauss (2005) pointed out, our philosophical assumptions or theoretical paradigms about the nature of reality are crucial to understanding the overall perspective from which a study is designed and carried out. In general, qualitative research, including leadership cartography, is based on a relativistic, constructivist ontology that posits that there is no objective reality. Rather, we impose order on the world as we perceive it in an effort to construct meaning; meaning lies in cognition not in elements external to us. The construction of meaning is the task of qualitative researchers and reflects the specific methods used in the qualitative data analysis process (Krauss, 2005). Lythcott and Dutschl (1990) took this issue a step further when they stated that the information impinging on our cognitive systems is screened, translated, altered, perhaps rejected by the knowledge that already exists in the system, resulting in knowledge that is idiosyncratic and purposefully constructed.

Leadership Cartography as Method

Qualitative research methods have evolved from the early days of grounded theory (e.g., Glaser & Strauss, 1967) to the current state which now includes an eclectic array of diverse methods beyond the most frequently used case study and interview method ranging from ethnography and phenomenology to arts-based research methods.

As a field of inquiry, we can also think of LC as a set of unique research methods. LC consists of several distinct elements; it employs some of the tools used by cartographers and geographers and combines them with cognitive mapping techniques for the purpose of constructing causal maps of leadership processes. As a research method, LC is based on the idea of using geographical maps as a framework for developing, generating, creating, depicting, capturing, and communicating nongeographic leadership concepts and theories relevant to women as global leaders. In other words, geographic maps are used as the basis for the construction of cognitive maps that allow leadership researchers to progress to causal maps of leadership processes that are context specific, have a history, and set temporal and spatial boundaries that can be empirically examined.

Leadership cartography is a comprehensive method that combines the use of comprehensive maps based on geography in time, space, and context (i.e., the social, political, economic climate summarized under the term *zeitgeist*), with cognitive mapping—a qualitative technique that can be employed to produce causal maps. Leadership cartography moves beyond topographical depictions and the assumption that a map is as accurate a representation of some external physical reality as the cartographer would perceive it. Instead, I take the cartographer's map and superimpose constructs, relationships, hypotheses, theories, and data so that the cartography base becomes a framework for representing information and ideas on other variables or measures relevant to women as global leaders.

Presently, the cartographic discipline has not been explored for combining with mapping cognitive processes, let alone applied to the leadership terrain. As in the analyses of other types of qualitative research methods such as qualitative interviewing (Kvale & Brinkman, 2009; Rubin & Rubin, 2012) or case study method (Stake, 2006; Swanborn, 2010; Yin, 2014) where computer assisted qualitative data analysis (CAQDAS) software programs are utilized, a number of powerful packages are available for cognitive mapping. The desired outcome is to develop techniques to produce rich, reliable, value-tapping data, amenable to qualitative (and quantitative) analyses.

LEADERSHIP CARTOGRAPHY: FROM GEOGRAPHIC MAPS TO CONCEPT MAPS

For much of human history, at least until mapmaking was developed as a craft in the ancient civilizations of the Fertile Crescent and China, explorers set out on their journeys without maps (Harley & Woodward, 1987). Women leaders are explorers too, and many are geographers in spirit, if not in disciplinary affiliation. Many of them set out on their leadership journey without a strategic map. They traverse organizations and engage in a venture of exploration such as charting unknown organizational territories or leading organizations on the edge of chaos. These female leaders approach risks they are confronted with or major change efforts without maps such as a compelling vision or effective strategy to guide them; they lack clarity of purpose about why their organizations exist and what their unique contributions are supposed to be. As a result, they are battered by waves of competition, globalization, significant shifts in demographics, and changing definitions of leadership effectiveness.

Maps and Mapmaking

Locations and spatial patterns are important elements in the description, explanation, or interpretation of many phenomena that interest leadership scholars; however, spatial patterns and spatial behaviors of leaders have not been virtually ignored. Maps are supposed to be scale models of reality, yet mapmakers, like leadership theorists, must choose what to show and how to show it. But our maps are much more than that. We want maps that go beyond geographic realities of locales—maps that tell much about society, culture, and leadership. Like the microscope and telescope, geographic maps can be an instrument of observation and discovery; they allow us to create or impose structure. Adding causally relevant characteristics can convert a map showing only geographic features to a map offering explanation or interpretation. For cognitive researchers who often use the idea of a map as an analogy, the basic idea is the same. Cognitive maps are graphic representations that locate people in relation to their information environments. Maps provide a frame of reference for what is known and believed; they exhibit reasoning behind purposeful action.

This anecdote by Karl Weick (personal communication, 2010) captures the importance of maps to a group or organization:

> A group of mountain climbers was in the process of ascending one of the most daunting peaks in the Alps when they were engulfed by a sudden snow squall. All were experienced climbers and each had their own idea of the direction they should go in to get back to the base camp. They wandered around for some time, arguing which way to go, while their circumstances became more dire and threatening with each moment of indecision. Finally, one of the climbers dug around in his backpack and found a map. Everyone huddled around the map, studied it and quickly determined their direction. Several hours later, they arrived safely at the camp. While they were warming themselves around the fire, regaling each other with the story of their misadventure, one of the climbers picked up the map they had used to descend the Alps. On looking at it more carefully, the group realized it was actually a map of the Pyrenees!

Maps, whether cartographic, geographic, cognitive, or LC have a purpose. As with positivistic science, maps are designed to represent the truth of the known world. But when we try to put purpose and truth into words, it turns out to be hard. Different maps show different selections from what is available in a medium where one cannot show everything at once. Therefore, all maps are selections from everything that is known, bent for the mapmaker's purpose. In fact, most maps are not at all what they seem to be. The map is a piece of history contextualized in time and place. Since history is one of the contexts for the study of leadership, we see immediately that the cartographic features of a map serve as a bridge from geography to the examination of social phenomena.

Mapmaking

There are many ways of making maps as there are truths to maps. As noted earlier, maps are descriptions of the ways things are, descriptions made to support the human purposes that summon the maps into being. Even today, people are as likely to hand-draw maps as they are to make them with computers. It is important to keep in mind that it is not how the map is made that makes the map. It is not the detail nor the quality of the printing. The value of the map is the degree to which it serves its purpose. Remember that maps are graphic objects that can preserve descriptions so that these descriptions can be used at other times and places. Mercator's map took the knowledge about the world that people had been gathering for millennia and put it in a form that sailors could sail away with and use when they needed to. Gerardus Mercator, one of the foremost cartographers of the 16th century when the Age of Discovery flooded mapmakers with information and made increasing demands on their skills and ingenuity, devoted 25 years of his life to his "atlas." In 1538, he published the first world map, faithfully depicting the new lands as they were revealed and nearly eliminating the medieval misconceptions (Jacobs, Dahl, & Conley, 2006; Monmeier, 2004). Mercator's atlas was as significant an achievement as his world map of 1569, drawn on a projection that bears his name.

As global women leaders and leadership scholars begin to think about developing leadership cartographic maps for ourselves, leaders we work with, leaders who inspire us, or leaders we wish to emulate, we need to keep in mind that every map comes packaged with a purpose. That purpose determines which properties the map needs to have, whether it needs to show true relative sizes or shapes, directions, or distances. It is these characteristics that make the map what it is—that enable the map to achieve its purpose.

The Power of Maps

The Mercator projection clearly illustrated that maps often have political agendas. Critical social theorists discovered years ago the hidden political agendas within cartography and maps, most particularly the nexus between maps, knowledge, and power that provided the initial entry point for the analysis of meanings of and in maps. Critiques of either colonial attitudes or Eurocentric approaches of global map representations, as well as those of the maps' presumed objectivity or neutrality, have been discussed for quite some time (Wood, 1992). LC promotes a new way of looking at how global women leaders can explore power through the lenses of maps and "the importance of asymmetries in leadership dynamics and the wider economic social, economic, political, and technological contexts of their countries of origin" (Collinson, 2014, p. 41). As Hardy (2013) recently pointed out, U.S. journals are "inexcusably behind the times, when it comes to addressing conceptualizations of power" (p. 454).

The cartographer's task is to design maps that will show the least distortion or no distortion in those properties that maps' intended users deem desirable. For this to be accomplished, a cartographer must draw from a repertoire of projections. The Mercator projection belongs to that class of maps called conformal, meaning "correct form." Such a map preserves the shape and small parts of the mapped surface, though it cannot preserve the shape of an especially large continent. Another class of maps is called equal area. While conformal maps are preferred by navigators, engineers, and military strategists, equal area maps are the choice of scientists, geographers, and others to whom a standard scale area is more important than correct shape.

WOMEN LEADERS AS CARTOGRAPHERS AND WOMEN'S LEADERSHIP AS LEADERSHIP CARTOGRAPHY

In this section, I offer some examples to demonstrate the application of leadership cartography to global women leaders. Although this is not a completed LC, as the software to do so it not yet available, it provides an idea of what might be included. The first case is Shirin Ebadi, the Iranian lawyer and human rights activist who was awarded the 2003 Nobel Peace Prize for her work promoting the rights of women in her home country. She was the first Iranian and first Muslim woman to receive the prize. According to Taheri (2004), awarding the Nobel Peace Prize to Ebadi was a strong signal from the democratic world to those Muslims who are fighting fascism disguised as religion, often at great personal risk. During her acceptance, Ebadi refused to wear the hijab that the Iranian government requires all women to wear during public appearances. Ebadi countered, "Instead of telling Muslim women to cover their heads, we should tell them to use their heads" (Taheri, 2003, para. 2). Her rejection of the hijab became one of the themes used by the Iranian propaganda machine launched against her by the state-owned media where women are forced to wear the hijab or have to face a 6-month jail term. She was repeatedly beaten but never wavered.

In her book, *Iran Awakening*, Ebadi (2006) explained her political and religious views of Islam, democracy, and gender equality. Ebadi, now 66 and the mother of two daughters, has been repeatedly beaten up by Islamist extremists who wish to turn religion into a weapon of rule by terror, as opposed to her perspective, which sees religion as a personal matter. She was part of a second generation of Iranian women who were able to attend the university where she studied law, a field expressly closed to women by the Islamists, and became a judge in 1974. The advent of female judges under the regime of the Shah was a truly revolutionary event, unprecedented in the 1,500 year history of Islam (Taheri, 2003). Ebadi has been imprisoned, kept under house arrest, prevented from working, and subjected to the most vicious media campaigns—and yet she has not wavered.

Since she was awarded the Nobel Peace Prize, Ebadi has received many other prestigious awards, including the International Democracy Award and numerous honorary doctorate degrees. She is also a co-founder of the Nobel Woman's Imitative, a group of Nobel Prize winning women working together to raise awareness in creating nonviolent social change. Ebadi now travels abroad lecturing in the West. In her most recent book, *The Golden Cage: Three Brothers, Three Choices, One Destiny* (2011), Ebadi narrates the story of three brothers who live deluded lives in the golden cages of ideology. She tells the story of the Iranian Revolution through three brothers: a monarchist, an anarchist, and a revolutionary Islamist. Of the three brothers, one was executed in prison and the other two left Iran; one of whom was executed in exile, presumably at the behest of Iran. Although Ebadi feels very strongly that she belongs to Iran, working on human rights issues in her home country has become virtually impossible. Despite the difficulties in her country, she refuses to give up hope or stop speaking the truth about injustice.

The LC of Ebadi commences with an ancient map of Persia and a contemporary map of Iran on which leadership constructs are superimposed. Leadership constructs may include her political and religious views, her exercise of invisible leadership as manifested in her compelling and deeply held devotion to a common purpose (Hickman & Sorenson, 2014). It would include her commitment to end discrimination on the basis of gender, race, and religion with other women of her generation, arguing that there is no future without human rights. It would also include her family of origin, which in part defines her leadership.

The second global woman leader I selected is Maria das Graças Silva Foster, CEO at Petrobras, Brazil's leading oil and gas company. Silva Foster's leadership could reshape the profile of Brazil; Petrobas produces 91% of Brazil's oil and 90% of its natural gas (Orihuela & Millard, 2012). Foster is facing tremendous challenges as Petrobras is confronted with rising debts, falling production, and its mandate to buy local. Complex regulation of the distribution of future oil profits has slowed down exploration activities and tough restrictions on contracting foreign companies have been blamed for increasing the company's costs (Pearson, 2012).

Silva Foster was raised by her mother together with her sisters in one of the most dangerous slums on the outskirts of Rio de Janeiro, where she collected recyclable cans and paper to pay for her books. She described her childhood as happy and joyful, but difficult since the family lived in poverty and endured a lot of domestic violence during her childhood. As a teenager, she wrote letters on behalf of illiterate immigrants and took on other odd jobs to help support her family, staying out of the way of the local drug gangs (Carneiro, 2012).

Foster joined Petrobras in 1978 and, over the next 30 plus years, worked her way up the corporate ladder. In 1981, she was hired as a chemical engineer and then moved into various managerial positions. Between 2003 and 2005, Foster served as Secretary of Oil, Natural Gas, and Renewable Fuels, and in 2007, former Brazilian president Gabrielli named Foster as Petrobas's first female director, the second-highest management-level position, and put her in charge of the gas and oil division. In November 2008, she was named Executive of the Year of Brazilian Finance Executives.

In January 2012, Brazilian President Dilma Rousseff appointed her as CEO of Petrobras. Foster had first worked with Rousseff when Foster managed the pipeline project importing natural gas from Bolivia. Petrobras stock jumped 3.8% on January 23, 2012, when Foster was named the company's first female CEO (Orihuela & Millard, 2012). Her career path to the top of Petrobras came as no surprise since, prior to her appointment as CEO, Silva Foster was one of the most prominent business women in Latin America. Her career trajectory underscores the value of education, hard work, and perseverance. Willpower, she has said, is everything to her.

Foster is known for her work capacity, competence, and seriousness with which she dedicates herself not only to Petrobras but also to everything in her professional life. She is known for her toughness and political acumen, and has been described as dogged, straight talking and, of course, the "Iron Lady," which is her nickname. She has a reputation as a hard-driving boss who demands results and sticks to deadlines. In addition, she is also known for her optimism which, as Dunkley (2012) noted, fuels the Iron Lady. A self-confessed Beatles enthusiast, she is married to British husband Colin and has two children.

Today Silva Foster and Brazil's president Dilma Rousseff are among the world's most powerful leaders. Rousseff became the first female president of Brazil in January 2011. According to Forbes, she is now the third most powerful women in the world and governs a country where 49% of entrepreneurs with companies less than 42 months old are women. Petrobas is currently 51% state controlled, but ultimately Foster, with guidance from Rousseff's government, will have to decide whether to continue to run the firm as a state-owned, job-creating bureaucracy or a modern public company (Orihuela & Millard, 2012).

The LC of Silva Foster begins with a geographical map of Brazil that highlights the country's rich oil resources. The leadership constructs superimposed on Brazil's geography would include her political savvy, perseverance, results orientation, optimism, and contextual intelligence, which Foster demonstrates as she applies her broad political skills not only in sizing up company politics but also in dealing with various stakeholders representing a broad spectrum of private and public firms. These personal characteristics will be constructed as flags, which will be placed strategically over the major oil depositories.

By comparing and contrasting LCs for global women leaders in different contexts, researchers would be able to analyze the commonalities and differences among global women leaders and develop a repertoire of skills requisite for effective leadership in the international arena. For example, Ebadi's LC can be compared to the LC of global business leaders such as Chanda Kockhar, CEO and managing director of the ICICI bank in India, or Maria Asuncion Aramburuzabala, called Marisun by her friends in Mexico, who heads the Grupo Modelo, brewer of Corona beer, founded by her grandfather. The benefits of such comparisons are derived from combined textual and visual analyses.

Effective global women leaders have the ability to manage uncertainty, balance the often powerful tensions between the need to respond to global issues and withstand local pressures. They must possess political savvy, collaboration, and negotiation skills, they must be culturally competent, exhibit both cultural and emotional intelligence, and embrace positive psychology constructs such as hope (e.g., Snyder, 2002; Snyder, Rand, & Sigmon, 2002), resilience (e.g., Crawford & Klenke, 2003; Masten & Reed, 2002), and optimism (e.g., Carver & Scheier, 2002; Peterson 2000; Youssef & Luthans, 2007), which characterized Ebadi's self-leadership during her time in jail and while under house arrest for a number of years. These are just a few constructs that provide the foundation of a leadership cartography perspective on global women leaders.

CONCLUSIONS AND IMPLICATIONS

In conclusion, in this chapter, I introduced leadership cartography as a future innovative qualitative methodology that is constructed based on the confluence of two foundational disciplines: cartography and cognitive mapping. I described leadership cartography as a paradigm based on a constructivist ontology and meaning making as the dominant epistemology. As a method, leadership cartography, utilizes specific techniques used in the construction of maps, both geographic and causal, employed by geographers and cognitive scientists. Currently, as in so many other cases, technology is lagging behind theoretical and conceptual development. Separate software is available to support a variety of cartography and cognitive mapping processes but a program that superimposes one on the other has yet to be developed for the academic market.

While waiting for technology to catch up with the conceptual development of LC presented in this chapter, it is critical for leadership scholars to remember that the global arena represents a unique context for women leaders and that contextual understanding is instrumental in discovering new avenues for expanding leadership theory and practice. Leadership and its effectiveness, in large part, is dependent upon the context (Osborn et al., 2002). In the global arena, context is more diversified, volatile, complex, and dynamic compared to other contexts, such as politics or the media. The diversity of cultures, languages, and values that prevails around the globe, such as African Renaissance and postcolonial leadership systems in East Asia, are challenges for global women leaders, yet they represent a significant portion of the global leadership talent pool because many leadership theories and practices from American or European descent have been difficult to export beyond Western boundaries. The complexity of the global context offers opportunities for global women leaders to capitalize on their strength, leadership competencies, and preparedness to serve their constituencies across all kinds of boundaries (Klenke, 2011). As a proposed work in progress approach, LC will enable researchers to pay more nuanced attention to where leadership is enacted as well as how leadership is enacted in the global context. With the rise of women leaders around the globe, an LC approach offers a different, interdisciplinary methodology empowered by the combination of textual and visual analyses. It therefore makes a unique contribution to the study of global women leaders by offering a multimethod, multiparadigm approach that currently is missing in research on women in leadership.

REFERENCES

Ackerman, F., Eden, C., & Cropper, S. (1992). *Getting started with cognitive mapping*. Tutorial paper, 7th Young OR conference. London, England: Banxia Software.

Adler, N. (1996). Global women political leaders: An invisible history, an increasingly important future. *The Leadership Quarterly, 7*(1), 133–161.

Alvesson, M., & Spicer, A. (2012). Critical leadership studies: The case of critical performativity. *Human Relations, 65*(3), 367–390.

Avolio, B., & Gardner, W. (2005). Authentic leadership development: Getting to the root of positive forms of leadership. *The Leadership Quarterly, 16*(3), 315–338.

Avolio, B., Gardner, W. Walumbwa, F., Luthans, F., & May, D. (2004). Unlocking the mask: A look at the process by which authentic leaders impact follower attitudes and behaviors. *The Leadership Quarterly, 15*(6), 801–823.

Avolio, B., Kahai, S., & Dodge, G. (2001). E-leadership: Implications for theory, research and practice. *Leadership Quarterly, 11*(4), 615–668.

Bougon, M. (1992). Congregate cognitive maps: A unified dynamic theory of organization and strategy. *Journal of Management Studies, 29*(3), 369–384.

British Cartographic Society. (n.d.). *About cartography & mapmaking*. Retrieved from www.cartography.org.uk

Brodbeck, F., & Eisenbeiss, S. (2014). Cross-cultural and global leadership. In D. Day (Ed.), *Leadership and organizations* (pp. 657–682). London, England: Oxford University Press.

Brown, M., & Treviño, L. (2006). Ethical leadership: A review and future directions. *The Leadership Quarterly, 17*(6), 596–616.

Carneiro, J. D. (2012, February, 8). Graca Foster takes charge at Brazil oil giant Petrobras. *BBC News Latin America & Caribbean*. Retrieved from http://www.bbc.co.uk/news/world-latin-america-16941382?print+true

Carver, C., & Scheier, M. (2002). Optimism. In R. Snyder & S. Lopez (Eds.), *Handbook of positive psychology* (pp. 231–243). New York, NY: Oxford University Press.

Chaleff, I. (2009). *The courageous follower: Standing up to and for our leaders* (2nd ed.). San Francisco, CA: Jossey-Bass.

Clarkson, G., & Hodgkinson, G. (2005). Introducing Cognizer: A comparative computer package for the elicitation and analysis of cause maps. *Organizational Research Methods, 8*(3), 317–341.

Cuilla, J. (2004). *Ethics: The heart of leadership*. Westport, CT: Praeger.

Collison, D. (2011). Critical leadership studies. In A. Bryman, D. Collison, K. Grint, B. Jackson, & M. Uhl-Bien (Eds.), *The Sage handbook of leadership* (pp. 179–192). London, England: Sage.

Collinson, D. (2014). Dichotomies, dialectics and dilemmas: New directions for critical leadership studies. *Leadership, 10*(1), 36–55.

Crampton, J. (2001). Maps as social constructions: Power, communication and visualization. *Progress in Human Geography, 25*, 16–32.

Crampton, J., & Krygier, J. (2006). *An introduction to critical cartography*. Retrieved from http://www.acme-journal.org/vol4/JWCJK.pdf

Crawford, D., & Klenke, K. (2003, April 11–13). *Dispositional traits and the implications for organizational change: The relationship between resilience and resistance to change*. Paper presented at the 18th conference of the Society of Industrial and Organizational Psychology, Orlando, FL.

Crone, G. (1978). *Maps and their makers: An introduction to the history of cartography* (5th ed.). London, England: Folkestone.

Curry, M. (2002). Toward a world without maps: Lessons from Ptolemy and postal codes. *Annals of the Association of American Geographers, 95*(3), 680–691.

Delgado, R., & Stefancic, J. (2012). *Critical race theory* (2nd ed.). New York, NY: New York University Press.

Dunkley, J. (2012, December 8). Maria Graças Silva Foster: Optimism fuels the "Iron Lady" of Petrobras. *The Independent*. Retrieved from http://www.independent.co.uk/news/business/analysis-and-features/maria-das-graas-silva-foster-optimism-fuels-the-iron-lady-of-petrobras-8393753.html

Ebadi, S. (2006). *Iran awakening: A memoir of revolution and hope*. New York, NY: Random House.

Ebadi, S. (2011). *The golden cage: Three brothers, three choices, one destiny*. Carlsbad, CA: Kales.

Fiol, M., & Huff, A. (1992). Maps for managers: Where are we? Where do we go from here? *Journal of Management Studies, 29*(3), 267–288.

Ford, J. (2006). Discourses of leadership: Gender, identity and contradiction in a UK public sector organization. *Leadership, 2*(1), 78–99.

Fry, L. (2003). Toward a theory of spiritual leadership. *The Leadership Quarterly, 14*(6), 693–727.

Fry, L. (2005). Introduction: Toward a paradigm of spiritual leadership. *The Leadership Quarterly, 16*(5), 619–622.

Glaser, B., & Strauss, A. (1967). *The discovery of grounded theory*. Chicago, IL: Aldine.

Glynn, M., & Raffaelli, R. (2010). Uncovering mechanisms of theory development in an academic field: Lessons from leadership research. *Academy of Management Annals, 4*(1), 359–401.

Hardy, C. (2013). Treading fine lines. *Journal of Management Inquiry, 22*(4), 452–456.

Harley, J. (1990). Cartography, ethics and social theory. *Cartographica, 27*, 1–23.

Harley, J., & Wooward, D. (Eds.). (1987). *Cartography in prehistoric, ancient, and medieval Europe and the Mediterranean*. Chicago, IL: Chicago University Press.

Harter, S. (2001). Authenticity. In R. Snyder & S. Lopez (Eds.), *Handbook of positive psychology* (pp. 382–394). New York, NY: Oxford University Press.

Hickman, G., & Sorenson, G. (2014). *Invisible leadership: How a compelling purpose inspires exceptional leadership*. Los Angeles, CA: Sage.

Huff, A. (Ed.). (1990). *Mapping strategic thought*. New York, NY: Wiley.

Jacobs, C., Dahl, E., & Conley, T. (2006). *The sovereign map: Theoretical approaches in cartography throughout history*. Chicago, IL: University of Chicago Press.

Klenke, K. (1996). *Women and leadership: A contextual perspective*. New York, NY: Springer.

Klenke, K. (2004a, January 29–February 1). *Qualitative research methods in leadership studies: Paradigm shift or paradigm paralysis*. Paper presented at the 5th international interdisciplinary conference on Advances in Qualitative Methods, Edmonton, AB, Canada.

Klenke, K. (2004b, April 14–16). *The trilogy of the leader's mind*. 21st annual conference of the Association of Management/International Association of Management, Norfolk, VA.

Klenke, K. (2005a, November 2–5). *Leadership cartography: Mapping leadership constructs geographically and cognitively*. Paper presented at the 7th annual meeting of the International Leadership Association, Amsterdam, The Netherlands.

Klenke, K. (2005b). The internal theater of the authentic leader: Integrating cognitive, affective, conative, and spiritual facets of authentic leadership. In W. Gardner, B. Avolio, & F. Walumbwa (Eds.), *Authentic leadership theory and practice: Origins, effects, and development* (pp. 155–182). New York, NY: Elsevier.

Klenke, K. (2008). *Qualitative research methods in the study of leadership*. Bingley, England: Emerald.

Klenke, K. (2011). *Women in leadership: Contextual dynamics and boundaries*. Bingley, England: Emerald.

Klenke, K. (2014). The leader's new work: Living with paradox. *Journal of Management Systems, 23*(1), 35–53.

Knight, P. (2002). *Conspiracy nation: The politics of paranoia in postwar America*. New York, NY: New York University Press.

Krauss, S. (2005, December). Research paradigms and meaning making: A primer. *The Qualitative Report, 10*(4), 758–770. Retrieved from http://www.nova.edu/ssss/QR/QR10-4/krauss.pdf

Kvale, S., & Brinkmann, S. (2009). *InterViews: Learning the craft of qualitative research interviewing*. Los Angeles, CA: Sage.

Lythcott, J., & Dutschl, R. (1990). Qualitative research: From methods to conclusions. *Science Education, 74*(4), 449–460.

Marion, R., & Uhl-Bien, M. (2000). Leadership in complex organizations. *The Leadership Quarterly, 12*(4), 389–418.

Masten, A., & Reed, G. (2002). Resilience in development. In R. Snyder & S. Lopez (Eds.), *Handbook of positive psychology* (pp. 74–88). New York, NY: Oxford University Press.

Mobley, W., & Dorfman, P. (2003). *Advances in global leadership* (Vol. 3). Bingley, England: Emerald.

Monmeier, M. (2004). *Rhumb lines and map wars: A social history of the Mercator projection*. Chicago, IL: Chicago University Press.

Niccolini, D. (1999). Comparing methods for mapping organizational cognition. *Organization Studies, 20*(5), 833–860.

O'Hara-Devereaux, M., & Johansen, R. (1994). *GlobalWork: Bridging distance, culture and time*. San Francisco, CA: Jossey-Bass.

Orihuela, R., & Millard, P. (2012, May 31). Petrobas first female CEO is Rousseff's response to delayed oil. *Bloomberg News*. Retrieved from http://www.bloomberg.com/news/2012-06-01/petrobras-first-female-ceo-is-rousseff-s-response-to-delayed-oil.html

Osborn, R., Hunt, J., & Jauch, L. (2002). Toward a contextual theory of leadership. *The Leadership Quarterly, 13*(6), 797–837.

Pearson, S. (2012, October). From a favela to the top table. *Financial Times*. Retrieved from http://www.ft.com/cms/s/0/9fc83078-0ecf-11e2-9343-00144feabdc0.html#axzz3ESA5Uquk

Peterson, C. (2000). The future of optimism. *American Psychologist, 55*(1), 44–55.

Pickles, J. (2004). *A history of spaces, cartographic reason, mapping and the geo-coded world*. London, England: Routledge.

Regine, B., & Lewin, R. (2000) Leading at the edge: How leaders influence complex systems. *Emergence, 2*(2), 5–23.

Rubin, H., & Rubin, I. (2012). *Qualitative interviewing: The art of hearing data*. Los Angeles, CA: Sage.

Schneider, M., & Somers, M. (2006). Organizations as complex adaptive systems: Implications of complexity theory for leadership research. *The Leadership Quarterly, 17*(4), 351–365.

Sim, S., & Van Loon, B. (2001). *Introducing critical theory: A graphic guide*. London, England: Icon.

Snyder, R. (2002). Hope theory: Rainbows in the mind. *Psychological Inquiry, 13*(4), 249–275.

Snyder, R., Rand, K., & Sigmon, D. R. (2002). Hope theory: A member of the positive psychology family. In R. Snyder & S. Lopez (Eds.), *Handbook of positive psychology* (pp. 257–276). New York, NY: Oxford University Press.

Sonpar, K., & Golden-Biddle, K. (2008). Using content analysis to elaborate adolescent theories of organization. *Organization Research Methods, 11*(4), 795–814.

Stake, R. (2006). *Multiple case study analysis*. New York, NY: Guilford.

Stoddart, E., Leach, C., & Dawson, C. (2000). Concept maps as assessment devices in science inquiry learning: A report of methodology. *International Journal of Science Education, 22*(12), 1221–1246.

Suutari, V. (2002). Global leader development: An emerging research agenda. *Career Development International, 7*(4), 218–233.

Swanborn, P. (2010) *Case study research: What, why, and how*. Los Angeles, CA: Sage

Taheri, A. (2003, October 17). Celebrating Shirin Ebadi. *National Review Online*. Retrieved from http://www.nationalreview.com/node/208300/print

Tolman, E. (1948). Cognitive maps in rats and mice. *Psychological Review, 55*(4), 189–208.

Tourish, D. (2014). Leadership, more or less? A processual, communication perspective on the role of agency in leadership theory. *Leadership 10*(1), 79–98.

Uhl-Bien, M. (2006). Relational leadership theory: Exploring the social processes of leadership and organizing. *The Leadership Quarterly, 17*(6) 654–676.

Uhl-Bien, M., Marion, R., & McKelvey, B. (2007). Complexity leadership theory: Shifting leadership from the industrial age the knowledge era. *The Leadership Quarterly, 18*(4), 298–318.

Wallis, H., & Robinson, A. (Eds.). (1987). *Cartographical innovations: An introductory handbook of mapping terms to 1900.* Tring, England: Map Collector.

Weick, K. (1979). *The social psychology of organizing.* New York, NY: McGraw-Hill.

Weick, K., & Bougon, M. (1986). Organizations as cognitive maps: Charting ways to success and failure. In H. Sims (Ed.), *The thinking organization* (pp. 102–135). San Francisco, CA: Jossey-Bass.

Wood, D. (1992). *The power of maps.* New York, NY: Guilford.

Yin, R. (2014). *Case study research: Design and methods.* Los Angeles, CA: Sage.

Youssef, C., & Luthans, F. (2007). Positive organizational behavior in the workplace: The impact of hope, optimism, and resilience. *Journal of Management, 33*(5), 774–800.

PART III

DEVELOPING WOMEN AS GLOBAL LEADERS

CHAPTER 8

ADVANCING WOMEN'S EXECUTIVE DEVELOPMENT

Effective Practices for the Design and Delivery of Global Women's Leadership Programs

Mary Ellen Kassotakis and Julnar B. Rizk

In the summer of 2013, the Women and Leadership Affinity Group of the International Leadership Association (ILA) hosted an inaugural conference at the Asilomar in Pacific Grove, California, where over 200 researchers, scholars, and practitioners gathered together to explore the state of women and leadership—past, present, and future. Presentations included topics about global women's leadership development as well as efforts toward the advancement of women in leadership in all sectors of society. Within hours of the start of the conference, a fierce and collective expression of frustration resounded from the majority of attendees regarding the progress still lacking for women reaching the upper echelons of all manner of industry, government, and society. Perhaps the recent calls for action that notables such as Anne-Marie Slaughter and Sheryl Sandberg had issued in the year leading up to this conference had fueled this urgency. Regardless, the frustration was clear and evident, and in the days following, we exchanged ideas with fellow attendees, ultimately giving voice to the resounding alarm that the time to excavate real answers was *now*.

As two practitioners and researchers in a large, global company, we are steeped in women's leadership topics, and we work to apply contemporary best practices in a large corporate environment for the benefit of our workplace. We are continually researching the literature of the past decade and examining key practices in leadership development for women that are offered by world-renowned universities and for-profit suppliers in order to remain abreast of our work efforts—to advance the development of future women leaders and better understand the most effective methods of achieving this goal through learning and development efforts.

We asked ourselves, "What is the impact of leadership programs that focus on women only?" In sheer numbers globally, women clearly continue to be underrepresented in senior levels of leadership. In our continual review of various academic and business sources, we remain curious about the recommendations being espoused by global industry thought leaders—academic institutions, commercial suppliers, and others. Following this women's conference, we were fueled by the collective alarm that more must be done. We embarked on a comprehensive review of current, global women-only leadership development programs in order to learn their approaches, compare them to our own, and then explore how these methods could augment current organizational solutions.

Based on our studies, we have drawn conclusions about what we believe to be the current implications and practices of leadership development with a women-only focus for global women leaders. For this chapter, we offer our recommendations for positioning leadership development as a solution for the organizational advancement and promotion of women, and we offer suggestions that should help produce superior programming for the cause of women's leadership development.

LEADERSHIP DEVELOPMENT: THE BEST SOLUTION FOR WOMEN'S ADVANCEMENT?

The training and development industry began in the United States in the 1960s, and it has now grown globally. In 2012 alone, the American Society for Training and Development (ASTD, 2014) estimated that approximately $164.2 billion was spent on employee training globally. According to Bersin by Deloitte (O'Leonard, 2014), U.S. companies spent more than $13 billion in leadership development in 2012 as well. Companies are investing more resources in developing leaders than ever before, with a 14% surge in spending in 2013 (ASTD, 2014). Of this total direct learning expenditure, 61% ($100.2 billion) was spent internally and the remainder was spent on external services (from suppliers and vendors), which accounted for 28% or $46 billion.

Why share these facts and figures? Clearly, teaching people "how to lead" is big money—for universities, corporations, third-party suppliers, and vendors. Per person, the cost of attending the leadership development programs of top business schools can reach up to $150,000. Executive MBA programs and education are top revenue generators for universities. Indeed, one perspective is that leadership development is an expensive undertaking wherein "armies of experts, including academics, coaches, and consultants ... make a living teaching leading" (Kellerman, 2012, p. 65). As the industry of leadership development has grown and proliferated, so too have programs focused on diverse audiences. In 2014, there were multiple programs offered to women-only audiences through top collegiate MBA executive education programs across the world, and several of these have been in operation for many years. Even for-profit conferences have generated moneymaking ventures by hosting women-only conferences (e.g., Professional Business Women's Conference, the California Women's Conference, Massachusetts Conference for Women). Given the attention and research regarding the gaps that continue to persist for women at the top levels of leadership—combined with an increased focus on executive leadership education efforts—we might assume that collectively, these efforts are improving the cause for the advancement of women to the most senior level positions.

This assumption, however, is incorrect. Both anecdotal and empirical evidence indicate this is a false perception of progress. Carter and Silva's (2010) "Delusions of Progress," published in the *Harvard Business Review*, noted that women represented roughly 3% of the Fortune 500 Chief Executive Officers and less than 15% of corporate executives worldwide. These low numbers are in great contrast to the fact that women make up approximately 40% of the global workforce with double-digit growth in several countries. Given the investment of a thriving and decades-old leadership development industry, it is difficult to understand why representation remains so low while such a large percentage of women comprise the global workforce and while organizations increase expenditures that are focused on women's development.

Several recent industry studies have set out to understand this perplexing problem and determine potential causes for the persistent underrepresentation of women at the top of corporate environments. Some studies have explored behavioral causes and examined whether a difference in male versus female characteristics of leadership may be a root cause for this persistent gap (Desvaux, Devillard, & Sancier-Sultan, 2011; Devillard, Sancier, Werner, Maller, & Kossoff, 2013; PDI Ninth House,

2012). Through interviews and other research, McKinsey & Company has, over several years, published a report series entitled *Women Matter* (e.g., Barsh, Craske, & Cranston, 2008; Desvaux, Devillard, & Sansier-Sultan, 2011; Devillard et al., 2013). These publications collectively showed that the corporate women they studied were results-focused, had a robust work ethic, and displayed both resilience and strong leadership—characteristics that are anecdotally attributed to masculine forms of leadership. From our own experience, these traits are also important in an era where employee engagement, customer focus, and change resiliency and competency are highly valued. Based on this study, women are delivering the right kind of leadership for these companies and their customers.

In 2012, a PDI Ninth House report entitled "Can Women Executives Break the Glass Ceiling?" confirmed the persistent gender gap between men and women in top leadership positions and set out to understand whether differences in competencies, motivations, and experiences were resulting in women not achieving roles with greater responsibilities. While the PDI Ninth House research revealed that women scored higher in overall competencies than men, the researchers found that men rank higher in the specific competencies often deemed critical at higher levels within an organization, including financial acumen and strategic thinking. In contrast, women ranked higher in competencies deemed "softer" such as team collaboration, prioritizing the customer, relationship building, pragmatic planning, and communication. Although these "soft" leadership competencies are important, capabilities such as financial acumen and strategic thinking are more concentrated at the top of an organization, and the researchers asserted these must be emphasized more in order to close the leadership gap between men and women at the top.

More recently, McKinsey & Company published the results of two different global surveys conducted in 2012–2013, which determined that, with regard to ambition, women respondents reported career ambitions that were just as high as their male counterparts (Devillard, Sancier-Sultan, Werner, Bannelier-Sudérie, & Kossoff, 2014). When it comes to doing what it takes to achieve those ambitions, women's intentions even exceeded those of their male peers. So why the continuing disparity? The McKinsey survey results also indicated that women are less confident they will be able to achieve their advancement goals, and that their ability to reach top management levels depended more on the collective corporate culture than on their own ambition or capability. Women surveyed reported an increased awareness of the challenges faced at work compared to the men surveyed, and in fact, male executives surveyed expressed skepticism that gender diversity issues still linger at all. Overcoming gender bias is especially trying when working to advance women in the historically male-dominated fields of science, technology, mathematics and medicine; in these disciplines, women are even more sparsely represented in leadership (Isaac, Kaatz, Lee, & Carnes, 2012).

In addition to examining the status and cause for the lack of women at the top of organizations, more attention in recent years has also focused on determining the status and trends of women holding seats on corporate boards. In 2013, the 20-first Consulting organization published *Global Gender Balance Scorecard: Where the World's Top Companies Stand*, based on the results of that organization's 4th annual survey (Wittenberg-Cox, 2013). This scorecard looked at a single measure of progress: the gender balance of the top 100 companies in the United States, Europe, and Asia. The results of this study indicated that, in 2013, both the United States and Europe were approximately equal in getting women on executive boards; however, Asia continues to lag behind. Interestingly, this survey's results indicated that the most gender-balanced companies spanned a wide range of industries—from retail to aerospace—implying that industry sector or even corporate culture was not a determining factor for the number of women on a corporate board. In fact, Wittenberg-Cox ultimately concluded, "Successful gender balancing depends primarily on where it sits on the CEO's list of priorities" (p. 1).

Despite substantial financial and time investments, current leadership development industry reports still point to a persistent gap in the advancement of women at top levels of organizations, and there is no clear statement of the root cause for this problem. Despite the concerted research toward examining this challenge, the metrics regarding the impact of efforts to remedy the problem are still lacking. Does this dearth of quantifiable metrics link to the fact that the pipeline for women in top leadership positions continues to move at a markedly sluggish speed, and by all accounts, remain shallow and unhealthy? It appears that people are flocking to the deployment of leadership development solutions to advance women without clearly understanding what specific problem they are addressing. From a learning and development perspective, it is troubling that the issues or problems that these programs are attempting to address remain unclear.

LOOKING FOR ANSWERS

As we examined the academic research, current market, and women-only leadership development solutions for clues, several questions guided our excavation:

- What best-practice recommendations does the academic research provide for the design and delivery of leadership development solutions targeted for only women?

- How well does women-only executive education (both academic and commercial) mirror the research with regard to program format and delivery methods that are both unique to women leaders as well as inclusive of methods that have been demonstrated to be relevant for both genders?
- What does research reveal about the root cause for underrepresentation of women at the top, and what does it reveal about solutions to this problem?

We believe that by answering these questions, clear practices that produce superior programming for the cause of women's leadership development can be identified.

Advocating for a Women-Only Approach in Leadership Development

In recent years, researchers and practitioners have identified the most current practices for adult learning theories and for developing leadership skills. Such practices include knowledge acquisition, self-awareness through 360-degree assessment feedback, feedback-intensive training, and skill-based training. Additional common practices include coaching and/or mentoring, virtual or social learning, pre- and posttraining work, formal project applications in home organizations, and the active engagement of the participant's manager (Beich, 2010; Knowles, Holton, & Swanson, 2011; McCall, 2010; Van Velsor, 1998; Van Velsor, McCauley, & Ruderman, 2010). Opportunities to ground development work in real experiences can have significant impact (McCall, 2004), yet significant barriers still exist with respect to effective mentoring and networking strategies (Linehan & Scullion, 2008). While these practices are for mixed gender groups, how have these practices been optimally applied as recommendations for women's-only solutions as well?

Hopkins, O'Neil, Passarelli, and Bilimoria (2008) proposed recommendations for an organizing framework of both formal and informal development practices for women's leadership development. These recommendations mirrored current practices for adult learning theory and leadership development for both genders, as noted earlier. The categories included assessment, training and development, coaching, mentoring, networking, experiential learning through "stretch" job assignments, action-learning projects, and career learning. These are all practices that many large for-profit organizations currently utilize in designing, developing, and deploying learning solutions and mesh with our own personal experiences in U.S. and global corporations.

Similarly, researchers Ely, Ibarra, and Kolb (2011) considered and categorized principles for approaching leadership development programs targeted for women, and they discussed three principles: "situate topics and tools in an analysis of second-generation gender bias," "create a holding environment to support women's identity work," and "anchor participants on their leadership purpose" (p. 486). Grounded in theories of both gender and leadership, they suggest a framework that also includes components like 360 assessments, feedback, coaching, and the development of leadership networks. They go further to highlight the importance of educating women leaders about institutional bias, particularly of the kinds of bias that are more subtle and cultural than blatant sexual discrimination. Moreover, their strong advocacy of women-only environments advocates for the importance of how these environments, often novel contexts for global women leaders, foster learning by placing women in a majority position compared to the male-dominated, more familiar environments.

In another study, a qualitative examination of leadership development initiatives for women, Debebe (2009) specifically explored the critical role of environment in learning and whether transformational learning and the nature of change might take place in a women-only classroom. Through observation and examination of a multistage framework that emphasized self-awareness and personal perspective change, Debebe concluded that transformational learning can, indeed, take place in the context of leadership development training and that internal change is key to fostering personal leadership growth for women. Debebe (2011) examined how the integration of key elements in a program with women-only participants and instructors created safety for participants and yielded participant willingness to break comfortable patterns. Debebe positioned individual change through transformational learning with a core assumption "that deep individual change is necessary for fundamental organization change" (p. 680).

In Debebe's (2011) qualitative study, she proposed an analytical framework to expand the transformational learning process. The focus was on all-women learners that included gender-sensitive pedagogical practices to create a sense of safety. All aspects of the learning environment were designed to affirm women's experiences and values—providing the freedom to talk about gender-related topics and listen carefully to the experiences of others, encouraging risk-taking and the willingness to speak up, and enabling participants to express their views confidently without fear of rejection. Further, Debebe argued,

> The presence of all-women learners and the use of gender-sensitive teaching and learning practices suggest that the opportunity to learn with women was critical in making participants feel that their experiences were valid and important. They immediately recognized their shared experiences, and there was an eagerness to share one's own experience but also to learn from

others. Furthermore, the egalitarian ethic established made participants feel safe to share their perspectives. Many said that they could not have imagined themselves opening up as they did had they been in a mixed-gender environment. (p. 703)

The study concluded that an environment for transformational learning was created through the coalescing of two primary elements: a women-only learning environment, and the use of gender-sensitive teaching and learning methodologies; thus, it produced favorable results for transformational learning. Debebe (2011) concluded that "for many women, being in an all-female environment is both rare and affirming, immediately putting them at ease" (p. 687).

Clarke (2011) affirmed the validity of a women-only learning environment. She was curious to learn how women might advance their careers through leadership development programs. The findings indicated that women-only development programs "provide a safe and supportive environment for improving self-confidence, learning new skills and learning from the experiences of successful role models" (p. 498). These programs help build social capital in organizations via networking and mentoring. Moreover, women-only development programs are uniquely suitable to helping participants learn new skills, to learn from others, and to develop enhanced self-confidence. In supportive women-only environments, the viewpoints of women are heard and not overshadowed by men.

As practitioners and developers of leadership development solutions for both genders, we wonder whether the absence of men in programs like the aforementioned prevent women from practicing new skills in a realistic environment that correlates more readily with their home organizations. Debebe (2011) acknowledged this challenge for women learners when they return to a work environment that has not changed; they return to an environment that may not be supportive of their growth as leaders. She recommended ways to mitigate these challenges that included (a) creating post-training opportunities for workshop participants to explicitly articulate their leadership dilemmas and use fellow workshop participants and coaches to resolve identified dilemmas, and (b) identifying methods to enable women learners to directly link their personal insights from the workshop to their work environments.

Developing Women Leaders in Real-World Contexts

The studies cited so far refer to learning environments that are largely designed and delivered in a face-to-face format, and, as will be later discussed, the current market women-only programs we examined for this chapter indeed reflect this in-person delivery format. Given the real-world complexity of global corporate environments and how learning will effectively translate to these work environments, we question whether learning programs always need to be done in person in order to be effective. What about remote, virtual development? Do these types of environments yield the same efficacies?

Garcea, Linley, Mazurkiewicz, and Bailey (2012) conducted a pilot case study at Thomson-Reuters (a multinational media and information firm) that leveraged a strengths-based development approach with emerging female talent and maximized the use of virtual technology for the delivery of this program. Globally, the company has a commitment to develop leaders who have a global mindset and can effectively leverage technology to communicate and influence virtually. Researchers concluded that, in addition to the strengths-awareness approach having positive impacts on participants' achieving their goals and abilities to influence, the training delivered virtually was as effective a format as for those who attended in-person.

This has important implications for global organizations in general. That is, in working virtually, it is helpful for people to understand how to influence in contexts when English is a second language. By helping participants understand their strengths, they can become more aware of the use of language and subtle cues that can positively increase their personal impact. Additionally, women can become savvier about cultural differences and identify ways to use their strengths to influence powerfully. In this manner, they can avoid major pitfalls and hopefully sidestep the common mistakes by embedding real work in leadership development efforts.

We cannot overemphasize the concept of embedding real work in leadership development efforts and translating the application of learning to real-world, global corporate environments. Consultant practitioners at McKinsey & Company echoed this in their article entitled "Why Leadership Development Programs Fail" (Gurdjian, Halbeisen, & Lane, 2014). The authors identified four common mistakes along with suggestions to overcome these mistakes, and one of these was "overlooking context" (p. 2). As a component to successful leadership, *context* of the organizational environment is critical, and a one-size-fits-all approach to developing a set of leadership skills or styles usually fails to translate to the real-world setting to which the program participant must ultimately return. Gurdjian et al. suggested incorporating real, on-the-job projects targeting a desired business impact and concurrently improving learning, and they further stated outright that the question "what, precisely, is the program for?" (p. 2) must be asked in order to directly understand the organizational context for which the leaders are being prepared.

A Survey Review of Women-Only Executive Education Programs

With this backdrop of academic and industry research, we set out to understand the key attributes of current leadership development programs targeted for women's executive education. Our hope was that they would mirror the studies we examined and demonstrate the efficacy in advancing the cause for professional women. In the pursuit to identify the best practices for the development of current and future women leaders and further understand what evidence-based practices in organizational learning are most relevant to women, we selected and analyzed 21 different women's leadership development multiday programs targeting corporate women leader audiences across the globe.

Selections of the programs were made using industry lists of top-rated global business schools, for example, *US News & World Report* (2014) and the *Financial Times* (2014), drawing upon firsthand experiences of the authors and considering program reputation within the learning and development field. The programs included in this dataset (see Table 8.1) included executive education programs designed and delivered by business schools in the United States and abroad, as well as a select handful of commercial leadership development suppliers which have further specialized in the delivery of women-only leadership development programs. We reviewed each of the programs' online and downloadable marketing materials stating program objectives, outcomes, and value proposition for their advertised programs, and gathered information with regard to three specific criteria: (a) participant audience targets with regard to organizational role, (b) program delivery and format elements leveraged, and (c) the most commonly taught topics.

Each of the program's marketing materials addressed a broader purpose of helping women to advance their careers as leaders within corporate environments, often quoting current industry statistics of the number of women at the highest levels in an organization and lamenting the reality of women representing a minority within the leadership of Fortune 500 companies. Across all the programs we studied, we noticed that they all included the intent to assist current corporate women leaders gain ground and successfully confront the pervasive "glass-ceiling" challenges that most female corporate leaders face within their organizations.

With regard to participant audiences that the leadership development programs targeted, we found that the majority of the programs targeted participant audiences with the organizational functional roles of manager and senior manager, as well as director and senior director functional roles. It is important to keep in mind that the topic of senior titles is complex because titles are subjective and frequently impacted by the size of an organization in addition to cultural practices. Comparatively, fewer programs targeted participants at the vice president (and above) levels within their organizations with an even smaller minority of programs focused on women who are ready and eligible for preparation to be hired for a corporate board role (see Table 8.2).

Table 8.1. Executive Education Programs Reviewed

U.S. Business Schools	Non-U.S. Business Schools	Commercial Vendors
Bentley University (Center For Women in Business)	CEIBS (China Europe International Business School)	Center for Creative Leadership (CCL)
Carnegie Mellon (Heinz Academy)	IMD in Switzerland (Lausanne)	International Women's Forum (IWF)
Dartmouth (Tuck)	Oxford SAID Business School	Linkage, Inc.
George Washington School of Business	University of Hong Kong	Women Unlimited Inc.
Harvard University		
Northwestern (Kellogg)		
Simmons College		
Smith College		
Stanford University		
UC Berkeley (Haas)		
UCLA (Anderson)		
UNC Chapel Hill (Kenan Flagler)		
U of New Hampshire (Pauls College)		

Table 8.2. Program-Identified Functional Levels of Target Audiences

Targeted Functional Level	% of Data Set
Manager, senior manager	52%
Director, senior director	57%
Vice president and above	43%
Corporate board preparation	10%

Upon examining the delivery format elements that each program advertised in their marketing, we discovered that all the programs leveraged faculty lectures, faculty instruction, and panels that included faculty and guest executives. A large majority (86%) of the programs also used interactive, break-out session formats to facilitate skill-building and more experiential forms of learning. In contrast, less than half of the programs used a 360 assessment instrument to establish performance and leadership efficacy baselines for each of the participants prior to the training programs or coaching methodologies as tools for learning before, during, and/or after the program. Less than half of the programs also marketed their programs' use of action and development planning processes once the participant returned to their home organization to capitalize on additional skill-building opportunities and practically apply the learning gained from the program (see Table 8.3).

Table 8.3. Delivery and Format Commonalities

Type of Delivery Format	% of Total Data Set
Faculty instruction/lectures/panels	100%
Interactive, break-out sessions	86%
360 assessment instrument	48%
Coaching (pre, during, or post)	48%
Action and development planning	43%
Peer coaching/mentoring	38%
Multiple month duration of the program	33%
Virtual, social learning, and pre/post work	14%
Formal project	5%
Active engagement of participant's manager	5%

Interestingly, as we further examined the delivery formats utilized by these programs, we calculated that approximately 40% or less of the programs reviewed actually utilized key learning approaches that have been well established within the corporate learning and development industry. As noted earlier, these approaches included methodologies such as peer coaching and/or mentoring, virtual or social learning, pre- and posttraining work, formal project applications in home organizations, and the active engagement of the participant's manager. In fact, only 33% of the programs offered options for learning over a multiple-month time frame; instead, the average duration of the programs was 3 to 5 days in length.

Finally, we examined the topics and descriptions that were noted in the programs' marketing collateral—looking for both commonalities and distinctions among the programs. This is where we discovered the most variability among the 21 programs examined (see Table 8.4):

- 67% of the program topics included topics such as developing influence and power as a leader, the management of politics and stakeholders within a corporate environment, the effective building of relationships, and leveraging influence and power with stakeholders as an effective leader.
- 62% of programs included instruction and activities exploring one's authenticity in a leadership context as well as clarifying one's leadership style and values that contribute to an individual's leadership approach.
- 52% of programs instructed on the topic of negotiation emphasizing gender perspectives with this capability; 52% of programs also reviewed the topic of leveraging social networks for building one's leadership capital and offered best practices and opportunities for networking.
- 48% of programs leveraged topics in gender psychology and how unconscious bias affects the success and advancement of women leaders within the corporate environment; 48% of programs also included instruction and skill-building on developing communication capabilities as an effective leader.
- 43% provided instructional opportunities for exploring the topic of emotional intelligence and awareness, and increasing the interpersonal skills to become a more effective leader; 43% of programs also included the topic of strategy and strategic thinking as part of their programs.

Table 8.4. Program Topic Commonalities

Leadership Development Topic	% of Total Data Set
Influence and power, politics management, stakeholder management and relationship building	67%
Authenticity, leadership style, values leadership	62%
Negotiation	52%
Networking, social networks	52%

(Table continues on next page)

Table 8.4. (Continued)

Leadership Development Topic	% of Total Data Set
Gender psychology, unconscious bias	48%
Leadership communication	48%
Emotional intelligence/awareness, interpersonal skills	43%
Strategy, strategic thinking	43%
Assertiveness and self-confidence, executive presence, presentation skills	33%
Giving feedback, coaching, mentoring, leading teams, people development	33%
Innovation management, product development, entrepreneurship	24%
Leadership vision development	24%
Change management	19%
Conflict management	19%
Career management and advancement	14%
Corporate board preparation (in noncorporate board prep programs)	14%
Global corporate finance	14%
Global leadership, leading multicultural teams	14%
Wellness, work-life balance	14%

When examining topics that were not broadly used or common among the topics, we identified several topics that are commonly included with gender-inclusive corporate leadership development programs. We found that less than 40% of the programs leveraged the following topics: self-confidence and executive presence; the leadership skills of coaching, mentoring, and the giving of feedback; leading teams and developing people; and the development of a personal vision for leadership.

DISCUSSION AND RECOMMENDATIONS

With all the attention in the media about the dearth of women in leadership positions, organizations have increasingly focused on doing what they believe are the best cost-effective measures to develop the leadership skills of women with an often-stated intention to increase the number of women in leadership positions. Development programs are big business, and organizations are hungry and eager to demonstrate impact to their employees and stakeholders. And these companies employ the current best practices in learning methodologies for general development programs and apply them to women-only programs.

The pace of this necessary shift, however, is glacial, and the question of why remains unanswered despite our examination of literature and reputable programs. How can we understand the initiating cause of this dilemma? Whether the root of the problem is due to behavioral styles of leadership, gaps in specific leadership competencies or capabilities, ambition and motivation, influence of the corporate culture, or even the agenda and whims of an organization's current CEO, further research is needed for a clear understanding of the cause. Until then, understanding the persistent gap still appears fleeting. Moving from entry-level to senior-level positions within large organizations teems with complexities, and there are a multitude of factors that influence this successful advancement (e.g., innate talent, individual motivation, luck, work and nonwork issues).

With the specific focus on assisting women's advancement success, women-only leadership development programs have proven to be a significant part of this career progression landscape, and one of many possible strategies for addressing the gender imbalance in organizations. We believe that a broad range of strategies and support structures that provide new ways of thinking about work and career progression are key for all employees.

Research of the past decade indicates that the organizations that have invested in women-only development programs are benefiting from this strategy and continue to leverage it as a solution. Yet to date, much of the research is qualitative in nature—for example, anecdotal testimonials about success collected from participants in these kinds of learning programs. Once quantitative analyses become more commonly implemented and available, our hope is that these programs will demonstrate a measurable, replicable impact, and we might even see a more visible move to parity in senior positions across organizations worldwide. Until we arrive at that ideal state, however, there are opportunities for change in this industry.

Defining the Problem and Designing to Solve This Problem

Research results and industry reports are slow to define a clear and well-defined problem statement for why women continue to be underrepresented, and with no central problem defined, a focused design framework for solving the problem has yet to be fully developed and executed. This lack was reinforced by our review of leading executive education programs, both commercial and academic, where we found neither of these key elements clearly articulated in the objectives and outcomes of a given program. What problems do the current leadership development program curriculums for women leaders aim to solve? It would appear that the deficit is in women's ability to navigate organizational environments powerfully and influentially, based on the high percentage (67%) of programs that emphasized topics such as influence and power, managing politics and stakeholders, and building relationships.

As learning and development practitioners, we highly recommend that organizations avoid the temptation to create a one-size-fits-all approach, and instead differentiate the learning product to a target need and niche. We also recommend using an approach of due diligence to research, define, and clearly articulate what a program is addressing and how success will be measured. Only then will organizations successfully create programs based on a framework of sound design that clearly and directly addresses the defined problem.

Measuring Program Efficacy

A goal for most learning development operations is to measure the effectiveness of these efforts. This is challenging to accomplish with scientific validity; however, there are advocates for return-on-investment studies (Brinkerhoff, 2006; Kirkpatrick, 2005; Phillips, 2012). Usually, there are often evaluations that follow the completion of the program, but most of these focus on basic reaction-level forms and surveys; that is, how well the participants liked or enjoyed the program. Training designers must do more than implement simple reaction-type evaluations. They must go further to garner the support and sponsorship for longitudinal studies in order to measure a leadership development program's observable impacts to the business.

We identified very few organizations that could demonstrate empirical evidence about the efficacy of their women-only leadership development programs. Perhaps this comes as no surprise: without a clear problem statement, how can practitioners determine what can be measured? We did not uncover any reported quantifiable evidence with program materials reviewed that would speak to the efficacy of the training advertised or even how the training would potentially be applied within the home organization in a quantifiable way (with a return on investment *and* value). Nor did we develop an understanding of how the program designers could effectively reproduce results, "course correct" in real time, and scale a working solution for a broader impact. It was more the exception than the rule that programs incorporated robust surveying tools, which involved a participant's manager or direct reports *following* the training.

Recalling the Gurdjian et al. (2014) article, "Why Leadership Development Programs Fail," the failure to measure results was another of the four mistakes they cited for why programs fail to meet expected outcomes. The caution noted is that if participant feedback is the only measure of efficacy, then the danger for program designers is to lean toward pleasing participants more than challenging them. The authors offered several suggestions for measuring efficacy such as assessing the extent of behavioral change with a 360 degree feedback tool administered both before the program and then again 6 to 12 months later. They also suggested monitoring the participants' career development and movement following the learning program, and in situations where training is tied to real-world projects within the home organization, monitoring business impact results.

With a program framework of sound design in place, then the task of measuring efficacy becomes solvable, and we recommend that at that point, both a quantitative and qualitative measurement system be put in place and reported along with program goals and objectives.

Delivery of Learning and a Lack of Application

We found that the vast number of learning programs have design formats that are rather traditional in their learning approach. By and large, they are *not* incorporating practices such as stretch assignments, posttraining projects, or even potentials for a job rotation in order to incorporate an application of the learning to the home organization (again, rare in most cases with the programs reviewed). We found a lack of virtual learning approaches that potentially span multiple months or the year following the training and encompass a larger spectrum of participant learning styles than face-to-face formats, listening to a lecture, or doing interactive activities in a limited multiple-day format. The lack of these less-traditional approaches left us wondering again about efficacy and how benefits were being measured after the attendance of a one-time, 3-to-5-day training program. As Garcea et al. (2012) concluded, in-person programs were as effective for participants who attended training virtually; it would appear that designers of these programs are missing some key opportunities for the application of learning after the completion of a program.

For those who embark on creating impactful women-focused leadership development training, we stress the importance of incorporating learning experiences that closely link the leadership development efforts to real-world, on-the-job projects that can have a visible business impact and concurrently, improve learning. Special-project assignments or job-rotation assignments (or both) can provide significant opportunities to amplify personal development. Instructional designers can embed experiential, action learning for the participants, and both managers and human resources professionals can be enrolled to identify and define an application project following a leadership development program.

When these assignments are a "stretch" for the individual pursuing new capabilities and skills, the learning gained is often impactful. Participants can apply the insightful reflection and learning epiphanies from an off-site learning experience and further validate and align them with the real work back at their home organizations. Furthermore, when such opportunities also include a high level of visibility with senior leaders, women in these situations gain greater opportunities to be highlighted within a corporate environment.

The Target Audiences

The majority of the programs reviewed targeted corporate leaders that were midcareer, and we found this strategy consistent with what the research indicates about the importance of building a "pipeline" of future, potential women leaders. In addition to enhancing financial results for an organization (Desvaux et al., 2011), the increase of women in leadership positions does enable organizations to tap into a larger, diverse pool of talent and thus secure the best people to fill leadership positions. In turn, these leaders serve as role models for younger, high-potential women and ultimately serve as a solid lure to potential employees. Research results imply the importance of having a plan that outlines how organizations can develop and retain their female talent at different levels.

In contrast, examining the target audiences identified revealed a lack of programs for the most senior level audiences of women leaders. Granted, a few options exist, and we reviewed select programs that are focused on preparing women for corporate board work. These are certainly excellent options for the most senior of women often at the height of their careers. However, these are a small minority of programs, and our analysis indicated that there are still fewer programs targeting the highest levels of corporate women leaders in the overall dataset.

We find this curious given collectively stated objectives to increase women leadership at the top of organizations. Does this lack of targeting development for the most senior level of women result because there are still small numbers of them and therefore the customer market is not a large one? Could this reflect that a women-only approach for these senior levels of women is perhaps *not* the most effective leadership development intervention to leverage? If so, are there other best practices with regard to leadership development for women at the highest levels of organizations not housed in a women-only leadership development approach? These are questions still to examine and perhaps a place for future research.

Topics and Content

Regardless of the identified target audiences, we did find it refreshing that, across the board, the programs examined did *not* appear to be attempting to duplicate the typical topics and competency-focused learning often included in gender-neutral leadership development programs that are designed in-house by organizations' learning and development teams. This would have been both redundant and would have lacked the advantage of an organization's institutional knowledge and context that these skill-building trainings require.

Given the ongoing investments in industry and in academic research to increase the numbers of women in senior leadership roles (i.e., to find advantageous methods that will advance women in their careers all the way to the coveted CEO position), it behooves the sponsors, designers, and implementers of women-only programs to stay abreast of and align with what researchers are currently determining in order to hone in on key success factors that these programs can address with their learning solutions.

Surprisingly, less than half of the current women-only programs we reviewed (48%) included the teaching of topics that included unconscious bias, gender bias, and the recognition of institutional barriers that prevent women from advancing in their careers. Instead, the lack of leadership capability on the part of women appeared to be at the core of the *implied* problem for most of these programs examined. Eagly and Carli's (2007) *Through the Labyrinth: How Women Become Leaders* noted that as women advance into leadership roles, they are expected to exhibit feminine behaviors; however, when they exhibit these behaviors, they risk being regarded as not being suited for leadership positions. They experience pressure to adapt to masculine behaviors and violate gender-role expectations. Sheryl Sandberg (2013) described this in her book *Lean In*, where she noted that women at more senior levels were not as likable. She said, "Success and likability are positively correlated for men and negatively correlated for women" (p. 40). The higher on the corporate ladder a woman climbs, the less likeable she is perceived to be. In the case of a man, the opposite holds true, and Sandberg presents substantial data to support these findings.

An important first step for women leaders is to become aware of cultural pressures and norms that impact their professional relationships, including hidden and overt behaviors. A key challenge is to actually tease out factors that influence "likeability" because of deep cultural mores and norms. How can designers of learning programs adopt learning methodologies that can be deployed in a gender-sensitive manner? And, if designed well, will this actually increase the number of qualified women in senior positions?

The Women-Only Approach

Despite the studies in favor of women-only programs, there are contrarian points of view (Kellerman, 2013; Vinnicombe & Singh, 2003; Wittenberg-Cox, 2013). Many argue that these kinds of learning programs still take an approach that could be reasoned as "fixing women," solving "the woman's problem" by providing women with even more training, and focusing these change efforts on women *instead* of creating solutions to effect deep cultural and institutional change. Given this either/or approach, we might certainly agree particularly if corporate interventions provide no other recognition of institutional barriers or persistent cultural biases that can often stand in the way of women's advancement.

In the arena of women-only development programs, however, the creation of holistic approaches toward leadership development has helped to create safe learning environments (Debebe, 2011; Ely et al., 2011). We found general support for a women-only approach and the benefit for participants of these programs in their ability to share experiences and learn from others at similar junctures in their careers within a safe, confidential environment. Gender-specific learning environments where women feel "safe" encouraged women to more fully and authentically embrace their personal learning experiences. For this reason, we advocate that at any stage of a career—midlevel to senior—a women-only leadership development program is a great choice, and it can (and perhaps *should*) be an addition to learning programs where the genders are mixed and balanced.

Such holistic practices include attention not only to pedagogy, values, norms, and affirmations, but also content. Our sincere hope is that with the continuation of women-only program formats, we will observe an increase in the number of programs discussing institutional barriers and topics like unconscious and gender bias. With careful instructional design, such programs could provide participants with the ability to recognize when these factors are at play and help to raise awareness of the unconscious factors that may prevent achievement of aspirational career goals. Furthermore, programs such as these can provide strategies to overcome the detrimental effects of institutional bias and empower women to positively impact their career advancement with these insights.

OUR CALL TO ACTION

Our firm conclusion for leadership development programs is that there is a place for mixed gender *and* women-only programs. Practitioners should avoid the temptation to create a one-size-fits-all approach for leadership development programs and instead differentiate the learning product to a target need and niche. We recommend researching, defining, and articulating the challenges that a program is addressing, and create programs based on well-designed frameworks that directly solve those challenges identified. Once programs like these are in place, then the task of measuring efficacy—quantitatively and qualitatively—is solvable, and results can then be reported along with program goals and objectives.

Second, we stress the importance of incorporating learning experiences that link leadership development to actual work projects; that is, work projects that are intended to improve learning and effect business impact. Additionally, we believe the best practices for leadership development include experiential learning (e.g., developmental job assignments and action learning projects) as well as "stretch" assignments and job rotations. For those who aspire to high visibility and/or international assignments, these experiences are vital. Participants can be encouraged to apply the learning so that insightful reflection and learning epiphanies from an off-site learning experience are further validated and aligned with the real work back at their home organizations.

Third, women-only development programs can be one key strategy in growing core talent, and we believe that a systems approach with a broad range of strategies and support structures can provide new ways of thinking about work. Career progression and opportunities are key for all employees globally. Once development opportunities become more available and accessible, quantitative and qualitative studies can be implemented to study impact. We might even see a more visible move to parity in senior positions across organizations worldwide.

In many countries, women have been entering the workforce in the same numbers as men, yet they have not attained similar parity in leadership roles. Indeed, women are greatly underrepresented in senior positions in almost all industries. The gap is even greater for women of racial minorities. In the face of laws that have been introduced to prevent discrimination, this is not only ironic but incredibly discouraging. Filling talent pipelines of qualified people, irrespective of gender and race, is woefully lacking.

While women continue to outpace men in educational achievement, we have ceased making real progress at the top. Clearly, something else is going on. The barriers and inhibitors to women's advancement are more complex than what appears on the surface. We must all continue to deconstruct this complexity in order to clearly define the root causes, and additional research is still needed on topics that are unique to women's issues in the workplace.

Furthermore, our male leaders, colleagues, and partners can equally play crucial roles in this cause of advancing women in leadership by becoming effective gender allies in the quest for what is just. As practitioners dedicated to this cause, our final call to action is to explore not just what has been done, but also what is possible—and right—and to go to work on implementing measures to address this situation.

REFERENCES

American Society of Training and Development (ASTD). (2014). 2013 state of the industry. *American Society of Training and Development*. Retrieved from http://www.astd.org/Professional-Resources/State-Of-The-Industry-Report

Barsh, J., Craske, R., & Cranston, S. (2008, September). Centered leadership: How talented women thrive. *McKinsey & Company*. Retrieved from http://www.mckinsey.com/insights/leading_in_the_21st_century/centered_leadership_how_talented_women_thrive

Beich, E. (Ed.). (2010). *The ASTD leadership handbook*. Washington, DC: ASTD.

Brinkerhoff, R. O. (2006). *Telling training's story: Evaluation made easy, credible and effective*. San Francisco, CA: Berrett-Koehler.

Carter, N. M., & Silva, C. (2010). Women in management: Delusions of progress. *Harvard Business Review, 88*(3), 19–21.

Clarke, M. (2011). Advancing women's careers through leadership development programs. *Employee Relations, 33*(5), 498–515. doi:101108/01-425451111153871

Debebe, G. (2009). Transformational learning in women's leadership development training. *Advancing Women in Leadership, 29*(7), 1–12.

Debebe, G. (2011). Creating a safe environment for women's leadership transformation. *Journal of Management Education, 35*(5), 679–712. doi:10.1177/1052563910397501

Desvaux, G., Devillard, S., & Sancier-Sultan, S. (2011). Women at the top of corporations: Making it happen. *McKinsey & Company*. Retrieved from http://www.asx.com.au/documents/media/2010_mckinsey_co_women_matter.pdf

Devillard, S., Sancier, S., Werner, C., Maller, I., & Kossoff, C. (2013). Gender diversity in top management: Moving corporate culture, moving boundaries. *McKinsey & Company*. Retrieved from http://www.mckinsey.de/sites/mck_files/files/womenmatter_13.pdf

Devillard, S., Sancier-Sultan, S., Werner, C., Bannelier-Sudérie, T., & Kossoff, C. (2014). Moving mind-sets on gender diversity: McKinsey global survey results. *McKinsey & Company*. Retrieved from http://www.mckinsey.com/insights/organization/moving_mind-sets_on_gender_diversity_mckinsey_global_survey_results

Eagly, A. H., & Carli, L. C. (2007). *Through the labyrinth: The truth about how women become leaders*. Boston, MA: Harvard Business School Press.

Ely, R. J., Ibarra, H., & Kolb, D. M. (2011). Taking gender into account: Theory and design for women's leadership development programs. *Academy of Management Learning & Education, 10*(3), 474–493.

Financial Times LTD. (2014). Global MBA ranking 2013. *FT.com*. Retrieved from http://rankings.ft.com/businessschoolrankings/global-mba-ranking-2013

Garcea, N., Linley, A., Mazurkiewicz, K., & Bailey, T. (2012). Future female talent development. *Strategic HR Review, 11*(4), 199–204.

Gurdjian, P., Halbeisen, T., & Lane, K. (2014, January). Why leadership-development programs fail. *McKinsey Quarterly*. Retrieved from http://www.mckinsey.com/insights/leading_in_the_21st_century/why_leadership-development_programs_fail

Hopkins, M. M., O'Neil, D., Passarelli, A., & Bilimoria, D. (2008). Women's leadership development: Strategic practices for women in organizations. *Consulting Psychology Journal: Practice and Research, 60*(4), 348–365.

Isaac, C., Kaatz, A., Lee, B., & Carnes, M. (2012). An educational intervention designed to increase women's leadership self-efficacy. *CBE—Life Sciences Education, 11*(3), 307–322. The American Society for Cell Biology.

Kellerman, B. (2012). *The end of leadership*. New York, NY: Harper.

Kellerman, B. (2013). Leading questions: The end of leadership—Redux. *Leadership, 9*(1), 135–139. doi:10.1177/1742715012455132

Kirkpatrick, D. L., & Kirkpatrick, J. D. (2005). *Transferring learning to behavior: Using the four levels to improve performance*. San Francisco, CA: Berrett-Koehler.

Knowles, M. S., Holton, E. F., & Swanson, R. A. (2011). *The adult learner* (7th ed). Oxford, England: Elsevier.

Linehan, M., & Scullion, H. (2008). The development of female global managers: The role of mentoring and networking. *Journal of Business Ethics, 83*(1), 29–40. doi:10.1007/s10551-007-9657-0

McCall, M. W. (2004). Leadership development through experience. *Academy of Management Executive, 18*(3), 127–130.

McCall, M. W. (2010). Recasting leadership development. *Industrial & Organizational Psychology, 3*(1), 3-19. doi:10.1111/j.1754-9434.2009.01189.x

O'Leonard, K. (2012, January 16). The corporate learning factbook 2012: Benchmarks, trends and analysis of the U.S. training market. *Bersin by Deloitte*. Retrieved from http://www.bersin.com/practice/Detail.aspx?id=15131

PDI Ninth House. (2012). Can women executives break the glass ceiling? Minneapolis, MN: *Personnel Decisions International Corporation*. Retrieved from http://infokf.kornferry.com/rs/korn_ferry/images/CanWomenExecBreakGlassCeiling.pdf

Phillips, J. (2012). *Return on investment in training and performance improvement programs* (2nd ed.). Burlington, MA: Butterworth-Heinemann.

Sandberg, S. (2013). *Lean in: Women, work and the will to lead*. New York, NY: Knopf.

US News & World Report. (2014). *Best business schools*. Retrieved from http://grad-schools.usnews.rankingsandreviews.com/best-graduate-schools/top-business-schools/mba-rankings

Van Velsor, E. (1998). Assessing the impact of development experiences. In E. Van Velsor (Ed.), *Assessing the impact of development experiences* (pp. 262–288). San Francisco, CA: Jossey-Bass.

Van Velsor, E., McCauley, C., & Ruderman, M. N. (2010). *Center for Creative Leadership handbook of leadership development* (3rd ed.). San Francisco, CA: Jossey-Bass.

Vinnicombe, S., & Singh, V. (2003). Women-only management training: An essential part of women's leadership development. *Journal of Change Management, 3*(4), 294–306.

Wittenberg-Cox, A. (2013). Global gender balance scorecard: Where the world's top companies stand. *20-first Consulting*. Retrieved from http://www.fccihk.com/files/dpt_image/5_committees/WOB/global_gender_balance_scorecard_2013_1%20%281%29.pdf

CHAPTER 9

A MASTER'S DEGREE IN GLOBAL LEADERSHIP

A Story of Development

Wendy E. Rowe, Cheryl Heykoop, and Catherine Etmanski

Women are increasingly an active force in the global context, working to bring improved dignity, well-being, living conditions, education, and economic prosperity to marginalized peoples in nations across the globe (Adler, 1997, 2007; Kellerman & Rhode, 2007). Many women have achieved prominence and are truly remarkable in terms of who they are and what they have achieved (Bengtsson, 2012; Paludi & Coates, 2011; Rehn & Sirleaf, 2002). They exhibit leadership skills and capacities of high intelligence, systems thinking, strategic analysis, relational perspectives, and intercultural capabilities while often maintaining compassion, sensitivity, and collaborative spirit. Many biographies and studies have documented how women have emerged as leaders, as well as their approach to leadership (Bengtsson, 2012; Fiorina, 2006; Ngunjiri, 2010; Sandberg, 2013; Sirleaf, 2010). These stories describe journeys of tremendous struggle to access educational opportunity. Some women describe challenges learning in a formal education system that is heavily weighted to male preference, patriarchal philosophies, and pedagogical models that reinforce hierarchical perspectives and management practices (Rhode & Kellerman, 2007; Smith, 1997).

Other authors note the masculine orientation of values and underlying assumptions in many management and leadership education programs (e.g., the MBA) (Simpson & Ituma, 2009; Smith, 1997), often biased against success for women as managers and leaders. Ely, Ibarra, and Kolb (2011) stated, "Educators lack a coherent, theoretically based and actionable framework for designing and delivering leadership programs for women" (p. 474), and they observed many programs adopt an "add-women-and-stir" approach (delivering the same programs to women that they deliver to men) or "fix the women" approach (endeavoring to teach women the same skills that males are taught on how to compete in a world still largely dominated by men). Ely et al. (2011) argued that leadership education for women needs to be oriented to identity formation and anchoring action to purpose as a leader. Further, this approach should align feminist relational values, perspectives, and communication skills with leadership purpose and strategies.

Consistent with the above perspective, we—a team of three women composed of two core faculty members in the School of Leadership Studies at Royal Roads University (RRU) and a scholar-practitioner with the International Institute for Child Rights and Development (IICRD)[1]—argue for an alternative educational program for women (and also men) who lead in the global context. We visualize a program that embraces knowledge (the mind), values (the heart), and actions (the hands) that are purposeful and focused on global issues. Drawing from our own unique and diverse backgrounds, perspectives, experiences, disciplines, and generations, we believe an approach to global leadership should include these key elements: (a) be intentionally grounded in understanding the global and local context and their intersection; (b) imbibe cultural awareness, relational capabilities, and collaborative practice; (c) apply an intersectional lens to break down structures and practices of inequality; and (d) mindfully act to support positive social change.

Additionally, we take the stance that an educational program suitable for female leaders (and in our minds also for male leaders) should be continually grounded in understanding the cultural context. Global leadership is a cultural activity "suffused with values, beliefs, language, rituals and artefacts" (Jackson & Parry, 2011, p. 71). All human beings are influenced by the cultural values, beliefs, and traditions of their families of origin, sociogeographical community, peer group, educational environment, and workplace, as well as by life experiences of joy or challenge. These factors shape cultural identity, which is further enhanced by intersecting elements like ethnicity, gender, age, generation, socioeconomic class, nationality, political or religious affiliation, (dis)ability, and sexual orientation (Gopaldas, 2013). As such, today's global leaders need to be aware of their own cultural values and orientations as well as work in ways that recognize the diversity of other people's complex cultural backgrounds. In keeping with current scholarship on gender and identity, to address complex challenges facing the world today, global leaders must navigate intersectionality—"the interactivity of social identity structures such as race, class, and gender in fostering life experiences, especially experiences of privilege and oppression" (Gopaldas, 2013, p. 90). These perspectives have informed the development of the new master's degree in global leadership program described in this chapter.

To develop the program, we adopted a collaborative development approach rather than falling into the trap of program development processes in a university environment similar to those characteristic of individualized, *heroic* leadership. While recognizing the potential for essentialism (Billing & Alvesson, 2000), this approach is reflective of women's ways of knowing and leading (Belenky, Clinchy, Goldberger, & Tarule, 1986; Court, 2005; Ferguson, 1984; Gilligan, 1982; MacNevin, 2002). The collaborative process also involved mirroring some of the competencies we wanted to inspire in global leaders, namely, the ability to truly listen to perspectives other than our own, to embrace mutual learning, to explore creatively, and to work together across perceived and real differences. In essence, the development of the program served as a playground to navigate some of the core competencies inherent in the program we were developing. The result is an educational program designed for all global leaders (both men and women), but having an orientation that is aligned with principles, practices, and perspectives commonly adopted by successful women in global leadership roles.

The next section of this chapter provides a brief overview of the new Master of Arts in Global Leadership (MAGL). We then describe and reflect upon the process of engagement we used with a consultative committee of scholars and practitioners to guide us in the development of the program. We conclude the chapter with a description of the program structure, competency framework, and type of courses.

PROGRAM OVERVIEW

When we began conceptualizing the program, we spoke with many leadership scholars as well as practitioners working in global contexts within international nongovernment organizations (INGOs), quasi-governmental international institutions (e.g., the United Nations, World Bank), and other global social purpose organizations (e.g., refugee organizations, humanitarian aid organizations, organizations seeking to expand education in the Global South). Through our consultations, it became clear these individuals wanted to see a program that was different from the typical university programs in global business development, international development, or international public policy. Rather, they were looking for something grounded in theory that supported their own leadership values and the leadership of others, and created the opportunity to enhance skills and practices for working collaboratively to improve the lives of people in the world. Practitioners, in particular, also spoke of the importance of being able to work and study at the same time and to apply learning within their professional contexts.

In response, we began to develop a 2-year master's degree program in global leadership focused on building and enhancing leadership capacities among officials, managers, and staff working in the international governance and social purpose public sector. Our goal was to create a credentialed degree that would provide academic legitimacy for those working in these fields while also providing opportunities, through coursework and a practical capstone project, to undertake projects that make a difference to a community, organization, or group of people. Additionally, the program needed to align with Royal Roads University's (RRU) learning and teaching model (RRU, 2013) with the following features:

- Offers a blended delivery model of intensive residencies and online courses allowing students to maintain their jobs (and living situations) while studying;
- Utilizes a competency learning and assessment model, including learning objectives in areas of knowledge perspectives, behaviors, and skills of relevance to their working realities;
- Supports adult learning principles and practices that encourage self-directed learning, empowerment, and accountability, as well as respect, dignity, and ethical practice;
- Adopts a cohort model so as to create a learning community that sustains students through the program and also facilitates the building of a global network;
- Offers flexible admission options for applicants who have extensive professional working experience but may lack the standard academic admission requirements (usually a bachelor's degree) required in most university graduate degree programs; and
- Utilizes faculty who are scholar-practitioners—academically qualified but also having years of practitioner experience.

DEVELOPING THE PROGRAM

Acknowledging our own limitations as coordinators of the program development process, we sought guidance from a range of people from within and outside of the University; we felt this was important to accurately develop a degree that would reflect students' wants and needs. Specifically, we invited input from 10 RRU core faculty from other programs (e.g., School of Humanitarian Studies, School of Communication and Culture, Office of Interdisciplinary Studies, Faculty of Management, School of Education and Technology); 6 RRU staff and administrators (Centre for Teaching and Educational Technologies, International Office); and over 35 external consultants—scholar-practitioners of varying cultural and racial backgrounds from various parts of the world and predominantly working in INGOs. We referred to this group as our MAGL Consultative Committee and reinforced their identity and role through regular communications, sharing of information resources, and offering opportunities to attend workshops or provide input on the program as it was developing.

Through the consultative process, we tried to remain cognizant of Arnstein's (1969) well-known ladder of participation that separates full citizen power from degrees of tokenism and nonparticipation. We endeavored to create a structure that enabled meaningful stakeholder input while not raising expectations that committee members had full control over program development. As such, we engaged with the Consultative Committee via monthly email and two face-to-face participatory meetings to seek their input into the design process. Specifically, this engagement contributed to the development of a working definition of global leadership, a competency framework for the program, and delineation of program courses.

Phase One: Defining Global Leadership

To define global leadership in a way that would resonate with potential students, we engaged the Consultative Committee in face-to-face dialogic sessions as well as through other Internet-based technologies. At the first face-to-face meeting, we used an arts-based method called Visual Explorer—essentially a large set of random images spread throughout a room—to elicit personal interpretations of global leadership through the symbolic images. Participants were invited to select an image that represented what global leadership meant to them; these images were used to facilitate introductions. In small groups, we also reflected on three key questions: (a) What defines global leadership? (b) What are the characteristics of a global leader? and (c) Why is global leadership important? To support this discussion, we reviewed the literature and compiled several definitions of global leadership (see Appendix). These definitions offered strong statements about how global leadership exists (or should exist) in the world; most of them differentiating global leadership from other approaches to leadership (e.g., Jokinen, 2005; Kets de Vries & Florent-Treacy, 1999, 2002; Mendenhall, Reiche, Bird, & Osland, 2012).

Notable elements highlighted in these definitions included the focus on the complexity of the global context; the role of a leader to inspire or influence (Beechler & Javidan, 2007; Mendenhall et al., 2012); the involvement of global stakeholders (Gregersen, Morrison, & Black, 1998); having a purpose to achieve positive change (Mendenhall, 2013); and achieving competitive advantage (Caligiuri & Tarique, 2009; Petrick, Scherer, Brodzinski, Quinn, & Fall Ainina, 1999) or world class performance (Brake, 1997). Kets de Vries and Florent-Treacy (2002) addressed the need for emotional intelligence capabilities and relational and cross-cultural process skills. Among these authors, only Adler (1997) stressed the importance of global leadership as improving quality of life for citizens around the world. Thus, what we recognized in compiling these definitions is that the concept of global leadership is not only complex, but is understood differently in different contexts, especially when addressed in a profit-making business setting versus the social purpose or humanitarian sector. Complexity further arises from leaders operating in multiple geographical contexts, engaging in multifunctional activities (e.g., multiple services or product lines), and dealing with heterogeneity in terms of different businesses, countries (cultures, legislations), and tasks. In other words, because global leaders function in many different contexts, they should be prepared to think, act, and communicate differently based on different situations.

We shared the literature on definitions of global leadership with the Consultative Committee, facilitating a lengthy discussion on how these matched with their own perspectives and experiences. Some remarked that they were surprised the definitions did not match their own understanding and experiences of global leadership. Some expressed cynicism about people working in ways that were less than authentic or sensitive to the cultural context in which they operated. The idea came up several times that all settings are, in fact, global settings. That is, in our current era of global interdependency, we are connected to people around the world in our daily interactions through trade, migration, and information technologies to name a few. There was also a strong feeling expressed that unqualified professionals working in the global context could do great harm in the country or to the people with whom they were working. Figure 9.1 summarizes how the Consultative Committee defined and conceptualized the global leader.

> **What is Global Leadership…**
>
> Anchored in values •A different way of being • A mindset • A new way of thinking as a member of the planetary community • Sustainability • Clarity of purpose • Collective wisdom • Understanding interrelationships between local and global communities, cultures, and contexts (global + local = glocal) • Awareness of difference (context, culture, needs, power) and connectedness to the other• Emergent and within all of us • Harnessing multiple values, beliefs, customs towards achievement of strategic goals • Transcending the present • Respecting past generations and generations to come • Accountable • Avoidance of harmful actions/consequences • Opportunistic • Builds from the strengths of cultures, contexts, and people • Empowerment and Participation • Understanding who we are and how we are related to the world around us • Non-hierarchical and addresses power imbalances • Creating space for people to connect • Not a one size fits all approach • Leadership improved by global challenges, interconnectedness and mutual vulnerabilities.
>
> **A Global Leader is…**
>
> Self-reflective; adaptive, integrative, fluid & flexible;connecting, networking, communicating & innovating; inspirational;an active listener; a facilitator, enabler & nurturer; understanding; sees the possibilities;influential; authentic; leading, following, supporting & transforming; humble; a proactive adaptor;"who she/he is."

Figure 9.1. Consultative committee members' perspectives on global leadership.

In short, through discussions it became clear that current definitions of global leadership did not adequately respond to the Consultative Committee's conceptualization and *lived realities* of global leadership in practice. Accordingly, we developed our own definition for the purposes of the MAGL program. Our intention was not to create a rigid prescription; rather, we hoped to create a working definition that would serve as a starting point and evolve over time. Drawing from the rich conversations amongst ourselves and members of the Consultative Committee, we arrived at the following definition:

> Global leadership is the capacity to lead and support oneself, others, organizations, communities, and complex systems in ways that enhance the well-being of communities and the planet, both today and in the future. An orientation to diversity and global citizenship is fundamental to our understanding of global leadership and allows us to recognize and value the multiple and evolving ways of being, doing, and knowing. Global leadership acknowledges that all communities are global communities and that we are fundamentally interconnected. Global leaders are guided by principles of mindfulness and compassion and work to promote dignity, humanity, prosperity, and justice for all.

What is noticeable about this definition, in contrast to those offered by many of the scholars cited in the Appendix, is the focus on thinking systemically and having globally oriented values that are respectful, humanizing, and understanding of multiple intelligences, and on behaviors and actions to improve dignity and justice for others in a complex world. Global leadership is not defined in terms of position or working in a specific geographical locations but in terms of how leaders think (the mind), feel (the heart) and work with others in a global context (the hands). By framing a working definition of global leadership in this manner, we encourage students in the program to explore their own ever-evolving concept of global leadership practice.

Phase 2: Developing a Competency Framework

We also sought to develop a contextualized competency framework to support the learning goals of global leaders in the MAGL program. To do so, we first reviewed existing literature pertaining to global leadership competencies. We noted a proliferation of competencies prescribed for global leaders (Bird, 2013; Jokinen, 2005; Mendenhall, 2013; Osland, 2013). Several scholars in the field have created typologies organizing the competencies into domains loosely pertaining to personality traits, cognitive capabilities, and behavioral skills (Bird, 2013; Brake, 1997; Jokinen, 2005). Much of the empirical literature focuses on managers who work in transnational business settings. Consequently, scholars and practitioners have emphasized various areas of business acumen and organizational skills as part of the critical characteristics of effective global leaders (Bikson, Treverton, Moini, & Lindstrom, 2003; Caligiuri, 2006; Kets de Vries & Florent-Treacy, 2002; McCall & Hollenbeck, 2002; Rhinesmith, 2003). For example, Bird (2013) summarized the necessary competencies as follows:

> They reflect global leadership on a larger scale, "at a distance" and are directed at the entire organization or to a global unit or initiative within the organization. Business and organization acumen appears to entail five composite competencies: vision and strategic thinking, business savvy, organizational savvy, managing communities and leading change. (p. 87)

In recent years, however, the debates around global leadership competencies have become more sophisticated and wide-reaching, generating new questions on what uniquely defines global leadership. While it is apparent there are various applications and different global environments, there is tremendous similarity in many of the knowledge, attitudinal, and behavioral competencies listed as necessary for the successful leader. Yet the framing or priority of these competencies shifts from context to context, as in a figure-ground exercise. For example, business leaders put greater emphasis on the business and organizational acumen skills, while those working in the humanitarian and nonprofit world place greater emphasis on the skills of collaboration and building capacity in local communities. Since we are a leadership program operating in the Faculty of Social and Applied Sciences, we decided to focus our efforts on the latter, especially so as to complement rather than compete with an already existing program at the University focused on international business (MA in Global Management Program).

After reviewing literature, universal competencies that appear to transcend both place and time include a global mindset, personal qualities of high self-awareness, flexibility, adaptability, resilience, cross-cultural sensitivity and communication skills, ability to work in a multicultural context building cooperative relationships and partnerships, and an orientation toward leading and managing change processes. Mendenhall (2013) provided a useful 5-level structure to conceptualize these universal global leadership characteristics: (a) global knowledge; (b) threshold traits of integrity, humility, inquisitiveness and self-resilience; (c) attitudes and orientations (the global mindset) toward a global context; (d) interpersonal skills for working cross-culturally in teams; and (e) systems thinking skills.

We shared the above literature and resource materials on various extant competency frameworks with the Consultative Committee at the first preparatory meeting and in subsequent emails following the meeting.

Building on the results of the first preparatory meeting as well as subsequent feedback from Consultative Committee members, we prepared a draft competency framework and set of learning capabilities consisting of three overarching domains: (1) personal leadership to work in a global context, (2) intercultural competency, and (3) competency to lead change in a complex environment. These domains were further broken down into nine subfactors: (a) leads self; (b) emotional adaptability; (c) managing self-in systems; (d) culture-general and culture-specific knowledge; (e) intercultural interaction and communication skills; (f) intercultural group facilitation skills; (g) knowledge of global political, social, and economic issues; (h) knowledge of international organization systems and change strategies; and (i) capability to lead change in complex environments. This competency framework was presented at the second face-to-face meeting of the Consultative Committee.

In an effort to engage a few members of the Consultative Committee who could not be physically present, we set up laptops at each of the discussion tables and linked them in using Blue Jeans (an Internet-based video conferencing technology). We invited the discussion groups to explore the foundational competencies and learning outcomes that they considered essential for students in the MAGL program. It was immediately apparent they viewed essential competencies of a global leader differently from many of the scholars who have published in this field. They chose to shift their focus away from the business and economic development sector (without ignoring it entirely) and placed greater emphasis on the competencies required of leaders working to improve quality of life, cultural empowerment, and dignity for people worldwide. Additionally, it was acknowledged that students in the program would likely be working professionals and would come equipped with many core characteristics and traits that have already predisposed them to work in the global arena.

Following this discussion on the competencies of a leader working in the global context, the MAGL competency framework was subsequently adapted and refined (Table 9.1). The nine capabilities within each of the three overarching domains relate to learning at the level of knowledge (the head), values/perspectives (the heart) and practice skills (the hands). We consider these capabilities to be foundational and in no way reflective of the broader domain of capabilities and wisdom that often emerges from long years of practice as a globally minded leader in multiple international and domestic settings.

We note that all the global leadership competencies make reference to diversity and cultural relevance. In the MAGL program, we approach the concept of diversity from an intersectional perspective, which includes ethnic heritage, language, religion, indigenous heritage, country of origin, and urban/rural community, as well as class, gender, sex, age, generation, (dis)ability, and more (Gopaldas, 2013). We also acknowledge that identity is not fixed; rather, it is fluid and changing over time. In short, this orientation to our competency framework reflects the diversity and complexity of the ever-changing and evolving nature of leadership in the global contexts.

Table 9.1. A Competency Framework for the MA Global Leadership

A. Personal Leadership Working in a Global Context

Entails understanding one's values, beliefs, and behaviors in the context of other people, being aware of one's orientation in the world, accountable for one's behavior and being open to learning. It includes being able to manage one's emotional reactions and being adaptive and resilient in complex changing environments.

> *A1. Self-Reflective Practice* entails orienting toward personal mastery and developing a supportive, self-reflexive practice. This inward focus entails continual self-reflection and approaching internal and external challenges through the lens of lifelong learning. Cultivating one's mental, physical, and spiritual health through regular inward-focused practices provides the foundation needed to serve others and to engage in global leadership from a healthy, professional, respectful position.

(Table continues on next page)

Table 9.1. (Continued)

A2. Resilience and Personal Adaptability refers to the ability to adapt, learn, and change in response to complex, challenging, and stressful environments through exercise of self-awareness and management of feeling and emotions, development of supportive and productive relationships, and through implementation of action plans that enhance self-management capabilities, resilience, and the ability to thrive in complex environments.

A3. Self-in-Systems Management Capability refers to awareness of self in relation to others in a global context (e.g., how one's actions affect others +/-) and in relation to broader social-ecological systems. Exercises responsibility and accountability in interactions with self and others. Looks for leverage points for positive change of self, regardless of position in a system.

B. Leading in a Diverse Global Context

Is the ability to engage in effective and appropriate interaction with others in a variety of cultural contexts (both globally and locally) and to honor differences in values, beliefs, and behaviors. Diversity reflects multiple ways of being, doing, and knowing across and within diverse contexts, populations, groups, and systems. Leading in diversity is grounded in an understanding of one's own cultural identity, being aware that other cultural values, beliefs, and behaviors exist, using appropriate communication practices, managing inevitable contact with others, working together, and engaging collaborative learning across real or perceived cultural divides.

B1. Culture-General and Culture-Specific Knowledge is defined as knowledge of the societal-level values and norms on which most cultures vary. This general understanding moves beyond cultural stereotypes and monocultural models toward fluid, emergent, and dynamic intercultural and intersectional understandings of the diversity and ever-changing nature of human experience. Culture-specific knowledge includes understanding one's own values, norms, beliefs, rites, rituals, and behaviors which result from having grown up within specific countries, cultures, and contexts (e.g., generation, socioeconomic background, historical conditions) in comparison with the values, norms, beliefs, rituals, and behaviors of those from other cultures and contexts—recognizing both similarities and differences.

B2. Intercultural Interaction and Communication refers to the ability to interact with and communicate in a variety of mediums with people of different cultures, ages/generations, and other dimensions of difference, demonstrating awareness of communication methods, protocols, and norms appropriate to the setting.

B3. Intercultural Group Facilitation refers to the ability to work effectively with groups and teams taking into account generational, gendered, cultural, and other differences, to include skills in forming working groups/teams, facilitating group performance, managing tension and negotiating conflict situations, and exercising hosting and fellowship behaviors.

(Table continues on next page)

Table 9.1. (Continued)

C. Leading Sustained Change in Complex Environments

Refers to the ability of a leader to understand the complex political, social, and economic issues in the world and how they impact communities and organizations. Such leaders can work within and mobilize the resources of the international organizations as well as community-based organizations to affect change in organizations or in communities.

> *C1. Knowledge of Global Political, Social, and Economic Issues* includes knowledge of the complex political, social, and economic drivers impacting communities (e.g., national borders, indigenous communities, environmental ecosystems, and generations), and their interrelationships across a variety of international and global systems. Drivers of change might include climate change and natural disasters, wars, conflict and forced migration, globalization and immigration patterns, new technologies, global conventions, treaties, agreements, and policies.
>
> *C2. Knowledge of International Organization Systems and Change Strategies* includes knowledge of organizational mandates, policies, structures, and performance systems of the United Nations (and its affiliates), international and local NGOs, governments, and civil society, in terms of how they deliver support for communities in need (e.g., humanitarian aid), support global markets, facilitate social/educational capacity development, and implement other change initiatives.
>
> *C3. Capability to Lead Change in Complex Environments* refers to the abilities to create vision and to organize and facilitate processes of change through collaboration with others and across multiple cultural, social, and political boundaries, exercising creativity and innovative thinking, and making use of collaborative and dialogic processes.

Phase 3: Developing Courses and Curriculum

The third phase in the development process was course and curriculum design. This process began at the second meeting with the Consultative Committee, where work teams were directed to begin conceptualizing courses that would fall into the following four domains:

1. Foundation concepts and experiences to orient students to the world of global leadership and strengthen their personal values, systems perspectives, resiliency, cultural sensitivity, and intercultural communication skills.
2. Courses focused on understanding and navigating the sociopolitical context of the diverse global communities, models, and approaches to community development and how to address tension and conflict operating across and within global communities.
3. Courses focused on understanding the structure and dynamics of global institutions and governance organizations that provide funding, humanitarian aid, health and educational resources to the

underdeveloped nations—their mandates and goals, policies, financial and business practices, operational procedures, and monitoring and evaluation requirements.
4. Courses focused on supporting student engagement in leadership work to address a need in an organization or community.

What emerged from this consultative process were general course-content domains. In subsequent planning meetings, content was organized into specific courses. We then wrote course titles and descriptions (see next section for details).

In developing the MAGL program, the Consultative Committee frequently noted that the program needed to be flexible and adaptive, recognizing prior learning and the specific learning interests of students (e.g., child rights and protection, international conflict, disaster management, poverty reduction, etc.). Initially, there was a request for multiple specializations in the program, but this soon proved to be unwieldy from a financial and operational perspective. Consequently, the group decided that mechanisms should be established for students to study in an area of specialization elsewhere—perhaps through a certificate at another university that could be transferred in and combined with the core knowledge and skills learning available through the MAGL program. In the end, it was decided the MAGL program would maintain its generic and foundational focus for all students while offering elective courses within two streams—community development and organizational management/development—and the opportunity to transfer in specialization courses from elsewhere.

COMPLETE PROGRAM STRUCTURE AND COURSES

The program is organized into required courses and electives. The first online course, *Personal and Theoretical Foundations to Global Leadership* (3 credits) and the first residency, *Personal Capacities for Working in Complex Global Systems* (9 credits), are foundational and required for all students before proceeding to the electives. Students are then required to take an additional 12 elective credits (typically four 3-credit courses) in the following manner:

- Four elective courses from the six courses offered in Streams A and Streams B, or
- Up to 9 credits transferred from an approved area of specialization (completed at RRU or through another institution), plus remaining credits from electives available in streams A or B (see Table 9.2).

Table 9.2. MAGL Courses

Required First Year Courses:

Online Course: Personal and Theoretical Foundations to Global Leadership (3 credits)

First Residency/Online Course: Personal Capacities for Working in Complex Global Systems (9 credits)

Elective Course Offerings (students are required to take a minimum of 4 courses in any combination from Stream A or Stream B or the Specialization Stream)

Stream A: Global Organizational Leadership

1. Social Structures and Dynamics within Social-Purpose Organizations (3 credits)
2. Strategic Analysis, Decision-Making and Evaluation (3 credits)
3. Business Development and Change Management within Social-Purpose Organizations (3 credits)

Stream B: Community Capacity Development

4. Navigating Geopolitical Dynamics of Global Communities (3 credits)
5. Community Development Models (3 credits)
6. Managing Difficult Relationships Within and Across Community Dynamics (3 credits)

Stream C: Specialization approved courses from other RRU programs or external educational institutions (up to 9 credits)

Required Second-Year Courses:

Second Residency: Project Planning and Partnership Building (3 credits)

Capstone Projec: (9 credits)

36 TOTAL COURSE CREDITS

In the second year of the program, students are required to attend a 2-week long residency: *Project Planning and Partnership Building* (3 credits), and then to complete an independent *Capstone Project* (9 credits). Calendar descriptions for the courses can be viewed through the program website at http://www.royalroads.ca/prospective-students/master-arts-global-leadership.

Figure 9.2 provides an integrative graphical representation of the program structure and courses. This diagram of program courses represents our conceptualization of the student's learning journey, beginning with the basic theoretical concepts about leadership in the global context, the development of personal awareness and interpersonal skills to work in a world of complexity and cultural diversity, and focusing on the knowledge and skills needed to work at the level of community or organizational management. The specialization stream is utilized for students who already have the knowledge and experience of working at the community or organizational level, providing them opportunity to direct this knowledge more deliberately to a specialized field of practice.

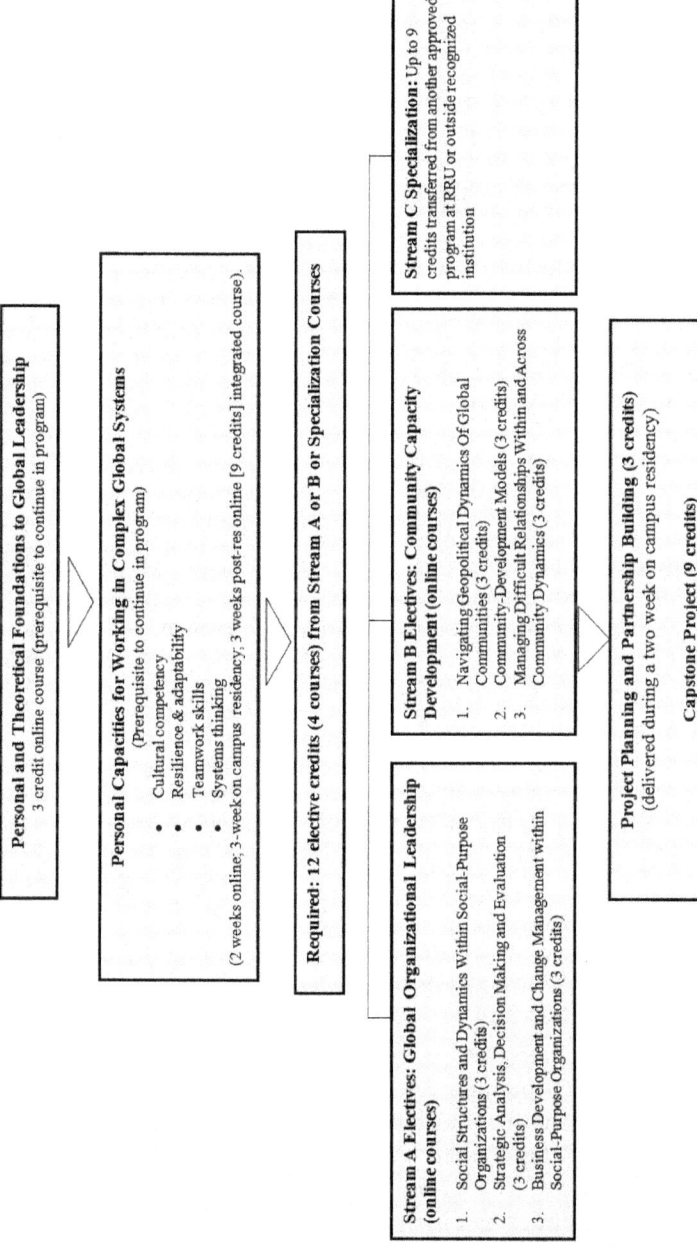

Figure 9.2. The MA Global Leadership Program: Building leadership capacity and sustainability for individuals, organizations and communities in a global context.

One could say that learning begins with "the head," moves to engage and expand "the heart," is accentuated through greater learning at the "the head" and transferred into practice at "the hands." The program is intentionally flexible to allow different pathways of learning while ensuring there is solid foundational knowledge that enhances the development of leadership competences to work in the global context and with a global perspective.

CONCLUSION

In this chapter, we have documented a process of collaboration for the development of a new degree in global leadership and the outcome in terms of a definition of global leadership, competency framework, and set of courses. This process took much longer than traditional program development, yet we believe the processes of consultation and engagement amongst ourselves and with the Consultative Committee offered a richness and diversity to the program design phase that likely would not have resulted otherwise. Creating opportunities for the Consultative Committee members to participate via technology also facilitated a process to pilot and adapt innovative and creative engagement tools and approaches for application in the MAGL program delivery. Moreover, the Consultative Committee provided a skilled and knowledgeable pool of scholar-practitioners to recruit as curriculum designers and instructors who would also endorse the program in their respective professional networks. It should be noted that the Consultative Committee continues to grow and attract additional scholar/practitioners, numbering over 70 individuals as of this writing. We continue to keep this group regularly informed about the progress of the program's development and implementation. In short, we feel the consultative process helped to ensure the development of a unique leadership program that responds to the ever-changing needs of scholar-practitioners—as global leaders—working to create a more equitable and just world.

We offer this development process not as a prescription for others, but rather as an example for interested readers to glean useful strategies that can be adapted to different settings. In sharing our story, we do not wish to offer a romanticized perspective. As mentioned at the outset, it took hard work, time, perseverance, patience, and openness for us to understand the various perspectives each one of us brought to the table. It also took deep dialogue for us to reach agreement on the nature of the degree program we wanted to put forward. These are the principles of interaction that we feel are critical for all leaders (women as well as men) working in a global context—the principles and values that are promoted in the curriculum and activities of the MAGL program.

In an era where leaders are challenged to be more self-aware and more globally competent, and leadership educators are challenged to model and teach these competencies in their programming, we hope our story has offered insight into what might be possible. We offer this educational program in global leadership as an alternative to more traditional management or business (often male oriented) pedagogical models; as such it may be more attractive to women but by no means targeted only at the female population. Hopefully, this type of program will be seen as a pedagogical model of the future for all leaders regardless of gender, generation, or cultural orientation.

ACKNOWLEDGMENTS

The authors would like to acknowledge Lisa Corak, who is an essential part of the program development team and without whom many of the activities documented here could not have transpired. We also thank the members of the MAGL Consultative Committee and our colleagues at Royal Roads University for their support throughout this process. For more information on the MA in Global Leadership Program, please see the program page at http://www.royalroads.ca/prospective-students/programs/leadership-studies

Correspondence concerning this chapter should be addressed to Wendy E. Rowe, School of Leadership Studies, Royal Roads University, 2005 Sooke Road, Victoria, BC, Canada, V9B 5Y2. E-mail: wendy.rowe@royalroads.ca

Appendix: Definitions of Global Leadership

Author	Definition	Orientation/Focus
Adler (1997, p. 174)	Global leadership involves the ability to inspire and influence the thinking, attitudes, and behavior of people from around the world. . . [it] can be described as a process by which members of the world community are empowered to work together synergistically toward a common vision and common goals resulting in an improvement in the quality of life on and for the planet. Global leaders are those people who most strongly influence the process of global leadership.	Influence others to common goals Improvement in quality of life of others
Beechler & Javidan (2007, p. 140)	Global leadership is the process of influencing individuals, groups, and organizations (inside and outside the boundaries of the global organization) representing diverse cultural/political/institutional systems to contribute towards the achievement of the global organization's goals.	Influences others to meet goals

(Appendix continues on next page)

Appendix: (Continued)

Author	Definition	Orientation/Focus
Brake (1997, p. 38)	Global leaders—at whatever level or location—will (1) embrace the challenges of global competition, (2) generate personal and organizational energies to confront those challenges, and (3) transform the organizational energy into world-class performance.	Leads organizational performance Transforms to be the best
Caligiuri (2006, p. 219)	Global leaders, defined as executives who are in jobs with some international scope, must effectively manage through the complex, changing, and often ambiguous global environment.	Able to work in complex environments
Caligiuri & Tarique (2009, p. 336)	Global leaders [are] high level professionals such as executives, vice presidents, directors, and managers who are in jobs with some global leadership activities such as global integration responsibilities. Global leaders play an important role in developing and sustaining a competitive advantage.	Has authority Global integration Achieve competitive advantage
Dorfman, Javidan, Hanges, Dastmalchian, & House (2012, p. 514)	Successful leaders enact core universally desired behaviors that comprise charismatic value based leadership.	Charismatic style Capability to motivate others
Harris, Moran, & Moran (2004, p. 25)	Global leaders are capable of operating effectively in a global environment while being respectful of cultural diversity.	Respectful of cultural diversity
Kets de Vries & Florent-Treacy (2002, p. 304)	Leaders with a cosmopolitan mindset ... requires cross-functional and cross-cultural process skills.... An outlook of cultural relativity, excellent relational skills, curiosity and emotional intelligence distinguish successful global leaders.	Mindset Cross cultural skills Emotional intelligence
McCall & Hollenbeck (2002, p. 32)	Global executives are those who do global work. With so many kinds of global work, again depending on the mix of business and cultural crossings involved, there is clearly no one type of global executive. Executives, as well as positions, are more or less global depending upon the roles they play, their responsibilities, what they must get done, and the extent to which they cross borders.	Leaders who cross borders

(Appendix continues on next page)

Appendix: (Continued)

Author	Definition	Orientation/Focus
Mendenhall, Reiche, Bird, & Osland (2012, p. 26)	An individual who inspires a group of people to willingly pursue a positive vision in an effectively organized fashion while fostering individual and collective growth in a context characterized by significant levels of complexity, flow and presence.	Inspires others towards a vision Works in complex environment
Mendenhall (2013, p. 20)	Global leaders are individuals who effect significant positive change in organizations by building communities through the development of trust and the arrangement of organizational structures and processes in a context involving multiple cross-boundary stakeholders, multiple sources of external cross-boundary authority and multiple cultures under conditions of temporal, geographical, and cultural complexity.	Effect positive change in organizations Works in structures Multiple stakeholders
Osland (2013, p. 75)	An individual who inspires a group of people to willingly pursue a positive vision in an effectively organized fashion while fostering individual and collective group in a context characterized by significant levels of complexity, flow and presence.	Influence and inspiration Works in complexity
Petrick, Scherer, Brodzinski, Quinn, & Ainina (1999, p. 58)	Global strategic leadership [...] consists of the individual and collective competence in style and substance to envision, formulate, and implement strategies that enhance global reputation and produce competitive advantage.	Enhance global reputation Competitive advantage

NOTE

1. IICRD is a Canadian nongovernmental organization (NGO) focused on child rights and protection, nationally and globally

REFERENCES

Adler, N. J. (1997). Global leadership: Women leaders. *Management International Review, 37*(1), 171–196.

Adler, N. J. (2007). One world: Women leading and managing worldwide. In D. Bilimoria & S. K. Piderit (Eds.), *Handbook on women in business and management* (pp. 330–355). Cheltenham, England: Elgar.

Arnstein, S. R. (1969). A ladder of citizen participation. *Journal of the American Institute of Planners, 35*(4), 216–224.

Beechler, S., & Javidan, M. (2007). Leading with a global mindset. In M. Javidan, R. Steers, & M. Hitt (Eds.), *Advances in international management: The global mindset* (Vol. 19, pp. 131–169). Oxford, England: Elsevier.

Belenky, M. F., Clinchy, B. M., Goldberger, N. R., & Tarule, J. M. (1986). *Women's ways of knowing*. New York, NY: Basic.

Bengtsson, J. (2012). *Aung San Suu Kyi: A biography*. Chicago, IL: Potomac.

Bikson, T. K., Treverton, G. F., Moini, J., & Lindstrom, G. (2003). *New challenges for international leadership: Lessons from organizations with global missions*. Santa Monica, CA: Rand.

Billing, Y. D., & Alvesson, M. (2000). Questioning the notion of feminine leadership: A critical perspective on the gender labelling of leadership. *Gender, Work, and Organization, 7*(3), 144–157.

Bird, A. (2013). Mapping the content domains of global leadership competencies. In M. E. Mendenhall, J. S. Osland, A. Bird, G. R. Oddou, M. L. Maznevski, M. J. Stevens, & G. K. Stahl (Eds.), *Global leadership: Research, practice, and development* (2nd ed., pp. 80–96). London, England: Routledge.

Brake, T. (1997). *The global leader: Critical factors for creating the world class organization*. Chicago, IL: Irwin.

Caligiuri, P. M. (2006). Developing global leaders. *Human Resource Management Review, 16*(2), 219–228.

Caligiuri P., & Tarique, I. (2009). Predicting effectiveness in global leadership activities. *Journal of World Business, 44*(3), 336–346.

Court, M. (2005). Negotiating and reconstructing gendered leadership discourses. In J. Collard & C. Reynolds (Eds.), *Leadership, gender and culture in education: Male and female perspectives* (pp. 3–17). New York, NY: Open University Press.

Dorfman, P., Javidan, M., Hanges, P., Dastmalchiand, A., & House, R. (2012). GLOBE: A twenty year journey into the intriguing world of culture and leadership. *Journal of World Business, 47*(4), 504–518.

Ely, R., Ibarra, H., & Kolb, D. M. (2011). Taking gender into account: Theory and design for women's leadership development programs. *Academy of Management Learning & Education, 10*(3), 474–493. doi:10.5465/amle.2010.0046

Ferguson, K. E. (1984). *The feminist case against bureaucracy*. Philadelphia, PA: Temple University Press.

Fiorina, C. (2006). *Tough choice: A memoir*. New York, NY: Penguin

Gilligan, C. (1982). *In a different voice: Psychological theory and women's development*. Cambridge, MA: Harvard University Press.

Gopaldas, A. (2013). Intersectionality 101. *Journal of Public Policy & Marketing, 32*, 90–94.

Gregersen, H. B., Morrison, A. J., & Black, J. S. (1998). Developing leaders for the global frontier. *Sloan Management Review, 40*(1), 21–22.

Harris, P. R., Moran, R. T., & Moran, S. V. (2004). *Managing cultural differences: Global leadership strategies for the 21st century* (6th ed.). Oxford, England: Butterworth-Heinemann/Elsevier.

Jackson, B., & Parry, K. (2011). *A very short, fairly interesting and reasonably cheap book about studying leadership* (2nd ed.). Thousand Oaks, CA: Sage.

Jokinen, T. (2005). Global leadership competencies: A review and discussion. *Journal of European Industrial Training, 29*(3), 199–216.

Kellerman, B., & Rhode, D. (Eds.). (2007). *Women & leadership: The state of play and strategies of change*. San Francisco, CA: Jossey-Bass.

Kets de Vries, M., & Florent-Treacy, E. (1999). *The new global leaders*. San Francisco, CA: Jossey-Bass.

Kets de Vries, M., & Florent-Treacy, E. (2002). Global leadership from A to Z: Creating high commitment organizations. *Organizational Dynamics, 30*(4), 295–309.

MacNevin, A. (2002). *Women and leadership*. Ottawa, ON: Canadian Research Institute for the Advancement of Women.

McCall, M. W., Jr., & Hollenbeck, G. P. (2002). *Developing global executives: The lessons of international experience*. Boston, MA: Harvard Business School Press.

Mendenhall, M. (2013). Leadership and the birth of global leadership. In M. E. Mendenhall, J. S. Osland, A. Bird, G. R. Oddou, M. L. Maznevski, M. J. Stevens, & G. K. Stahl (Eds.), *Global leadership: Research, practice, and development* (2nd ed., pp. 1–20). London, England: Routledge.

Mendenhall, M. E., Osland, J. S., Bird, A., Oddou, G. R., & Maznevski, M. L. (Eds.). (2008). *Global leadership: Research, practice, and development*. London, England/New York, NY: Routledge.

Mendenhall, M. E., Reiche, B. S., Bird, A., & Osland, J. S. (2012). Defining the "global" in global leadership. *Journal of World Business, 47*(4), 493–503.

Ngunjiri, F. W. (2010). *Women's spiritual leadership in Africa: Tempered radicals and critical servant leaders*. New York: State University of New York Press.

Osland, J. S. (2013). An overview of the global leadership literature. In M. E. Mendenhall, J. S. Osland, A. Bird, G. R. Oddou, M. L. Maznevski, M. J. Stevens, & G. K. Stahl (Eds.), *Global leadership: research, practice, and development* (2nd ed., pp. 40–79). London, England: Routledge.

Paludi, M. A., & Coates, B. E. (2011). *Women as transformational leaders: From grassroots to global interests* (Vol. 1). Santa Barbara, CA: ABC-CLIO.

Petrick, J. A., Scherer, R. F., Brodzinski, J. D., Quinn, J. D., & Fall Ainina, M. (1999). Global leadership skills and reputational capital: Intangible resources for sustainable competitive advantage. *Academy of Management Executive, 13*(1), 58–69.

Rehn, E., & Sirleaf, E. J. (2002). *Women, war and peace: The independent expert's assessment on the impact of armed conflict on women and women's role in peace-building*. New York, NY: United Nations Development Fund for Women.

Rhinesmith, S. (2003). Basic components of a global mindset. In M. Goldsmith, V. Govindarajan, B. Kaye, & A. Vicere (Eds.), *The many facets of leadership* (pp. 215-228). Upper Saddle: NJ. Prentice Hall.

Rhode, D., & Kellerman, B. (2007). Women and leadership: The state of play. In B. Kellerman & D. Rhode (Eds.), *Women & leadership: The state of play and strategies of change* (pp. 1–62). San Francisco, CA: Jossey-Bass.

RRU. (2013). Learning and teaching model. Victoria, BC. Retrieved from http://media.royalroads.ca/media/marketing/viewbooks/2013/learning-model/

Sandberg, S. (2013). *Lean in: Women, work, and the will to lead*. New York, NY: Knopf.

Simpson, R., & Ituma, A. (2009). Transformation and feminization: The masculinity of the MBA and the "un-development" of men. *Journal of Management Development, 28*(4), 301–316.

Sirleaf, E. J. (2010). *This child will be great: Memoir of a remarkable life by Africa's first woman president.* New York, NY: Harper Perennial.

Smith, C. (1997). Gender issues in management education: A new teaching resource. *Women in Management Review, 12*(3), 100–104.

CHAPTER 10

WOMEN'S LEADERSHIP LEARNING THROUGH GLOBAL STUDY IN CENTRAL AND SOUTH AMERICA

Paige Haber-Curran and Kaitlin Hartley

An important angle through which to examine women's leadership is to understand the experiences of younger women, the next generation of leaders. To narrow the gender gap in leadership, it is vital we focus on and invest in young women in order to understand their leadership development experiences and prepare them for future global leadership. Effective leadership in an increasingly global society requires global understanding and the ability to interact effectively within and across cultures (Earnest, 2003; Hofstede & Hofstede, 2004). This chapter addresses these needs by focusing on the experiences of four college women who participated in a 4-week global leadership program. Through examining the experiences of these women, we provide implications to inform future global leadership education for college women, including study abroad experiences and leadership curriculum.

GLOBALIZATION AND STUDY ABROAD IN HIGHER EDUCATION

Higher education continues to place a growing emphasis on globalization, making global and cultural understanding hot topics within curricula and programmatic development (Currie & Newson, 1998). As a result, institutions offer and encourage participation in international experiences to enhance global understanding. The variety of skills and knowledge gained through an international experience is shown to have a positive effect on cognitive and psychosocial development, as well as employability and career preparation (Drexler & Campbell, 2007; Franklin, 2010). Through developing global perspectives, students are able to incorporate intercultural knowledge into their beliefs and sense of self, aiding in overall student development (Braskamp & Engberg, 2011).

Study abroad is identified as high-impact educational practice within higher education that facilitates meaningful student learning (Kuh, 2008) and provides benefits both for student participants and institutions (McKeown, 2009). Short-term programs (8 weeks or less) in particular have had increased national participation over the last decade and are said to create powerful learning experiences for students (Institute of International Education, 2012). Global and intercultural competence is a central learning outcome and priority of study-abroad programs (AAC&U, 2011), providing students key and desirable skills to effectively engage in our increasingly global society.

LEADERSHIP-FOCUSED STUDY ABROAD PROGRAMS

Beyond traditional study-abroad programs are those programs with an emphasis on leadership. The number of leadership-focused study-abroad programs has increased in recent years (see May 2012 issue of *The Journal of Leadership Studies*). This increase of leadership-focused study-abroad programs is warranted, as "anyone who wants to study or to exercise leadership successfully needs to be educated about the world, about diverse cultures and interests, and about different ways of working with others to influence an increasingly complex, connected, and conflicted system" (Robinson, 2005, p. 82). Through participating in leadership-focused study-abroad programs, students are able to examine and challenge their previously held worldviews and lenses as a way to shift and broaden their thinking about themselves, leadership, and the world (Montgomery & Arensdorf, 2012; Robinson, 2005). These programs allow students to learn skills and competencies for operating in a global society as well as promote opportunities for self-discovery and insight into one's own leadership capacities (Earnest, 2003). Broadening one's worldview and engaging with people and cultures that are different from one's own culture can also enable students to expand their understanding of multiculturalism and diversity, concepts central to contemporary perspectives on leadership (Montgomery & Arensdorf, 2012; Ostick & Wall, 2011).

As we see this influx of globalization and a growing interest of leadership, it is important that "knowledge about and the exercise of cutting-edge leadership [be] informed by an appreciation of growing internationalization, both locally and abroad" (Robinson, 2005, p. 79). One way to facilitate this is providing students with opportunities to engage in new cultures and communities around the world, enabling them to develop their global competency (Earnest, 2003).

LEADERSHIP DEVELOPMENT OF WOMEN

As the focus on understanding leadership in a global context increases, there is a need to consider the leadership development of women. Although women are attending and graduating from colleges and universities in higher rates than men (Allen, 2011) and hold approximately half of professional and managerial roles in the workforce, there remains a substantial gap in women holding top leadership roles across all major sectors of the American workforce, even those sectors that have a large majority of women in the workforce (Lennon, 2013). It is in these top roles that key decisions are made affecting the following: major companies; educational institutions; health and human services; local state and national government; and the everyday life of people and communities served by these organizations and institutions. Due to this gender gap in top leadership roles, often women's voices are not at the table or are at the table in disproportionately small numbers. This not only has the potential to result in decisions that do not take into consideration the needs and voices of women, but also has been shown to negatively impact the organization, as research demonstrates that the presence of women in top leadership roles results in greater organizational performance and success for organizations (Eagly & Carli, 2007; Lennon, 2013). The impact of this gender gap in leadership is often focused on domestic implications, such as on the implications for American society and American women. As society is becoming more global in nature and practice, it is imperative that we consider the impact of this gender gap on the state of women both domestically and internationally. Further, we must identify ways to help women advance in leadership beyond just the confines of American organizations and American society.

Although there are many systemic issues and barriers in place preventing women from advancing in leadership that must be tackled in order for substantial change to take place (Eagly & Carli, 2007), there are ways we can proactively prepare and equip women for leadership with a global emphasis. One such way is to focus global leadership education efforts on college women. College women, more so than college men, actively pursue student involvement and student leadership development experiences while in college (Allen, 2011; Sax, 2008), and college women demonstrate higher self-assessed scores on measurements of contemporary, socially responsible leadership behaviors as compared to men (Dugan, Komives, & Segar, 2008).

Although women's self-assessed leadership behaviors tend to be higher than men, women tend to report less confidence and self-efficacy for leadership as compared to men (Dugan & Komives, 2007; Offerman & Beil, 1992). Further, a report on college women's leadership at Princeton University (2011) revealed many college women undersell themselves, do not take credit for their accomplishments, and shy away from or are discouraged from pursuing top, elected leadership roles. A study focusing on college women holding top leadership roles in student organizations revealed women were anxious about what leadership would be like postcollege in the "real world," expressing concerns that the environment may not be as female-friendly and supportive (Haber, 2011). If this is how women were feeling about the "real world" in the society where each of them was raised, one can imagine that the women have similar, if not greater, concerns about leadership globally. It is important that as we work to prepare women for leadership postcollege, we consider the broader context, seeking to prepare women for global leadership. In this chapter, we address this need by examining the experiences and learning of four women participating in a short-term leadership-focused study-abroad course.

BACKGROUND OF GLOBAL LEADERSHIP EXPERIENCE

The study-abroad course examined in this chapter took place as part of *Semester at Sea*, a program dedicated to providing a global comparative education to undergraduate students. Semester at Sea is operated through the Institute for Shipboard Education, a nonprofit organization, and has academic sponsorship through the University of Virginia. Semester at Sea's mission focuses on influencing social change by educating students from around the world and developing global understanding to tackle global challenges (Institute for Shipboard Education, 2014). The specific leadership course examined in this chapter was part of a 4-week short-term voyage through Central and South America. Ports of call included cities in Costa Rica, Ecuador, Peru, Panama, and Belize.

The voyage had a common theme focused on the United Nation's (2005) Millennium Development Goals (MDGs). The MDGs are eight specific goals established as part of a concrete 10-year action plan from the United Nations for overcoming global challenges. The goals range in focus from reducing extreme poverty by half, to offering universal primary education, to promoting gender equality and the empowerment of women by 2015 (United Nations, 2005). These goals provided the framework for the courses and field experiences on the voyage.

The specific course examined in this chapter was entitled *Adaptive Leadership for Social Change: An International Context*. Situated within the frameworks of the social change model of leadership (HERI, 1996; Komives & Wagner, 2009) and adaptive leadership (Heifetz & Linsky, 2002), the course focused on preparing students to be effective agents of social change through self-examination and self-exploration; exposure to contemporary leadership frameworks; and examination of social issues and social responsibility in a global context.

The social change model of leadership is a values-based model that emphasizes the goal of leadership as facilitating "positive change for the betterment of others, community, and society" (Cilente, 2009, p. 45). The model promotes seven values to support the overall goal of change; these values focus on self (consciousness of self, congruence, and commitment), others (collaboration, controversy with civility, and common purpose), and society/community (citizenship). This is an accessible model, promoting the idea that anyone has the ability to engage in leadership regardless of whether or not they hold a positional leadership role.

Adaptive leadership similarly promotes the idea that leadership is about affecting change for the betterment of something beyond oneself (Heifetz & Linsky, 2002). The framework focuses on mobilizing people to address and tackle substantial *adaptive* challenges to which there are not readily available answers. In order to address these challenges, people must be aware of the larger system in which the leadership process exists and must be willing and able to adjust their current belief systems and behaviors (Heifetz & Linsky, 2002). Specific behaviors enabling adaptive leadership include getting on the balcony (i.e., seeking a broader perspective), thinking politically (i.e., developing and facilitating relationships to gain support), orchestrating the conflict (i.e., allowing conflict to arise and regulating the temperature in order to facilitate productive conflict), giving the work back (i.e., enlisting and empowering others to take responsibility and action), and holding steady (i.e., remaining stable in the face of pressure and challenges in order to keep focus on the issues) (Heifetz & Linsky, 2002).

In addition to the social change model of leadership and adaptive leadership frameworks, the curriculum focused on personal and cultural values, leadership from various cultural perspectives, social responsibility, and systemic/ecological perspectives on leadership. Complementing the in-class curriculum was examination of leadership and social change efforts aligning with the UN MDGs that took place in the regions visited in the voyage. This included episodes from the PBS Series, *The New Heroes*, which focused on social entrepreneurs making a substantial positive impact in their communities, and the book *The Last Flight of the Scarlet Macaw*, which examines the journey of Sharon Matola, an American woman who ran the Belize Zoo, in her fight against environmental destruction and corruption within Belize. Additionally, students participated in two field experiences wherein they learned firsthand about social issues affecting the region and leadership efforts addressing these issues. The first field experience was a service trip to an orphanage in Panama, and the second was a visit to Veragua Rainforest Research and Adventure Park in Costa Rica. Students' final group projects examined one of the MDGs within one of the countries visited and focused on leadership efforts addressing the goals.

In addition to this course, all students were required to take the *Global Studies* course, which provided a study of the region and individual countries visited. The course focused on the economics, history, language, and culture of each country. In addition, groups of students were challenged with choosing an individual MDG and developing a creative project to address the challenges. Information taught in *Global Studies* enhanced the overall learning experience for students and allowed a deeper look at the countries visited in order for meaningful conversations to take place and to provide greater context for the study of leadership and social change in the countries. Further enhancing students' experiences were the opportunities to participate in additional in-country field experiences not associated with the course; each student participated in at least a few additional cultural experiences, including participating in an indigenous homestay, visiting the Galapagos Islands, and engaging in service projects.

The curriculum, overall voyage, and in-country experiences provided an excellent framework for learning about and experiencing leadership in an international context. The next sections provide an overview of the case study and a presentation of the themes that emerged about students' experiences and learning through the course.

OVERVIEW OF THE CASE STUDY

A case-study approach was used to examine the experiences of four women who were enrolled in the course *Adaptive Leadership for Social Change: An*

International Context. Case study is an approach to qualitative research that "involves the study of an issue explored through one or more cases within a bounded system" (Creswell, 2007, p. 73). There were a total of four women in the course, and they each were invited to participate in the study once the course had commenced; all four of the women agreed to participate in the study. Three of the women were undergraduate students and one was a graduate student. One woman was from the West Coast, one was from the south, and two were from the northeast. They each had active student leadership experiences at their home institutions and had an expressed interest in leadership. They had a range of past experiences with international travel and study.

This study focused on the students' experiences and learning as it relates to themselves, leadership, and culture/global issues. Participants' reflective journals and course assignments were analyzed using thematic content analysis to identify key themes within the data (Boyatzis, 1998). Pseudonyms are used to identify the four women. Jennifer was a senior from the northeast who was a Spanish major. Camille was a junior from the West Coast who was a Liberal Studies major. Veronica was a sophomore from the northeast studying International Relations. Kelly was a graduate student from the south studying Higher Education.

PRESENTATION OF THEMES

Each of the four women identified salient experiences and learning in three key areas: self, leadership, and culture/global issues. The women also each identified salient experiences as part of the course and the overall voyage that contributed to their learning; these key experiences are noted within the presentation of themes.

Salient Experiences and Learning: Self

At the beginning of the voyage, the students were tasked with setting intentions for themselves and their learning; they considered their goals for the voyage in the classroom, on the ship, and in port. Students' intentions and expectations for themselves varied, yet common themes that emerged across the four women's reflections included having a desire to get out of one's comfort zone, being open to experiencing new things, and trying to suspend preconceived notions of what each country would entail. Jennifer was a Spanish major and was excited to experience the countries she had learned about in her coursework. She wrote, "I hope to break out of my shell earlier rather than later … live in the moment everyday of this voyage and truly be aware of everything I am doing." Camille expressed nervousness about the experience and had not traveled much prior; she focused her intentions more on the shipboard community, challenging herself to get out of her comfort zone by meeting other students on the voyage. Veronica, the International Relations major, had traveled in the region prior and was intentional about how she wanted to approach her travels within the countries:

> How can we, as affluent Americans with the responsibility to aid the world, affect positive social change through the creation of programming if we are not exposed to those cultures we are trying to support? I am hoping to gain perspective and insight into this region of the world.... In order to ensure that I am able to fully understand and enjoy the countries we visit, it will be important for me to put my prior knowledge gained from traveling to other countries in the region out of my mind ... each country is unique. Comparisons are okay, but I have to make sure to objectively view each difference as just that; no country is better or worse.

Kelly, who had been a student on two prior voyages, was intentional about what she wanted to get out of this experience, "I expect to encounter ideas with new knowledge and think critically about how I could impact the world, specifically relating to the United Nations MDGs.... I must better understand what role my generation has in being the change towards improvement." The women's varied intentions and expectations reflected differences based on past travel experiences and areas of study.

In-class discussions and reflection papers challenged students to consider their own sense of self and to learn more about themselves throughout the voyage. Learning about and being exposed to other cultures challenged the women to explore their own perspectives and worldviews. This often stemmed from interactions with people from the local cultures. Veronica, who spoke Spanish fluently, had a conversation with a fisherman in Ecuador that challenged her to consider Ecuadorian culture and her worldview:

> The fishing boat *Tiuna* was unloading its cargo: one month's worth of yellow fin tuna, selling for about $100 each fish. I went over to where they were unloading and struck up a conversation with some of the men about what life is like on the boat. One man explained to me that when the nets start to fill and the men begin to haul it in, it is his job to jump into the net and extract, by hand, any dolphins that he finds in an effort to preserve them. He literally jumps into the center of a net filled with hundreds of thrashing tunas, possibly sharks, and wild dolphins to remove them. My jaw literally hit the floor when I heard him talk about his work. He said it with such a look of resolution, pride, and a maturity I will never possess.... I work hard to do well in school and work hard in whatever jobs I have held, but never will I have to do the type of life-threatening, back-breaking work required by jobs

such as the dolphin saver man in order to make money. I have always had the choice of where I want to work, gotten paid well, and been treated decently. The man who saved the dolphins is admirable and courageous, that is true ... [but] he is working this job because he needs the money. Where I will always be able to choose, he will never be so lucky.

As is depicted in Veronica's story, realization of one's worldview was often connected to recognition of one's own privilege, such as the privileges of being American, having educational opportunities, and having the ability to travel. Camille wrote, "Throughout this whole trip, going to each country I have gained much more appreciation for the house I live in, that I am able to go to school, and that I live in a safe community." The women recognized that these experiences they often took for granted were not commonplace for the citizens of the countries we visited, and particularly not commonplace for the women in the region.

Class discussions within this course and curriculum within the global studies course emphasized the lack of educational and economic opportunities for women in these countries as well as the presence of the *machismo* mindset within many of the cultures visited. Kelly reflected on this, sharing,

> It's interesting to see the role of women in the communities we are entering. We visited a scientific research center run solely by men; however, in visiting an orphanage, the leadership was entirely women. There is a clear divide in the roles of women versus men, and it is probably not common for women to earn a college degree.

Each of the women also experienced personal development and growth as it related to their vocational exploration. Jennifer reflected on her life's purpose in her time visiting Machu Picchu, Peru:

> I realized how much I want to do with my life. Standing among the mountains, feeling so much smaller in the large scheme of things, I couldn't help but reflect on my experience at the orphanage. I read in one of the readings for today a quote by Anne Frank that really resonated with me and brought all of this together; "How wonderful it is that nobody need wait a single moment before starting to improve the world." Whether it's in the U.S. or across the world, I want to make an impact.... It is not that I do not want to teach anymore, but rather I now think there is so much I can do at the same time. I can teach and during the summers do service trips. I can create programs that help the youth in my community. Basically, I've realized how much I really can do within the field. I am passionate about using my knowledge, my experiences, and my motivation.

Similarly, Kelly reached a sense of empowerment as it related to her vocational calling as an educator, "What I learned most about myself is how

I can influence social change as a leader ... as I gain more education and experience, I have the authority and leadership ability to lead students to do things that impact the world."

One of the texts used in the course was Bruce Barcott's *The Last Flight of the Scarlet Macaw*. The students really connected with this story and saw it as an inspiring and empowering case study for concepts of social change and leadership covered in the course. Camille wrote, "All I want to do is make a difference. I don't want to become the next 'zoo lady' but in some way I do want to make a difference in someone's life personally and in the community." The women left the course with a more developed desire to make a positive impact on others, the community, and even the world, which connects to the next set of themes below, students' learning about leadership.

Salient Experiences and Learning: Leadership

The students had varying experiences with leadership education prior to the voyage. When asked in their first paper to share what the concept of leadership meant to them, the definitions varied slightly but tended to focus primarily on leadership as positional, wherein a leader has the ability to delegate to others, motivate others, and empower others. The students also used words such as *integrity*, *humility*, and *passion* as desirable leader qualities.

By the end of the course students' understandings of leadership had become more developed, as they recognized the complexity of leadership at both the micro (personal and group) and macro (societal/cultural) levels. Many of the students resonated with aspects of adaptive leadership (Heifetz & Linsky, 2002) when discussing their views of leadership at the end of the course. Camille, who had initially described leadership as a person with integrity, humility, and an open mind, concluded at the end of the course, "Leadership is not defined by an individual. It takes a whole team along with delegating (give the work back), keeping calm in a difficult situation (hold steady), and knowing your audience (think politically)." Veronica's changing view of leadership moved beyond the importance of listening to others to instead empower others' voices, "Speech is empowerment and is the way that change starts. Before, I just believed in the power of the voice, but now I understand more fully how to find those voices and raise them up."

Jennifer also resonated with aspects of adaptive leadership, recognizing the limitations of merely focusing on technical solutions and grappling with how this relates to her passion for volunteerism. She discussed this in connection to two service trips to orphanages:

I kept thinking, are we here for the kids, or are we here for ourselves? Sure we brought supplies and made the children smile, but both of these experiences, in Peru and Panama, made me want to do more service learning with bigger projects. I felt like I was just doing sporadic volunteer work fixing technical problems rather than participating in a larger program bringing more of an adaptive change to the area.... I love to volunteer because I love the feeling that comes with it, I love the experience. But is that a bad drive to have? Should my motivation be for the people I am helping rather than what I get out of it? How do I ensure that I am giving back for the right reasons and not for myself? ... When returning home I want to become more permanently involved in a project I am passionate about and really work for the individuals, not for myself.

Jennifer's quote also suggests a movement toward recognizing leadership as adaptive work that affects social change, a common theme among the women. Viewing leadership as making positive change in something beyond oneself was also evident in Veronica's reflections on her visit to the orphanage in Panama:

Even if there is nothing that I can do for Doris the blind and deaf girl, or the seven-year-old diva with Down Syndrome or the cutie whose legs were amputated after receiving severe burns, I can use these experiences to remind me of what great leadership can do for the world. These nuns lead by example and believe that through hard work, persistence, kindness, and love all will be provided. Not a single person there was driven by selfish motives. They are there for the collective good of all the children reliant on the orphanage. If more businesses, communities, and organizations could align themselves around a common goal as well as these women have been able to, the world would be a better place. Exposing youth, such as myself, to experiences like these reminds us of the virtues of humility and kindness.

The nuns at the orphanage made a substantial impact on the students and their understanding of what it means to lead and serve. Additionally, in class we watched episodes of PBS's *The New Heroes*, a few of which featured women affecting substantial social change in their countries. One episode in particular was touching for the women; it featured Albina Ruiz, who led an initiative to introduce a community-managed waste collection system in order to address health and environmental problems stemming from garbage in Peru. The women often referred back to Albina Ruiz's story when discussing leadership for social change in the region. Kelly described these women as "inspirational ... [they demonstrated] the importance of giving back once we have received so much knowledge, it's our moral responsibility." Camille was also really inspired by the women, recognizing the importance of their leadership efforts: "The women [in the documentaries] changed their country by starting in a small way with little money and now have successfully saved many lives ... I really look up to them."

The voyage focused on the United Nation's MDGs, and the students had an opportunity to examine these goals within the countries visited both within this course and the *Global Studies* course. At times this was daunting for the students, often viewing these issues as so large that they were intangible, but through understanding the impact that one person can have in a community or even a country, the students were hopeful, encouraged, and even empowered about the possibilities that lie ahead. Kelly wrote,

> All of the students on *Semester at Sea* have the ability to make an impact, no matter how big or small. Although achieving the MDGs seems farfetched and unrealistic, small changes add up and we must remember this when we make decisions in our future. By living as responsible citizens, we can all make an impact on the future of our world. Being cognizant of our waste, what we purchase, what we eat, and how we live can establish change. I strive for this in my daily life upon return home.

Overall, the students developed more complex understandings of leadership and in many cases left with more questions than answers. They grew to view the world in terms of adaptive challenges and recognized the importance of moving beyond technical fixes to a place of empowerment and social change.

Salient Experiences and Learning: Culture and Global Issues

The final cluster of themes revolved around students' experiences with and learning about culture and global issues. As was previously noted, the four women had varying prior experiences with international travel. Additionally, their major fields of study also varied, with two students' majors having a cultural or global focus (International Relations and Spanish). The students' past experiences with travel and fields of study seemed to influence how they approached and interacted with local cultures.

Two of the women expressed initial feelings of uncertainty and concerns prior to entering Peru, the first country visited on the voyage. Semester at Sea deans and staff, along with Peruvian diplomats who were on the ship, provided the students with a preport security and safety briefing, which left some students concerned about their safety and what they may experience in the country. Kelly wrote, "I was very skeptical and apprehensive of the environment ... [they] did a good job of scaring everyone before we arrived. I have traveled extensively, visiting many 'unsafe' countries, but the stories and accounts shared left me with a feeling of anxiety." Some specific words of advice stuck with Camille: "Girls should not walk alone, keep your money and passport on your body, and if you end up in a situation that you should not be in then just give them what they want and get back to the ship." Camille also recalled some of her initial observations of the country: "Dogs walking down the street without leashes ... a man pulled down his pants right in front of all the people and peed right on the curb.... The city equivalent to our 'middle class' smelt of pee, old dogs, trash, and smog."

The students discussed their understanding and experiences of each country and culture through comparison; they compared their experiences to the United States, to what textbooks and experts had taught them, or to other countries visited. Jennifer wrote,

> The most interesting thing that I have come away with is the similarities and differences between each of the countries we visited, especially in the general "vibe" of the country. I don't know a better way to explain it but each country has its own feeling and it's something you can only get by going there.

Veronica was particularly in tune with comparing her experience in Lima to what she had learned about Peru on the voyage with a critical lens:

> I tried to keep in mind the information that we had discussed about the country. The social divide between the indigenous and Mestizo peoples, the desert climate of the coastal region Lima inhabits, and the recent economic boom were all on my mind. I chose to pay close attention to these facts because they were all gathered and disseminated to me by people from the developed world, principally the United States. I wanted to compare the Western perspective of the political, economic, and social situation in Peru to the people's own.... As I expected, the cultural, as well as physical climates of the country were not quite what we thought. But what truly surprised me was how right we were about some observations.

Throughout the voyage, Veronica moved to a place of wanting to understand and experience the cultures in each country *as is*, deemphasizing the need to make comparisons: "Now I have learned to research (objectively) the culture and history of the countries where I visit. I try not to listen to the stereotypes and prejudices associated with the cultures.... I will do my best to enter humbly."

The women expressed their greatest learning about the cultures through interacting with people from the countries we visited. Camille wrote, "Even though I saw the cities and some history museums, the greatest learning I took out of this trip was hearing the stories of the people's lives." Kelly had a particularly moving conversation with a woman in Ecuador and wrote, "A conversation can truly paint a picture of the culture in which you are immersed.... She was such a sweet lady and influenced my view of Ecuadorians in such a positive light." Jennifer had the unique experience of participating in an indigenous family homestay in Ecuador. Through this experience she was able to stay with a family and participate in local and cultural customs. She described this experience, particularly her interaction with the women in the family and village, as "transformational" and "life changing."

Through interacting with and observing people in each of the countries, the students came to the place of recognizing not only differences, but also similarities across the cultures and across human nature in general. While sitting in a restaurant, Camille observed a touching scene between a young Ecuadorian boy showing some elderly women, perhaps family members, that he could ride his bike. From this experience Camille took away a feeling of connection and home: "The two women clapped and smiled at the accomplishment of the boy riding his two wheeler bike.... It was really comforting to know that no matter what country you are in there are still some traditions that everyone goes through." Kelly visited the Embera Indian Village in Panama and got a glimpse into the culture of the native Indian tribe. She reflected, "I wouldn't be surprised if our values showed alignment. Perhaps we both value family, education, health and love. People aren't all that different when you look at the core of their being." Similarly, Veronica wrote, "I must constantly remind myself that each person is just like me: has a family, worries about the future, likes to have fun every once in a while, and wants to be successful in his or her own society." As the women began to make these connections, they also expressed greater comfort with themselves and with engaging within the culture.

Another key theme emerged around better understanding the social issues affecting countries in Central and South America. Framed primarily around the MDGs, students learned about a variety of social issues through our course as well as through the *Global Studies* course. Veronica discussed this in a reaction paper to the book *The Last Flight of the Scarlet Macaw*:

> I have been given a snapshot into the political, social, cultural, and environmental apparatus that is the Belizean government. Furthermore, after reading about these issues in Belize, I realized that they are prevalent in most other governments, especially in Latin America. We always wonder why change is so slow, and this is why. Politics, corruption, money, and lack of resources are more important factors in decision-making than effective leadership or what is right.

Although much of this learning was content-based through curriculum, the students also experienced and observed some of the social issues while in country. Kelly participated in a service-learning project focused on bringing a water filtration system to a village in Belize. She saw the challenges of poverty and insufficient infrastructure within this village and its connection with education, "The children in this village aren't even able to have a drink of safe water while they are at school all day, something we take for granted every single day in the U.S." Veronica had a conversation with a taxi driver in Lima that brought to light the issues of violence and terrorism in the country:

> His wife and daughter had been killed in a terrorist attack by a drug cartel in the north, on the border of Ecuador where his daughter had been visiting her police boyfriend stationed there. He was devastated, especially when forced to identify their bloated, bullet-ridden bodies in the morgue in Lima. The issues Peru faces with drugs are real, and they affect people all over the country, not just on the Ecuadorian border.

The students were able to connect their learning about social issues within the country to challenges of adaptive leadership, which was discussed earlier in the presentation of themes. Their in-country experiences also enabled them to see these countries beyond their challenges; they were able to see hope and light within the darkness. Kelly was touched by how the Peruvians valued their faith, "On Sunday, the streets filled with people praising a saint and rallying to celebrate Catholicism. It's interesting to understand the supreme importance that Peruvians place in their religion." Veronica, after discussing the heartbreaking terrorism story from her taxi driver, wrote,

> Peruvian people care about so much more than counter-narcotics, politics, and income gaps. They take great pride in their food, an example of the syncretism embodied by Peruvian culture. They love to dance and spend time celebrating the important things in life such as family and religion. They realize that their country isn't perfect, but they love it despite of that. These people work hard to deserve the breaks they take, and live whole-heartedly in that moment. They don't dwell on the past, but embrace it and strive for a better future.

Summary of Themes

When examining the experiences of the four women in the course, themes emerged related to salient experiences and learning about self, about leadership, and about culture and global issues. Key themes related to self included setting intentions and expectations of being open and getting the most out of the experience, examining one's own perspectives and world views, acknowledging privileges, and exploring one's vocational interests and values. Key leadership themes emerged around students developing a more complex understanding of leadership, recognizing the need for adaptive leadership, viewing leadership with an emphasis on positive change, and feeling empowered and inspired to lead. Finally, the key themes that emerged related to culture and global issues were feelings of uncertainty and concern for safety; comparing cultures to the United States, to past experiences, and across countries; learning through interacting with people across cultures; acknowledging similarities across cultures; learning about and experiencing social issues within the countries visited; and seeing past the challenges to find hope and light within the darkness.

DISCUSSION OF COURSE AND THEMES

The course focused on preparing students to be effective agents of social change through self-examination and self-exploration, exposure to contemporary leadership frameworks, and examination of social issues and social responsibility in a global context. Analysis of the four women's reflection papers and course assignments suggested meaningful learning in each of these areas. We focus this discussion on two key areas: leadership education through study abroad and women's leadership. Within the discussion below are conclusions that can be drawn from this case study along with implications for practice and suggestions for future research.

Leadership Education Through Study Abroad

The women expressed considerable shifts in their understanding of the concept of leadership, wherein they moved away from leadership as positional and involving certain traits or characteristics to a more complex understanding of leadership as more relational and encompassing the facilitation of positive change. Similarly, a few of the women began to see leadership as about being a change agent and were able to recognize the drive and desire within them to facilitate positive change. This shift in students' understandings of leadership reflects movement from more traditional to more contemporary conceptualizations of leadership (Northouse, 2012) as well as movement toward more complexity in one's leadership identity development (Komives, Longerbeam, Owen, Mainella, & Osteen, 2006).

Although it is not entirely surprising that the women's understandings of leadership reflected the more contemporary and complex conceptualizations of leadership included in the curriculum, this shift within a 4-week period of time can be viewed as substantial, as research suggests that students' leadership identity development takes considerable time, reflection, relationships, and experiences (Day, 2001; Komives et al., 2006) and thus may not be so easily shifted through course content alone. In their reflection papers, the women identified a number of in-country and regional case studies and experiences that were salient in their shifting understanding of leadership. Further, they often connected their experiences in-country to the UN MDGs, which seemed to provide a tangible framework from which to learn about leadership for social change. These "real-life" experiences and examples reflected the course curriculum; this alignment of course content and "real-life" content and experiences likely provided an environment supportive of examining and exploring new ways of conceptualizing leadership. Without the opportunity to engage within the cultures and learn from those who had facilitated positive social change, it is possible that the curriculum may not have provided such a meaningful learning experience.

Thus, as leadership educators continue to design leadership education opportunities abroad, it is suggested they find ways to meaningfully connect with the culture and countries visited and seek to understand and experience the leadership challenges and learn about leadership initiatives taking place within the country. In fact, the same implication can likely be made about domestic leadership programs, whereby meaningfully connecting with and learning from the community may provide significant opportunities for learning.

The students also expressed a desire to be open to new experiences and to take in as much as they could within the 4-week voyage, yet that looked different for each woman; each woman enrolled in the course for different reasons, had different fields of study, and had varied past experiences with travel. The setup of Semester at Sea provided a good balance of structured group activities and class time along with opportunities for individual and noncourse-related travel and experiences. This environment was very conducive to the students' varying backgrounds and intentions for the experience. For example, Jennifer participated in an overnight indigenous homestay, which may have been too much of a stretch for some of the other women in the course. Accordingly, an implication for designing study-abroad programs is to consider blending structured group and class activities with opportunities for individualized experiences to help meet students where they are in their educational and life journeys.

With the recent emergence of leadership-focused study-abroad programs, it is not surprising that the research base on such programs is limited. The research base that does exist is focused on single programs, and considering the range of purposes, curriculum, and experiences within these courses, this is fitting. The themes in students' learning and experiences from this course suggest that consideration of both the curriculum and the in-country experiences is important. Similarly, and particularly for future quantitative studies, it is important to consider students' precourse experiences from the onset including their goals, intentions, and previous travel experiences. Last, it would be interesting to examine a range of leadership-focused study-abroad programs to discern patterns of meaningful learning experiences across different contexts and cultures.

Women's Leadership

This course did not have an explicit curricular focus on women's leadership; rather, this case study examined the experiences of four women in this leadership-focused study-abroad course. Despite this, though, content-based learning about women in Central and South American society and about women in leadership resonated with the women. Through the in-country experiences and through studying the UN MDGs, the participants recognized the lack of education, lack of opportunity, and lack of status women had in comparison to men. In contrast to this, though, many of the participants were drawn to the women who were positively affecting social change, whether it was the nuns at the orphanage, Albina Ruiz from PBS's *The New Heroes*, or Sharon Matola from *The Last Flight of the Scarlett Macaw*. In fact, these women were the ones who set the leadership examples that helped open up the participants' eyes to a broader understanding of leadership for social change. Interestingly, in each of these examples the women were leading in less traditional position roles and were able to make a substantial positive impact through grassroots leadership efforts; this provided a refreshing contrast to the more masculine, positional views on leadership (e.g., political and business leaders) some may have when examining a country and culture.

The participants may not have actually been conscious of the contrasting impressions of women (lacking opportunity and leading/facilitating change) to which they were exposed during their experience; in fact, it was not evident for us until analyzing the reflection papers for this case study. There may have been a missed learning opportunity for the students in the course on intentionally examining and discussing the role of gender as it related to leadership within the countries visited. Even if a leadership study-abroad course does not explicitly focus on gender, enough evidence exists within the leadership literature to support examination of gender, and specifically women, when studying leadership (Eagly & Carli, 2007; Kellerman & Rhode, 2007). Leadership educators planning a study-abroad course should consider this, even if it is not an explicit learning outcome of the course.

The women expressed a more complex view of leadership throughout this course as well as feelings of motivation and empowerment to make a positive difference in the lives of others and in their communities. Much of this motivation and empowerment came from seeing and reading about change makers, who happened to primarily be women. Considering this course did not intentionally focus on women's leadership, yet the women found empowerment and motivation through this, there appears to be a great opportunity to capitalize on opportunities to learn from women who are leading and affecting positive change in their countries and communities. Knowing this, leadership educators can more intentionally focus on this in study-abroad programs; this could be accomplished through course content as well as field experiences. As an example, students could meet with, hear the stories of, and learn from women who are leading change initiatives and making a positive impact in their countries and communities. This may be a particularly effective way to help women reflect upon and focus on their leadership self-efficacy, an area in which research suggests women are lacking as compared to their male peers (Dugan & Komives, 2007; Offerman & Beil, 1992).

CONCLUSION

Women's leadership in a global context, and specifically women's leadership development and learning through study abroad, is an underresearched area. As society continues to become more global, it is imperative intentional efforts are made to develop women for global leadership. One way this can be done is through international learning experiences. In reviewing literature for this chapter, we did not find any research directly addressing this topic. Research, not just on global leadership, but on *women's* global leadership, deserves attention. Although women's leadership was not a purposeful curricular component of the course examined in this case study, it is clear that the course provided an opportunity for the four women to develop as leaders and reflect upon the role of gender in an international leadership context. We are left considering what the opportunities and outcomes could be in a course purposefully addressing the goal of developing women for global leadership. We encourage others to take what we have learned here to inform future efforts to prepare women for global leadership.

REFERENCES

Allen, E. J. (2011, April). Women's status in higher education: Equity matters. *ASHE Higher Education Report, 37*(1), San Francisco, CA: Jossey-Bass.
Association of American Colleges and Universities (AAC&U). (2011). *VALUE: Valid Assessment of Learning in Undergraduate Education*. Retrieved from http://www.aacu.org/value/
Boyatzis, R. (1998). *Transforming qualitative information*. Thousand Oaks, CA: Sage.
Braskamp, L. A., & Engberg, M. E. (2011). How colleges can influence the development of a global perspective. *Liberal Education, 97*(3/4), 34–39.

Cilente, K. (2009). An overview of the social change model of leadership. In S. R. Komives & W. Wagner (Eds.), *Leadership for a better world: Understanding the social change model of leadership development* (pp. 43–77). San Francisco, CA: Jossey-Bass.

Creswell, J. W. (2007). *Qualitative inquiry and research design: Choosing among five approaches* (2nd ed.). Thousand Oaks, CA: Sage.

Currie, J., & Newson, J. (1998). *Universities and globalization: Critical perspectives.* Thousand Oaks, CA: Sage.

Day, D. V. (2001). Leadership development: A review in context. *Leadership Quarterly, 11*(4), 581–613.

Drexler, D. S., & Campbell, D. F. (2011). Student development among community college participants in study abroad programs. *Community College Journal of Research and Practice, 35*(8), 608–619.

Dugan, J. P., & Komives, S. R. (2007). *Developing leadership capacity in college students: Findings from a national study.* College Park, MD: National Clearinghouse for Leadership Programs.

Dugan, J. P., Komives, S. R., & Segar, T. C. (2008). College student capacity for socially responsible leadership: Understanding norms and influences of race, gender, and sexual orientation. *NASPA Journal, 45*(4), 475–500.

Eagly, A. H., & Carli, L. L. (2007). *Through the labyrinth: The truth about how women become leaders.* Boston, MA: Harvard Business School Press.

Earnest, G. W. (2003). Study abroad: A powerful new approach for developing leadership capacities. *Journal of Leadership Education, 2*(2), 46–56.

Franklin, K. (2010, Fall/Winter). Long-term career impact and professional applicability of the study abroad experience. *Frontiers: The Interdisciplinary Journal of Study Abroad, 19,* 169–190.

Haber, P. (2011). Iron sharpens iron: Exploring the experiences of female college student leaders. *Advancing Women in Leadership Journal, 31,* 86–101.

Heifetz, R. A., & Linsky, M. (2002). *Leadership without easy answers.* Cambridge, MA: Harvard University Press.

Higher Education Research Institute (HERI). (1996). *A social change model of leadership development* (3rd ed.). Los Angeles, CA: Higher Education Research Institute.

Hofstede, G., & Hofstede, G. J. (2004). *Cultures and organizations: Software of the mind* (2nd ed.). New York, NY: McGraw-Hill.

Institute for Shipboard Education. (2014). *Semester at sea.* Retrieved from http://www.semesteratsea.org/

Institute of International Education. (2012). Open doors report on international educational exchange: Duration of U.S. study abroad. Retrieved from http://www.iie.org/opendoors

Kellerman, B., & Rhode, D. L. (Eds.). (2007). *Women and leadership: The state of play and strategies for change.* San Francisco, CA: Jossey-Bass.

Komives, S. R., Longerbeam, S. D., Owen, J. E., Mainella, F., & Osteen, L. (2006). A leadership identity development model: Applications from a grounded theory. *Journal of College Student Development, 47*(4), 401–418.

Komives, S. R., & Wagner, W. (2009). *Leadership for a better world: Understanding the social change model of leadership development.* San Francisco, CA: Jossey-Bass.

Kuh, G. D. (2008). High-impact educational practices: What they are, who has access to them, and why they matter. *American Association of Colleges and Universities*. Retrieved from http://leap.aacu.org/toolkit/high-impact-practices/2011

Lennon, T. (2013). Benchmarking women's leadership in the United States. *University of Denver*. Retrieved from http://www.womenscollege.du.edu/benchmarking-womens-leadership/

McKeown, J. (2009). *The first time effect: The impact of study abroad on college student intellectual development*. New York, NY: State University of New York Press.

Montgomery, J. F., & Arensdorf, J. (2012). Preparing globally competent leaders through innovative study abroad experiences. *Journal of Leadership Studies, 6*(1), 64–71.

Northouse, P. G. (2012). *Leadership: Theory and practice* (6th ed.). Thousand Oaks, CA: Sage.

Offerman, L. R., & Beil, C. (1992). Achievement styles of women leaders and their peers. *Psychology of Women Quarterly, 16*(1), 37–56.

Ostick, D. T., & Wall, V. A. (2011). Considerations for culture and social identity dimensions. In S. R. Komives, J. Dugan, J. E. Owen, C. Slack, & W. Wagner (Eds.), *Handbook for student leadership programs* (2nd ed., pp. 339–368). San Francisco, CA: Jossey-Bass.

Princeton University. (2011). *Report of the steering committee on undergraduate student leadership*. Retrieved from http://www.princeton.edu/reports/2011/leadership/

Robinson, B. D. (2005). Bringing "worldmindedness" to students of leadership. *Journal of Leadership Education, 4*(1), 79–89.

Sax, L. J. (2008). *The gender gap in college: Maximizing the developmental potential of women and men*. San Francisco, CA: Jossey-Bass.

United Nations. (2005). *United Nations millennium development goals*. Retrieved from www.un.org/millenniumgoals

PART IV

STORIES OF WOMEN AS GLOBAL LEADERS

CHAPTER 11

WHAT FILMS REVEAL ABOUT WOMEN AS GLOBAL LEADERS

Margie A. Nicholson

As our understanding about the subject of women as global leaders evolves, leadership scholars, educators, and practitioners may find that films—particularly films that portray the lives of real leaders, whether in documentary or docudrama formats—can be a rich resource. Watching films through the lens of leadership theories can bring theories to life, challenge some of our thinking about women as global leaders, and open up new lines of inquiry for future research.

The films and documentaries that serve as primary "texts" or resources for this chapter—*The Lady*, *Bhutto*, *Taking Root: The Vision of Wangari Maathai*, and *Chahinaz: What Rights for Women?*—have been widely seen and reviewed. *The Lady* (Besson, 2011), a dramatic film based on real people and events, profiles Aung San Suu Kyi, who was awarded the Nobel Peace Prize in 1991 for her resistance to a military junta that assassinated her father and continues to oppress the people of Burma. The documentary *Bhutto* (Baughman & O'Hara, 2010) explores the life of Benazir Bhutto, who fought to avenge the execution of her father, restore democracy to Pakistan, and warn the world about the threat of radical terrorism. Wangari Maathai, founder of the Green Belt Movement in Kenya and the first African woman and first environmentalist to win the Nobel Peace Prize, is the subject of the documentary *Taking Root: The Vision of Wangari Maathai* (Dater & Merton, 2008). Finally, Mary Robinson, the former President of Ireland and UN High Commissioner for Human Rights, and Sheikha Haya Rashed Al Khalifa from Bahrain, former president of the General Assembly of the UN, are both featured in the documentary *Chahinaz: What Rights for Women?* (Chala, 2007). Chahinaz, a young Algerian woman, interviews them and other women activists while examining her life options and opportunities within the broader context of global rights for women.

What makes someone a global leader? Adler (1997) said that global leaders "address people worldwide" (p. 175) and "the vision of a global leader, by definition, must be broader than the particular organization or country that he or she leads.... As society goes global, the audience of a leader also goes global" (p. 176).

Research into the evolution and impact of women as global leaders is increasingly relevant because, as Adler (1997) has observed, the number of women global political leaders is increasing and will continue to increase in the 21st century. The attention paid by filmmakers and programmers to the emergence of women as leaders is also growing, as evidenced by the number of films about women leaders and the success of projects such as the recent ITVS (2014) series, *Women and Girls Lead*, which showcased more than 50 documentaries and attracted a worldwide audience of more than 100 million viewers.

This chapter will highlight theories that are relevant to our thinking about leadership and about women as global leaders, drawing from research conducted by Nancy Adler, Beverly Metcalfe, Virginia Schein, Adam Galinsky, and others. Film scenes will be analyzed in light of leadership research on the following topics: the importance of vision; women leaders as images of culture, spirit, and hope; sources of support; the influences of role models, mentors, and family; the impact of media; the value of multicultural experience; power and leadership styles; and how respecting tradition and culture can be an obstacle to the evolution of women.

The Importance of Vision

Women who emerge as leaders are typically motivated by a vision, mission, or cause, not by a desire for power or hierarchical status (Adler, 1997). As their leadership attracts broader attention, these women become global citizens, taking up causes beyond domestic interests and national borders (Adler, 1997). When faced with the choice between self and service, they are willing to sacrifice their personal goals, comfort, freedom, and safety for the greater good. Adler (1997) claimed that women are motivated by a compelling agenda that they want to achieve, not primarily by either a desire for the hierarchical status of being president, prime minister, or CEO, or a desire for power per se. Power and the presidency are means for achieving their mission, not the mission itself. (p. 189)

And what is that vision? Typically, it is not just about the rights of women. That goal alone may not be enough to attract and mobilize a global audience. Schein (2001) studied global psychological barriers to women's progress into management in the 1970s, identifying the "think-manager, think-male stereotype" as a barrier. In 2001, she reviewed the work of scholars who had replicated her research in the 1980s and 1990s. The newer studies found that the stereotype was gradually eroding among women in management and female management students in the United States, but that it still had significance for managers and male management students in the United States and men and women in other countries, including the United Kingdom, Germany, China, and Japan. Given the challenges of overcoming the stereotypes held by men and women and the resistance to expanding rights for women, it appears that one path to global leadership for women is to shift from promoting rights for themselves and other women to a focus on broader concerns such as human rights, the environment, and freedom for all.

Wangari Maathai organized rural women to protect the environment and worked for freedom, human rights, and democracy in Kenya, ultimately winning the Nobel Peace Prize in 2004 and seeing her ideas spread worldwide. In early scenes in *Taking Root: The Vision of Wangari Maathai* (Dater & Merton, 2008), she accused the government and authorities of overseeing the destruction of forests and public lands. Later she told tribal elders and citizens that they were responsible for most of their problems, and she conducted seminars on civic and environmental education to help people learn how to govern themselves. Her concerns and vision expanded from soil erosion in rural Kenya to the global challenges of environmental protection and civic participation. Her voice was powerful and she spoke to all people:

> Today we are faced with a challenge that calls for a shift in our thinking so that humanity stops threatening its life support system. We are called to assist the earth to heal her wounds and in the process to heal our own. (Dater & Merton, 2008)

The tumultuous life of Benazir Bhutto, who took up the progressive political causes of her charismatic father, Prime Minister Zulfikar Ali Bhutto, after he was deposed in a military coup, is depicted in the documentary *Bhutto* (Baughman & O'Hara, 2010). General Mohammad Zia ul-Haq, leader of the coup, imprisoned and eventually executed Ali

Bhutto; Benazir spent the following 9 years in detention or exile. When she returned to Pakistan to challenge General Zia, she told her cheering followers, "Seeing you, the people, makes me feel that Bhutto is alive before my eyes. He told me at our last meeting at Rawalpindi jail that I must sacrifice everything for my country" (Baughman & O'Hara, 2010).

After Bhutto was elected prime minister, she freed all political prisoners and gave freedom to the press. Later she built thousands of schools, ended polio, and brought water and electricity to the villages. But her terms in office were marred by charges of corruption and incompetence; she eventually left Pakistan to raise her family in Dubai and travel the world giving speeches about the threat of radical Islamic terrorism. In the spirit of her father's legacy and in spite of death threats, Bhutto returned to Pakistan to speak up on behalf of her people. She was assassinated at a public rally in December 2007.

The docudrama, *The Lady* (Besson, 2011), profiles the life of Aung San Suu Kyi, Burma's national heroine and a global symbol of resistance to dictatorship. Suu Kyi, like Bhutto, was born into a progressive political family, and her father was also assassinated, leaving Burma in the hands of a military dictatorship that was considered "one of the world's most oppressive and secretive regimes" (Besson, 2011). Suu Kyi studied in England, married a British citizen, and raised a family there. When she returned home to care for her aging mother, activists approached her saying that she was the only one who could unite the people and bring democracy to Burma.

Suu Kyi traveled throughout the country, telling villagers, "I urge you all to embrace democracy and basic human rights. We must do this peacefully. We are here to insure that you the people all have a voice" (Besson, 2011). Her emergence on the political scene was greeted with enormous public enthusiasm, but once the military recognized her threat to their power, she was put under house arrest where she spent 15 of the next 21 years. In 1991, while still under house arrest, she was awarded the Nobel Peace Prize. Her son accepted the award in her honor, telling the gathering that his mother was "part of a larger struggle for the human spirit" (Besson, 2011).

Chahinaz: What Rights for Women? (Chala, 2007) is an aptly named documentary about Chahinaz, a young Algerian woman who questioned women's rights in Algeria, Ireland, India, France, the United States, and at the United Nations. The filmmakers followed Chahinaz as her questions and vision evolved from the personal to the global:

> Why should a man control my life? How can change be brought about? Should we demonstrate? Who can intervene? How do things work in other countries? If religion is not as prominent, are things different? What can international organizations, particularly the United Nations, do for women? (Chala, 2007)

During her travels Chahinaz met with Mary Robinson, the first female president of Ireland and the High Commissioner for Human Rights at the United Nations. She also met Sheikha Haya Rashed Al Khalifa, former president of the UN General Assembly, who organized cross-cultural dialogues at the United Nations on topics such as the fight against poverty, women's rights, civilization, and religion. As Chahinaz walked through Paris near the end of her journey and contemplated staying there, she considered her options: "If I want to do what I want, this is where I need to be. My country needs to change, but I want a good life, which is not possible at home" (Chala, 2007).

Women who emerge as global leaders have faced a basic choice about their priorities. Like Chahinaz, they have had to decide whether they want to work for change or focus on their own well-being. Should they step forward to take on ever greater leadership responsibilities, staying in the public sphere to fight for all even though the outcome is uncertain and potentially dangerous? Or should they leave for a more welcoming and supportive environment, taking advantage of their social and cultural opportunities, leaving the battle to others? Should they focus on the political or the personal? Will they "lean in," as Sheryl Sandberg (2013) might say, or step back?

Courage, Spirit, and Hope

Bolman and Deal (1995) described two images that dominate our understanding of leadership: one is the "heroic champion with extraordinary stature and vision," the other is "the policy wonk, the skilled analyst who solves pressing problems with information, programs, and policies." Yet both images "miss the essence of leadership" and neglect the "deeper and more enduring elements of courage, spirit and hope" (p. 5). Although it could be argued that women have not been given the institutional opportunity or support to emerge as global leaders from backgrounds as "heroic champions" or "policy wonks," we can find images and stories of women who represent the "enduring elements of courage, spirit and hope" in all of these films (p. 5). These women were steadfast in the face of social ostracism, imprisonment, solitary confinement, and death threats, often standing up and speaking up with remarkable force.

When Benazir Bhutto's father was deposed in a military coup and imprisoned, her brothers fled the country, but she bravely stayed in Pakistan to support her father and visit him in prison. In the documentary *Bhutto*, we learn that she later survived years of imprisonment, including 7 years in solitary confinement during which she had so little opportunity to speak that her jaws locked from lack of use. As she considered whether to challenge General Zia in an election, Bhutto went on a pilgrimage to Mecca, deciding that she was on a holy mission to return democracy to her country, and then flew to Pakistan where she was welcomed by cheering crowds. She was "a young frail girl" who challenged the military dictator who imprisoned and executed her father; "people who were afraid to speak out when her father was being hanged, came out for her" (Baughman & O'Hara, 2010). During her tenure as prime minister, she "brought cell phones and CNN to Pakistan, dispelled myths about women in leadership roles, and never shied away from a fight" (Baughman & O'Hara, 2010). After her exile to Dubai, the political turbulence in Pakistan inspired her to return, one final act of spirit and defiance, in the face of almost certain assassination.

When Wangari Maathai led mass protests in Kenya, former friends crossed the street to avoid meeting her; the president called her a "wayward woman" and told her followers, "I ask you, women, can't you discipline one of your own?" (Dater & Merton, 2008). During her years of protest, she was divorced, fired from her professional position at the university, threatened, beaten, and imprisoned. Yet she maintained her spirit and her sense of humor. At one point, she challenged male politicians and tribal leaders to improve their decision-making, telling them, "just use the anatomy that matters right now, from the neck up!" (Dater & Merton, 2008). After she was elected to office with 98% of the vote, Maathai, holding a tree in her right hand and a gun in the left, met with soldiers and encouraged them to plant trees around their barracks. When she accepted the Nobel Peace Prize in 2004, her words were stirring and prophetic:

> In the course of history there comes a time when humanity is called to make a shift, to reach a higher moral ground, a time when we have to shed our fear and give hope to each other. That time is now. (Dater & Merton, 2008)

Finally, in thinking about Suu Kyi, a wife and mother who has emerged as a globally respected voice for freedom and nonviolence, it is clear that her power is primarily derived from the image of courage, spirit, and hope that she represents to her followers. Early in her ascendance to leadership, soldiers with weapons surrounded her to stop her from holding a rally. In a dramatic and heart-stopping moment, Suu Kyi, much like the Chinese dissident who faced the tanks in Tiananmen Square, calmly walked toward the soldiers, who had their rifles raised and ready to shoot her, and then passed them to address her followers. Her courage inspired the Irish rock band U2 to write their award-winning song, *Walk On* (2001).

Popular Versus Traditional Support

Adler (1997) observed that women leaders tend to develop and use broad-based popular support rather than relying primarily on traditional, hierarchical party or structural support. Because there are so many barriers to entry for women as leaders on a global level, including tradition, culture, psychology, religion, institutional, and social constraints, it is not easy for women to gain support and move ahead within traditional, hierarchical organizations and institutions.

How do women leaders attract broad-based popular support? In some cases their popularity is inherited. Both Bhutto and Suu Kyi walked into webs of loyalty created by their charismatic fathers; they took up the leadership roles that were virtually bequeathed to them. But for the most part, women leaders, even those who inherited popular support, went out and met their constituents, person to person. In one of the most memorable scenes from *The Lady*, Suu Kyi traveled around Burma during her first political campaign, driving through stunning vistas along the coastline and through the mountains, meeting villagers in striking outfits who greeted her with great enthusiasm (Besson, 2011).

A sequence in *Chahinaz* (Chala, 2007) depicts the situation in Ireland during the 1980s, when a woman could not open her own bank account and was required to leave her job when her first child was born. These and other restrictions on women's rights, including strict anti-abortion laws, motivated Mary Robinson, an attorney with a deep commitment to personal rights, to run for office. Unnoticed and underestimated by her political enemies until it was too late, she visited virtually every corner of the country, winning the hearts of citizens who were glad that a candidate for high office "had come to listen to them rather than to wave at them from a helicopter" (Finlay, 1990, p. 107). Robinson was elected as Ireland's first female president in 1990.

Bhutto (Baughman & O'Hara, 2010) includes a sequence showing the joyous response when Benazir Bhutto returned from exile to challenge General Zia in 1986. Hundreds of thousands of people turned out to welcome her back during a 9-hour procession through the streets of Lahore. Until that triumphant return, even her own party did not take her seriously. Like Robinson, Bhutto campaigned in more communities than any politician before her (Adler, 1997). Two years later, at age 35, she became the youngest and first female prime minister of a Muslim state.

The tendency of powerful people to overestimate themselves and underestimate others may work to the benefit of emerging women leaders. It is notable that the traditional hierarchy often dismisses them; this lack of attention offers women an opportunity to hone their skills and develop a base of support. A biographer of Mary Robinson pointed out that she was "unnoticed by her political enemies until it was way too late" (Finlay, 1990, p. 151). And the documentary *Bhutto* (Baughman & O'Hara, 2010) reveals that General Zia once told a U.S. diplomat, "The worst mistake of my life was allowing Benazir to live." Attracting broad-based popular support and international media attention are signifiers of global leadership and might also be strategies that prolong the lives of these emerging women leaders.

Mentors, Role Models, and Family

Eagly and Carli (2007) noted that "a successful mentor of either gender can ease a woman's career path" (p. 1). Linehan and Scullion (2008) found that "female managers can miss out on global appointments because they lack mentors, role models, sponsorship, or access to appropriate networks—all of which are commonly available to their male counterparts" (p. 29).

The importance of fathers as role models and mentors is evident in these films. Benazir Bhutto and Aung San Suu Kyi had role models in their fathers, both charismatic leaders with strong popular support. Bhutto's father was a mentor as well as a role model, coaching her on leadership during her visits to him in prison. He cried when he saw Benazir wearing a burka for the first time and told her to go without it (Baughman & O'Hara, 2010). Chahinaz's mother had died, but her father, a progressive university professor, supported her inquiry and independence.

Although the mothers of Benazir Bhutto and Aung San Suu Kyi both served in diplomatic positions, we do not see their influence in these films. Mothers are not shown as role models or mentors as these daughters evolve from national to global leadership. There is also little evidence in the films that these global women leaders are consciously following paths that others have forged. In fact, many of these women are "firsts"—first president or first prime minister. As Adler (2007) observed, "Of the 68 women who have served in their country's highest political leadership position—either as president or prime minister—half came into office in just the last decade … more than 80 percent (57 of the 68) are the first woman their country has ever selected" (p. 331). Incidentally, the Council of Women World Leaders was not even founded until 1996.

Chahinaz represents the dawning of a new era. As a young woman with a vision, she traveled the world to seek out and learn from women who already had experience as global leaders. Emerging leaders of this next generation may not have to be pioneers; they are finding that it is possible to get advice, encouragement, and support from women who have already forged a path into global leadership.

In how many instances have patriarchal expectations within the home smothered the aspirations of potential women leaders? Eagly and Carli (2007) observed that "for women to advance to equality, men will need to take on more domestic responsibilities" (p. 1). Sandberg (2013) concurred, arguing that her own success as a global leader would not have been possible without her supportive spouse. A woman architect advised Chahinaz to "marry someone calm who won't overpower you." Later Chahinaz said, "I hope I'll find a person that I can live with in equality. To raise children as decent people with respect for women and sisters, a daughter who can speak up for herself, and a son who respects women" (Chala, 2007).

Based on scenes in these films, it would be interesting to explore the role of brothers in the lives of women who emerge as leaders. Mary Robinson talked about the benefits and challenges of growing up as a girl in a family with four brothers. Benazir Bhutto stayed behind with her father when he was imprisoned even while her brothers fled the country; later there was a family battle because Ali Bhutto had passed on his legacy to Benazir rather than the eldest son. Observe the role of the brother in a more contemporary family: Chahinaz' brother complained that because of the death of his mother and his father's progressive views, he had to help around the house, something that was not required of his male friends. As Chahinaz traveled the world to explore her opportunities as a woman, it appeared that one obstacle to her liberation may have been at home in her own family.

Impact of Media

Numerous studies have shown that media, and particularly advertising, promote stereotypical images of women. But being a woman can be an advantage when it comes to attracting media coverage. As Adler (1997) noted, women leaders often get more media coverage and exposure simply because they are women: "Because women leaders are new, they have the advantage of global visibility. Their unique status as their countries' first woman president or prime minister attracts worldwide media attention" (p. 191). Following the election of Mary Robinson as Ireland's first female president, newspapers and magazines in virtually every country in the world carried the story (Finlay, 1990).

Adler (1997) shared a telling story: In contrast to Benazir Bhutto's male predecessor

> who not only complained about receiving insufficient worldwide press coverage while abroad but also fired the Pakistani embassy's public relations officer when too few journalists showed up to cover his arrival in London, Pakistan's former Prime Minister Benazir Bhutto always received extensive media coverage no matter where in the world she travelled. (p. 191)

Globalization has affected the way in which we communicate and use media. Yes, it is important to be multilingual in this new global village, but there is a limit to how many languages one can learn. The content of the message may lessen in importance as communicators begin to rely more heavily on images and action. Much as Hollywood filmmakers have revised the content of their films to incorporate more action and less dialogue in order to appeal to global audiences, women leaders are also using—perhaps unconsciously—the power of the media to synthesize concepts to their visual essence as a way of communicating ideas in a media-saturated, postverbal world. Millions of people worldwide may not be able to identify a quote from Suu Kyi, but they will recognize the image of a solemn Asian woman with a flower tucked behind her ear. They may not recall what Benazir Bhutto said during her triumphant return to Pakistan, but they recognize the glamorous woman speaking powerfully and wearing her *chador* with confidence. A smiling African woman in a colorful headdress holding a tree can only be Wangari Maathai; she is known even in small villages in Mexico where environmentalists are adopting her tree-planting strategy.

The filmmakers who were involved in creating these films certainly drew from the extensive media coverage—print and electronic—of their subjects. Both Suu Kyi and Bhutto have been featured more than once on the cover of *Time* magazine. Wangari Maathai and Aung San Suu Kyi were awarded Nobel Peace Prizes, garnering worldwide acclaim. Extensive footage of women global leaders is readily available online and through various news sources, providing inspiration for students, role models for emerging leaders, and resource material for future researchers.

Viewers of *The Lady* may notice the end title card:

> After 15 years under house arrest, Aung San Suu Kyi was released in 2010. Yet according to Amnesty International the Burmese military continues to have one of the worst human rights records in the world and the charges against them include mass murder, torture, rape, and forced labor of both adults and children. There are currently 2100 political prisoners in detention, 17 are video journalists, some of whose colleagues courageously supplied footage for this film. (Besson, 2011)

Films and filmmakers contribute to—and benefit from—the worldwide reputation and recognition of women leaders, sometimes at great risk to themselves.

David and Goliath

Another factor might influence the media coverage of women as they emerge as global leaders: the David and Goliath effect. The media loves this storytelling frame and women often follow paths and put themselves into situations that fit right into this mediagenic storyline. For example, contemplate the images of cheering crowds and public acclaim as Benazir Bhutto emerges from an airplane in Pakistan after her visit to Mecca, clearly prepared to challenge General Zia, the man who imprisoned and executed her father. Watch the dramatic confrontation between Suu Kyi and the military as she faces down the soldiers and walks forward to deliver her campaign speech. Listen as journalists announce her arrival on the political scene by saying, "An Oxford housewife and mother of two emerged today as Burma's bright new hope for the future" (Besson, 2011). And notice how Wangari Maathai seems to consciously evoke the David versus Goliath imagery during her speeches, by saying that her success shows people that even one person, "one little woman of no significance," can stand up to a dictator and change the government (Dater & Merton, 2008).

While evoking the David and Goliath storyline can be effective in attracting attention from the media and inspiring public response, it may also provide a deeper insight into the effectiveness of women's leadership. As Gladwell (2009) points out, "David can beat Goliath by substituting effort for ability—and substituting effort for ability turns out to be a winning formula for underdogs in all walks of life" (p. 4). He added,

> We tell ourselves that skill is the precious resource and effort is the commodity. It's the other way around. Effort can trump ability ... because relentless effort is in fact something rarer than the ability to engage in some finely tuned act of motor coordination. (p. 11)

If there is any common thread through the lives of these heroic women, it would have to be relentless effort. Even in the face of enormous obstacles, these women persevere. This advice is disseminated in popular media; witness the popularity of Sheryl Sandberg's call to action in her successful 2013 book, *Lean In: Women, Work and the Will to Lead*. Calls for relentless effort are seen and heard in these films, as, for example, Sheikh Haya tells Chahinaz, "You said it can't have been easy for me. No, it wasn't. People would tell me, 'It's a sin to work with men.' I'd ignore it. I was determined to succeed at all costs. The message is: to succeed you need perseverance" (Chala, 2007).

Multicultural Experience

Journeying outside one's culture can be a powerful experience and there is evidence of the transformative power of interacting with other cultures in each of these film biographies. According to Leung, Maddux, Galinsky, and Chiu (2008), multicultural experience confers distinct beneficial effects on creative performance. They noted that there are

> numerous examples of high-profile individuals having life-changing experiences during short visits in a foreign country: The late Boris Yeltsin indicated that his ideas of reforming Russia's political economy were inspired by a visit to a Houston supermarket.... Similarly, Malcolm X's views on racial prejudice were transformed during a pilgrimage to Mecca, where he was stunned to see Muslims of all nationalities and ethnic backgrounds living and worshipping in harmony. (p. 179)

Even in the corporate world, exposure to other cultures can be transformative and a key to leadership development. John Pepper, former CEO and Chairman of Procter and Gamble, credited much of his professional development and global leadership capabilities to the time and experience gained in international assignments. He said, "Of all the career changes that I have had, the international assignment was the most important and developmental. It changed me as a person" (Bingham, Felin, & Black, 2008, p. 287). Among the competencies he developed from this international experience, Pepper cited his ability to deal with uncertainty and act in the face of ambiguity, understand the subtleties and nuances of differences in customer needs and preferences, appreciate diversity, and communicate across cultures.

The transformative impact of traveling, living, studying, or working in other cultures is clearly evident in these films. As a student at Harvard during the height of the Vietnam War protests in the United States, Benazir Bhutto saw the power of the people and said, "That early experience shaped my political being" (Baughman & O'Hara, 2010). Mary Robinson also attended Harvard during the era of student activism and anti-Vietnam war protest (Finlay, 1990). Suu Kyi grew up in Burma, but then lived, studied, and raised her family in Oxford. Wangari Maathai won a Kennedy scholarship to study in the United States and reflected on that experience:

> My five and a half years in America transformed me. What to be a good citizen was. What to be respected was. It was not easy to come back and try to apply that to my society. My society had hardly changed, but I had been completely changed. (Dater & Merton, 2008)

Culture as Obstacle

Experiencing other cultures may spur a woman's vision, creativity, and leadership, but culture can also be an obstacle to the development of women's rights and the evolution of women as leaders. Metcalfe's (2008) research into women's rights and leadership in the Middle East showed that cultural and ethical values in society and patriarchal traditions in the workplace inhibited opportunities for women. As Schein (2001) observed, "Embedded in all cultures are traditions, practices and views that impede women's equality" (p. 686).

In *Chahina*, it is evident that tradition and culture often trump the rights of women in societies as seemingly disparate as Ireland and Algeria. Algerian women are "formally under the custody of men and, in case of an inheritance, girls get only one-half of what boys get" (Chala, 2007). When Chahinaz complained to her friends about these and other injustices, one of them told her, "It's required by our religion. You can rebel against anyone, but not against God" (Chala, 2007).

Can another higher power—the United Nations—help in the struggle for women's rights? The outlook is not encouraging. Bessis (2004) has observed that some UN agencies have shown a commitment to gender agendas and women's rights, but "at the heart of many UN agencies is a legitimate concern to take into account the plurality of cultures and avoid imposing a single standard of conduct ... this policy has mainly reassured dominant ideologies of masculine superiority" (p. 637). Metcalfe (2008) has stated that globalization is not gender neutral and that men "tend to hold power in the highest positions in the hierarchies of international organizations such as the World Bank, World Trade Organization and the United Nations" (p. 9). The unwillingness of men in power—at the UN, transnational corporations, and international nongovernmental organizations—to challenge traditional cultures and customs perpetuates the lower status of women.

Power

Do women bring particular qualities to leadership based on their gender? Or are the attributes ascribed to women leaders due to cultural influences or strategic choices rather than any innate differences between men and women? Scholars have assigned particular attributes to women leaders in order to differentiate their leadership style from that of men. It is possible that these stylistic differences emerge more from women's experiences as the less powerful sex in most social, cultural, religious, and political milieu, than from any inherent qualities of gender.

Research into the relationship between power and leadership finds that people with power tend to acquire characteristics such as less ability to see things from other people's points of view, less willingness to consider the opinions of others or to be influenced by their emotions, and a greater likelihood to see others through the lens of self-interest (Galinsky, Jordan,

& Sivanathan, 2008). Since men have traditionally held the reins of power, these traits are more closely associated with masculine leadership styles. Can we assume that because of the social and cultural traditions that have circumscribed women's behavior, they have, conversely, become more likely to see things from other's points of view, more willing to be influenced by others, and more likely to take a selfless approach to leadership? As women accumulate greater power over longer periods of time, will they take on the positive and negative attributes that are now more associated with masculine styles of leadership? The existing research on the differences between leadership styles defined as masculine and feminine, the sources of those differences, and any impact of those differences in the real world is inconclusive and "open to debate" (Eagly & Johannsen-Schmidt, 2007, p. 298). Further research may shed new light on this nature versus nurture controversy.

Shein (2001) suggested that rather than focusing on the glass ceiling that is inhibiting women's upward mobility, "perhaps we also need to learn more about factors contributing to the male manager's need to have a 'protective power shield.' How can we change stereotyping views held by men and even some women?" she asked (p. 685). Why do men and even many women not see the problem of stereotyping? Perhaps the research by Galinsky et al. (2008) can help answer these questions. After years or even decades of having greater power, is it possible that men's ability to empathize and to listen has been commensurately diminished?

There are also strategic options for emerging leaders to consider in confronting a more powerful institution or authority figure. Over the past century, many of our greatest leaders—Wangari Maathai, Benazir Bhutto, and Aung San Suu Kyi, as well as Mahatma Gandhi, Martin Luther King, Jr., and Nelson Mandela—have emerged in battles against traditional social, cultural, and political institutions. Even Mary Robinson faced entrenched social, cultural, religious, and political authorities in Ireland, who imposed restrictions on women's rights that are hard to believe looking back only 30 years. It appears that these leaders were taking action based not on any qualities inherent to their gender but rather on their analysis of the best strategic approach.

How can a leader without power—without the ability to provide or withhold resources or administer punishment—motivate others toward a shared goal? Galinsky et al. (2008) used Nelson Mandela and Rosa Parks as exemplars, both of whom inspired millions despite lacking the traditional tools of power. People without power have to build their strategy based on that reality, often by taking what might be called a more stereotypically feminine approach. Those who recklessly challenge power, using what might be termed a more stereotypically masculine strategy, may be more likely to be literally or figuratively assassinated.

In studying the battle between David and Goliath, Gladwell (2009) cited the work of political scientist Ivan Arreguin-Toft, who studied wars between very large and very small countries to see how often the bigger side wins. The answer was 71.5% when the weaker side fought using conventional methods. Surprisingly, when the smaller entities were willing to use unconventional or guerilla tactics rather than confronting their enemies "straight on," their winning percentages "climbed from 28.5 percent to 63.6 percent" (p. 3).

QUESTIONS AND CHALLENGES

One discovery from my earlier research into leadership was that the people who emerged as leaders were not afraid to reach out and ask for help (Nicholson, 2009). In reviewing documentaries about both women and men as leaders, including *Taking Root: The Vision of Wangari Maathai* (Dater & Merton, 2008), *Blindsight* (Walker, 2006), and *Emmanuel's Gift* (Lax & Stern, 2005), I found that the person who was willing to reach out across social, economic, political and geographic boundaries to ask for help was often the person who emerged as a leader. Further research might tell us whether women are more willing to ask for help and how valuable that willingness might be in collecting information and building relationships as women evolve into their roles as leaders.

A final observation about the path of women as global leaders is that each woman faces, sometimes repeatedly, the decision about whether to stay or leave. Chahinaz beautifully illustrated the quandary faced by potential women leaders. At the end of the documentary, Chahinaz considers her future: Should she stay in Algeria and fight for women's rights and human rights or should she move to a country with greater legal, social, and cultural support for women? In these films and stories, it is the women who stayed—or the women who chose to return—who emerged as leaders. Even though greater freedoms were available to them elsewhere, they returned out of a sense of responsibility to all, out of a sense of dedication to the greater good. A decision to participate is the first, and perhaps the most essential, choice for the next generation of women leaders.

ACKNOWLEDGMENTS

The author thanks Sally Jo Fifer, President and CEO, Independent Television Service (ITVS), and Debra Zimmerman, Executive Director, Women Make Movies, for their contributions to this research.

REFERENCES

Adler, N. J. (1997). Global leadership: Women leaders. *Management International Review, 37*(1), 171–196.

Adler, N. J. (2007). One world: Women leading and managing worldwide. In D. Bilimoria & S. K. Piderit (Eds.), *Handbook of women in business and management* (pp. 330–355). Cheltenham, England: Elgar.

Baughman, B., & O'Hara, J. (Directors). (2010). *Bhutto* [Documentary film]. Los Angeles, CA: Bhutto Film.

Bessis, S. (2003). International organizations and gender: New paradigms and old habit. *Signs: Journal of Women in Culture and Society, 29*(2), 633–647.

Besson, L. (Director). (2011). *The lady* [Feature film]. Japan, France & UK: Europacorp, Left Bank Pictures, France 2 Cinema.

Bingham, C., Felin, T., & Black, J. S. (2000). An interview with John Pepper: What it takes to be a global leader. *Human Resource Management, 39*(2,3), 287–292.

Bolman, L. G., & Deal, T. E. (1995) *Leading with soul: An uncommon journey of spirit.* San Francisco, CA: Jossey-Bass.

Chala, S. (Director). (2007). *Chahinaz: What rights for women?* [Documentary film]. US: Article 2 & ITVS International.

Dater, A., & Merton, L. (Directors). (2008). *Taking root: The vision of Wangari Maathai* [Documentary film]. Los Angeles, CA: Soundchef Studios.

Eagly, A. H., & Carli, L. L. (2007). *Through the labyrinth: The truth about how women become leaders.* Boston, MA: Harvard Business School Press.

Eagly, A. H., & Johannesen-Schmidt, M. C. (2007). Leadership style matters: The small, but important, style differences between male and female leaders. In D. Bilimoria & S. K. Piderit (Eds.), *Handbook of women in business and management* (pp. 279–303). Cheltenham, England: Elgar.

Finlay, F. (1990). *Mary Robinson: A president with a purpose.* Dublin, Ireland: O'Brien.

Galinsky, A. D., Jordan, J., & Sivanathan, N. (2008). Harnessing power to capture leadership. In J. B. Ciulla, C. L. Hoyt, G. R. Goethals, D. R. Forsyth, & M. A. Genovese (Eds.), *Leadership at the crossroads* (pp. 283–299). Westport, CT: Greenwood.

Gladwell, M. (2009, May 11). Annals of innovation: How David beats Goliath; When underdogs break the rules. *The New Yorker.* Retrieved from http://www.newyorker.com/reporting/2009/05/11/090511fa_fact_gladwell?currentPage=all

Independent Television Service (ITVS). (2014). *Women and girls lead film catalog.* Retrieved from http://www.itvs.org/women-and-girls-lead/resources

Lax, L., & Stern, N. (Directors). (2005). *Emmanuel's gift* [Documentary film]. United States: First Look International.

Leung, A. K., Maddux, W. W., Galinsky, A. D., & Chiu C. (2008, April). Multicultural experience enhances creativity: The when and how. *American Psychologist, 63*(3), 169–181.

Linehan, M., & Scullion, H. (2008). The development of female global managers: The role of mentoring and networking. *Journal of Business Ethics, 83*(1), 29–40.

Nicholson, M. A. (2009, November 14). *Reel leaders: Coaching for transformation*. Workshop given at the International Leadership Association's 11th annual Global Conference, Prague, Czech Republic.

Sandberg, S. (2013). *Lean in: Women, work and the will to lead*. New York, NY: Knopf.

Schein, V. E. (2001). A global look at psychological barriers to women's progress in management. *Journal of Social Issues, 57*(4), 675-688.

U2. (2001). Walk on. On *All that you can't leave behind* [CD]. New York, NY: Island Records.

Walker, L. (Director). (2006). *Blindsight* [Documentary film]. United States: Robson Entertainment.

CHAPTER 12

MALALA YOUSAFZAI

The Power and Paradox of Global Celebrity

Carol Burbank

In only 5 years since she gave her first public speech at the age of 12, Malala Yousafzai has evolved from a vocal advocate for girl's education in Pakistan into a Taliban culture-war survivor, global activist, and winner of the Nobel Peace Prize. Now she has become a nearly mythic icon, not only representing continuing Pakistani resistance against the Taliban and the struggle for girls' education in her home nation, but also the fight against Muslim fundamentalism, terrorism, and the equal rights of girls and women all over the world.

Yousafzai's activist leadership offers an extraordinary case study for a rare but pivotal role that marginalized women can claim in global leadership. Her alchemical blend of activism, celebrity, mythopolitical identity, and vision create an irresistible narrative framework that has elevated her into near-sainthood. In this chapter, I will explore this iconic role as an example of leadership by synecdoche, in which one person comes to represent, symbolically, emotionally, and strategically, a whole population and cause. After a summary of Yousafzai's life and work, I examine the leadership power of this one-as-all, all-as-one position, an effective tool for gathering attention and concrete support internationally. The role is nonetheless problematic, requiring great sacrifice on the part of the representative leader and potentially obscuring more complex, politically nuanced intersectional identities for the representative leader and other less prominent Islamic women activists.

CONTEXT: YOUSAFZAI'S REMARKABLE LIFE SO FAR

Yousafzai's is an undeniably inspiring story. I will tell it to offer a context for my discussion of her influential leadership role, based primarily on a strategically mythopolitical interpretation of her biography, and bolstered by her power as a speaker and her persistent vision for equal education for women and girls in Pakistan and the world.

She was born in 1997 to a Pashtun family in Pakistan's Swat Valley. Devoted to centrist Islam and progressive democratic reform, her activist, educator father and traditional Purdah-observing mother raised her and her two brothers in Mingora, Swat's main city. She was educated in her father's often-struggling school, which welcomed both girls and boys and trained them separately, as was the custom. When the Taliban seized power in 2007, the increasing violence against girls' schools threatened her family's life and livelihood. Coached by her father, she gave her first public speech, "How Dare the Taliban Take Away My Basic Right to an Education?" at a protest in Peshawar in 2009.

That same year, she began to write an anonymous blog for the British Broadcasting Corporation (BBC) Urdu about life under the Taliban. Although she was already a vocal activist, having been interviewed on television and speaking at rallies, this was a dangerous move because she shared highly critical stories of daily life under Taliban repression in an international forum. She took the pseudonym, Gul Makai (Cornflower), a heroine in a Pashtun folk story about lovers who cause and then stop an ethnic war (Yousafzai & Lamb, 2013, p. 155). Soon afterward, during ceasefire talks between the Taliban and the Pakistani government, Malala was a featured guest, talking about the value of girls' education on national TV with influential host Hamid Mir, increasing her visibility even more.

When the ceasefire collapsed only months later, the Yousafzai family was separated when Malala fled the Swat Valley with her mother and brothers. After the conflict ended with Pakistan's army controlling Swat, she returned to her devastated town to rebuild her life. At this point, her father revealed that she was the BBC Blogger, and *New York Times* reporter Adam Ellick filmed a documentary about her activism and life. The Taliban continued to dominate the Swat Valley, however, and she and her father both received death threats because they continued to criticize the ongoing violence and incorrect interpretations of Islamic law and texts. They persisted in rebuilding the school and speaking out against the Taliban. Yousafzai became famous in Pakistan in 2011 when she was nominated for the International Children's Peace Prize and won Pakistan's National Youth Peace Prize for her activism.

In October 2012, a masked gunman stopped her school bus and shot her and some of her schoolmates. She was hit just over her left eye, and the bullet traveled through her head and neck to lodge in her shoulder blade. Yousafzai's biography reported that the British doctor who cared for her commented that

> she had never been in a situation quite like this. Not only was Peshawar dangerous for Westerners, but after googling me she realized this was no ordinary case. "If anything had happened to her it would have been blamed on the white woman.... If [Malala] died I would have killed Pakistan's Mother Teresa." (Yousafzai & Lamb, 2013, p. 263)

When bone shards in her brain threatened her life, she was moved to Birmingham, England, for surgery. She was joined by her family and recovered there. The Pakistani government covered her extensive medical bills, and she received global attention in the media and thousands of cards and gifts (Yousafzai & Lamb, 2013). By November, she was conscious and recovering, and continued her activism from her hospital bed, speaking to the press, and becoming the iconic representation of the-girl-who-survived a Taliban attack. She remained in Birmingham with her family, granted asylum because of ongoing death threats in her home country.

In the 2 years since her relocation to the West, she has received numerous awards and nominations. In December of 2012, Pakistan's president established a $10 million education fund in her name, and she was declared a runner-up for *Time Magazine*'s Person-of-the-Year. Other awards, in no particular order, include honorary Canadian Citizenship, the 2013 Sakharov Prize, the RAW in WAR Anna Politkovskaya Award, the Clinton Global Initiative Global Citizen Award, the Amnesty International Ambassador of Conscience Award, the Simone de Beauvoir Prize, the OPEC Fund for International Development's Annual Award, the Rome Prize for Peace and Humanitarian Action, the Oklahoma City National Memorial Reflections of Hope Award, the Mother Teresa Memorial Award for Social Justice, and finally the Nobel Peace Prize itself (2014), and *Glamour Magazine*'s 2013 Woman of the Year (Yusufzai 2013). In 2013, she created the Malala Fund; initially under the umbrella of Vital Voices Women's partnership, it was an NGO dedicated to supporting education for girls in Pakistan and all over the world.

The Malala Fund's first grant created "a program in Pakistan to ensure that 40 girls ranging in age from 5–12 who would otherwise be engaged in domestic labor ... attend school," offering stipends to the girls' families as well as enrolling them in school and paying for "resources to adapt to an educational environment, such as school uniforms, shoes and learning materials" (Vital Voices, 2014, para. 7). As of the writing of this chapter, the most recent Malala Fund initiative was a partnership with the Vodaphone Foundation to use mobile phones "to promote mobile-based literacy and education projects all over the world," particularly for girls and women (Vodaphone Foundation, 2014, para. 1).

Yousafzai's rallying cry for universal education for girls has been heard at prestigious universities, international conferences, and the United Nations, where she spoke on June 12, 2013, her 16th birthday, named "Malala Day" by the Secretary-Generals' Global Education First Initiative. It was a straightforward, beautifully delivered speech. The core of her message, then and now, is

> Dear brothers and sisters, do remember one thing. Malala Day is not my day. Today is the day of every woman, every boy and every girl who have raised their voice for their rights. There are hundreds of Human rights activists and social workers who are not only speaking for human rights, but who are struggling to achieve their goals of education, peace and equality. Thousands of people have been killed by the terrorists and millions have been injured. I am just one of them.
>
> So here I stand ... one girl among many. I speak—not for myself, but for all girls and boys. I raise up my voice—not so that I can shout, but so that those without a voice can be heard. Those who have fought for their rights:
>
> Their right to live in peace.
> Their right to be treated with dignity.
> Their right to equality of opportunity.
> Their right to be educated....
>
> The terrorists thought that they would change our aims and stop our ambitions but nothing changed in my life except this: Weakness, fear and hopelessness died. Strength, power and courage was born. I am the same Malala. My ambitions are the same. My hopes are the same. My dreams are the same.... I am here to speak up for the right of education of every child. I want education for the sons and the daughters of all the extremists especially the Taliban. (Yousafzai, 2013, paras. 4–6)

LEADERSHIP BY SYNECDOCHE

When Malala Yousafzai frames her activism, as shown in her speech, as the choice to speak for those who cannot raise their voices, she raises her leadership discourse from the personal to the universal. In essence, she does her best to turn the considerable recognition she has received for her courage and persistence away from her biography and toward the political and social constraints on women and girls in Pakistan and the world. She also makes a concerted effort to expand even that broad call to include everyone "struggling to achieve their goals of education, peace and equality" (Yousafzai, 2013, para. 4).

I believe this rhetoric is genuinely heartfelt. From her earliest activism, she has stepped forward when others hesitated. One example out of many from her autobiography expressed her clarity and heartfelt desire to support change despite the obvious dangers:

> When I overheard my father talking about [her schoolmate's father forbidding his daughter from writing the BBC Urdu blog], I said, "Why not me?" I wanted people to know what was happening. Education is our right, I said. Just as it is our right to sing. (Yousafzai & Lamb, 2013, p. 154)

Although any autobiography must be interpreted with an eye to strategic self-representation, this story is only one of many moments when Yousafzai explained her choices as, "Why not me?" As the near-fatal 2012 attack demonstrated, she placed herself in great danger, since less obviously political choices led to the many executions, with bodies dumped regularly in the public square. In her autobiography, she tells the story of one of these victims, the traditional dancer Shabana, whose corpse was left as a warning to other women (Yousafzai & Lamb, 2013, p. 147). This report is confirmed by a BBC News story of the long-term display of the bodies of people tortured and killed in public executions, a common tactic by the Taliban in Pakistan and Afghanistan (Hundreds witness, 2010).

Creating an identity as a spokesperson for those who cannot speak frames her leadership identity beyond national, faith, and gender boundaries, expanding from her grounding in her special experiences. It is a way to resist the "Great Man" leadership stereotype, which would weaken her activist celebration of everyday resistance. Further, it establishes her as what Haslam, Reicher, and Platow (2011) called an in-group prototype; in Yousafzai's case an ordinary girl with the same desires as all girls. In-group prototypes create a resonant narrative of inclusion. Specifically,

> the more representative an individual is seen to be of a given social identity—the more he or she is clearly "one of us"—the more influential he or she will be within the group and the more willing other group members will be to follow his or her direction. (Haslam et al., 2011, p. 75)

Augoustos and deGaris (2012) analyzed American President Obama's strategic construction of his identity as a classic in-group prototypical role, neither black nor white, but American. In the process, Obama became "truly representative of the diverse and varied experiences within America" (p. 572). Being perceived as prototypical or in-group means representing a group's shared beliefs and values rather than being typical or ordinary.

> Thus, it is possible for a leader to emerge who at face value is atypical (as in Obama's case), but who in time is able to craft and project an identity that is perceived to embody the emergent identity of the group as a whole or, as in the case of those who seek to radically transform and change their society, political leaders who offer an alternative identity that the group comes to value over time. (Augoustinos & deGaris, 2012, p. 566)

As a person of color, Obama's choice to ground his identity in American nationalism and corresponding ideologies embracing diversity is often seen as a leadership strategy to resist the "Magic Negro" stereotype of exceptionalism that generally masks implicit racism (King, 2011, p. 79). His effectiveness as a biracial president depends on being perceived as American to the bone, because of his specific role and its challenges in U.S. culture today. As a young woman of color, and a Muslim, Yousafzai's choice of identity prototype is of a different sort, as is her role: global in nature, international in scope, and nationalist only in details of her cause and her development as an activist. At the same time, rather than resisting identity assignment based on gender, religion, and race, she emphasizes these differences because they were the reason she herself had to stand to claim equality. These differences could serve to inspire other marginalized people to stand against terrorism and oppression.

Yousafzai is simultaneously an ex-patriot and an exile, an activist and a politician, a victim and a survivor, a citizen of the world and of Pakistan, as well as a Muslim and an activist. These potentially contradictory categories are more complex than her public global identity. Perhaps most challenging is her contested and controversial role in Pakistan (Masood & Walsh, 2013). Despite her honors from the Pakistan government and the pride she expresses for her country, she is a hero/villain in her own nation. She has been called a "western puppet," and a "global brand" (Ghosh, 2013, para. 10). But one reporter found ways her story inspired activists and progressive citizens in Pakistan as they waited for news about her 2013 nomination for the Nobel Prize:

> There are still hopes that the mere fact that Malala was nominated can push education to the forefront of Pakistan's development agenda. "The Peace Prize would have been a good symbol," says Zaidi, the education advocate, "but Malala's voice is still deeply resonant." At the school, Azka says that the moment shouldn't be wasted. "We shouldn't just be satisfied with a nomination or a prize," she says. "We need to use this moment to do more for girls'

education in Pakistan. There are thousands of Malalas in Pakistan. (Ellison, 2013, p. 29)

In this way, she does represent many others, specifically and accurately, in Pakistan. As a girl/woman, her resistance is at the heart of some of that Muslim nation's most difficult cultural and legislative issues (Jamal, 2006). But she is undeniably a hero in Western global circles, representing a typical girl with atypical courage. In this way, she is generating considerable social capital with her role as global activist, an in-group prototype designed to inspire others to demand the same emergent identity—full citizen—as both followers and leaders.

But there is another element to her identity that exaggerates and expands the strategic in-group prototyping and generosity of her rhetoric, bringing her leadership firmly into the realm of iconographic global celebrity. As if she has become a mythic figure, we have adopted her as an official, out-of-cultural-context representative for all Muslim women and girls, by definition repressed and struggling, a kind of leadership by synecdoche that has more to do with her role as iconic survivor than her cause. Many marginalized leaders employ the motivating power of synecdoche, a symbolic turn of identity in which a part is made to represent the whole, because of the weight of the narratives, stereotypes, and cultural assumptions projected on them. Yousafzai has gone so far that she may be in danger of becoming a "Magic Muslim" for the Christian West.

In this role, she is simultaneously "one of us" and an extraordinary "other," which gives her voice greater power and influence. Because her story represents subjugation by Taliban fundamentalists, it has been easy to expand that synecdoche of suffering Muslim women and symbolically adopt her as "everybody's daughter," as her father has called her (Topping, 2012). Further, her call for fundamental human rights is so universal, at least in its liberal appeal in the West, that it is easy to adopt her as a member of our democratic "family." Because she is a child, we are even more drawn to her, even more willing to hold her up as a placeholder for the universal girl-child oppressed by the Taliban and terrorism. The result is that she is a leader with enormous clout, considering her age and origins. Simply reviewing her accomplishments, clarity, and partnerships demonstrates another reason behind this synecdoche—we want to *be* Yousafzai, to have her courage. If we cannot be her, we want to protect her. She says she speaks for the voiceless; to us she represents all those who need a voice, particularly the innocent and the vulnerable, again, women and girls under the Taliban. She asks us to stand for justice and equality; whether we do or not, she has taken that leadership role in a way that marks her as a saint, and perhaps, martyr, wise beyond her years. Synecdoche has made her larger than life, for good or ill.

LEADING BY SYNECDOCHE: MYTHOPOLITICAL INFLUENCE AND THE PARADOX OF IN/VISIBILITY

Yousafzai's is a powerful position and her paradoxical identity may be one of the necessary conditions of global activist celebrity. Leading by synecdoche gives her unprecedented visibility, which ensures access to money, institutions, alliances, media, celebrities, and socially minded entrepreneurs and politicians. But the iconic identity that gives her that access also blurs her more specific message, reinforcing Western ignorance of Islam, women's varied roles in Muslim nations, and the complexities of the psychosocial politics of Islamic nationalism in Pakistan.

Strengths of Yousafzai's Global Leadership Role

It is hard to argue with Yousafzai's obvious success. However long it lasts (and I expect her leadership influence will continue long after her survivor celebrity has cooled), she has seemingly unlimited access to opportunities to make change and inspire local and global initiatives. She has been given, and taken without hesitation, a stage from which she can share her message, create partnerships, and find funding to take practical steps toward equal education.

Her current leadership life seems to embody what I call "mythopolitical activism"—social movement leadership that mythologizes autobiographical details to inspire political action and social transformation. I take this phrase partly from the activist/author Audre Lorde's (1982) term, "biomythography," from her groundbreaking autobiography, *Zami: A New Spelling of My Name*, in which she creatively integrated archetypes, magical realism, biographical fact, and the contradictions of her identity as a lesbian of color from Grenada. The idea is also influenced by my research in transformational leadership and archetypes, and through Storyweaving, my training program for mastering the shapeshifting roles and mythic narratives at the core of leadership processes. These often paradoxical expectations and identities require resilience and self-awareness in order to be sustainable and effective (Burbank, 2012a, 2012b, 2014). In activist contexts, these mythic roles and performed/projected identities are even more important in leading change.

Mythopolitical activism is, by its nature, leadership by synecdoche because it accesses universal archetypes that excite trust, inspiration, and imitation. Yousafzai embodies a heroic survivor's story with activist focus and personal transcendence, made even more appealing by her youth and clarity of vision. In her autobiography, she offered a playful, earnest glimpse into her own biomythography, which could be called the making of an activist. Even the sections that described children's games and fantasies have political ramifications and are meant to inspire or justify activism as well as tell the story of her experiences. In the book, she became a compelling and independent character, given extraordinary freedom and responsibility by her father. Ironically, her *wildness*, which seems quite conservative in Western terms, was in itself heretical to the Taliban ideas about proper training for girls. Further, she is steadfast in representing the challenges and history of Pakistan, an admirable educational project in itself.

The irreverent, brave, and cosmopolitan biomythographical narrative of her youthful perspective can be quite powerful, giving a sense of a rebel streak behind her saintly public presence and simple speeches. One of the clearest examples is her description of the Taliban, when they arrived to dominate Swat Valley:

> I was ten when the Taliban came to our valley. Moniba [her best friend] and I had been reading the Twilight books and longed to be vampires. It seemed to us that the Taliban arrived in the night just like vampires. They appeared in groups, armed with knives and Kalashnikovs.... They were strange-looking men with long straggly hair and beards and camouflage vests over their shalwar kamiz.... They had jogging shoes or cheap plastic sandals on their feet, and sometimes stockings over their heads with holes for their eyes, and they blew their noses dirtily into the ends of their turbans.... They looked so dark and dirty that my father's friend described them as "people deprived of baths and barbers." (Yousafzai & Lamb, 2013, p. 111)

This vision of the Taliban as unkempt, militaristic vampires offered a glimpse into the private jokes and resistance to their presence during their rise to power. This dramatic, archetypal framing captures the political imagination by seamlessly connecting Western fear and hatred of terrorism with a description of Taliban arrival in Mingora, and the disdainful if distrustful reception they received before they seized power. These are not holy men, it is clear. Seen through this literary version of a child's eyes (and I say that because I do not know the relationship or process by which Lamb helped Yousafzai write this autobiography), her attraction is clear. She is both amusing and wise, young, and brave, and the juxtapositions in her narrative make her mythopolitical synecdoche even more compelling.

In reality, though, that synecdoche does not come from Yousafzai, or even her father, whose quiet hand clearly guides his charismatic daughter's development. It was progressive politicians, ordinary citizens, and NGOs in the Western world that put her up on this pedestal as a representative of all girls. While Yousafzai was still in the hospital, on the 15th of October in 2012, Gordon Brown, then UN Special Envoy for Global Education and a former British Prime Minister, launched the "I am Malala" campaign—a petition in her name to support her campaign for girl's education (NDTV,

2013). The petition demanded equal education by 2015. Brown called especially for every country to create "a national plan setting out exact teacher needs, and the building and financing requirements for achieving the 2015 target, ... including strategies for policing an end to child labour, child marriage, and discrimination against girls" (Brown, 2012, para. 14).

This UN petition was only the beginning of her global role, and it happened before she had completed physical therapy to restore her ability to move and speak normally. The name of the campaign, "I am Malala," was emblazoned on buttons worn by thousands of supporters, only the beginning of the romanticized, powerful identification that has led to Yousafzai's potent presence as a leader with a prototypical universal identity. Synecdoche thus functions by creating an idealized, mythic aura with a heroic mirror effect that engages followers as potential leaders. In its most complete sense, with the part becoming the whole metaphorically and the whole yearning to become that part that symbolizes all of us, synecdoche is a powerful, iterative process of persuasion and inspiration.

Now, mostly recovered and lovely, especially when her scars are airbrushed in celebrity magazine photo shoots, she brings a charismatic visibility to many issues around the oppression of women and girls across the world. Her presence, as a representative of an oppressed and rising class, encourages outpourings of global support. Her ability to project personal authenticity while shapeshifting into daughter, sister, warrior, and hero roles makes her story powerfully persuasive. Her reputation, oratory, and story inspires girls and women to stand up authentically as leaders in their own right. Thanks to her articulate presence and her allies and partners, she is rapidly becoming as recognizable and beloved as Nelson Mandela, another larger-than-life leader who symbolized his cause, his nation, and people of color all over the world. It remains to be seen what Yousafzai will become once she receives her full education and becomes an adult. However, it is clear from her example that leadership by synecdoche creates a platform for marginalized women to tell their stories strategically with global partners, amplifying and extending their reach.

Challenges of Her Global Leadership Role

Leadership by synecdoche is not an easy role to maintain. Yousafzai's dependence on mythopolitical celebrity, the temporary nature of the fame from her surprising survival, and her developing womanly maturity mean that she will probably have to adapt her leadership style in order to sustain her influence. In addition, her global celebrity involves great danger because she is still under threat of death. In 2013, the Taliban renewed their fatwa, complained (with some justification) that she has been used in Western propaganda, and were quoted as saying,

> She is not a brave girl and has no courage. We will target her again and attack whenever we have a chance. She accepted that she attacked Islam so we tried to kill her, and if we get another chance we will definitely kill her and that will make us feel proud. Islam prohibits killing women, but except those that support the infidels in their war against our religion. (Nolan & Duell, 2013, paras. 5–6)

These threats only strengthened her celebrity, giving the press an opportunity to review the earlier shooting, quote her pacifist response with telling headlines like "Malala Yousafzai turns the other cheek to the Taliban" (Simpson & Brumfield, 2013), and remind us of her much-cited personal goals. "I will be a politician in my future," she told the BBC. "I want to change the future of my country and I want to make education compulsory" (Simpson & Brumfield, 2013, para. 28). However, the threats are real, even though they only make her seem more precious and powerful and the Taliban less in control.

There are other, perhaps equally problematic but less personal issues with leadership by synecdoche, along with its mythopolitical sensibility and globalized liberal universalism. First, celebrity such as Yousafzai's may obscure more complex, culturally embedded, less visible activist work by other Muslim women in the Middle East, regardless of her best efforts to educate Westerners about the situation there. The struggle for women's rights in Pakistan has created a unique and complicated new kind of woman leader, defining her leadership role within devout or secular Muslim values. Whatever their connection to Muslim culture, these leaders invariably come up against the "Islamization" implemented by fundamentalists, and the dominance of Shariah laws (religious courts) over civic legal protections for women citizens. Where the dominant arbiters of personal and public regulation are fundamentalist, there is also pressure for the secular legal system to mirror the oppression of women and girls. Therefore Muslim women activists work in a contentious, evolving Islamic context, culturally and legally complex and fraught with moral and civic controversies that are difficult to understand from the outside.

This complexity in part explains why we hear a great deal about Malala, but we do not hear as much about some of the women activists in Pakistan who work from within Islam. Yousafzai's simple, universal-seeming message requires very little cultural translation, but the work of more embedded activists needs nuanced and detailed contextualization. It is more difficult to create an inspiring sound byte from the work of Farhat Hashmi, who founded an Islamic movement called Al-Huda, "a network of schools in which women study the Quran and other religious texts, and share a conviction that they can reform Pakistani society by spreading their version of Islamic belief and practice" (Mushtaq, 2010, p. 3). Nor do we hear about the in-country work of peace activists like Sameena Imtiaz, the founding head and Executive Director of the Peace Education and Development Foundation, conducting culturally impactful trainings for youth on peace and conflict resolution as well as on gender and human rights issues (for details about Imtiaz' work, see Habib, 2013).

I believe Yousafzai overshadows these and other activists, not because she sets out to take center stage, but because her message is one of fundamental rights, and her iconic role is framed in terms of good/liberal, bad/fundamentalist, Western constructions. These binary constructions obscure the reasons it is so difficult to challenge ongoing Taliban control over women, and make other stories less "marketable" in the media. We do not become aware of what we cannot see, and therefore we lose many of the nuances of the struggle. "The unstable constructions of 'woman' and 'citizen' that emerge through the interaction between the discourses of Islamization and modern nation-state formation in Pakistan" are not easily translated into a Westernized discourse of universal rights (Jamal, 2006, p. 285). They are embedded in a culture deeply ambivalent about the negotiation between secular Muslim democracy and traditional Muslim fundamentalism. According to Homi Bhaba, these ambivalent personal negotiations are the key to effective social change toward moderate and inclusive solutions.

> In order for there to be political change from fundamentalism to moderate Islam, it becomes necessary to motivate the movement between positions, to acknowledge the ambivalence within any site of identification or enunciation.... It is the ambivalence in their coexistence—the proximate relation between persons—that becomes the basis for the performance of moderation as a practice of life. (Bhaba, 1997, pp. 434–435)

It could be argued that Yousafzai's mythopolitics interferes with these necessary negotiations, trading on the polarization of the vampire Taliban with liberatory Western secular culture. Her synecdochic role may motivate more support for initiatives from outside Pakistan while working against relationships that mitigate polarized positions within the embattled nation. The Taliban's violent protection of rigid gender roles is at the core of its interpretation of Islam, and Western societies tend to impose our secularized beliefs about women's roles and rights without examining the psychosocial realities of other cultures. Granted, it may seem like common sense to educate girls, and there is ample proof that educating girls and women raises per capita income nationally, increases family security and class mobility, fosters democracy, and saves children's lives (Women Deliver,

2014). There is also a great deal of specific and complicated cultural resistance to the movement for equal and improved education for all in Pakistan. According to Leon Wieseltier (2012), "The war against schools is not just a war against schools," and the battle has only begun (para. 2).

This cultural misunderstanding, based in unexamined assumptions and stereotypes, results in attitudes that make the complexities of women's position in Muslim nations largely invisible, turning women into symbols of Taliban oppression, although not always resulting in the creation of celebrity, as in the case of Yousafzai.

> Discourses about Muslim women's victimization, which have intensified during the U.S.-led "war on terror," position Muslim women as objects in a debate of Islam versus the West, tradition versus modernity, and threaten to erase accounts of Muslim women's agency and activism within their own societies. We need to examine Muslim women's ambivalent positioning within religion, society and politics, and family and nation and recuperate the ways in which women appropriate contradictory discourses to assert their identities as daughters and citizens. (Jamal, 2006, p. 283)

In other words, we may have adopted Malala as "everybody's daughter," but she and other Muslim feminist activists have a very specific struggle with emerging identities and leadership challenges that we need to understand in order to offer sustainable partnerships and support. Leadership by synecdoche obscures these complexities in exchange for charismatic headlines and mythopolitical storytelling.

As leadership scholars and practitioners, it is important to consider the role of multiple identities in framing a leader's role, especially for marginalized leaders. Intersectionality is an approach that "reveals the connections between multiple identities and personas of social actors; it suggests that the analysis of complex social situations should not be reduced to singular categories but should include connected roles and situations" (Sanchez-Hucles & Davis, 2010, p. 176). Tracking the intersectionality of identities that lie behind the master frame of a leader's narrative is equally important, especially the call for dignity and fundamental human rights. For synechdochic leaders like Malala Yousafzai, whose call for action is experienced as universal, intersectionality reveals the specific cultural forces and roles she participates in, hidden behind her mythic status.

These roles are deeply gendered reflections of social identity, as are the discourses that hide them. Interestingly, Singerman (2013) suggested that dignity is not a universal topic, but culturally gendered. In the right rhetoric, with culturally engaged partnerships,

> the master frame of dignity has the potential to support campaigns for women's access to public space, for the integrity of women's right to protest,

and for protection from arbitrary coercive authority (torture, sexual violence, arbitrary arrest without due process) through the rule of law and the justice system. (p. 20)

Accordingly, the Western tendency to universalize diversity in order to categorize activists in generic, unexamined discourses of fundamental rights, means that culturally embedded movements and their partnerships with NGOs stay below mainstream media outlets. The well-intentioned elevation of iconic leaders like Yousafzai also elevates rhetoric that makes activism seem too one-size-fits-all. Referencing the work of McEwan (2001), Mohanty (1988), Narayan (1998), and Udayagiri (1995), Habib (2013) wrote,

> Though it is important to pay attention to women's needs, it is equally crucial to avoid representing all women as a group, either in the case of security needs, or in any other field.... Women's diverse experiences cannot be understood without a reference to the context in which they live; therefore, it has been with this in mind that women from outside the West have criticized Western feminists' perceptions that they can speak on behalf of all women. (p. 11)

Finally, the mythopolitics of Yousafzai's representation of the Taliban, however real an experience it was, has been tightly framed by the binary good/evil equation that makes Taliban supporters seem monolithic and evil. This rhetorical shift makes her elevation to near-sainthood even more problematic. Politically useful for Western politicians and UN alliances, the opposition, the seductive role of Yousafzai as victim triumphant has more power as propaganda than policymaking. According to Khattak (2004), Yousafzai is not the first case of this strategic propaganda. The United States has framed its fight against the Taliban through criticism of their "war on women" since the first Bush administration, echoing an approach made most famous by Great Britain, which justified its colonization of India, in part, as a way of "introducing [their] subject populations to civilized norms, and rescuing brown women from brown men" (p. 221). Further,

> the obscurantism of the Taliban is symbolized in western discourse by their attitude in three key areas: the imposition of the veil, women's right to education and their right to employment. This depiction only reproduces Afghan women as victims to reinscribe racism and empire. Women's needs and priorities are rarely addressed by the politics and policies entrenched within the current system of unequal social relations. Women are frequently used as pawns in colonial and neocolonial discourse, and the recent example of Afghanistan is no exception. In the present context, the process that reversed the few gains regarding women's rights over the course of a century began with the takeover by the Mujahideen, who were assisted by western countries

including the USA and Britain, as well as China, Saudi Arabia and Egypt. (Khattak, 2004, p. 230)

In the Western imagination, then, we have embraced Yousafzai as an embodiment of resistance against these three symbols of Taliban evil. Whatever good she may do—and she is doing considerable good—there is an equal danger that she will become entirely symbolic and unable to reconnect meaningfully to her home culture or her cause. In mythopolitical terms, she is rapidly becoming "the girl who lived," a real-life Harry Potter being pitted, rhetorically and in reality, against Voldemort (i.e., the Taliban). In the real world, these absolutes cannot hold the compromises that sustainable reform and culturally meaningful leadership must create.

CONCLUSION

Malala Yousafzai is an extraordinary individual, and her work in the 5 short years since she became an activist has been inspiring. This chapter does not question that well-documented fact, nor do I mean to criticize her choices. She is a talented, dedicated 16-year-old activist who has been swept up into historical events and global debates. Her clarity of vision, focused rhetoric, and articulate presence makes her elevation to a high position of celebrity leadership seem not only natural but inevitable, despite the remarkable and dangerous path she has taken to get there.

Her role as a leader who represents all Muslim women and girls, and increasingly all girls and children who want an education, is both positive and problematic. She leads first through her mythopolitical narrative of survival and resistance. Second, she embodies leadership by synecdoche, largely imposed by her Western allies and the publicity machine they have marshaled to use her to galvanize support for her call for universal education for girls and social reform against the Taliban. Both strategies are potent forms of sociopolitical leadership but will require sacrifice and strategy to maintain integrity without losing the focus of her cause in the complex elaborations of iconic celebrity.

As a young woman of color and a devout Muslim, she cannot be globalized without consequences, either to herself or her cause. She has created a persuasive master frame to challenge the exclusion of girls and women from access to education under Taliban rule. However, there is little room in her inspiring mythopolitical activism to express the complex and culturally specific intersectionality of identities that shape women's cultural roles as emergent leaders in the Islamic world. This chapter is an initial effort to respectfully contextualize those possible consequences in a way that sheds light on the need for an intersectionality framework and effective cross-cultural alliances as we consider the impact of leadership roles for women in global arenas.

REFERENCES

Augostinos, M., & de Garis, S. (2012). Too black or not black enough?: Social identity complexity in the political rhetoric of Barak Obama. *European Journal of Social Psychology, 42*, 564–577.

Bhaba, H. K. (1997). Editor's introduction: Minority maneuvers and unsettled negotiations. *Critical Inquiry, 23*(3), 431–459.

Brown, G. (2012, October 25). Malala Yousafzai's courage can start new movement for global education. *The Guardian.* Retrieved from http://www.theguardian.com/global-development/poverty-matters/2012/oct/25/malala-yousafzai-courage-global-education

Burbank, C. (2012a). Leadership is a lived story: A call for radical embodiment and soul resilience in transformational leadership development. *Integral Leadership Review.* Retrieved from http://integralleadershipreview.com/8586-leadership-is-a-lived-story-a-call-for-radical-embodiment-and-soul-resilience-in-transformational-leadership-development

Burbank, C. (2012b). Shapeshifter leadership: Responding creatively to the challenges of a complex world. In C. Pearson (Ed.), *The transforming leader: New approaches to leadership for the 21st century* (pp. 140–151). San Francisco, CA: Berrett-Koehler.

Burbank, C. (2014). *Lead me on: Spirited thoughts about leadership, transformation, and survival.* Retrieved from http://leadershipspirit.wordpress.com/

Ellison, J. (2013). The 2011 global women's progress report. *Newsweek, 158*(13), 27–29.

Ghosh, P. (2013). Malala Yousafzai: Backlash intensifies. *International Business Times.* Retrieved from: http://www.ibtimes.com/malala-yousafzai-backlash-intensifies-pakistani-girl-western-puppet-global-brand-1426298

Habib, Z. (2013). *Women's perspectives of peace: Unheard voices from Pakistan.* George Mason University, UMI Dissertations Publishing. (UMI No: 3564260)

Haslam, A., Reicher, S., & Platow, M. (2011). *A new psychology of leadership.* Hove, East Sussex, England: Psychology.

Hundreds witness Pakistan Taliban public execution. (2010, June 8). *BBC News South Asia.* Retrieved from http://www.bbc.co.uk/news/10265522

Jamal, A. (2006). Gender, citizenship, and the nation—state in Pakistan: Willful daughters or free citizens? *Signs, 31*(2), 283–304.

Khattak, S. G. (2004). Adversarial discourses, analogous objectives: Afghan women's control. *Cultural Dynamics, 16*(2/3), 213–236.

King, R. H. (2011). Becoming black, becoming president. *Patterns of Prejudice, 45*(1/2), 62–85.

Lorde, A. (1982) *Zami: A new spelling of my name.* Trumansburg, NY: Crossing.

Masood, A., & Walsh, D. (2013, October 11). Pakistani girl, a global heroine after an attack, has critics at home. *New York Times.* Retrieved from http://www.nytimes.

com/2013/10/12/world/asia/pakistanis-cant-decide-is-malala-yousafzai-a-heroine-or-western-stooge.html?_r=0

Mushtaq, F. (2010). *New claimants to religious authority: A movement for women's Islamic education, moral reform and innovative traditionalism.* Northwestern University. UMI Dissertations Publishing.

NDTV. (2013, October 11). *Malala Inc: Global operation surrounds Pakistani girl.* Retrieved from http://www.ndtv.com/article/world/malala-inc-global-operation-surrounds-pakistani-girl-430931

Nolan, S., & Duell, M. (2013, October 7). "We will attack her whenever we get the chance": Taliban renews threat to kill schoolgirl Malala, 16, who survived terrorist shooting on her school bus. *Mail Online.* Retrieved from http://www.dailymail.co.uk/news/article-2449329/Malala-Yousafzai-Taliban-say-We-attack-chance.html#ixzz2w3rGT38Y

Sanchez-Hucles, J., & Davis, D. D. (2010). Women and women of color in leadership: Complexity, identity and intersectionality. *American Psychologist, 65*(2), 171–181.

Simpson, D., & Brumfield, B. (2013, October 9). Malala Yousafzai turns the other cheek to the Taliban. *CNN World.* Retrieved from http://www.cnn.com/2013/10/07/world/asia/taliban-malala/

Singerman, D. (2013). Youth, gender, and dignity in the Egyptian uprising. *Journal of Middle East Women's Studies, 9*(3), 1–27.

Vital Voices. (2014). *Support the Malala Fund.* Retrieved from http://www.vitalvoices.org/node/3326

Topping, A. (2012, October 26). Malala Yousafzai "is everybody's daughter," says father. *The Guardian.* Retrieved from http://www.theguardian.com/world/2012/oct/26/malala-yousafzai-everybodys-daughter-father

Wieseltier, L. (2012, October 19). Why the Taliban shot the schoolgirl. *New Republic.* Retrieved from http://www.newrepublic.com/article/politics/magazine/108847/why-the-taliban-shot-the-schoolgirl

Women Deliver. (2014). *Girl's Education.* Retrieved from http://www.womendeliver.org/knowledge-center/facts-figures/girls-education/

Yousafzai, M. (2013, July 12). Malala Yousafzai's speech at the Youth Takeover of the United Nations. *A World at School.* Retrieved from https://secure.aworldatschool.org/page/content/the-text-of-malala-yousafzais-speech-at-the-united-nations/

Yousafzai, M., & Lamb, C. (2013). *I am Malala: The girl who stood up for education and was shot by the Taliban.* New York, NY: Little, Brown.

Yusufzai, R. (2013, October 12). Malala won 17 awards before failing to win Nobel Peace Prize. *The International News.* Retrieved from http://www.thenews.com.pk/Todays-News-2-207727-Malala-won-17-awards-before-failing-to-win-Nobel-Peace-Prize

Vodaphone Foundation. (2014). *Vodafone Foundation and Malala Fund Partnership to tackle female illiteracy and expand girls' access to education* [News release]. Retrieved from http://www.vodafone.com/content/index/media/vodafone-group-releases/2014/malala-fund.html

CHAPTER 13

BEYOND THE APPENDAGE SYNDROME

The Life and Meaning of Golda Meir

Norman W. Provizer

In his book, *King of the Mountain: The Nature of Political Leadership*, Arnold Ludwig (2002) wrote, with depressing accuracy, that while some degree of intelligence and stability are not necessarily inflexible barriers to holding political power,

> you can be the ruler of a nation if you have never read a book, do not know how to make a budget, still count with your fingers, take delight in murdering and torturing people, stay zonked out on drugs or alcohol during cabinet meetings, pay more attention to the imaginary voices in your head than to your advisors, or, simply put, are ignorant, demented, or crazy. With notable exceptions the one thing you cannot be as a ruler is a woman. (p. 6)

Ludwig, a psychiatrist by training, highlighted that proposition with numbers drawn from his examination of 20th century political leaders. In his calculation, there were 1,941 such leaders and only 27 of them (1.4% of the total) were women. Beyond that, only one half of that small number of women global leaders (or .78% of the total) came to power without coattails provided by their husbands or fathers (pp. 22–23). The first of those women was Golda Meir, Israel's prime minister from March 1969 to June 1974.

Other women had come to power on the world stage before Meir. Sirimavo Bandaranaike emerged as the prime minister of Sri Lanka (Ceylon) in 1960 following the assassination of the country's leader who was her husband. Some 6 years later, Indira Gandhi, the daughter of India's first leader Jawaharlal Nehru, became prime minster of the vast Indian subcontinent. Yet Meir was different. Born into poverty and oppression in Kiev, Ukraine (then a part of Russia), Meir was twice an immigrant to new lands, coming to America at the age of eight in 1906 and departing for British Palestine to pursue her dream of Labor Zionism in 1921. With Meir, in the words of Antonia Fraser (1994), there was at last

> a female leader who owed nothing to the Appendage Syndrome, one who was neither the daughter or widow of a famous man, nor the regent-mother for some form of infant princeling. To secure her place without the benefit of any specific male connection was in itself a remarkable achievement; and one far rarer in the history of women than is generally supposed. (p. 311)

Certainly, Meir had male mentors along the way with whom she had close relations, but she was nobody's appendage.

The more a woman leader's career follows a path that resembles the one taken by her male colleagues, Genovese (2013) noted, the harder it is to ignore the flaws of the "exclusionary assumptions" which keep women from power (p. 5). And that is exactly the trail-breaking road taken by Meir—a nonappendage road that is now well paved and, as such, followed by an increasing number of women leaders (Bauer & Tremblay, 2011; Jalalzai & Krook, 2010).

On the one hand, since Meir, the upward spiral in the number of women holding a position of primary, chief-executive power has continued, adding legitimacy to the idea that the term leader is losing its "gender reference" (Genovese, 1993a, p. ix). Yet, on the other hand, the fact that we have moved from a point where there were three women leading their nations in the 1960s to one in which a total of more than 70 women have done so during the four decades that have followed does not erase the reality of the vast gender gap that remains relative to those possessing pivotal political power across the globe.

In similar fashion, while the Appendage Syndrome has not disappeared, nations have moved beyond it in many important ways. As Jalalzai (2013) pointed out, while 78% of women holding power in dominant presidential systems have made their way to the top with family ties that mattered, that number shrinks to 23% when it comes to women who occupy the dominant prime ministerial role in parliamentary systems. Obviously, the coattails provided by kinship ties still matter, including cases in which established women leaders "help propel members of their own immediate family into power" (Jalalzai & Krook, 2010, p. 15). But those ties, overall, now matter less and less, and that's where Golda Meir comes into the picture.

The Woman Called Golda

The second of three daughters (five other children, four boys and another girl; all died at a very young age), Golda was born Goldie Mabovitch on May 3, 1898. She was named for her maternal great-grandmother, Golde, who was known "for her will of iron and for her bossiness," terms that would be frequently used to describe the woman who carried her name as well (Meir, 1975, pp. 16, 18).

While Meir's older sister, Sheyna, was the one who played the role of the public activist in Russia, in America that mantle would quickly fall on Golda. Not too long after the Mabovitch family (sometimes spelled Mabowehz, as it appears on her father's application for American citizenship in 1917, as well as Mabowitz) settled in Milwaukee and Golda was in the fourth grade, she moved into the public arena to solve what she saw as a problem, a wrong that needed to be put right. Though the public schools in Milwaukee were free, there was a nominal fee charged for the textbooks used. Together with a close friend, Golda created an "organization" in name only that called for a public meeting on the textbook issue and raised money to insure that all children had the books they needed (Meir, 1975). At 11, Golda displayed the qualities she would carry with her throughout her life: the drive to right a perceived wrong, the ability to organize and persuade in order to achieve a focused goal, fundraising skills, and the ability to deliver an effective speech in ad-lib fashion. In exhibiting her willingness to, in Sheryl Sandberg's (2013) term, "lean in," Golda displayed at an early age that there were no gender boundaries to what Theodore Roosevelt (1910) praised as the willingness to get off the sidelines and enter into the arena of doing.

When she was 14, Golda also offered a clear indication of her namesake's iron will with her unannounced departure from Milwaukee to live with her older sister in Denver. Determined to continue her education and avoid any form of an unwanted marriage, Golda ran away from home. In Denver, she would later write, "Life really opened up for me" (Meir, 1975, p. 45). She continued high school, while living with her sister and brother-in-law, and listened intently to the political ideas discussed by the stream of visitors coming through their home. It was here that she was especially drawn to the concept of Socialist Zionism (Meir, 1975). It was also here that she met the man, Morris Meyerson (also spelled Myerson), whom she would later marry after reconciling with her parents and returning to Milwaukee. Before that return, Golda's stubbornness further emerged when she had enough of her sister scolding her as if she were a child and "marched out" of Sheyna's home to search for other living arrangements with only the clothes on her back (Meir, 1975, p. 50).

With the seed of Socialist/Labor Zionism firmly planted in her, Golda became an immigrant again in 1921 when she and her husband, despite his opposition to the move, left for Palestine on the *SS Pocahontas*. The final and longest chapter in her life was about to unfold. That chapter began with Golda and a reluctant Morris joining the Merhavia kibbutz, where they stayed for two and a half years. Despite the kibbutz's hesitation in accepting the Americans, Golda quickly made her mark and was named to Merhavia's policymaking committee, launching her public career in what would become Israel in 1948. Golda's life in the public arena escalated when her husband's illness and his refusal to have children raised communally brought their stay at Merhavia to an end (Meir, 1975).

In his examination of Meir, Thompson (1993) described the three themes that ran throughout her life: her sense of Jewish identity, her commitment to a public-political existence, and her gender. In their own way, each of these themes highlights the importance of the idea of duty to Meir. In the words of Richard Nixon (1983), who certainly understood such things,

> Many leaders drive to the top by the force of personal ambition. They seek power because they want power. Not Golda Meir. All of her life she simply set out to do a job, whatever that might be, and poured into it every ounce of energy and dedication she could summon. (p. 300)

From this perspective, at least, the tough but grandmotherly Meir captured several (though by no means all) of the key points contained in the notion of servant leadership. After all, the servant leader

> begins with the natural feeling that one wants to serve, to serve first. Then conscious choice brings one to aspire to lead. That person is sharply different from one who is a leader first, perhaps because of the need to assuage an unusual power drive or to acquire material possessions. For such it will be a later choice to serve—after leadership is established. (Greenleaf, 1995, p. 22)

"In short, it is the lure of power versus the call to exercise it through service" (Provizer, 2001, p. 198).

Of course, an emphasis on the servant side of Meir's leadership cannot and should not erase other facets of her political character. Responding to the call to power is not the same as passivity in exercising it, however power is defined. Nor does responding to a call mean a complete absence of other motivations. Steinberg (2008), for example, noted, in her psychoanalytical examination of Meir, "there is something of a mythical quality" to the notion that Golda, despite her self-effacing behavior, was always a reluctant candidate in the pursuit of political power (p. 179).

And yet, in Steinberg's comparative study of Meir, Indira Gandhi, and Margaret Thatcher, it is Meir who, by far, ranks lower than the other two women prime ministers when it comes to being motivated by the lure of power. In the personality-profile inventories generated by Steinberg in *Women in Power* (2008), the drive for power represents 44% of Gandhi's motivation and 22% of Thatcher's motivation. For Meir, that number is just under 10%. That tells us something. If there is a certain "mythical quality" to Meir's image as a reluctant figure when it came to pursuing power, there is ample empirical evidence upon which the myth is built.

Despite Meir's strong sense of duty and dedication, along with her projection of humility and wry humor, "the Old Lady" (as she was widely known in the Arab world) would, in fact, be the last person to claim that she was a saint or someone without weaknesses or shortcomings. After all, in a telling letter about her inner life, written to her son Menahem in 1945 from Iran, Golda explained her long silence this way:

> Suffice it to say that it has its origins in the same deep, dark well as other aspects of my troubled existence, and is one other facet of a life utterly unhinged and frustrated, which has been the bane of my lot for oh so many ages. (M. Meir, 1983, p. 19)

A deep and dark well that would also have her say, "I know myself too well to like myself. I am not what I would like to be" (Provizer, 2007, p. 299).

When Meir finally agreed, after much hesitation, to produce an autobiography for publisher Sir George Weidenfeld, she said, "I will not write about my private life. I will not settle political or other scores with anyone. I will not take advantage of the high office I have just left, or anything I learned there" (M. Meir, 1983, p. 231). The final, international best seller (ghost written by Rinna Samuels with added input from Meir's friend and biographer Marie Syrkin) clearly stayed within Meir's stated boundaries (Kessner, 2008). In that sense, it's not surprising that Yaron Ezrahi described Meir's *My Life* as falling in the tradition of the "how-I-helped-build-the-country approach" so prevalent in Israeli autobiographies—autobiographies that "do not address the inner life of the author nor do they provide honest, reflective narratives of the writing, or speaking self" (1997, p. 95). Still, it strongly reinforces in many ways the role played by duty and service in Meir's extended political career.

Moving on Up

That career began in 1928 when she became Secretary to the Woman's Labor Council—a year that also produced her initial separation from her husband that would eventually lead to a formal ending of their marriage without ever involving a divorce. Some 2 years later, she was one of the founders of Mapai (the Labor Party). And 2 years after that, she emerged as the head of Histadrut's Political Department, actively involved with ending Britain's restrictive policy regarding the immigration of Jews into Palestine.

In 1946, Golda was named acting head, and then head of the Jewish Agency's Political Department, the unofficial government of Palestine's Jewish community. The following year, she met secretly with Jordan's King Abdullah in Amman. At that meeting, Abdullah promised not to join any attack on the Jews of Palestine. Just weeks later, the United Nations Security Council approved a partition plan for the region, carving the territory into both a Jewish state and an Arab one. Under those emerging conditions, there was a second clandestine meeting with Abdullah. During the secret 1948 discussion, Abdullah announced he could not now resist joining the other Arab nations in opposing, by force, the creation of a Jewish state. But he did offer his plan to avoid war. The Jewish territory would become part of Jordan and the Jewish people there would be treated well by him.

As Meir (1975) recalls the meeting, Abdullah (who was assassinated at the Al-Aqsa Mosque in Jerusalem in 1951) asked, "Why are you in such a hurry to proclaim your state? What is the rush? You are so impatient!" Disguised in Arab dress to get to the secret meeting, Meir responded in her typical manner saying, "I don't think that a people who had waited for 2,000 years should be described as being 'in a hurry'" (p. 218). And not long after her meeting with Abdullah ended, Meir, who had just turned 50, was at the Tel Aviv Museum as one of two women signing the document proclaiming Israel's independence as the British mandate over Palestine came to an end.

Then the war came and the government led by David Ben-Gurion sent Meir to raise money for the fledgling state. Armed with a cause and a command of American English, Meir returned with pledges for what was viewed at the time as the astronomical sum of some $50 million and she would raise even more during a return visit, all of which led Prime Minister Ben-Gurion to comment that when the history of Israel is written it will say "there was a Jewish woman who got the money to make the state possible" (Meir 1975, p. 214).

In 1948, Meir was also named Israel's first ambassador to the Soviet Union, drawing massive crowds when she visited a synagogue in Moscow during the Jewish high holidays. Interestingly, it was also in 1948 that the British Consulate General in Jerusalem sent a cable after meeting Golda, describing her as "a tough American Trades Union and Labour boss ... not overtly intelligent but honest" in contrast "to the cultured, elegant woman ambassador from India" whom he also met (British Embassy, 1948, p. 1).

The following year, she was elected to the country's new parliament (the Knesset) and was asked by Prime Minster Ben-Gurion to be his deputy prime minister. While she declined that offer, she accepted the position as minister of labor, involved with the integration of hundreds of thousands of Jews from Arab nations. Then 7 years later, in 1956, she was named Israel's foreign minister and served in that position for 10 years. During that time, the country was embroiled in the Suez crisis and the international controversy surrounding the trial of Adolf Eichmann in Jerusalem, as well as the implementation of a Golda-driven effort to provide significant developmental assistance to the emerging nations of sub-Saharan Africa. It was also in 1956 that Golda Meyerson (formerly Golda Mabovitch) became Golda Meir. Ben-Gurion believed that Israel's leaders, who were from various lands, should Hebraicize their names and Golda took the name Meir, meaning "to illuminate" in Hebrew. Meir is also the Hebrew version of Morris, Golda's husband and her father's name.

Following her decade as Israel's foreign minister, Meir left the government and became the Labor Party's secretary general while keeping her seat in the Knesset. Then in 1969, she was elected to be the nation's prime minister (the fourth person to hold that office) and came to power with decades of experience in both the legislative and executive arenas of government, if not with culture and elegance.

At each step on her move up the political ladder, Meir responded, often with self-effacing candor, that she was simply a worker called upon, rightly or wrongly, to perform a task. Whatever her misgivings, Meir would act, regardless of the impact on her role as a mother and wife, because, as she put it, "I'm only a soldier called upon to do my duty" (M. Meir, 1983, p. 112). When she was asked to be foreign minister in 1956, at first she dismissed the idea, saying, "I as foreign minister? What do I know about diplomacy? or protocol?" (M. Meir, 1983, p. 156). Prior to that in 1949, when Ben-Gurion invited her to be deputy prime minister and coordinator of development, Meir said, "If you insist on my being in the government, I have no desire to be deputy prime minister, nor do I want to be coordinator of development, of which I know little" (Meir, 1975, pp. 156, 135).

Then in 1969, the call came to head the government as prime minister. According to Meir, she could not make up her mind about taking the position. She recognized that, if she failed to step in, there would be a battle between Moshe Dayan and Yigal Allon for power, and that was a divisive struggle the country did not need. At the same time, Meir, just shy of her 71st birthday, "didn't want the responsibility, the awful stress and strain of being prime minster" (M. Meir, 1983, p. 185). As she explained,

> I had never planned to be prime minister; I had never planned any position, in fact, I had planned to come to Palestine, to go to [kibbutz] Merhavia, to be active in the labor movement. I became prime minister because that was how it was, in the same way that my milkman became an officer in command of an outpost on Mount Hermon. Neither of us had any particular relish for the job, but we both did it as well as we could. (Meir, 1975, pp. 378–379)

Her son recalled the telephone call he received from his mother, while he and his wife were living in the United States. She told him about the offer to become prime minister and wanted his opinion. Among the several items that worried her, there were significant health issues. She had been plagued by numerous medical problems, including malignant lymphoma that she dealt with through secret treatments. But the most serious concern was, in the words of her son, "whether she really wanted the job or not." As he noted, "For mother to say yes meant, as she saw it, no less than taking upon herself personal responsibility for each and every casualty ... and more than that, the responsibility for Israel's continued if much challenged existence" (M. Meir, 1983, pp. 184-185).

She accepted the office and, in the wake of the 1973 Yom Kippur War, that specter of responsibility would come to haunt her with a vengeance. Believing however, that the future of the labor movement was at stake, Meir, at that stage of her life, simply could not stay out of the arena and turn a blind eye on either her principles or her colleagues regardless of the risks involved (Meir, 1975).

In a telling 1972 interview with the noted and strongly anti-Zionist Italian journalist Oriana Fallaci (1976), Meir responded to a comment made by Fallaci that the prime minister was "the symbol of Israel," saying, "I, a symbol? Some symbol! Are you pulling my leg? I've done what I've done, that's true. But I can't say that if I hadn't done what I've done, Israel would have been any different" (pp. 117-118). But if she was not a symbol, Fallaci continued, "Why do they say you're the only one who can hold the country together." To which Golda responded,

> Nonsense ... it was by accident that Golda Meir got to lead the country. [Prime Minister Levi] Eshkol was dead, someone had to take his place, and the party thought I might replace him because I was acceptable to all factions. In fact, I didn't even want to accept. (pp. 117–118)

At the time of the 1972 interview with Fallaci, Meir was 74 years old. When asked about possible retirement, Golda remarked that she sometimes thought, "To hell with everything, to hell with everybody. I've done my share now others do theirs, enough, enough, enough! If I've stayed this long ... it's out of duty and nothing else" (p. 119). Meir then went on to give Fallaci a retirement date, October 1973, following the elections scheduled for that month. "Once they're over, goodbye!" (p. 119). History, of course, would not cooperate with Meir's retirement plans. In October 1973, instead of elections, Israel, led by Golda, found itself in a war that involved an existential threat to its very existence.

In Shakespeare's *The Two Gentlemen of Verona*, Proteus betrays his close friend Valentine to the Duke of Milan, saying, "My duty pricks me to utter that which else no worldly good should draw from me" (Staunton, 1979, p. 20). And throughout her life, Meir "realized that in a conflict between my duty and my innermost desires, it was my duty that had the prior claim" (Meir, 1975, p. 98). Perhaps more than anything else, it was this sense of duty and the aura of credibility it created that helps explain why someone such as Fallaci could write, "even if one is not at all in agreement with her, with her politics, her ideology, one cannot help but respect her, admire her, even love her" (p. 88).

Fallaci was not the only unusual suspect attracted to Meir. Fidel Castro would refer to her as "one of the greatest women of the twentieth century" and requested Spanish copies of her autobiography for key colleagues (Benes, 2003, p. 1). Even Egyptian President Anwar Sadat "jumped on the Golda bandwagon," suggesting that the Israeli leaders following Meir paled in comparison to the Old Lady, saying, "I prefer dealing with a strong leader like Golda" (Burkett, 2008, p. 374).

In late 1977, Meir had been out of power for more than 3 years and was just a year away from death. She was in New York for the premiere of William Gibson's unsuccessful play *Golda* when President Sadat's historic trip to Israel was announced. To say the least, Meir was wary of the meeting between her enemy in war, Sadat, and her internal political enemy, Prime Minister Menachem Begin. Earlier in the year, after all, his Likud Party had driven Golda's beloved Labor Party from power, for the first time in Israeli history. But placing her misgivings aside, in typical Golda style she returned to Israel and was on hand to greet Sadat upon his arrival. Smiling, Sadat took her hand and said, "Madam, for many, many years I wanted to meet you." To which Golda replied, "Mr. President, so have I waited a long time to meet you. Why didn't you come earlier?" (Burkett, 2008, p. 376)

On War and the Question of Gender

If there were those who found her, as French Prime Minister George Pompidou did, to be "une femme formidable" or, as Richard Nixon (1983) put it, "an elemental force of nature," Meir was not without her critics (p. 298). Leah Rabin (1997), the widow of the assassinated Israeli prime minister, who first gained that leadership position in the wake of Meir's resignation and final departure from office in June 1974, has argued that

Meir was "not selflessly dedicated" and that she "didn't advance the pursuit of peace during her administration" (pp. 139, 246).

Chaim Herzog (1996), who became Israel's sixth president in 1983, took the view concerning Meir that

> she believed that she had the common touch and was one of the people. The fact is that as prime minister, she was very much out of touch with ordinary citizens. Doctrinaire and obsessed with the trappings of power, she believed that only she was right about any subject under discussion. Her stubborn blindness to outside influences cost Israel much. (p. 173)

In his assessment of Meir, Gideon Rafael (1981) wrote, "Sustained by an unwavering faith in the uncontestable justice of the cause, she had little use and patience for the refined counter argument" (p. 380). From his perspective, Golda's perception of leadership was "to hold doggedly to concepts, even if they had long been overtaken by events" and to never forget (p. 381). While her Spartan office and extremely modest home call into question the idea that she was obsessed with "the trappings of power," certainly the issues that are raised by her "domineering streak" and her tendencies toward stubbornness, dogmatism, and oversimplification are real enough—even if complex in their consequences (Herzog, 1996, p. 173). As an editorial in the *Jerusalem Post* (published after Meir's death on December 8, 1978 at the age of 80), put it, "The strength of Golda's leadership derived from the same source as her weakness" (1978, p. 5).

Though she faced numerous challenges during her time in office, including the static War of Attrition with Egypt across the Suez Canal (that would end with a cease fire in 1970), the terrorist massacre of Israeli athletes at the 1972 Munich Olympics and its aftermath, and Chancellor Bruno Kreisky's closing of the Austrian transit point for Russian Jews leaving the Soviet Union, it was the Yom Kippur War in October 1973 that most defined Meir's years as prime minister. Concerning the failure of her government, including its military and intelligence establishments, to see that the war was coming and to mobilize its military reserves in a timely manner, she said, "But I know that I should have done so, and I shall live with that terrible knowledge for the rest of my life. I will never again be the person I was before the Yom Kippur War" (Meir, 1975, p. 425). "The war," Henry Kissinger later observed, "had devastated her" (Rabinovich, 2004, p. 489).

The Agranat Commission's investigation into that war distinguished between political and military responsibility for the failure to anticipate the October attack. Though it declined to issue any judgment concerning the political side of things, it did examine whether Meir and Defense Minister Moshe Dayan were personally responsible for what occurred. While there were clearly political repercussions produced by the war for Meir and the Labor Party, the commission concluded that neither minister was negligent

(Lahav, 1997). But official findings never allowed her to forgive herself for not acting on her own instincts rather than listening to the military and intelligence advice that claimed war was not imminent (Meir, 1975; Tarnir, 1988).

In September 2013, Israel released Meir's 40-year-old testimony before the five-person commission headed by the Chief Supreme Court Justice Shimon Agranat. Though she noted that just days before the attack occurred on October 6, all of the major figures involved in the decision-making process agreed that an immediate war was unlikely, she chastised herself for not recommending a call-up of the reserves at a cabinet meeting on October 5, though not one of the military leaders present suggested such action. She did however listen to her instincts on Yom Kippur morning when the self-confessed amateur in military matters issued the call-up only hours before the attack began at 2 p.m., though there were still those arguing against that move (Ginsburg, 2013).

Once it was clear to all that an attack was indeed imminent, there was an added decision to be made: whether to launch an immediate preemptive strike against the Egyptian army massed on the western side of the Suez Canal. While her heart was drawn to a preemptive air strike, Meir displayed considerable contextual intelligence with her refusal to strike first. "I knew then, and I know now," she said, "that's it's possible, maybe we can even say certain, that boys who are no longer would still be alive." Yet she believed that 1973 was not 1967, and if Israel had fired the first shot, then the United States would have claimed that it was Israel that had started the war. Under those circumstances, her fear was that when Israel would need assistance from America it would not be forthcoming. Without that support, which she was able to muster most effectively, Meir said, "I don't know how many other boys would have fallen due to a lack of equipment" (Ginsburg, 2013, pp. 1–2).

Despite the traumatic defeats suffered by Israel at the outset, the tide soon turned and, in the process, Meir proved her mettle as a wartime leader. In fact, when it came to how that war was conducted, even Meir's strong critics had to give her high marks. Herzog (1996), for example, while condemning her "nearsightedness" that almost caused Israel's defeat, also wrote that

> once the war began she showed great strength of character and enormous composure ... her inflexibility proved to be an enormous asset in the war. She used common sense to make military decisions, often opposing the choices made by lifelong military men—and her choices were usually correct. (p. 188)

And, like Herzog (1996), Rafael (1981) admitted that Golda's stubborn inflexibility gave her the "strength of resistance" required by an embattled people even as it impaired her ability to adapt to new situations (p. 381). During the war, the 75-year-old, grandmotherly Meir, who was known for making coffee and tea in the kitchen for her guests, proved she could also play the role of Mars.

Rudyard Kipling, in his poem *If*, provides advice that can be readily applied to leadership. That poem begins with the line, "If you can keep your head when all about you are losing theirs and blaming it on you" (Moran, 2011, p. xvi). That's exactly what Golda, more than many of her male colleagues, did during the 19-day war that produced heavy casualties and sent shock waves through the small state she led.

Playwright William Gibson captured that theme in his second and much more successful attempt to project Meir's meaning on stage, *Golda's Balcony*. That play opened in 2003, 36 years after his initial failed effort and went on to set a record as the longest-running one-woman play in the history of Broadway (Simonson, 2004). The balcony in the title refers to a platform at Israel's now not-so-secret nuclear facility Dimona. On that balcony, Meir reflects on her life, the war, and the recommendation by some during the early, dark days of the conflict to use nuclear weapons. Golda's son Menahem and her daughter Sara Rahabi pointed out that, while authors certainly have literary license, they found no support from cabinet officials in their mother's government that the use of such weapons was ever brought up for serious discussion, though, certainly, there might have been individuals who mentioned it in passing (M. Meir & Rahabi, personal communication, June 8, 2003). But whatever the exact facts, the portrayal of Golda as a woman keeping her head while many of those around her were losing theirs highlights a fundamental leadership truth about her.

On the subject of the war, there is one further item to consider briefly. It involves the charge made by many of Meir's critics that entire trauma of the Yom Kippur conflict could have been avoided if Golda had been less intransigent toward the Arab world and therefore more open to peace feelers sent out by Egypt's president before the war came. Meir's defenders, including Mordechai Gazit (1983), noted that she was in fact more flexible than the portrait of intransigence painted by her critics. Gazit, for example, wrote that Sadat, in the view of a French journalist close to the Egyptian president, was impressed by Meir's reported comments in early 1970 that if she learned that an Arab nation was seriously interested in peace, she would pursue that opportunity even though doing so would risk breaking up her government of National Unity.

The problem, from the perspective of Meir and others, was that the offer on the table from Sadat was not a serious one but rather the same old unacceptable song heard before (Gazit, 1983). While the debate on this question continues, in this context it is worth keeping in mind the clear statement from Sadat's wife Jihan: "I do not agree with those among us and among you who assert today that Sadat tried to achieve a real peace before 1973." In reality, as she put it, "Sadat needed one more war in order to win and enter into negotiations from a position of equality" (Burkett, 2008, p. 378). A sentiment that is not really out of line with the references in the Egyptian president's autobiography (published in 1977, four years before his assassination) concerning how the 1973 October War established new conditions and facts on the ground that finally enabled negotiations toward peace to move forward (Sadat, 1977).

On the gender front, Meir's tendency toward dualities has also produced debate. Gender was always there, and if Meir's views on that subject seem enigmatic to some, they were anything but that to her. From some feminist perspectives, Golda was a Queen Bee, not a worker, whose *if-I-made-it-any-woman-can* attitude displayed a blind spot toward her own gender and was "ultimately disappointing for her limited vision and for failing to use her power to greater effect." And for these reasons, she is "not a worthy role model" (Pogrebin, 1991, p. 151).

True, Meir did not create an avalanche of women in political leadership roles in Israel (Sharfman, 1994); and the world had to wait until 2006 for another woman, Tzipi Livni, to become the country's minister of foreign affairs, 50 years after Meir was named to that post. As for the position of prime minister, Meir remains the only woman to occupy that office in Israel, though Livni came very close to leading the government in the aftermath of the 2009 election.

In terms of movements, Meir was a "hedgehog" and the big idea she pursued was that of a democratic-socialist Zionist state led by the Labor Party, not one that focused on the collective empowerment of women. Yet it is a mistake to read too much into this. In an interview on the British television show *Panorama* (1971), for example, Meir commented on how strange it was "that men think the highest compliment they can pay a woman is to say that she is a man. I was never a feminist but that I absolutely refuse to accept" (p. 3). In other words, she found nothing positive in Israeli Prime Minister Ben-Gurion's earlier comment that she was "the ablest man" in his cabinet. If she was tough minded, it was because of who she was and to always add "as tough minded as any man" was neither welcome nor a compliment (Fallaci, 1976, p. 112).

Additionally, while she was in the cabinet, there was a rash of assaults on women in the country. In an effort to deal with the situation, a fellow minister suggested a curfew for women that would keep them off the streets after dark and protect them. In response, Meir said, "Men are attacking the women, not the other way around. If there is going to be a curfew, let the men be locked up, not the women" (Shenker & Shenker, 1970, p. 7). In fact, she had failed to be named mayor of Tel Aviv in 1955 due to the opposition of orthodox members of the town council, who objected to having a woman in such a position. Gender, after all, was woven into the very fabric of Meir's life whatever her expressions concerning organized or structured feminism.

Meir's blend of gender roles allowed her to be blunt yet prudent, firm yet cautious, and stubborn yet compromising. Long before the terms were used, Meir showed that "hard" and "soft" leadership (like "hard" and "soft" power) are not at all mutually exclusive categories. When Meir's political advisor Simcha Dinitz spoke to the press, he announced that the new prime minister possessed "the best qualities of a woman—intuition, insight, sensitivity, and compassion—plus the best qualities of a man—strength, determination, practicality, purposefulness" (Opfell, 1993, p. 33). Though that announcement contained more than a few questionable elements, it did serve as reminder of the role played by the perception of roles in leadership and of what Genovese (1993b) called "an androgynous style" of leadership in which the most successful leaders are those who are "adept at recognizing what the situation requires and adapting his or her style of leadership to fit that situation" rather than those who rigidly follow "one style of leadership in all situations" (p. 215).

In similar fashion, Cho (2001) summarized her examination of a dozen women who served as world leaders with the proposition "that integrated or balanced leadership is more successful than either masculine or feminine leadership" (p. 37). Given that leaders need to exercise judgment, leadership is found less in the qualities possessed than in the judgment involved in their application to a given set of conditions. Whatever their differences, one half of the human population does not possesses a monopoly in this matter nor does the other half exist without it.

As Eagly and Carli (2012) concluded, "Effective leadership thus reflects a wide range of traits and skills, none of which empirical research has placed strongly in the domain of one sex" (p. 450). That point is reinforced by an analysis of more than a dozen studies, which indicated that significant differences along gender lines do exist. Carothers and Reis (2013) examined the data from those studies and reported that

> one conclusion stood out: instead of dividing into two groups, men and women overlapped considerably on attributes.... Even stereotypical traits, like assertiveness or valuing close friendships, fell along a continuum. In other words, we found little or no evidence of categorical distinctions based on sex. (p. SR 9)

While they do not dispute the idea that gender differences on average exist, they do dispute the notion idea "of consistently and inflexibly gender-typed individuals " (Gray, 2013).

That is a conclusion that might well produce a smile and nod of approval from Golda. Returning to the conversation between Golda and Fallaci that

Avner (2010) labeled a romance, Meir reflected on the question of whether "women really react differently to war than men" and answers the question in the negative.

> I've so often found myself having to make certain decisions for instance, to send our soldiers to places from which they wouldn't come back, or commit them to operations that would cost the lives of who knows how many on both sides. And I suffered ... I suffered. But I gave those orders as a man would have given them. And now that I think of it, I'm not at all sure that I suffered any more than a man would have. (Fallaci, 1976, pp. 94–95)

Lighting the Way

Meir was able to overcome the "incongruity" problem that plagues so many women who seek positions of leadership, in part because she had the advantage of being a political-party insider in a governing structure, a parliamentary system, that, in short, is more open to women leaders historically than a direct-election presidential system (Jalalzai & Krook, 2010). Further, when it comes to being a leader on the world stage, if the bias against women is reasonably assigned to "the incongruity that people often perceive between the characteristics *typical* of women and the requirements of leader roles," Meir's entire persona, rooted in her long history in the arena, provided a significant antidote (Carli & Eagly, 2012, p. 453, emphasis added). Gender typing the formidable package that made up Golda was not an easy task. She was selected, after all, not to transform the requirements for effective leadership in Israel, but to navigate the leadership channels already in place in an effective manner.

On the issue of the West Bank (Judea and Samaria) territory captured during 1967 War, and the growth of often unregulated Israeli settlements there, Meir, though fiercely Zionist and a known hardliner on the Palestinian question, retaining her contextual intelligence, said, "It is unthinkable that there should be under our rule a population composed partly of citizens of Israel and partly of non-citizens" (Burkett, 2008, p. 299). And yet, facing the realities of domestic Israeli politics at the time, she accepted the expansion of a problem that has only worsened over time.

This brings us back to Steinberg's (2008) study of Golda, Gandhi, and Thatcher and the question of motivation. According to Steinberg's methodology, Meir was extremely well balanced when it came to ideology and pragmatism. The percentage-point gap between her number one motivator, ideology, and pragmatism was only 17.1. Ideology was first, but pragmatism was a close second. In contrast to Golda, Thatcher was more ideological and less pragmatic, producing a gap of 34.7 percentage points.

As for Gandhi, pragmatism was way on top generating a percentage-point gap of 35.2.

Writing about Golda, Syrkin (1969) said that, "Her peculiar virtue lies in a fierce moral assurance always translated into action to which her whole life testifies" (p. 11). A "peculiar virtue" that would also connect to the label of intransigence so often attached to her. But importantly, that virtue (which was also a vice) never completely erased Meir's problem-solving orientation toward leadership—an orientation that was not without its adaptive dimension, though of the incremental kind. So, while Meir was known for her firm, uncompromising stand toward the Arab world in general and the Palestinians in particular, she also, in Yossi Beilin's (1993) words, "supported a solution based on territorial compromise" (p. 16).

In line with Steinberg's (2008) analysis, Meir, Israel's Iron Lady, had a dominant/controlling personality. Yet hers was also a personality that came with an attractive wrapping of "maternal appearance, self-effacing humor and supreme confidence" (Pogrebin, 1991, p. 175). "Nobody," Abba Eban (1995) said, "has ever called Golda an easy personality" (p. 8). But easy or not, nobody can ignore her meaning for the evolving role of women as global leaders. When Liswood (1995) studied 15 women world leaders, she wrote, "Golda Meir was in fact the sole specific woman named by these prime ministers and presidents" (p. 99). Anyone who looks at her life and career understands that the very notion that women political leaders must have some sort of "gender deficit" that would adversely affect their performance is a prejudice without any basis in reality.

If a "gender deficit" in fact exists, it might well flow the other way. After all, from this perspective, women leaders can not only offer solutions, they may well offer the kind of solutions most appropriate for a postindustrial world dominated by change (Ball, 2013). Though as the battle between the dueling political matriarchs of Bangladesh (Sheikh Hasina and Begum Khaleda Zia) reminds us, that proposition comes with absolutely no guarantees (Barry, 2014). Still, to return to Ludwig (2002),

> Since men have held center stage as leaders of nations for so long, perhaps it is time to have more women rulers to see if they can do a better job of keeping nations from destroying each other ... it may not make a difference. But it is worth a try. (p. 376)

REFERENCES

Avner, Y. (2010). *The prime ministers: An intimate portrait of Israeli leadership*. New Milford, CT: Toby.

Ball, M. (2013, May). Why both political parties now think that voters prefer female candidates. *The Atlantic, 312*(4), 15–17.

Barry, E. (2014, January 12). Matriarchs' duel for power threatens to tilt Bangladesh off balance. *The New York Times*, p. A6.

Bauer, G., & Tremblay, M. (2011). *Women in executive power: A global overview*. New York, NY: Routledge.

Beilin, Y. (1993). *Israel: A concise political history*. New York, NY: St. Martin's.

Benes, B. (2003, May 25). *Letter to the author.* Golda Meir Archive (Box 1). Golda Meir Center for Political Leadership, Metropolitan State University of Denver, Denver, CO.

British Embassy in Moscow. (1948, September 17). *Cable to London*. Golda Meir Archive (Box 5). Golda Meir Library, University of Wisconsin, Milwaukee, WI.

Burkett, E. (2008). *Golda Meir*. New York, NY: HarperCollins. (Published in Great Britain as *Golda Meir: The Iron Lady of the Middle East*. London, England: GibsonSquare.)

Carothers, B., & Reis, H. (2013, April 21). The tangle of sexes. *The New York Times*, p. SR 9.

Cho, K. (2001). Do women lead differently? Leadership styles of top women leaders. In S. Wilsey, L. Matusak, & C. Cherrey (Eds.), *Building leadership bridges 2001* (pp. 32–44). College Park, MD: Burns Academy of Leadership.

Eagly, A., & Carli, L. (2012). Leadership and gender. In D. Day & J. Antonakis (Eds.), *The nature of leadership* (2nd ed., pp. 437–476). Los Angeles, CA: Sage.

Eban, A. (1995). *The political legacy of Golda Meir*. Milwaukee, WI: Golda Meir Library.

Ezrahi, Y. (1997). *Rubber bullets: Power and conscience in modern Israel*. New York, NY: Farrar, Strauss and Giroux.

Fallaci, O. (1976). *Interview with history*. Boston, MA: Houghton Mifflin.

Fraser, A. (1994). *The warrior queens*. New York, NY: Vintage.

Gazit, M. (1983). *The peace process 1969–1973: Efforts and contacts*. Jerusalem, Israel: Magnus Press/Hebrew University.

Genovese, M. (1993a). Preface. In M. Genovese (Ed.), *Women as national leaders* (pp. ix–xi). Newbury Park, CA: Sage.

Genovese, M (1993b). Women as national leaders: What do we know? In M. Genovese (Ed.), *Women as national leaders* (pp. 211–218). Newbury Park, CA: Sage.

Genovese, M. (2013). Introduction. In M. Genovese & J. Steckenrider (Eds.), *Women as political leaders: Studies in gender and governing* (pp. 1–13). New York, NY: Routledge.

Gibson, W. (Writer) & D. Filshelson (Director). (2003). Golda's balcony—A one woman play.

Ginsburg, M. (2013, September 24), Golda Meir: My heart was drawn to a preemptive strike. *The Times of Israel*, pp. 1–7.

Gray, E. (2013, February 6). Men and women's differences aren't actually distinct, confirms study. *Huffington Post*. Retrieved from http://www.huffingtonpost.com/2013/02/04/men-women-differences-minimal-mars-venus-study_n_2618199.html

Greenleaf, R. (1995). Servant leadership. In T. Wren (Ed.), *The leader's companion* (pp. 1–23). New York, NY: Free Press.

Herzog, C. (1996). *Living history*. New York, NY: Pantheon.

Jalalzai, F. (2013). *Shattered, cracked, or firmly intact? Women and the executive glass ceiling*. New York, NY: Oxford University Press

Jalalzai, F., & Krook, M. L. (2010). Beyond Hillary and Benazir: Women's political leadership worldwide. *International Political Science Review*, *33*(1), 5–23.

Jerusalem Post. (1978, December 10). Editorial. Golda Meir Archive (Box 5). Golda Meir Library, University of Wisconsin, Milawaukee, WI.

Kessner, C. (2008). *Marie Syrkin: Values beyond the self*. Waltham, MA: Brandeis University Press.

Lahav, P. (1997). *Judgment in Jerusalem: Chief Justice Simon Agranat and the Zionist century*. Berkeley, CA: University of California Press.

Liswood, L. (1995). *Women world leaders*. San Francisco, CA: HarperCollins.

Ludwig, A. (2002). *King of the mountain: The nature of political leadership*. Lexington, KY: University Press of Kentucky.

Meir, G. (1975). *My life*. New York, NY: Putnam.

Meir, M. (1983). *My mother Golda Meir*. New York, NY: Arbor House.

Moran, D. (2011). *If you will lead*. Chicago, IL: Agate/B2.

Nixon, R. (1983). *Leaders*. New York, NY: Warner.

Opfell, O. (1993). *Women prime ministers and presidents*. Jefferson, NC: McFarland.

Panorama. (1971, August 9). Transcript. Golda Meir Archive (Box 1). Golda Meir Center for Political Leadership, Metropolitan State University of Denver, Denver, CO.

Pogrebin, L. C. (1991). *Deborah, Golda, and me*. New York, NY: Crown.

Provizer, N. W. (2001). In the shadow of Washington: Golda Meir, duty, and the call to power. In K. Cope (Ed.), *George Washington in and as culture* (pp. 197–211). New York, NY: AMS.

Provizer, N. W. (2007). Moving on up: From Dolley Madison to Golda Meir. In W. D. Pederson & F. J. Williams (Eds.), *Creative breakthroughs in leadership* (pp. 293–303). New Delhi, India: Pencraft.

Rabin, L. (1997). *Rabin*. New York, NY: Putnam.

Rabinovich, A. (2004). *The Yom Kippur war*. New York, NY: Schocken.

Rafael, G. (1981). *Destination Peace*. Briarcliff Manor, NY: Stein & Day.

Roosevelt, T. (1910). The man in the arena. *Theodore Roosevelt*. Retrieved from http://www.theodore-roosevelt.com/trsorbonnespeech.html

Sadat, A. (1977) *In search of peace: An autobiography*. New York, NY: Harper & Row.

Sandberg, S. (2013). *Lean in: Women, work, and the will to lead*. New York, NY: Knopf.

Sharfman, D. (1994). Women and politics in Israel. In B. Nelson & N. Chowdhury (Eds.), *Women and politics worldwide* (pp. 380–395). New Haven, CT: Yale University Press.

Shenker, I., & Shenker, M. (1970). *As good as Golda*. New York, NY: McCall.

Simonson, R. (2004, September 23). Golda's balcony becomes the longest-running one-woman show in Bway history. *Playbill*. Retrieved from http://playbill.com/news/article/goldas-balcony-becomes-longest-running-one-woman-show-in-bway-history-oct.--122091

Staunton, H. (Ed.). (1979). *The Globe Shakespeare: The complete works*. New York, NY: Gramercy.

Steinberg, B. (2008). *Women in power: The personalities and leadership styles of Indira Gandhi, Golda Meir, and Margaret Thatcher*. Montreal, Canada: McGill/Queen's University Press.

Syrkin, M. (1969). *Golda Meir: Israel's leader*. New York, NY: Putnam.

Tarnir, A. (1988). *A soldier in search of peace*. New York, NY: Harper & Row.
Thompson, S. (1993). Golda Meir: A very public life. In M. Genovese (Ed.), *Women as national leaders* (pp. 135–160). Newbury Park, CA: Sage.

CHAPTER 14

WHAT KIND OF LEADER WAS MRS. THATCHER?

Stephanie Jones

As women continue to reach leadership positions, it is critical to understand where women lead as well as how women lead within the global arena. Enacting leadership within a globalized context includes understanding cross-cultural complexity, national boundaries, and multiple legal systems. It also requires an acknowledgement and response to global concerns such as reducing emissions, sustainability issues, and human rights concerns. Most definitions of global leadership also incorporate the need for a global perspective or mindset, intercultural competency, and behavioral adaptability/flexibility (Gosling, Jones, Sutherland, & Dijkstra, 2012).

As one of the most famous global leaders of the last century, Margaret Thatcher was a great inspiration for women aspiring to leadership roles. Or was she? She was seen as a powerful leader, and she was a woman, but she did surprisingly little to advance the cause of promoting women in business and politics, except by example. It was widely observed, by many living in Britain at the time, that she showed that a woman could reach the highest office in the land. However, was this the result of her personality and level of ambition rather than her gender?

In which context did Thatcher lead? This was certainly global, but she was always the leader of Britain first. As Prime Minister, she led the government in the United Kingdom for 11 years (1979–1990), but her influence was strongly felt internationally. She championed Britain's continuing autonomy in Europe, whilst embracing the emergence of the Common Market and the subsequent establishment of the European Union. Through her friendship with Ronald Reagan and George Bush Sr., she became a staunch ally of the United States during challenging times of international conflict. She negotiated with China to secure the future of the former British colony of Hong Kong to continue its way of life for 50 years. She took her country to war and saved a British colony against what she saw as a terrorist invasion. She handled terrorism on her own doorstep with attacks from the Irish Republican Army. She strongly believed in freedom of choice, independence, autonomy, and being in charge of one's own destiny.

Thatcher also celebrated the end of the Cold War with the fall of the Berlin Wall. Speaking to journalists outside 10 Downing Street (the British Prime Minister's official residence), she spoke of "the joy on people's faces and ... what freedom means to them ... you cannot stifle or suppress people's desire for liberty" (Thatcher, 1989, para. 2).

How did she lead, especially in this global context? She was not necessarily famous for understanding cross-cultural complexity, although she appreciated the significance of national boundaries in her pursuit of international diplomacy. As a lawyer, she could grasp the significance of multiple legal systems. In her era, environmental issues such as reducing emissions and the sustainability of the planet were fairly new, and human rights concerns were underdeveloped. Her main goal was restoring the economy of Britain, and she refused to tolerate a continuing postwar decline in Britain's role internationally. She was a leader of global standing, but as an individualist rather than a team player, she cannot be said to have developed synergy in an international team. She represented Britain globally, but often in conflict rather than cooperation. This chapter aims to help aspirational readers by offering a practical example of one of the most famous women leaders of the 20th century, who made a huge impact globally, and who was widely seen as an "alchemist" leader—a style described as transformational and epoch-making (Rooke & Torbert, 2005).

A Personal Reflection

Margaret Thatcher, who passed away in 2013, was a global leader who changed society, politics, and the economy of Britain. As a teacher of leadership, when I ask students all around the world to name well-known leaders they admire, often the famous former British Prime Minister is mentioned. She was the only female to achieve this office and one of the longest-serving prime ministers. Indeed, a Kazakh student interviewed on video during the 60th anniversary of my school, the Maastricht School of Management, went to great lengths explaining the inspiration she gained from "The Iron Lady." Many students, from all over the globe, point to the celebrity status enjoyed by Thatcher, as well as Hitler, Stalin, and Mao, as having changed the world. This is widely seen as a definition of leadership greatness, for better or for worse.

Looking back to when I was living in London in the 1970s and 1980s as an undergraduate and graduate student, teaching assistant, and aspiring author during Thatcher's lengthy tenure of office, she changed my world. She deliberately set out to create a landed middle class with conservative values (a small "c" possibly leading to a big "C"). Attracted to study at the London School of Economics for its left-wing image, I could be described as a "pinko" if not an out-and-out "red." But when buying a small flat in London gave me a 150% capital gain a year later, thanks largely to her tough economic policies, I saw the world in quite a different way.

When delivering my classes in leadership at the Maastricht School of Management, I can hear myself being asked, "What kind of leader was Margaret Thatcher?" As I sorted through piles of newspaper reports in the days following her death and her funeral, I found several quotations regarding her leadership which might help to answer this question.

Thatcher was clearly authoritarian. The oldest and most popular joke about her in Britain is the one about Thatcher dining in a restaurant with members of the Cabinet (created by a popular TV show called *Spitting Image* in 1989).

> Waitress: Would you like to order, sir?
> Thatcher: Yes, I will have the steak.
> Waitress: How would you like it?
> Thatcher: Oh, rare, please.
> Waitress: And what about the vegetables?
> Thatcher: Oh, they [the Cabinet] will have the same as me!

When her deputy prime minister resigned, he reflected on the problems he encountered in this role (No ordinary politician, 2013):

> As the deputy prime minister left, he summed up ... the difficulty of trying to work with Mrs. Thatcher: "It is rather like sending your opening batsmen [in the game of cricket] ... only for them to find, the moment the first balls are bowled, that their bats have been broken before the game by the team captain." (p. 28)

She was bossy and decisive, evidenced by her famous blunt advice to former U.S. president George H. W. Bush on August 26, 1990, when the

United States and Britain were enforcing an embargo against Iraq and clamping down on those breaking the sanctions. Thatcher (2011), in her memoirs, recalled telling Bush when he telephoned from Kennebunkport: "We must use our powers to stop Iraq shipping. This was no time to go wobbly. Information we had gleaned from secret sources must be published to show up sanction-busting. The President agreed" (pp. 823–824).

Thatcher was not just bossy, but could also be caring and kind. As reported in many newspapers, the funeral address given by the Bishop of London described a classic anecdote: "I was once sitting next to her at some City function and, in the midst of describing how [various economic theories] … had influenced her thinking, she suddenly grasped my wrist and said, 'Don't touch the duck pate, Bishop—it's very fattening'" (Stevenson, 2013, para. 4).

Thatcher's Leadership Style

There are many examples where Thatcher was effective and where she made many disastrous mistakes. However, she was essentially pioneering at a time when many of her colleagues did not take her seriously and when there were very few female role models in leadership for women to follow.

Thatcher came to power in the British parliament at a time "when women had to be twice as good to get half as far as men," a commonly heard expression in the 1970s and 1980s. Not everyone agreed with her politics, but many agree on the range of her achievements in an eventful period and especially on her stance as a role model for would-be women leaders all over the world. Thatcher was not viewed as a feminist or women's liberation fanatic; she most likely saw herself as a leader first and a woman second. With the challenge of defining what we mean by typical "male" attributes compared with "female" characteristics of leaders, it could be that Thatcher was more masculine than feminine in the way she saw the world and operated (Rajan & Krishnan, 2002; Stoeberl, Kwon, Han, & Bae, 1998). She was often described as "the only European leader with balls" (Nixon, 2012, para. 1) and "the only man in the Cabinet" (Warner, 2009, para. 2). Warner (2009) explained,

> The opening, under the 30-year rule, of archives revealing Margaret Thatcher's governmental processes makes one long for the days when Britain was in secure hands. You did not have to agree with The Lady on every term of policy to recognize that here was a formidable patriot who could be relied upon to put Britain first. (para. 1)

It may be that the new 21st century woman leader, by contrast, can be more of a woman than a man, whatever that means. Perhaps the most important concern for a woman leader now is to be more of herself rather than what she thinks she should be. This consideration may not have bothered Thatcher. So, if she was not trying to be something she was not, what was she really like, beyond the initial impression of being authoritarian and a combination of bossy, decisive, and caring?

The Eight Questions of Leadership

Jones and Gosling (2005) developed a set of "eight questions of leadership" for use in trying to understand a historical leader. In this section, these questions are used to analyze Thatcher's approach to leadership. Firstly, why did Thatcher want to be a leader? It was her destiny; she wanted to improve the economy and society and stop the postwar decline, and she believed she was the one to do it. She was strongly influenced by her father: "Her father taught her how to lead. She watched how he was the one who was prepared to go for it," according to journalist Michael Brunson, quoted by Bryon (2012), in a detailed documentary titled *Margaret Thatcher: The Iron Lady* graphically portraying Thatcher's journey to leadership.

Second, did Thatcher have to be an expert in her field to be a leader in this field? What preparation can be made for a life in politics? As a grocer's daughter, she felt that she was in touch with her voters and constituents and able to represent their interests and needs. Winning a scholarship to Oxford and being a lawyer, she had taken a typical route for many venturing into public leadership roles. She served in several ministries with different portfolios, where she adopted a generalist role, learning aspects of her job through her advisers and using market research for feedback.

Furthermore, did she lead from the front or practice quiet leadership? There is no doubt that she was in-your-face and larger-than-life, and she was always visible. It was never her way to take a back seat. In *Margaret Thatcher*, writer Giles Brandeth was quoted saying,

> She was a very adept politician but she gave the impression of leadership. She led from the front. She appeared to be strident and clear while at the same time ... moderating her views. So she had the style of a leader but the acumen of a politician. (as cited in Bryon, 2012)

Fourth, how did she handle the possible clash between public life and private life? Perhaps she did not; her passion for leadership took precedence over everything else in her life. Her husband and two children realized her strong sense of mission and only revolted occasionally.

Fifth, what was her attitude to teamwork? She took a negative view here: she had made a decision, whether conscious or not, to avoid the sharing of power. She saw it as pursuing consensus, a weak and vacillating option. At best she would ask for advice, which she might or might not take. She took a dim view of many of her subordinates, and when she was ousted from power, her lack of confidence in many of them turned to disgust (Lloyd, 2011).

Sixth, why did people follow her? She had many fanatical adherents and opponents; the country was divided between feelings of love and hate. Nick Robinson (2013), BBC Political Editor, argued that "in an era in which politicians are all too often greeted with indifference, it is easy to forget that Britain was once led by a woman who inspired passion—both love and loathing" (para. 1). Few were indifferent. Expatriates based overseas, nostalgic former politicians, and many Commonwealth heads held her in high esteem, feeling that she signaled a return to British imperial ascendancy. This is evidenced by her battle for Britain's position in Europe: as she stated after a European Council meeting, "We are not asking for a penny piece of Community money for Britain. What we are asking is for a very large amount of our own money back" (Thatcher, 1979, para. 1). Labor union leaders disliked her intensely, seeing her as heralding more unemployment and poverty as she sought higher productivity and balancing Britain's books.

Seventh, was she a manager as well as a leader? She prided herself on a sense of meticulous detail, knowing the price of every item in a housewife's shopping basket. She decided that schoolchildren no longer needed free milk every morning, then provided to all children attending school. This cost-saving, she felt, could be easily made. But here she miscalculated the outbursts then leveled against her. Popularly labeled by many observers as "Thatcher the milk-snatcher" and widely seen as the least popular woman in Britain, she carried on making radical moves to restore Britain's economy with what she regarded as simply good housekeeping (Lloyd, 2011).

Finally, what was the nature of her legacy? She stood up for Britain. In her famous "Bruges Speech," Thatcher insisted that "we have not successfully rolled back the frontiers of the state in Britain only to see them re-imposed at a European level, with a European super-state exercising a new dominance from Brussels" (Thatcher, 1988, para. 70). Many saw her as paving the way for dramatic change in the party lines in Britain, pushing the alternative Labor Party into a more centralist role, although her own party was subsequently to spend many years in the political wilderness. To be a woman in politics, business, or any senior position was no longer so unusual and was no longer seen by men as necessarily risky. A new generation of citizens took charge of their own destinies and became less dependent on the state in the reforms she envisaged, although many suggested that the rich got richer and the poor got poorer.

The Use and Abuse of Power

Another context in which approaches to leadership might be understood is the use and abuse of power. Jones and Gosling (in press) outlined eight different ways in which power might be manifested. The leader can have different ways to gain and retain power. Thatcher enjoyed the power of patronage and mentoring from others and also played the role of patron to her younger acolytes, but to a limited degree, and it did not last. In *Margaret Thatcher*, Brandreth stated that

> after you've been in power for a number of years ... you've promoted those who are going to be promoted and those who haven't been promoted know they never will be. So the leader has no longer got any patronage to offer ... they then turn on the leader. (as cited in Bryon, 2012)

Thatcher was not interested in creating a political dynasty, unlike the case of the Bush family, the Gandhi family in India, or other leading families. She neither benefited from dynastic succession nor provided it for others. She showed and used merit power as a campaigner, making an effort to know what the electorate wanted. Tireless in administrative work and able to absorb detail, her decisiveness and energy were seen as remarkable. Much of her power came from her endless capacity for sustained effort and refusal to compromise her beliefs. She used her charm and powers of physical attraction to captivate colleagues and fellow leaders all over the world, charismatically getting her way. In *Margaret Thatcher* journalist Nicholas Owen stated that "she had something about her and you could see why she could dominate a room full of men ... there was something about her ... riveting personality" (as cited in Bryon, 2012). Despite the skepticism of Britain's traditional sparring partners in Europe, such as France and Germany, she could get her way. As French President Mitterand (2005) put it, "She has the eyes of Caligula but the mouth of Marilyn Monroe" (para. 9). Made over and groomed by media experts, she became even more persuasive, convincing her party in an internal leadership battle. This was her chance to opportunistically seize power, later consolidated in general elections. Although she did not use the power of fear as such, she could be intimidating, especially as she herself was never frightened by anything (Bryon, 2012). At her first job interview in 1948, the Imperial Chemicals Industry personnel department turned her down; the interviewer recorded, "This woman is headstrong, obstinate and dangerously self-opinionated" (BBC News, 2013, para. 21). In her own words quoted in *Margaret Thatcher*, "I didn't believe that the job of a Prime Minister was just to be chairman of a Committee.... Leadership is very important in politics. I chose my way of doing it" (Bryon, 2012).

With her overwhelming personality, her fellow Cabinet and Opposition members were often afraid to confront her. It was not so much what she did to people or threatened to do, but she could be fear-inducing through her own force of will. Was Thatcher manipulative? Did she play people off against each other? It could be argued that most of the time she did not need to. She could win by popular election, by her fellow party members, and by the voters, but she could lose this way too. The patriotic fervor following the defeat of the Argentine forces and the return of the Falklands to British rule ensured her reelection, but the hated poll tax was to bring her down in the end, despite many warnings to this effect. According to Kaiser and Kaplan (2013), "Her fighting spirit left her with a cabinet that had learned its lesson ... it was pointless to contradict or challenge her. She denied herself a loyal opposition—a counterforce to keep her honest, to challenge thinking, to test out ideas, and elevate understanding" (para. 7).

Key Concepts of Leadership

Thatcher was seen as highly competitive; she needed to win every battle and was intuitive in following the path she thought was right (Gosling et al., 2012). Instinctive rather than reflective, she was authoritarian with her Cabinet members and made her own decisions, deploring consensus and compromise. Kaiser and Kaplan (2013) further reported that "her interpersonal style [was based on an] assertive, forceful approach vs. a participative, enabling approach" (para. 3).

Involved in everything in an analytical and task-oriented way, she rarely avoided painful decisions. Always visible and extroverted in her leadership role, she tried to gain broad-based support from her newly created class of citizens who were busy enriching themselves. Leading profound change in all aspects of the economy, politics, and society, she was seen as a "leadaholic": she was obsessed with gaining and preserving the leader role, and was only happy leading. Highly directive in telling others what to do, she could be a prima donna but would give no room to others with a tendency toward this role. With her own individualistic leadership brand, she would refuse to compromise and often would not cooperate or collaborate. In a BBC interview, she said "There is no such thing [as society]. There are individual men and women and there are families" (Keay, 1987). She was not necessarily people-oriented; apart from her committed disciples, she did not see it as her role to develop others and preferred a loyal and supportive team around her who would implement her ideas and policies without unwelcome challenges. She could be effective with volunteers, and all political parties depend on volunteer party workers, but her more senior colleagues were more difficult for her to lead, and eventually they rebelled.

Although she operated in a global context, Thatcher was not especially worldly or cosmopolitan (Gosling & Mintzberg, 2003). Exhibiting features of extreme Britishness, she embraced the concept of the European Union, but on British terms. Thatcher was task-oriented, principled, and goal-driven; she hung in for the long term. She might not necessarily be described as toxic, but she was not exactly nurturing.

Leadership Dimensions

The leadership role typically requires leaders to operate on several different dimensions (i.e., cognitive, emotional, spiritual, and behavioral) (Gill, 2004). Thatcher knew what needed to be done; she had the cognitive ability or expertise to see solutions to problems and to seize an opportunity. The cognitive dimension to leadership can be seen in another way; it has been argued that power creates both temporary and enduring cognitive changes that transform the way that leaders differentiate themselves from others. Power can change a leader's self-perception. For example, Thatcher, especially after the Falklands war, suddenly saw herself as a leader without limits. When she was reelected for the third time, she began to feel invincible. Power perceptions of the leader also impact on followers, making them feel more powerful or more powerless. At first, Thatcher was empowering but then tended to disempower as she became more power-struck. As she accumulated more power, she was less and less inclined to let it go, or maybe she was always like this. As Klenke (1996) stated, "Thatcher had promised she would assemble a cabinet of like-minded colleagues because she could not waste time having internal arguments" (p. 63).

Thatcher's charisma was part of her emotional appeal. She was emotionally swayed by patriotism and her refusal to see Britain decline. Although brought up a church-goer, she was more material than spiritual, with her focus on balancing Britain's books and good housekeeping. But she was moral. According to Klenke (1996), "Other personality traits studied by leadership theorists which were manifest in Margaret Thatcher include her driving ambition and her moral certitude, which threw her opponents on the offensive" (p. 63). She was also infamous for her controversial and slightly sacrilegious observation that "nobody would remember the Good Samaritan if he had only good intentions. He had money as well" (BBC News, 2013, para. 6). Her authoritarian behaviors reinforced her message backed by her strong beliefs. She used these dimensions of leadership and power in the five key areas of effective leadership: creating a vision and mission; demonstrating shared values; formulating strategy; the empowerment of others; and the process of motivating, influencing, and inspiring followers (Gill, 2004). Arguably, she began to decline as an effective leader when she relapsed into hanging onto power, refusing to listen to feedback. Her values, including the virtue of living within your means, tightening your belt, being stoical, and trying to better yourself, became unattractive to many of her weary followers and electors. She empowered some of the population with material wealth but alienated many others. Her string of election victories and her disparaging remarks about her opponents led her to mistakenly assume that her strategies and policies would always win. Surrounding herself with willing sycophants lost her the ability to motivate, influence, and inspire. Although she said, according to the BBC News (2013), "I love argument. I love debate. I don't expect anyone just to sit there and agree with me—that's not their job," (para. 1); she also said "I don't mind how much my ministers talk, as long as they do what I say" (para. 3).

Transactional or Transformational

Although Thatcher was interested in her most loyal and committed followers and could transform them into strong potential leaders for the future, she found several of her colleagues to be barely tolerable. Those whom she liked could be rewarded with coaching and support, and they found her to be an inspirational role model. But these were not necessarily her female colleagues. Thatcher was transactional insofar as she would reward loyalty with positions; however, she was looking out for any mistakes and shortcomings, cancelling meetings if the colleague entrusted with a job was ill-prepared. She was never a laissez-faire leader: she never let go and she carefully monitored everything as something of a "control-freak," according to many observers. She was probably more transformational with her country than with individuals. The current (2014) British Prime Minister David Cameron described her as "the patriot prime minister" and said she had "taken a country that was on its knees and made it stand tall again" (Swinford & Kirkup, 2013, para. 4).

Emotional Intelligence

At first, Thatcher found it challenging to empathize with her constituents. Those from the middle-class background from which she came were relatively straightforward to understand, but she often failed to grasp why the working class was so loyal to their coal mines, even if they were depleted and therefore unprofitable. She appeared to develop self-awareness through accepting feedback and receiving a superficial "make-over" when she bid for the party leadership. Although supremely self-motivated, self-controlled, and disciplined in her work habits, she could not hide her contempt for many around her and would lose her patience, a dangerous characteristic for a leader (Goleman, Boyatzis, & McKee, 2001). She could be charming, sociable, and diplomatic when she had to be, but it was always for a purpose. Her lack of affinity with the voters brought her down in the end, and at that point the only person who could get through to her was her long-suffering husband. By that stage, her emotional intelligence, particularly self-awareness and self-control, were being called into doubt. According to Goleman (1998), the lack of these characteristics can be seen as producing ineffective leadership.

CONCLUSION

In what ways did Thatcher see her identity as a woman as helping in her global leadership role? There were not many. She was quoted as saying that "any woman who understands the problems of running a home will be nearer to understanding the problems of running a country" (Blundell, 2008, p. 193). She also said, "I've got a woman's ability to stick to a job and get on with it when everyone else walks off and leaves it" (McGregor, 2013, p. 4).

The hindrances she encountered to being a leader were more frequent. For example, at a dinner to select potential candidates, the customary practice followed at the time was for the women to leave the dining table after dinner while the men drank port. The men then had a private conversation without the women present (an old-fashioned tradition in England). When she was elected as a Member of Parliament [MP], the bar at the House of Commons was for men only, and the other MPs brought in an ironing-board and iron as a welcome gift for her (Lloyd, 2011). Thatcher was also affected by long-recognized barriers to women in senior roles, such as overcoming a perception that women do not like and are not good at politics (Mann, 1995), and that women are passive; when she married, she made it clear that she would not be there just to hang off her husband's arm and wash-up teacups (Lloyd, 2011). She originally lacked financial support and status; this was then provided by her husband, despite the conditions she imposed on him. She faced the negative perceptions often inherent in being in a minority. She had to break into a male-dominated power network despite a significant increase in women in the workplace in the 1970s and 1980s in Britain (Lahtinen & Wilson, 1994).

For the first time, the media became interested in the prime minister's clothes, hairstyle, and her ability to manage her family life *and* the job of being Prime Minister at the same time. Journalists did not seem to notice this before, perhaps because there were mostly only men in government.

According to Klenke (1996), "Margaret Thatcher was a woman leader in a man's world who neither demanded nor received concessions to her femininity" (p. 63). The most she would say was that there was a "need for a few more women in parliament" as then each one of them would be less conspicuous (King, 1972, para. 1). Yet it was felt in some quarters that "while she was Britain's most successful female politician ever, she regarded feminism as 'poison,' and did little to encourage women to follow her" (Johnson, 2011, para. 7; see also Skidelskey, 2013). This was echoed by Hanson (2012), who asked, "Where were the women in her Cabinet? Only one managed to get in briefly. Margaret seemed to prefer men, especially handsome ones ... or others with whom she could flirt vaguely, or boss about" (para. 19).

Thatcher was widely seen as promoting the idea and acceptability of women in global leadership positions and was inspirational to many ambitious females around the world, but this was not necessarily how she saw herself. She realized she was a trailblazer and was breaking through the glass ceiling, although she would not have used this terminology, and this was not her first intention. The fact that there are now many more women in global leadership attests to her achievement, even if promoting women in leadership as a goal was not her first priority. It could be suggested that because she was a leader first and a woman second, and that she had no interest in positive discrimination in favor of women, she took on the men at their own game, was effective against the odds, and was successful on their terms. Not only was she Britain's first and so far only woman prime minister, she was one of the longest-serving and one of the very few accorded a state funeral. Her passing was front-page news in nearly every newspaper on the planet, and this had little to do with her being a woman.

REFERENCES

BBC News. (2013, April 8). In quotes: Margaret Thatcher. Retrieved from http://www.bbc.com/news/uk-politics-10377842

Blundell, J. (2008). *Margaret Thatcher: A portrait of the Iron Lady*. London, England: Vintage.

Byron, A. (Director). (2012). *Margaret Thatcher: The iron lady*. [Documentary film]. London, England: Revolver Entertainment.

Gill, R. (2004, July). Leadership development in MBA programmes. *Business Leadership Review, 1*(2), 1–4.

Goleman, D. (1998, November/December). What makes a leader? *Harvard Business Review, 76*(6), 93–102.

Goleman, D., Boyatzis, R., & McKee, A. (2001, December). Primal leadership: The hidden driver of great performance. *Harvard Business Review, 79*(11), 42–51.

Gosling, J., Jones, S., Sutherland, I., & Dijkstra, J. (2012). *Key concepts in leadership*. London, England: Sage.

Gosling, J., & Mintzberg, H. (2003, November). The five minds of the manager. *Harvard Business Review, 81*(11), 54–63.

Hannan, D. (2013, May 17). The woman who saved Britain [Review of the book *Margaret Thatcher—The authorized biography. Volume I—Not for turning*, by C. Moore]. *Wall Street Journal*. Retrieved from http://online.wsj.com/news/articles/SB10001424127887324216004578481112955176562

Hanson, M. (2012, January 5). Margaret Thatcher: a feminist icon? *The Guardian*. Retrieved from http://www.theguardian.com/politics/the-womens-blog-with-jane-martinson/2012/jan/05/margaret-thatcher-feminist-icon

Johnson, P. (2011, March 12). Failure of the feminists. *The Spectator*. Retrieved from http://www.spectator.co.uk/features/6766663/failure-of-the-feminists/

Jones, S., & Gosling, J. (2005). *Nelson's way: Leadership lessons from the great commander*. London, England: Nicholas Brealey.

Jones, S., & Gosling, J. (in press). *Napoleonic leadership—A pact with power*. London, England: Sage.

Kaiser, R. B., & Kaplan, R. E. (2013, April 16). Thatcher's greatest strength was her greatest weakness. *Harvard Business Review*. Retrieved from http://blogs.hbr.org/2013/04/thatchers-greatest-strength-was

Keay, D. (1987, September 23). Interview for Women's Own ("no such thing as society"). *Margaret Thatcher Foundation*. Retrieved from http://www.margaretthatcher.org/document/106689

King, A. (1972, January 14). Women in politics. *BBC Archive*. Retrieved from http://www.bbc.co.uk/archive/thatcher/6310.shtml

Klenke, K. (1996). *Women and leadership: A contextual perspective*. Amsterdam, The Netherlands: Springer.

Lahtinen, H. K., & Wilson, F. M. (1994). Women and power in organizations. *Executive Development, 7*(3), 16–23.

Lloyd, P. (Director). (2011). *The Iron Lady*. [Motion picture]. UK, USA, Australia: 20th Century Fox, The Weinstein Company, Icon Productions.

Mann, S. (1995). Politics and power in organizations: Why women lose out. *Leadership and Organization Development Journal, 16*(2), 9–15.

McGregor, J. (2013, July). Turn if you want. The lady's not for turning. *The Washington Post*, quoted in *Executive Leadership*, p. 4.

Mitterand, F. (2005, November 20). In quotes: Margaret Thatcher. *BBC News*. Retrieved from http://www.bbc.com/news/uk-politics-10377842

Nixon, S. (2012, June 12). Merkel still waiting for Thatcher moment. *TheOligarch.Com*. Retrieved from http://www.theoligarch.com/simon_nixon_thatcher_needed.htm

No ordinary politician. (2013, April 13). *The Economist, 407*(8831), 26–28.

Rajan, S., & Krishnan, V. R. (2002). The impact of gender on influence, power and authoritarianism. *Women in Management Review, 1*(5), 197–206.

Robinson, N. (2013, April 8). Margaret Thatcher—a woman who inspired passion and shaped a political generation. *BBC News*. Retrieved from http://www.bbc.com/news/uk-politics-22067985

Rooke, D., & Torbert, W. R. (2005, April). Seven transformations of leadership. *Harvard Business Review, 83*(4), 66–76.

Skidelsky, R. (2013, April 18). Margaret Thatcher: A strong leader, but a resolute failure by any other measure. *The Guardian*. Retrieved from http://www.theguardian.com/business/economics-blog/2013/apr/18/margaret-thatcher-leader-failure-strong

Spitting Image. (2013, April 8). *Margaret Thatcher: Cabinet of vegetables* [Video]. Retrieved from https://www.youtube.com/watch?v=DPzzgE34YQY

Stevenson, A. (2013, April 17). Analysis: Bishop of London's Margaret Thatcher funeral address. *politics.co.uk*. Retrieved from http://www.politics.co.uk/comment-analysis/2013/04/17/analysis-bishop-of-london-s-margaret-thatcher-funeral-addres

Stoeberl, P. A., Kwon, I. W. G., Han, D., & Bae, M. (1998). Leadership and power relations based on culture and gender. *Women in Management Review, 13*(6), 208–216.

Swinford, S., & Kirkup, J. (2013, April 8). Margaret Thatcher, the Iron Lady, who made a nation on its knees stand tall. *The Daily Telegraph*. Retrieved from http://www.telegraph.co.uk/news/politics/margaret-thatcher/9980285/Margaret-Thatcher-Iron-Lady-who-made-a-nation-on-its-knees-stand-tall.html

Thatcher, M. (1979, November 30). Press conference after Dublin European council. *Margaret Thatcher Foundation*. Retrieved from http://www.margaretthatcher.org/speeches/displaydocument.asp?docid=104180

Thatcher, M. (1988, September 20). The Bruges Speech. *Margaret Thatcher Foundation*. Retrieved from http://www.margaretthatcher.org/document/107332

Thatcher, M. (1989, November 10). Remarks on the Berlin Wall (fall thereof). *Margaret Thatcher Foundation*. Retrieved from http://www.margaretthatcher.org/document/107819

Thatcher, M. (2011). *The Downing Street years*. New York, NY: Harper. Retrieved from http://www.margaretthatcher.org/archive/displaydocument.asp?docid=110711

Warner, G. (2009, December 31). The Thatcher years. No time for soundbites when we felt the handbag of history on our shoulders. *The Telegraph*. Retrieved from http://blogs.telegraph.co.uk/news/geraldwarner/100021002/the-thatcher-years-no-time-for-soundbites-when-we-felt-the-handbag-of-history-on-our-shoulders

Appendix: Further Reading

Authors	Title of Book
Aitken, J.	Margaret Thatcher: Power and Personality (2013)
Aldous, R.	Reagan and Thatcher: The Difficult Relationship (2012)
Berlinski, C.	There is no Alternative: Why Mrs. Thatcher Matters (2008)
Campbell, J.	Margaret Thatcher, Volume One: The Grocer's Daughter (2007)
Campbell, J.	Margaret Thatcher, Volume Two: The Iron Lady (2008)
Cosgrave, P.	Thatcher: The First Term (1990)
Dale, I. (Ed.)	Memoirs of Maggie: A Portrait of Margaret Thatcher (2000)
Dale, I. (Ed.)	Margaret Thatcher: In Her Own Words (2010)
Gardiner, G.	Margaret Thatcher: From Childhood to Leadership (1975)
Gilmour, I.	Dancing with Dogma: Britain Under Thatcherism (1992)
Harris, R.	Not for Turning: The Life of Margaret Thatcher (2013)
Hoskyns, J.	Just in Time: Inside the Thatcher Revolution (2000)
Junor, P.	Margaret Thatcher: Wife, Mother, Politician (1983)
Lewis, R.	Margaret Thatcher: A Personal and Political Biography (1975)
Money, E.	Margaret Thatcher: First Lady of the House (1975)
Murray, T.	Margaret Thatcher (1979)
Ranelagh, J.	Thatcher's People: An Insider's Account of the Politics, the Power and the Personalities (1991)
Renwick, R.	A Journey with Margaret Thatcher: Foreign Policy Under the Iron Lady (2013)
Ridley, N.	My Style of Government: The Thatcher Years (1991)
Smith, G.	Reagan and Thatcher (1990)
Thatcher, M.	The Path to Power (1995)
Thomson, A.	Margaret Thatcher: The Woman Within (1989)
Watkins, A.	A Conservative Coup: The Fall of Margaret Thatcher (1992)
Young, H.	One of Us: A Biography of Margaret Thatcher (1991)

ABOUT THE AUTHORS

THE EDITORS

Faith Wambura Ngunjiri, EdD, is the Director of the Lorentzsen Center for Faith and Work, and associate professor of ethics and leadership at the Offutt School of Business at Concordia College. She has research interests in women and leadership, particularly at the intersections of identities and locations; spirituality in the workplace; and culturally appropriate qualitative methods. Her work has been published in books and various journals, including *Journal of Research Practice, International and Intercultural Communication Annual, Journal of Business Communication, Journal of Pan African Studies*, and *Journal of Educational Administration*, among others. She authored *Women's Spiritual Leadership in Africa* (SUNY, 2010) and co-authored *Collaborative Autoethnography* with H. Chang and K. Hernandez (Left Coast Press, 2013). Faith serves as co-editor for this *Woman and Leadership* book series (ILA/IAP) and *Palgrave Studies in African Leadership* (Palgrave McMillan) and serves on the editorial boards of several journals. She earned a doctorate in leadership studies from Bowling Green State University.

Susan R. Madsen, EdD, is the Orin R. Woodbury Professor of Leadership and Ethics in the Woodbury School of Business at Utah Valley University. She has been heavily involved for the last decade in researching the lifetime development of prominent women leaders. She has personally interviewed a host of women university presidents, U.S. governors, and international leaders, and has two books published on her results. Susan has conducted related research in the United States, the six Arab Gulf countries, China, and recently in Eastern Europe. She has published over 60 articles in scholarly journals and presents often in local, national, and international settings. She has been an invited speaker at the *New York Times* and in NGO sessions at the United Nations. Susan is the founder of numerous networks, including the International Leadership Association's (ILA) Women and Leadership Affinity Group. She has received numerous awards for her teaching, research, and service. She is co-editing the new ILA/IAP book series titled *Women and Leadership*. She received her doctorate from the University of Minnesota in human resource development.

THE CONTRIBUTORS

Nancy J. Adler, PhD, is the S. Bronfman Chair in Management at McGill University. She conducts research and consults worldwide on global leadership, cross-cultural management, and arts-inspired leadership practices. She has authored more than 125 articles, produced three films, and published ten books and edited volumes. She is a Fellow of the Academy of Management, the Academy of International Business, and the Royal Society of Canada and has been recognized as one of the top university teachers in Canada. Nancy is also a visual artist and has been an artist-in-residence at the Banff Centre. Her paintings and monotype print are held in private collections worldwide.

Roya Ayman received her PhD in cross-cultural organizational social psychology from the University of Utah. She is a fellow at Leadership Trust in the UK and is a professor and director of the Industrial and Organizational Psychology Program in the Department of Psychology, Lewis College of Human Science, at the Illinois Institute of Technology. Roya's main area of research is in leadership, culture, and the work-family interface. She has conducted a variety of research in many private and public organizations in the United States and in other countries. She was a co-editor of *Leadership Theory and Research: Perspectives and Directions* and has published more than 40 chapters and scientific articles on topics of leadership across culture, gender, and the role of support in work-family balance. Roya is currently a member of a multinational research team that is engaged in a 10-country study of the work-family interface (Project 3535).

Joanne Barnes, EdD, is the dean of the graduate school and associate professor of organizational leadership at Indiana Wesleyan University (IWU) and has been involved in higher education since 1996. Joanne retired from Delphi Electronics & Safety in 2008, in Kokomo, Indiana after nearly 37 plus years of service, where she held various management and leadership positions. Her position upon retirement was the Global Quality Systems Manager for the entire enterprise. As an active member of ILA, she has served in various leadership roles. Her current research involves cultural intelligence, multicultural leadership, and the cross-transferability of Western-based theories and assessments to Eastern European and Asian cultures. Joanne currently teaches global leadership and theory, organizational behavior and theory, and adult and organizational learning. She earned her EdD in organizational leadership from Indiana Wesleyan University.

Julie R. Breithaupt, PhD, has more than 15 years of experience in global clinical research and development in the multinational pharmaceutical industry. Throughout her career, she has worked with colleagues to conduct successful global clinical trials in more than 25 countries. Her work experience as a clinical development manager fueled an interest that led to doctoral research exploring women's global leadership. At GlaxoSmithKline she received an award for Exceptional Science in 2004. She is a member of the National Association of Professional Women and was recognized in 2012–2013 as Woman of the Year for demonstrated excellence and dedication within her profession. She earned a PhD in organizational leadership from Eastern University (St David's, PA).

Carol Burbank, PhD, is an educator, independent scholar, and coach specializing in the connections between leadership, cultural stories and archetypes, and identity (both organizational and personal). She has a PhD in performance studies from Northwestern University, served as a Senior Fellow at the Burns Academy of Leadership at the University of Maryland, College Park, and served as visiting professor for Union Institute and University's Interdisciplinary Leadership PhD program. She currently teaches at Pacifica Graduate Institute, Sofia University, and in the University of New England's PhD in Educational Leadership. Her reviews and articles have appeared in *Integral Leadership Review*, *Indigenous Issues and Culture*, *Business Leadership Review*, and *Transformational Thinking for 21st Century Leadership*. Her blog, Lead Me On, tracks trends and paradoxes in leadership theory and practice (http://leadershipspirit.wordpress.com/).

Paige Haber-Curran, PhD, is assistant professor and program coordinator for the Student Affairs in Higher Education master's program at Texas State University-San Marcos. Paige earned her doctorate in leadership studies from the University of San Diego. Her research focuses on college student leadership development, women and leadership, student leadership programs, college student learning, and emotional intelligence. Paige is actively involved with the International Leadership Association, ACPA-College Student Educators International, and the LeaderShape Institute. She consults across the United States and internationally on leadership programs, leadership development, and women and leadership.

Catherine Etmanski, PhD, is assistant professor in the School of Leadership Studies at Royal Roads University (RRU) and one of the program heads for the school's Master's of Arts in Leadership Studies program. She has been a key member of the design team for the new Master's of Arts in Global Leadership program. Having engaged extensively in international work, studies, and travel over the past two decades, Catherine promotes global solidarity throughout her research and teaching. She has also published in areas related to the learning and teaching of action-oriented, community-based participatory research, mindful leadership, environmental adult education, transformative education, and arts-based research. Her recent book is titled *Learning and Teaching Community-Based Research: Linking Pedagogy to Practice* (University of Toronto Press, co-edited with B. Hall and T. Dawson, 2014).

Kaitlin Hartley, MA, is the coordinator of Student Leadership for Student Affairs at The University of Alabama. Kaitlin earned her master's of arts in higher education administration from The University of Alabama. Since the fall 2009 voyage of *Semester at Sea*, Kaitlin has taken an active role in promoting leadership development and service-learning. Her active involvement includes serving on the Associate Board of Directors for the $100 Solution, serving as the program coordinator for UA's session of the LeaderShape Institute, and engagement in National Association for Student Personnel Administrators (NASPA).

Cheryl Heykoop, DSocSci, is the child participation and protection advisor with the International Institute for Child Rights and Development (IICRD) and a member of the Master of Global Leadership design team at Royal Roads University. She has over 11 years of experience as a scholar-practitioner working in Uganda, Sierra Leone, Timor-Leste, Brazil, Thailand, Zambia, and the United States. She has collaborated with a range of nongovernmental organizations, national governments, academic institutions, civil society, and young people themselves in Canada to strengthen child and youth participation, protection, and empowerment. Cheryl has a BSc in Biomedical Science (University of Guelph), a MSC in Humanitarian Studies (University of Liverpool), and a Doctorate of Social Sciences (Royal Roads University). Her current areas of interest include participatory action research; child and youth engagement in planning, monitoring, and evaluation; child and youth protection; and engagement with at-risk young people (e.g., post-conflict, disaster recovery, violence).

Stephanie Jones, PhD, is Associate Professor of Organizational Behavior in the Maastricht School of Management, Maastricht University, the Netherlands. She has recently focused on research into leadership lessons and insights from historical figures—Admiral Lord Nelson, the Emperor Napoleon, and Mrs. Margaret Thatcher. She is also interested in cultural challenges facing leaders and teams. She teaches MBA classes in leadership, change management, corporate social responsibility, teamwork, human resource management, and cross-cultural issues worldwide—especially in emerging markets. The author of over 30 books on leadership and management, she has taught classes and conducted research in Africa, the Arab Gulf countries, Egypt, China, Vietnam, South America, and in Eastern Europe, such as Kazakhstan. She also supervises doctoral and masters students in many locations and teaches thesis-writing workshops. She has published many articles in scholarly and practitioner journals—especially on leadership—and has presented conference papers and seminar discussions in countries like the United States, United Kingdom, Dubai, Cairo, New Delhi, and Lima. She collaborates closely with Professor Jonathan Gosling of the University of Exeter, United Kingdom. She received her doctorate from the University of London in the field of economics.

Mary Ellen Kassotakis, EdD, has responsibility for Oracle's Leadership & Professional Development Center within Oracle's Global Organization and Talent Development (Human Resources) group. She has more than 20 years of leadership experience in large, global companies. Her areas of expertise include performance improvement, organization development, leadership development, women's leadership development, strategic planning, diversity and inclusion, coaching and change management. Mary Ellen serves as the 2013–2014 President of the International Society for Performance Improvement (ISPI), and she is also a member of the International Leadership Association. In 2010 she co-authored *Social Media at Work: How Networking Tools Propel Organzational Performance* (2010, Jossey-Bass). Mary Ellen earned her doctorate from the University of Southern California's Rossier School of Education.

Barbara Kellerman is the James MacGregor Burns Lecturer in Public Leadership at the Harvard Kennedy School. She is the Founding Executive Director of the School's Center for Public Leadership; from 2003 to 2006 she served as Research Director. Kellerman has held professorships at Fordham, Tufts, Fairleigh Dickinson, George Washington, Uppsala, and Dartmouth. For the last several years, she has also been Visiting Professor of Business Administration at the Tuck School of Business at Dartmouth. She also served as Dean of Graduate Studies and Research at Fairleigh Dickinson, and as Director of the Center for the Advanced Study of Leadership at the University of Maryland. Kellerman received her BA from Sarah Lawrence College, and her MA (in Russian and East European Studies), MPhil, and PhD (in Political Science) degrees from Yale University. She was awarded a Danforth Fellowship and three Fulbright fellowships. At Uppsala (1996–97), she held the Fulbright Chair in American Studies. Kellerman was cofounder of the International Leadership Association (ILA), and is author and editor of many books. She has appeared often on media outlets such as CBS, NBC, PBS, CNN, NPR, Reuters, and BBC, and has contributed articles and reviews to the *New York Times*, the *Washington Post*, the *Boston Globe*, the *Los Angeles Times*, and the *Harvard Business Review*.

Karin Klenke, PhD, is Graduate Dissertation Chair at Northcentral University, where she supervises doctoral dissertations across a variety of disciplines. She is also the Chief Leadership Development Officer at the Leadership Development Institute (LDI) International, an international consulting firm specializing in the design and delivery of customized and public leadership development and education programs. Karin holds a PhD in organizational psychology, served as the founding and editor-in-chief of the *Journal of Management Systems* and *Leadership and Leaders*, was past president of the Association of Management/International Association of Management, and currently serves on the editorial board of several leadership, management, and methodological journals. Her research interests include women in leadership, qualitative and visual methodologies, leadership cartography, and the role of social media in leadership.

Karen Korabik, PhD, is an emeritus professor at the University of Guelph, where she is affiliated with the faculty of Industrial/Organizational Psychology and the Centre for Families, Work, and Well-Being. She is a Fellow of the American Psychological Association. Karen has carried out research in a wide variety of public and private sector organizational settings both in Canada and internationally. She has published more than 50 book chapters and scientific articles on topics such as leadership and conflict management; work/family balance; stress, coping, and social support; job change; gender issues; acculturation; and program evaluation. She was a co-editor of the *Handbook of Work-family Integration: Research, Theory, and Best Practices*. She is currently a member of a multinational research team that is engaged in a 10-country study of the work-family interface (Project 3535). She received her PhD in evaluative/applied psychology from St. Louis University.

About the Authors

Margie A. Nicholson, MBA, is associate professor in the Business and Entrepreneurship Department at Columbia College, Chicago, where she teaches management and leadership. She has been a board member of the International Leadership Association (ILA) since 2004 and currently serves as ILA's treasurer and finance committee chair. In addition to chairing the ILA's international leadership conference in Chicago in 2006, she has given presentations at leadership conferences in the United States, the United Kingdom, Mexico, and the Czech Republic. Drawing upon her earlier career experience in independent media, Margie has developed a database of more than 100 feature films and documentaries that can be used to study, teach, and inspire leaders. Her blog on leadership and media can be found at reelleadersblog.wordpress.com. Margie has an MBA from the Kellogg Graduate School of Management at Northwestern University and an MA in radio, TV, and film and a BA in English literature from the University of Wisconsin-Madison.

Joyce Osland, PhD, Case Western Reserve University, is the Lucas Endowed Professor of Global Leadership and Executive Director/Founder of the Global Leadership Advancement Center at San Jose State University. Her current research addresses repatriate knowledge transfer and global leadership expertise and development. She has received numerous awards for both teaching and scholarship, most recently the Academy of Management's International Management Division's Outstanding Educator Award. With over 90 publications, Dr. Osland's research appears in journals such as *Academy of Management Journal*, *Human Resource Management*, *Journal of International Business Studies*, and *Organizational Dynamics*. Her recent co-authored books are *Global Leadership: Research, Practice and Development*, *Advances in Global Leadership* (Volume 8), and *The Organizational Behavior Reader*. Joyce is also a senior partner in the Kozai Group.

Valerie Claire Petit, PhD, is professor of leadership at EDHEC Business School in France. She teaches, writes, and does research on strategic leadership and ethics. She has been head of the EDHEC Leadership Teaching Chair (2005–2008) and Director of the EDHEC Leadership & Corporate Governance Research Centre (2007–2011). Recently, she has launched a research initiative on leadership and diversity to promote inclusive leadership practices and diverse leaders. A graduate in political sciences (MSc), communication (MA), and social psychology (MSc), Valerie obtained her PhD in strategic management in 2006. She is a member of the ILA, the European Business Network (EBEN), and the Association Française de Psychologie Positive (AFPP). Her work has been published in the *European Management Journal*, and the *Journal of Business Ethics*. She is also the author of *The Art and Science of Strategic Leadership* (Pearson, 2013).

ABOUT the AUTHORS

Norman W. Provizer, PhD, is professor of political science and the director of the Golda Meir Center for Political Leadership at Metropolitan State University of Denver. His writing on leadership has appeared in journals such as *The Leadership Quarterly*, the *Journal of African Studies*, and *Comparative Politics*. Most recently, he has published chapters in a number of edited volumes, including *Fictional Leaders: Heroes, Villains and Absent Friends*, *Leadership Studies: The Dialogue of Disciplines*, *Lincoln's Enduring Legacy*, and *A Companion to Franklin D. Roosevelt*. He is also the editor of *Analyzing the Third World* and the co-editor of two books on the Supreme Court, *Leaders of the Pack: Polls and Case Studies of Great Supreme Court Justices* and *Great Justices of the U.S. Supreme Court*. His PhD is from the University of Pennsylvania.

Julnar B. Rizk, MPT, is a member of the Global Learning & Development team at Facebook, providing expertise in the area of Diversity & Inclusion Education. Prior to joining Facebook, she was an internal consultant with Oracle Women's Leadership, supporting the engagement and development of current and future Oracle women leaders, as well as the establishment of community leadership throughout the Americas, Europe, Middle East, and Africa. Julnar has worked as an organizational and leadership consultant for Fortune 50, 100, and 500 companies throughout multiple industries and has been a professional coach since 2004. Prior to becoming a coach, she worked as a licensed physical manual therapist with a specialty in spine and advanced orthopedics. Julnar earned her master's in physical therapy from East Carolina University and a master's certificate in learning and organizational change from Northwestern University.

Wendy E. Rowe, PhD, is a faculty member and scholar practitioner at Royal Roads University in Victoria, Canada. She teaches in the School of Leadership and is program head for the MA Global Leadership program. She is committed to promoting the role of women in leadership and management and serves as a teacher, mentor, and researcher to promote change that breaks down institutional barriers and creates a healthier work environment. Wendy has worked extensively across Canada and the United States, in addition to various international locations (India, China, New Zealand, Australia), developing and evaluating programs in the not-for-profit sector. She has a BA and MA degree in psychology (Simon Fraser University), an MBA (Western Washington University), and a PhD in organizational and human systems (Fielding Graduate University). She has published and is engaged in a number of research initiatives in areas of health system change, evaluation planning and methodology, action research methodology, and personal and organizational resiliency, thriving, and leadership.

Sarah E. Saint-Michel, PhD, is assistant professor of human resources management at Toulouse University. Her research focuses on gender and leadership, work-family conflict, and diversity in organizational context. She received her PhD from Paris Sorbonne University.

CPSIA information can be obtained
at www.ICGtesting.com
Printed in the USA
FSOW04n0824180515
7199FS